WHERE IN MOSCOW

Paul E. Richardson, ed.

The ultimate directory,
including maps,
telephone listings,
and essential goods
and services.

GW00630567

EDITION 4

Russian Information Services, Inc.
Montpelier, VT

Русская Информационная Служба
Москва & Санкт-Петербург, Россия

Every attempt has been made to make this guide the most up-to-date collection of business information available. Given the swift rate of change in Russia and the new Commonwealth, mistakes in phone numbers, addresses, and on other points of fact are inevitable. The authors, editors and publishers accept no liability for any consequences which may arise from the use of information in this guide.

First edition: August 1991
Second edition: March 1992
Third edition: May 1993
Fourth edition: March 1994

Published by:
Russian Information Services
89 Main Street, Suite 2
Montpelier, VT 05602 USA
ph. 802-223-4955
fax 802-223-6105

in cooperation with:
Russkaya Informatsionnaya Sluzhba
B. Kondratyevskiy per. 4, kor. 2, kv. 168
Moscow, Russia 125056
ph./fax 095-254-9275

Cover design by:
Marketing Arts
Bridge Street Marketplace
Waitsfield, VT 05673, USA

Moscow City Street Map by:
Northern Cartographic, Inc.
4050 Williston Rd.
South Burlington, VT 05403

Quotes on page four as translated in The Heritage of Russian Verse, *Dimitri Obolensky, ed. (Indiana University Press, 1965) and* Moscow, a Traveler's Companion, *by Lawrence Kelly (Atheneum, 1984).*

Russian Information Services, Montpelier, VT USA

Library of Congress Catalog Card Number: 94-65295
ISBN 1-880100-19-3

Where in Moscow

Where in Moscow is published with the independent traveler in mind. In this sense it stands alone. You won't find historical information on the Kremlin or a compendium of tourist sights in this guide. But you will find information on where to eat, where to get a suit dry cleaned, where to send a fax, where to spend your evenings, and much more.

Where in Moscow contains the most useful and up-to-date information available for traveling to or living in Moscow. It's the kind of information that thousands of Western business people and travelers have come to depend on *Where in Moscow* to provide, with its no-nonsense, no-directions-required style.

Where in Moscow has been **totally updated** and **significantly expanded** in this fourth edition. Each bit of information was reverified just prior to publication. An important point, when you consider the swift and unpredictable nature of change in Moscow. It is something we can achieve because of our fine staff that is resident year-round in Moscow, gathering information, sifting and verifying it. No other travel or tourist guide offers that kind of resume.

Among the fine members of the RIS team responsible for this trying work are Stephanie Ratmeyer, S. Todd Weinberg, Bella Gubnitskaya, Yuri Pankratov, Ken Pafford, Clare Kimmel, Scott D. McDonald, Patrick Ryan, Glenn Holstein, Jennifer Krebs, Nina Goryachyova, Tatyana Subbotina, Julia Gubnitskaya, Marina Gershtein, Anna Subbotina, Galina Levina, Katya Alekseyeva, Irina Petrova and Dmitri Katsyzny.

Corrections and comments are enthusiastically encouraged. If you would like your company to be listed in the next edition of this guide, simply send your information to either of our addresses given on the page facing.

Where in Moscow is just one of a series of publications of Russian Information Services on doing business in Russia and the Commonwealth, including:

Where in St. Petersburg (2nd edition)
Russia Survival Guide: Business & Travel (5th edition)
Russian Travel Monthly
Business Russian
The New Moscow: City Map and Guide (2nd edition)
The New St. Petersburg: City Map and Guide (1st edition)

Ask at your local bookseller or see the back of this guide for ordering information.

The Publisher
March 1994

"My hero was of Moscow. That is why
I scorn the Neva's fog, and hate and mock it....

"Moscow, my home – I love you as a son,
Love like a Russian, strong and fierce and gentle!"

– Mikhail Lermontov

"In Moscow, every foreigner is taken to look at the
great cannon and the great bell – the cannon which
cannot be fired and the bell which fell down before it
was rung. It is an amazing town in which the objects of
interest are distinguished by their absurdity..."

– Pyotr Chaadayev

Moscow Business Telephone Directory

City Codes Within the CIS

To direct-dial long distance within the Commonwealth of Independent States, dial 8, wait for a dial tone, then dial the city code as listed below and then the local number. You will need to add zeroes or twos between the city code and the local number to make a total of 10 digits if the number of digits does not already equal ten.

Almaty	327	Kurgan	35222
Arkhangelsk	818	Kursk	07100
Ashkabad	363	Lipetsk	0740
Astrakhan	85100	Lvov	0322
Baku	8922	Magadan	41300
Barnaul	3952	Magnitogorsk	35137
Bishkek	331	Minsk	0172
Blagoveshensk	41622	Moscow	095
Borodino	39168	Mozhaisk	238
Bratsk	39531	Murmansk	815
Brest	01622	Nikolaev	0510
Bryansk	08322	Nizhny Novgorod	8312
Bukhara	365	Noginsk	251
Cheboksari	8350	Novgorod	8160
Chelyabinsk	351	Novosibirsk	3832
Cherkassy	0472	Odessa	048
Chita	30222	Omsk	38122
Dagomys	8620	Orel	0860
Dnepropetrovsk	0562	Orenburg	35300
Donetsk	0622	Pavlodar	3182
Dushanbe	3772	Penza	8412
Fergana	373	Perm	3422
Gomel	02322	Petropavlovsk	3150
Grozny	8712	Petrozavodsk	81400
Irkutsk	3952	Pinsk	01653
Ivanovo	09322	Poltava	05322
Izhevsk	3412	Pskov	81122
Kaliningrad	01122	Rostov	08536
Kaluga	08422	Rostov-on-Don	8632
Karaganda	3210	Rovno	0360
Kaunas	0127	Ryazan	0912
Kazan	8432	St. Petersburg	812
Kemerovo	38422	Samarkand	366
Khabarovsk	4210	Saransk	8342
Kharkov	0572	Saratov	8452
Kiev	044	Semipalatinsk	3222
Kirov	833	Sergeyev Posad	254
Kostroma	09422	Sevastopol	0690
Krasnodar	8612	Simferopol	06522
Krasnoyarsk	3912	Smolensk	08100
Kuybyshev	8462	Sochi	8620

Stavropol	86522
Sukhumi	88122
Sumgait	89264
Suzdal	09231
Syktyvkar	82122
Taganrog	86344
Tambov	07522
Tashkent	3712
Tbilisi	8832
Termez	37622
Tomsk	38222
Tula	0872
Tver	08222
Tyumen	3452
Ufa	3472
Ulan-Ude	30122
Ulyanovsk	84222
Uralsk	31122
Vitebsk	02122
Vladimir	09222
Volgograd	8442
Vologda	81722
Volokolamsk	236
Voronezh	0732
Vyborg	278
Yakutsk	41122
Yalta	0600
Yaroslavl	0852
Yekaterinburg	3432
Yerevan	8852
Zaporozhe	0612
Zhitomir	041

☑ **For other cities, or if you have difficulties with dialing, or if you want the number for directory assistance for a certain city, call 07.**

☑ **Note that Moldova, Estonia, Lithuania and Latvia now have their own country dialing codes (see chart on page 130).**

A

	Phone	Fax	Telex
A & A Relocations, Krapivinskiy p. 3, bldg. 2	299-2960	924-0782	
A&G Relocations-Russia, Ltd., Staropanskiy p. 4	923-7813	117-6001	
A.C.P., see Litwin			
A1 Trade Int'l. Systems Ltd., ul. Myasnitskaya 15/17	923-1353	921-0593	411700
ABB Asea Brown Boveri AG, Gazetny p. 17	956-9810	230-2833	413229
ABB Inc./ABB Lummus, Gazetny p. 17/9, 9th Floor	956-9810	956-9809	
ABB Industry, Inc., ul. Profsoyuznaya 23	120-3030	120-3490	
ABB Oy, Gazetny p. 17	956-9810	956-9809	413229
Abbott Laboratories, Gruzinskiy p. 3, kv. 162	254-1774	230-2462	413340
ABC Opel, ul. Sergeya Eyzenshteyna 1	181-0407		
ABC/TIEMPO, B. Spasskaya 12, kv.11			
ABD Company, Staropanskiy p. 4	921-7641		
Abkhaskiy Dvor Restaurant, Nakhimovskiy prosp. 35	124-9833		
ABR Consortium, 1st Kolobovskiy p. 27/3	921-2952		
Abramtsevo Museum,			
from Yaroslavskiy Railway Museum	2-543-2470		
Absolut, Pokrovka ul. 12	227-3985	925-8057	
Academinvest JV (Austria), ul. Gubkina 14, kv. 11	129-0443	938-2278	
Academy of Agricultural Science,			
B. Kharitonyevskiy p. 21	124-7724	207-3762	
Academy of Medical Sciences,			
see Russian Academy of Medical Sciences			
Academy of Sciences, see Russian Academy of Sciences			
Accent, ul. Krzhizhanovskovo 14, k. 3	124-4504		
Acotech JV, B. Kommunisticheskaya ul. 36, str. 4	272-3262	271-9924	
Adams and Reese, Dmitrovka B. ul. 4/2, #1b	925-8430	925-9992	
Adidas-Moscow Ltd., Leningradskiy prosp. 39A	213-6525	213-2938	614408
Adventist Health Center,			
60-Letiya Oktyabrya prosp. 21a	126-7906	126-3391	
AEC, ul. Skakovaya 3	945-2477	251-1538	
AEG Aktiengesellschaft,			
Pokrovskiy bul. 4/17, k. 3, 1st fl.	208-5413	230-2313	413265
Aektra, Kalanchevskaya ul. 16, kv. 4	972-6132	972-6119	414536
Aengevelt Immobilien KG, ul. Burdenko 14a	248-1855	248-2350	
Aero Traders Pvt. Ltd,			
Krasnopresnenskaya nab. 12, Office 1105a	255-5751	253-2675	413069
Aerocom Corp., Leninskiy prosp. 32A	938-1811	938-1704	411809
Aerofirst JV, Sheremetevo 2 Airport	578-5749	230-2351	411954
Aeroflot, Leningradskiy prosp., 37	155-6641		411969
Arrivals	578-7518		
Departures	578-7816		
Sheremetevo 2 Airport	578-9101		411969

All numbers and addresses in the Telephone Directory were individually verified prior to printing and are therefore judged to be the best available at the time of publication. Given the swift nature of change in Moscow, it is expected that some numbers will not be correct even soon after printing. If you have corrections or additions to suggest to the Telephone Directory, please call Russian Information Services at (Moscow) 254-9275 or (US) 802-223-4955; fax 802-223-6105.

	Phone	Fax	Telex
Aeroflot Airport Information, Leningradskiy prosp. 37	155-0922		
Aeroflot Bank, Leningradskiy prosp.37a	292-0759	292-0759	
Aeroflot-Lufthansa and Partners JV,			
Sheremetevo I Airport, K-340	578-0540	578-2743	
Aerofreight, P.O. Box 47	954-8879	954-8879	
Aeroimp JV (Canada), Leningradskiy prosp. 37, k. 9	155-5987	155-6614	
Aeromar JV (USA), Sheremetevo I Airport	578-4141	578-2714	
Aeroprima JV, Ul. Pudovkina 6, k. 2	147-1051	143-2919	
Aeroservice JV, Sheremetevo 2 Airport	578-9030	578-2753	911718
Aerostar Hotel, Leningradskiy prosp. 37, k. 9	155-5030	155-6614	414831
Borodino Bar	155-5030		
Business Center	155-5030		
Cafe Taiga	155-5030		
K-Boutiques	155-5030		
Terrace Bar	155-5030		
Aerovokzal, Leningradskiy prosp. 37a	155-0922		
AES, Ltd., Shmitovskiy pr. 33	259-2876	959-2876	
Aescom, Ul. Parshina 23, Ap. 89	197-6760	292-6511	
Aesop Center, PO Box 27	141-8315	141-8315	
AF Computers, Sudostroitelnaya ul. 15	112-6204	112-6204	411700
AFCO-Pager, prosp. Mira 51	290-2704	197-7831	
Africana Beauty Center, The, ul. Zelenodolskaya 41	172-7671		
Aftonbladet, ul. D. Ulyanova 16,k. 2, kv. 320	124-3361	124-0364	
AG Plan, Mezhdunarodnaya assotsiatsiya 'Moskva',			
prosp. Mira 176	286-6316	283-0259	
Agat-Credit JV (USA), Krymskiy val 10/14	238-8558	230-2576	
Agence France Presse,			
ul. Sadovaya-Samotechnaya 12/24, kv. 67-68	292-3175	200-1946	413321
Agency for International Cooperation and			
Development, ul. Vozdvizhenka 18	290-0903	975-2253	
Agenzia Nazionale Stampa Associata (ANSA),			
Kutuzovskiy prosp. 9, kv. 14,12	243-7393	243-0637	413451
Agimpex, Detskiy Mir, 4th floor			
Agip, Staropimenovskiy p. 13	973-0572	973-0585	
Agora USA, Inc., ul. Tuchkovskaya 6, kv.3	145-0583	145-0583	
Agrica Commercial Bank, ul. Timiryazevskaya 26	210-1129	979-0116	911008
Agrika (Poland), ul. Profsoyuznaya 128	338-7266	338-4055	412152
Agrina (Steepler Publisher), Bobrov p. 4/2	928-0637	921-0996	
AgroEngineering JV, ul. B. Sadovaya 2/46	254-8842	253-9203	411756
Agroimpex JV (France), ul. Lesnaya 43	258-9563	973-2017	411274
Agroindustrial Complex, Economy and Mgmt			
Journal, ul. Sadovaya-Spasskaya 18	207-1662	207-2870	
Agrokhim Association, Znamenskiy B. p. 2/16	203-2352		114507
Agrokhimbank, Znamenskiy B. p. 2/16	202-3847	202-6185	
Agromark JV (Austria),			
Novogireyevskaya 24, k. 1, kv. 6	176-9572		
Agropribor, ul. Skakovaya 36	257-1898		
Ahlstrom ABB Stromberg, Mamonovskiy p. 4, kv. 3	209-6417	200-0254	413483
Aideks JV (Italy), 1st Krasnoselskiy p. 7/9, str.5, kv. 224	264-0664	263-0389	411700
AIG Trading, Slavyanskaya-Radisson Hotel, #812/843	941-8228	941-8229	
Aikon JV (UK), Uglovoy p. 27	972-3135	973-3741	413523
AIOC (American International Ore Corp.),			
ul. Mytnaya 1, kv. 5	230-6647	238-0700	

	Phone	Fax	Telex
Air Algerie, Koroviy val 7, section 11	237-5257		
Air Charter Service	939-0200		
Air China, Kuznetskiy Most 1/8, Str. 5	292-3387	292-5136	413080
Sheremetevo 2 Airport	578-2725		
Air France, Koroviy val 7	237-2325	230-2005	
Sheremetevo 2 Airport	578-2757		
Air India, Koroviy val 7, k. 1	237-7494		
Sheremetevo 2 Airport	578-2747		
Air-BI JV, Sheremetevo 2 Airport	578-8268	578-2777	
Air-Troyka, Kuznetskiy Most 6/3	927-8303	924-3582	
Airborne Express, Spasoplinishchevskiy B. p. 9/1	262-9515		
Airline Ticket Booking, Leningradskiy prosp. 37	155-5003	155-2618	
International	156-8019		
AISI International JV (Italy), Dmitrovka M. ul. 8	209-7553	200-4287	
AISI JV, P.O. Box 332	925-7158	200-3219	
Aist, M. Bronnaya 1/8	291-6692		
AIT Information Systems, Lyusinovskaya 72	236-3717	236-3717	
AJT Air International,			
ul. Varvarka 6, Hotel Rossiya, #503	298-1404	298-1504	
AK III/Steepler Intl, ul. Prechistenka 40	193-1624	246-4752	
Akademicheskaya I Hotel, Leninskiy prosp. 1	238-0902		
Akademicheskaya II Hotel, see Rossiyanka Hotel			
Akademkniga, ul. Tverskaya 19			
Akko-Universal, ul. Kosmonavta Volkova 6A, #1206	155-5644	150-8329	411182
Akonis, ul. Radio 17	267-2022		
AKPS Marcom VT JV (Austria), ul. Kedrova 15	124-1711	200-0260	114526
Aktsia Art Gallery, Krymskiy val 10/14	291-7509		
Akva, ul. Fonvizina 5a	210-6546	979-5014	
Akvales JV Filial, B. Kisselny p. 13/15	200-4282		411647
Akzent Media Russia, ul. Malomoskovskaya 21	286-2666	286-4783	
Al-Hayat, Rublyovskoye sh. 26, k. 1, kv. 18	415-4253	415-4254	
Alain Manoukian Shop, ul. Druzhinnikovskaya 11	255-9140		
Alankom, ul. Letchika Babushkina 26	186-5301	470-8274	
Alarm Center, Lomonovskiy prosp. 27	939-0098		
Alberto Beski - Products of Italy, GUM, 3rd line, 1st fl.	926-3246		
Alcatel BSR, Pokrovskiy bul. 4/17, #21	207-9998	230-2688	
Alcatel Trade International, Spasonalivkovskiy p.2. 4	230-0334	230-6875	413558
Alcoholics Anonymous (English),			
ul. D. Ulyanova 37, k. 1	243-4260		
Aleks Detective Agency	255-2901		
Alexander Blok Hotel, see Inflotel			
Alexander Industries, Ltd.,			
ul. Kosmonavta Volkova 14, 8th floor	156-9604	450-3147	
Alexander's, Kolonny Zal, Entrance 6, Dmitrovka B. ul. 1	292-7123		
Alfa Technology, Dmitrovka B. ul. 4-2-10	923-4476	925-2512	
Alfa-Echo, ul. Novatorov 7, k. 2/ ul. Novyi Arbat 21	936-1777	936-2195	411792
Alfa-Laval, Pokrovskiy bul. 4/17, kv. 29	207-6478	230-2146	413355
Alfa-Star, ul. Kedrova, 5	125-3978	125-2061	
Alfa-Systems JV (FRG), ul. Vorontsovskaya 35A	924-4161		
Algemeen Dagblad, ul. Akad. Koroleva 4, k. 2, kv. 79-80	215-1966	215-1966	413644
Alisa Construction Exchange, Leninskiy prosp. 45	137-6819	137-6525	
Alitalia, ul. Pushechnaya 7	923-9840		
Sheremetevo 2 Airport	578-2767		

	Phone	Fax	Telex
Alkodes, ul. B. Ordynka 46	233-5941	257-2707	
Alkort Ltd, prosp. Mira 18, room 234	477-7289	908-2866	
All American Renovation, Tverskoy bul. 152	229-7097	956-3301	
All Express Services (AES), Shmitovskiy pr. 33	256-4502	259-0832	
All Nippon Airways,			
Hotel Mezhdunarodnaya II, room 1405	253-1546	253-1549	
Sheremetevo 2 Airport	578-5744	578-2720	
All Russian Commodity Exchange,			
B. Matrosskiy p. 1/1	217-6027	217-6051	
All Russian Exchange Bank, Yaroslavskoye sh. 13	188-8136	188-8674	
All-Russia Decorative and Folk Art Museum,			
ul. Delegatskaya 3	921-0139		
All-Star Jazz Club, ul. Generala Yermolova 6			
Alla JV (Switz.), Sokolnicheskiy val 1	269-2697	269-3098	
Allen-Bradley Co., B. Strochenovski p. 22/25 office 403	230-6010	230-6015	
Alliance Brokerage House,			
Brodnikov p. 7, str. 2, entr. 2	222-1306	238-8556	
Allied Pickfords, ul. B. Dorogomilovskaya 16, #12	243-7609	243-7609	
Allimpex JV (FRG), 1st Varshavskiy pr. 2	111-8497	111-7178	207301
Alma, ul. Kluchevaya 8	342-8848		
Almaz Cinema, ul. Shabolovka 56	234-1002		
Almaz Independent Group, Kutuzovskiy prosp. 35	249-5049		
Almazyuvelirexport, Zubovskiy bul. 25, k. 1	245-3420	956-6326	411115
Almeko JV, Leningradskiy prosp. 80	158-8927	158-5671	
Alpa JV, ul. Kosmonavta Volkova 16	450-3500	943-0072	411080
Alpha Design, Inc., ul. 2nd Baumanskaya 9/23	265-7236		
AlphaGraphics Inc., ul. 1st Tverskaya-Yamskaya 22	251-1208	230-2207	
ALS JV, B. Strochenovskiy p. 13	236-1041		
Altair JV (France), Profsoyuznaya ul. 84/32	333-3145	333-4513	411498
Altay Cinema, Kubanskaya ul. 29	350-4033		
Altay Hotel, Botanicheskaya ul. 41	482-5703		
Alternativa JV (Sweden), Seliverstov p. 2, 4	207-5758	975-2425	414-20
Alternative JV & IPLV, Orlyonok Hotel			

Less *is* more.

Our philosophy in compiling *Where in Moscow* is that less advertisements means more information. In this sense, *Where in Moscow*'s content is driven by its users, not its advertisors. As a result, *Where in Moscow*, now in its fifth year, enjoys a reputation for concise, easy-to-access and objectively-presented information. Further, we allow only full page advertisements, because we feel that this provides the advertisor with a more exclusive and more reasonable amount of space to present their pitch, while not breaking the "flow" of information for the reader. We don't think you should have to fish through advertisements to get the phone number or address you need. And we don't feel our advertisors should have to fight for your attention. We also rely on the considerable amount of feedback and input from readers. If you have suggestions or ideas for helping us continually improve this or any other RIS publication, please do not hesitate to contact us.

HOTEL
METROPOL
MOSCOW

A MEMBER OF INTER-CONTINENTAL HOTELS GROUP

METROPOL RESTAURANT

Buffet Style Dining, International Cuisine.
Breakfast 7 am to 10:30 am
Lunch: Noon to 3:30 pm
Dinner: 6:30 pm to 11 pm
Sunday Brunch 11:30 am to 3:30 pm

EVROPEYSKIY RESTAURANT

French Cuisine, 11 am to 11 pm

BOYARSKIY RESTAURANT

Russian Fine Dining
Monday to Saturday, 7 pm to 11 pm

ARTIST BAR

Open Noon to Midnight

SHALYAPIN BAR

Open 7 am to 2 am

CAFE CONFECTIONARY

Open 10 am to 8 pm

BUSINESS CENTER

Open 8 am to 10 pm weekdays
8 am to 8 pm weekends

1/4 Teatralny Proezd, 103012 Moscow, Russia
Telephone: 7(501) or 7(095) 927-6000
Telefax: 7(501) or 7(095) 927-6010

Sunday Brunch available in the Metropol Restaurant
American Express cards preferred
All major credit cards accepted

Russia has never
been this accessible!

This **essential guide** to doing business in the new Russia is the current version of the most widely-read book on doing business in the new Russia. This guide includes valuable information like: how to get a visa, customs regulations, rubles and what you can do with them, dealing with transportation, accommodations and telecommunications, including up-to-date contact information for travel and business in Russia's 77 largest cities, hotel prices and ratings, how to make contacts, business etiquette and customs, and a complete review of investment, trade and enterprise legislation, including import/export, currency and taxation laws.
ISBN 1-880100-18-5
March 1994, 232 p., $18.50

...and St. Petersburg will
never be the same!

This companion guide to *Where in Moscow* is the first complete guide to the new St. Petersburg. It includes St. Petersburg's best (all-new and in full color) city street map, the city's first English language yellow pages and only white pages directories. Whether you are going to the Imperial City for business, study or pleasure, you can't afford to go without this guide!
If you like *Where in Moscow*, you'll love *Where in St. Petersburg*!
ISBN 1-880100-13-4
March 1994, 184 p., $13.50

*Ask at your local bookseller, or see last page of book for ordering information.

	Phone	Fax	Telex
Altromash JV (Austria), 2nd Vladimirskaya ul. 6, k. 2	176-1472	176-2130	414712
Alybiross JV (England), Nikitskaya, B. ul. 47, str. 2	291-7831	230-2571	
Alyusvislonza Produkte, ul. Usacheva 35	245-5042	244-2966	
Amadeus Cafe, Radisson-Slavyanskaya Hotel	941-8333		
Ambassador, ul. Prechistenka 29	201-4014		
Ambiz, Inc., Chistoprudny bul. 23, kv. 25	208-5254	208-5254	
Ambulance	03		
AMC, see American Medical Center			
Amca Chimie et Plastiques, see Groupe Litwin			
AMCA International, see Litwin			
Amerex, Inc., ul. Krasnobogatyrskaya 42	963-4902	963-4881	
American Business Club	273-3101		
American Cultural Center Library,			
Nikoloyamskaya ul. 1, 2nd floor, Foreign Lit. Library	297-6985		
American Drug Store, Shmitovskiy proyezd 3	259-7181		
American Express, ul. Sadovo-Kudrinskaya 21a	956-9000	253-9372	413075
American Food Companies, The,			
ul. Tallinskaya 2, kv. 172, box 5217	942-3787	292-6511;	
American Found. for Diplomacy and Cooperation,			
Smolenskiy bul. 17	244-0042	230-2200	411939
American International Group (AIG),			
Radisson-Slavyanskaya Hotel	941-8879	941-8879	
American International Ore Corp.,			
ul. Mytnaya 1, office 5	230-6647	238-0700	413807
American Medical Center, Shmitovskiy pr. 3	256-8212	973-2142	911626
American Office Supplies, Inc., ul. Ostrovityanova 1	434-7617	434-6183	
American Store, ul. Profsoyuznaya 84/32	333-2313	333-6466	
American Technology, Raushskaya nab. 4/5	239-3046	230-7363	
American Trade Center, Radisson Slavyanskaya Hotel	941-0015	941-8376	
American Trade Consortium (Mercator),			
nab. Shevchenko 3a	243-1404	243-9777	412100
American Video Store, B. Gnezdnikovskiy p. 10, kv. 834	229-7459		
American Wholesale Center: Pervomaiskiy Center,			
9th Parkovaya ul. 62	468-4119		
American Women's Club, The	202-7175		
Americom Business Center,			
Radisson-Slavyanskaya Hotel	941-8427	941-8376	
Ameritrade, ul. Krasnoproletarskaya 9, kv. 164, ent. 3	258-5339	258-5339	
Amerkand JV, 3rd Cherepkovskaya ul. 15a			
Amersham Internationl, ul. Tverskaya 22A, floor 5	299-5438	299-5325	
Ameta, VVTs	181-9988	181-9988	
Amfora JV (Austria), Gogolevskiy bul. 14	291-1688	291-2911	
Amigo JV (Spain), Komsomolskiy prosp. 19	248-2225		412164
Amitra Inc., ul. Nezhdannaya 15, 4th fl., kom. 70	925-1991	924-9120	
AMMO JV (Holland), ul. Kosygina 4	137-8241	938-2156	112790
Amnesty International	291-2904	291-2904	
AMO Ltd., Kashirskoye sh. 57, k. 2	344-6604		
ul. Avtozavodskaya 5, 'Ogonyek'	275-4314		
Amoco Eurasia Petroleum Co.,			
Moscow Region, Krasnogorsk, Gorki-6, #3	418-4359	418-4359	411133
Amro Bank, Krasnopresnenskaya nab. 12, Office 1209	253-1476	255-0513	413301
Amru-Star JV (US), ul. Aviamotornaya 53	273-9388	273-1937	412176

	Phone	Fax	Telex
Amskort International JV (US),			
prosp. Mira, VVTs, Pavilion 4	187-8386	187-9657	411089
Amsovinvest JV (US), ul. Mytnaya 18	238-5914	230-2360	
AmSovMed JV (USA), ul. Dostoyevskovo 4	288-9837		
Amstroi JV (US)	243-2792	243-2488	
AMT JV (Finland), Khoroshevskoye sh. 42a	941-3092	253-9911	412225
Amtel Exports Private Ltd.,			
Krasnopresnenskaya nab. 12, Office 503L	253-1944	253-1949	411636
Amtorg Trading Corp., Trubnikovskiy p. 19	202-5794	202-5794	
ANA, see All Nippon Airways			
Ana-1, ul. Lublinskaya 117/4	351-4028		
Anatolian News Agency, Rublyovskoye sh. 26, kv. 279	415-2934		413641
Anchor Restaurant,			
Palace Hotel, ul. Tverskaya-Yamskaya 19	956-3152	956-3151	
Ancor Agency	261-9262	261-9262	
Andre & Cie S.A., Pokrovskiy bul. 4/17, k. 3, kv. 2, 4	207-2959	208-9942	213296
Andrei Rublyov Museum of Early Russian Art,			
Adronyevskaya pl. 10 (Andronnikov Monastery)	278-1489		
Andrew Corp., ul. Volkhonka 3/4, 2nd fl.	203-0280	203-6005	
Andy's Fashion, prosp. Vernadskovo 9	131-0420	131-0420	
Angara Cinema, Chongarskiy bul. 7	110-5602		
Anglo-American School, B. Devyatinskiy p. 8	255-0326		
Leninskiy prosp. 78	131-8700		
Anglo-Soviet Shipping Co. Ltd.,			
Pokrovskiy bul. 4/17, kv. 25	230-2955	230-2955	413158
Angolan Airlines, see Linhas Aereas de Angola			
Angolan Radio, see Embassy of Angola			
ANGOP News Agency, ul. Olaf Palme 6	143-6531		413402
Angst Film and TV, Rublyovskoye sh. 26, k. 1, kv. 130	415-4211	415-2946	412631
Angstrome JV, prosp. Mira, VVTs			
Angus Fire Armour Ltd., ul. Musorgskovo 4, office 62	403-1465	403-1465	
Anima Box, ul. Volkhonka 5/6, stroenie 8	203-4115	203-3933	
Animal Theater, ul. Durova 4	281-2914		
Anna Mons Restaurant, ul. Krasnokazarmennaya 3	261-8626	267-9726	
Annik JV, Leningradskiy prosp. 47			
Annushka Tea Tram	236-8272		
Anson Trade Ltd., Staraya Basmanaya 18/1	267-4130	261-6414	
Antenne 2, Leninskiy prosp. 45, kv. 427	135-1172	230-2010	413304
Antiakhilskoye Podvorje, Arkhangelskiy p. 15a	923-4605		
Antikvar, ul. 1st Tverskaya-Yamskaya 14	251-6548		
Antikvariat, ul. B. Yakimanka 52	238-9545		
Antique - Bukinist, Teatralny pr., 1	971-6181		
ul. Arbat 36	241-3387		
Antiques, ul. Arbat 9	291-7034		
Antonika, ul. Arbat 4	291-7444		
AO Vartecon, ul. 1st Tverskaya-Yamskaya 14	251-0500	250-1302	
AOT Limited, Krasnopresnenskaya nab. 12, office 534	253-2534	253-2534	413795
Aoyama Motors Ltd., ul. Tverskaya 29/3	209-6490		
Zemlyanoy val 41/2	297-4128	297-4128	
APCO, see Most JV (USA)			
Apco Associates, Inc., Varshavskoye sh. 46, ent. 3, #512	111-4320	230-6295	
Apiko Ltd., ul. Sretenka 36	975-4342	207-1025	
APN (Novosti News Agency), see IAN			

	Phone	Fax	Telex
Apollo Store, ul. Arbat 32	241-6060		
Apple Computer (RUI a.r.), Petrovskiy p. 8	229-1136	229-7414	
Kazenny M. p. 12/1, apt.20	207-4570		
Apricot Computers PLC, Koroviy val 7, office 4	236-2135	230-2488	413905
Apteka, Beskudnikovskiy bul. 59A	905-4227		
Bolshaya Polyanka 30	238-4134	202-4920	
Detskiy Mir, 4th floor			
ul. Pyatnitskaya 16	231-7013		
APV Pasilac, Mamonovskiy p. 4, Office 6	209-2823	200-0241	413308
APV PLC, Mamonovskiy p. 4, kv. 6	209-2823	200-0241	413308
Aquarius Systems Integral, Dmitrovka B. ul. 32	200-0459	229-8459	
Arab School, ul. Ulofa Palme 5	147-4083		
Aragvi Restaurant, ul. Tverskaya 6	229-3762		
Araks cafe, Sirenevy bul. 11, korp. 2	164-3630		
Arbat Blues Club, Aksakov p. 11, kor. 2	291-1546		
Arbat Hotel, Plotnikov p. 12	244-7635		
Arbat Inc. 90 JV, ul. Durova 36	921-2820	200-2265	
Arbat International JV (UK), Arbatskiy p. 6/2 kv. 7-8	291-5904	291-6078	411700
Arbat Irish House, Novy Arbat 13	291-7641		
Arbat Trade Company, Novy Arbat 21	291-7767	291-7790	
Arbeiderbladet, Leninskiy prosp. 148, kv. 43	434-4697		
Arbitration Board, Council of Ministers of Russia	208-1194		
Arbitration Board, Moscow City Council,			
Novobasmannaya ul. 10	297-7583		
Arbitration Board, Moscow Regional Council,			
Vetoshny p. 9	228-8388		
Arch Technology Corp., prosp. Vernadskovo 41, #800	431-0554		
Architecture Museum (Shchusev Museum of			
Architecture, Don Monastery, Donskaya pl. 1	232-0221		
ul. Vozdvizhenka 5	291-2109		
Area Travel Agency Ltd., ul. Rozhdestvenka 3	929-8665		
Arena cafe, ul. 10-letiya Oktyabrya 11	245-2972		
Arena Hotel, ul. 10-letiya Oktyabrya 11	245-2802		
Arendmash JV (Finland),			
ul. Zoi i Aleksandra Kosmodemyanskikh 26/21	150-9700	943-0050	411085
Argoteknics Stil JV (Syria), Dmitrovskoye sh. 107	332-8555		
Argumenti i Fakti, Myasnitskaya ul. 42	923-3541	200-2252	
Argus Trading Ltd., ul. Skakovaya 9, floor 4	945-2777	945-2765	612171
Ariana Afghan Airlines, Koroviy val 7, fl. 2, kv. 8a	238-9779	238-9779	414459
Sheremetevo 2 Airport	578-2719		
Ariplan, International Association JV			
Aris Co. Ltd., Tsentralny pr. 1, #246	536-5196	534-2735	
Ark, Mnevniki 7, k. 1, office 1	946-6549	946-6549	411418
Arkadia Jazz Club, Teatralny pr. 3	926-9008		
Arkadia Restaurant, Teatralny pr. 3, str. 4	926-9545		
Arkom JV (Holland), ul. Simonova 3b	152-0717		411263
Arksim JV Filial (China), Glazovskiy p. 3/14	241-9124	241-6858	
Arktika Cinema, ul. Menzhinskovo 6	472-5979		
Arlecchino Restaurant JV (Italy),			
ul. Druzhinnikovskaya 15	205-7088	973-2029	411070
Arlekin, Inc., pl. Zhurolova 1	928-6841	267-1557	
Armadillo, VVTs, bldg. 1, #15, prosp. Mira 120	181-7074		
Armadillo Bar, Khrustalny p. 1	254-2832		

	Phone	Fax	Telex
Armco International, Inc., 1st Vrazhskiy p. 4	248-1865	248-1582	
Armed Forces Museum, ul. Sovetskoy Armii 2	281-1880		
Armoury Palace, Kremlin	221-4720		
Arnold & Porter, Khvostov p. 3A	238-5525	238-1574	
Aromat Restaurant, ul. Rogova, 12, kor 2	947-0024	947-0024	
Arrange Media Service, ul. Lesnaya 27	251-5602	251-1841	
Arrow, GUM, 1st line, 1st fl.	926-3474		
ART, Leninskiy prosp. 93, kv. 42	138-3477		
Art and Electronics JV (US), ul. Sadovaya-Triumfalnaya 14-12	209-6247	200-2232	
Art Gallery of the USSR, see State Tretyakov Art Gallery			
Art Moderne Gallery, ul. B. Ordynka 39	242-0175	281-8955	
Art Salon, Ukrainskiy bul. 6-185	264-4109		
Art Zone Gallery, Pullman Iris Hotel	488-8267		
ART&C, ul. Parfenova 11	134-0495	383-0292	
Artel, ul. Myasnitskaya 26	925-2901	924-1198	
Business Center, Novy Arbat 2	245-0026	291-3374	
Arthur Andersen & Co., ul. Staraya Basmannaya 14	262-5077	262-7336	
Artists' Bar, Hotel Metropol, Teatralny pr. 1/4	927-6159		
Artmodern, Izvestkovy p.3	928-2431	975-2316	
Artromed International JV (Australia), 2nd Tverskaya-Yamskaya ul. 52, kab. 6	450-3811	200-2217	411700
AS JV (France), Lubyanskiy pr. 4	445-0787		411630
Asahi Shimbun, Kutuzovskiy prosp. 7/4, k. 6, kv. 63	243-0989	230-2772	413383
Asea Brown Bauer, see ABB Asea			
ASET Consultants, Inc., Zagorodnoye sh. 9	958-6273	958-6273	
Ashkhabad Cinema, Chertanovskaya ul. 17a	315-1268		
Asikulo JV (Finland), Nikitskaya M. ul. 16, kv.4	258-8957		411700
ASK JV (Austria), Tverskoy bul. 13	433-0981	433-0981	
ASK JV (USA), Smolenskiy bul. 17	244-0042	230-2200	411939
Asko Consulting, Petrovskaya pl. 12	209-1208		
Asko Insurance Company, Universitetskiy prosp. 21	143-4692	143-8658	
Asko Moden JV (FRG), Dmitrovskoye sh. 7	216-2779	216-2809	
Askot JV (Switz.), Nikitskiy bul. 11	291-3218	200-2284	
Asmaral JV (UK), Kotelnicheskaya nab. 1/15, kv. 28, k. V	928-9760	227-4286	411823
ASP Equipman, Leningradskiy prosp. 36, BSA, ent. 1	213-4321	214-9829	413723
Aspect JV (UK), Gagarinskiy p. 25	241-2206	230-2658	412156
Aspek JV (Spain), ul. Fedotovoy 11/2, kv. 14	241-9500	291-6880	
Assess-Moskva JV (Austria), Zubovskiy bul. 4	201-3548	201-4545	411323
Associated Press, Kutuzovskiy prosp. 7/4, k. 5, kv. 33	243-5153	230-2845	413422
Association 'Moscow', ul. Varvarka 8b	298-3398	298-3398	
Association Amikst JV (France, Germany), Novinskiy bul. 18a	291-7505	230-2884	
Association of Joint Ventures, Leningradskiy prosp. 55, pod. 6	943-9481	943-0020	
Association of Post Graduate Education, ul. Sadovaya-Triumfalnaya 2/30	299-7636		
Assotiation of Tchaikovskiy Prize winners, Nikitskaya, B. ul. 14/2	201-6092	201-6956	411625
Asteis JV (UK), Verkhniy Taganskiy tupik 2	272-1176	271-9215	411355
Astek JV (Australia), ul. 3rd Cherepkovskaya 15a	414-6932	414-6985	112454
Astiko JV (US), ul. Tverskaya 5	291-9924	200-3210	
Asto, ul. Gorbunova 14	447-3804		

	Phone	Fax	Telex
Asto (Avtoexport-Satra) JV (Italy, Germany),			
ul. Marksa-Engelsa 8	202-8626	975-2218	411436
ASU-Impuls, ul. Nelidovskaya 18, kv. 38	497-2047	497-2047	
AT&T, Chernysheskovo p. 1	284-3215	284-3491	
Atel JV (Switzerland)	939-3784		
Atelier, Leninskiy prosp. 21			
Lomonosovskiy prosp. 23			
Mozhayskiy val 4			
ul. B. Yakimanka 19			
Atelier Modnie Golovnie Ubori, Nikitskaya, B. ul. 16	229-0663		
Atemi JV, ul. Trubnaya 4	207-3113	208-4836	
Athens Medical Center, Michurinskiy prosp. 6	143-2387		
Athens News Agency/ET-2 TV/NEA,			
Rublyovskoye sh. 36, k. 2, kv. 255-6	415-4306	415-4306	
Atlant Commercial Bank, prosp. Mira 50	280-1302		
Atlant JV (Yugoslavia), Nakhimovskiy prosp. 32	129-0933	310-7026	411163
Atlantik International JV, ul. Vavilova 44, k. 2	236-0555		
Atlantikstrom JV, Dmitrovka B. ul. 9	229-4229		
Atlas, Zemlyanoy val 14/16	297-4937	297-7816	
Atlas Language Service, Vorontsovskiy p. 2, office 206	272-6257		
Atochem, see Elf Aquitaine			
Atoll Firm, Kashirskoye sh. 66, k. 1, entrance 2	324-0728	324-3020	
Atomenergoexport, Ovchinnikovskaya nab. 18/1	220-1436	230-2181	411397
Atrium Cafe, Leninskiy prosp. 44	137-3008		
Audi Sales and Service, see Fisherman's Harbor			
Auditing Council of the USSR	206-7187		
Auriga Int'l, Kostyaniskiy p. 9, kv. 45			
Aurora 80, Lavrushinskiy p. 17, kv. 83	231-3507	230-2096	413616
Australian Broadcasting Corporation,			
Rublyovskoye sh. 26, kv. 19	415-4015	415-2904	413639
Australian Down Under Club, Kropotkinskiy p. 13			
Australian Pie Co., Ltd., Varshavskoye sh. 46	111-0522		
Australian-Soviet Bakery, Pyatnitskaya ul. 29/8			
Austrian Airlines,			
Krasnopresnenskaya nab. 12, Office 1805	253-1670	253-1669	413127
Sheremetevo 2 Airport	578-2734	578-2770	413901
Auto Clemert, ul. Vorontsovo pole 3	297-2271	297-5273	
Auto Sun JV (Japan), Grokholskiy p. 29	280-3600	280-4428	414753
Sheremetevo 2 Airport	280-3600		
Auto-Lux International JV (FRG), ul. Oktyabrskaya 6	288-8785	970-2015	412126
Autobank, ul. Lesnaya 41	258-9412	258-9412	
Autoclave Engineers, Inc., Leningradskiy prosp. 36	212-7482	214-9829	
Autodesignservice JV (Japan), Trubnikovskiy pr. 1	290-2322		
Autohaus 'Helbig', Dobrolyubova ul. 2A	218-1613	218-1613	
Autosensor (represens Volkswagen in Moscow),			
1st Tverskaya-Yamskaya 46, office 6	251-0500	250-1302	
Autoserve JV, ul. B. Molchanovka 36	291-9631	292-6511	411700
Autoshop Toyota, prosp. Marshala Zhukova 49/1	199-5977	199-5977	
Avangard Cinema, ul. Generala Belova 18	394-7900		
Avantat, Dmitrovka B. ul. 2	292-1175		
AVEX Commodities Exchange	921-1430		
Aviabank, Ulanskiy p. 16	207-5856	207-0467	411761
Aviaexport, Trubnikovskiy p. 19	290-0176		

	Phone	Fax	Telex
Aviation and Cosmonautics Journal,			
Petrovsko-Razumovskaya alleya 12	155-1328		
Aviation and Space Travel Museum (Frunze			
Central Museum), Krasnoarmeyskaya ul. 4			
Aviation stock company VOLARE,			
Novoryazanskaya ul. 26	267-6545	261-6608	
Avicenna JV, 2nd Romyatnicheskiy p. 11/16	229-5593	288-9563	411685
AVIS Car Rental - main office, prosp. Vernadskovo 7	930-1323	930-5995	
Sheremetevo 2 Airport	578-5646		
Avkom JV, Sheremetevo 2 Airport, K-340	578-5212		
Avon, Lavrushinsky p. 15, 2nd fl.	230-6532	230-6534	
Avon Cosmetics Store,			
Petrovskiy Passage, 1st fl. (see Passazh)			
Avrora Cinema, ul. Profsoyuznaya 154	337-2600		
Avrora Publishers, Sushchyovskiy val 64	971-0245		
Avstrokop-Lisow AG,			
Hotel Mezhdunarodnaya II, room 1548	253-1317	253-9090	
Avstrosoft JV, ul. Garibaldi 21b	128-8072	310-7060	
Avto JV (UK), ul. Marksa-Engelsa 8	203-5430		411436
Avtobank, ul. Delegatskaya 11	973-3216		
Avtodom, ul. Zorge 17	943-1001		
Avtoexport, ul. Marksa-Engelsa 8	203-0662	202-6075	411135
Avtoimport, ul. Marksa-Engelsa 8	202-6221	202-6075	
Avtokhozyaistvo, Dmitrovskoye sh. 98	488-3112		
Avtopromimport, Pyatnitskaya ul. 50/2	231-8126	238-3318	411961
AvtoVAZ Bank, ul. Novy Arbat 36	926-7663		411961
Awer, ul. Olkhovskaya 16/6	265-0535	261-5998	
Axel Johnson AB, Kutuzovskiy prosp. 13, kv. 131-132	243-5025	230-6348	413154
Axelsen Industries Ltd.,			
Krasnopresnenskaya nab. 12, Mezh-II, office 621	253-2621	253-9481	411432
Ayastan Restaurant,			
Flotskaya 3, summer on board 'Sviatoy Giorgiy'	456-9503		
Azerborn AG, Khamovnicheskiy val 34	242-3158	242-5566	

B

	Phone	Fax	Telex
B&B&A, Frunzenskaya Nab. 30, pavilion 11	201-1929	248-2524	
B*O*Y* & Co., Inc., Leninskiy prosp. 66, kv. 30	137-0003	133-4335	
Babcock, see Deutsche Babcock			
Babylon Ltd., Pokrovka ul. 40b	227-0127	227-0143	
Baginskiy Fashion,			
Sovintsentr, Mezhdunarodnaya Hotel I, 1st fl.	253-2697		
Bai JV (US), Altufyevskoye sh. 2	401-1422		
Baikal Cinema, Mikhalkovskaya ul. 4	154-1324		
Baikonur Cinema, ul. Dekabristov 21	404-5119		
Bain and Company, Inc., ul. Shcherbakovskaya 40-42	369-5948	166-6867	
Bakas AB JV, ul. Nagornaya 7, k. 3	127-6829		
Baker & Botts, L.L.P., Dmitrovka B. ul. 10	921-5300	921-5390	
Baker & McKenzie, B. Strochenovskiy 22/25	230-6036	230-6047	413671
Baker Hughes Russia, Inc.,			
Leningradskiy prosp. 36, Dinamo Stadium, Adm. Build.	212-7471	213-7934	612279

	Phone	Fax	Telex
Bakery, The,			
Olympic Penta Hotel, Olympiskiy prosp. 18/1	971-6101		
Bakhrushin Theater Museum, ul. Bakhrushina 31/12	235-3820		
Baku Cinema, ul. Usiyevicha 12/14	155-0006		
Baku Restaurant, ul. Tverskaya 24	299-8506		
Baku-Livan Bakery, ul. Tverskaya 24	299-2322		
Baku-Livan-Nasr Restaurant, ul. Tverskaya 24	299-8506		
Balkan Air, Kuznetskiy Most 3	921-0267		
Sheremetevo 2 Airport	578-2712		
Balli Trading ltd., ul. Myasnitskaya 13, str. 5, floor 2	928-2261	928-2446	413826
Baltes Moebelspedition, Vekovaya ul. 5, kv. 14	274-0746	200-2217	411700
Baltika Cinema, Skhodnenskaya ul. 54	493-1571		
Baltimore Sun, ul. Sadovaya-Samotechnaya 12/24, kv. 18	200-2153	200-0265	413426
Baltschug Kempinski Hotel, ul. Baltschuga 1	230-6500		
Baltschug Bar	230-6500		
Bistro Restaurant	230-6500		
Cafe Berlin	230-6500		
Champagne Bar	230-6500		
Gourmet Restaurant	230-6500		
Le Romanoff	230-6500		
Restaurant Baltschug	230-6500		
Bamford, J.C., Escavators Ltd., Zelenograd, P.B. 38	535-9737	536-0296	
Banca Commerciale Italiana, Mamonovskiy p. 6, kv. 9	209-6518	209-6569	413482
Banca Nazionale Del Lavoro,			
Krasnopresnenskaya nab. 12, Office 1602	253-1802	253-9472	413500
Banco Central - Madrid, ul. Mytnaya 1, Office 4	230-0388	238-9082	413042
Banco di Napoli,			
Krasnopresnenskaya nab. 12, Office 1008	253-2590	230-2952	413105
Banco di Roma, Mamonovskiy p. 4, kv. 8	209-6625	200-0233	413294
Banco Do Estado De Sao Paulo,			
Serpukhovskaya pl. 7, Office 220	238-9724		
Banco Exterior de Espana,			
Krasnopresnenskaya nab. 12, Office 1408	253-2263		413345
Banco Hispano Americano,			
Krasnopresnenskaya nab. 12, Office 1301	253-8176	253-8172	413302
Bang and Olufsen, Kutuzovskiy prosp. 8	243-0229		
Bank Austria, Dolgorukovskaya ul. 19	200-5221	200-4271	413700
Bank fur Gemeinwirtschaft AG, see BFG Moscow			
Bank of America NT & SA,			
Krasnopresnenskaya nab. 12, Office 1605	253-7054	253-9512	413189
Bank of Scotland, Pokrovskiy bul. 4/17, kv. 34	207-5998	230-2386	413121
Bank-Melli-Iran, Smolenskiy bul. 22/14, kv. 3	248-2153		
Banque Nationale de Paris,			
Pokrovskiy bul. 4/17, kv. 19	207-5888	274-0054	413243
Banque Paribas, Pokrovskiy bul. 4/17, kv, 31	297-5511	230-2188	413209
BANSO Real Estate Agency, ul. Novozavodskaya 21	148-0806	142-3939	
Banzai, ul. Novopeshchannaya 12	157-7552		
Baptist Services, M. Tryokhsvyatitelskiy p. 3	297-5167		
Bar, The, Novotel Hotel, Sheremetyevo-II	578-9407		
Barass JV, Perovskoye sh. 9	173-8352	975-2008	
Barbie, Detskiy Mir, Teatralny pr. 5			
Barclays Bank PLC, Mamonovskiy p. 4, kv. 14	209-6452		413224

	Phone	Fax	Telex
Barocenter (Center of Social Reabilitation), ul. Bolshaya Kosinskaya 139	700-0445	246-8565	
Baroid Trading International, Milyutinskiy p. 9, 3-d floor, office 'D'	208-0784	208-0784	
Barrikadi Cinema, Barrikadnaya ul. 21	252-0680		
Barrington Development, Nikoloyamskaya ul. 13	297-3454	956-3454	
Barry Martin Travel, ul. Vorontsovskaya 26	271-9232	253-9374	413197
Bars JV (Germany), Rublyovskoye sh. 16, k. 4	415-9818	415-9814	
Barus Video JV (Holland), Skatertny p. 20	290-4258	200-1286	411114
BASF AG, B. Gnezdnikovskiy p. 7	200-2749	200-3420	413167
Baskin Robbins, Lesnaya alleya 1111, Zelenograd	530-9091		
ul. Arbat 20	291-7114		
ul. Graivoronovskaya 19			
ul. Tverskaya 27/5	299-5829	299-5829	
ul. Udaltsova 19A			
ul. Varvarka 6, Hotel Rossiya	298-3594		
Baskin Robbins Moscow JV (US), ul. Metallurgov 29	305-3610	305-7990	
Bat Cabaret Theater, B. Gnezdnikovskiy p. 3	229-8661		
Batterymarch Financial Management JV (US), Merzlyakovskiy p. 8	290-2952	200-4256	411089
Bayer, ul. Mytnaya 1, 9th fl., Office 22-3	230-0042	230-0042	413947
Bayerische Hypotheker u. Wechselbank AG, see Hypo Bank			
Bayerische Vereinsbank, ul. Babayevskaya 1/8, kv 23	269-2743	268-1250	
Baykal Hotel, Selskokhozyaystvennaya ul. 15/1	189-7515		
Baytur Construction and Contracting Co., Krasnopresnenskaya nab. 12	253-1315	253-9506	413593
BBC TV News, Gruzinskiy p. 3, kv. 1-2	253-9360	253-1144	413613
BBDO Marketing, Staromonetny p. 31	231-3906	238-3088	411238
BBN, Radisson-Slavyanskaya Hotel, Press Club	941-8961	941-8659	
BC Business Car, Ovchinnikovskaya nab. 18/1	233-1796	231-4924	
Showroom, prosp. Marshala Zhukova 49/1	199-5977		
Bear Travels, prosp. Andropova 35, k. 2, apt. 172	114-4223	114-4223	
Bechtel International Inc., Povarskaya ul. 21	230-2006	291-3747	
Beckman Instruments, Inc., ul. Bolshaya Pirogovskaya 6, 11-th floor	871-4848	248-4836	
Beden & Co., Idex JV (Italy), 1st Krasnoselskiy p. 7/9, str. 5, kv. 224	264-0664	263-0389	
Beer House, Sadko Arcade (Expocenter)	940-4062		
Begemot, M. Bronnaya 20a	202-1652		
Bekar Advertising Agency	110-3993		
Belaya Rus, ul. Krasnoprudnaya 26/28, #3	264-2572		
Belcom, ul. Usacheva 35	245-5766	205-0653	
Belgian Air, see Sabena Belgian World Airlines			
Belgian Investment Group, PO Box 42, 117049	237-5195	234-5395	411663
Belgrade I Hotel, Smolenskaya pl. 5 (see also Zolotoye Koltso)	248-1643		
DAB Beer Bar	248-2684		
Centaur Shop	248-2828		
Belgub Ltd., ul. Korolenko 9, korp. 2, #48	268-7267		
Belka Trading Corp., B. Cherkasskiy p. 4	923-1403	288-9501	
Bell, Teterinskiy p. 10	208-6734		
Bell Atlantic, Degtyarny p. 2	209-6256	209-7854	

	Phone	Fax	Telex
Bely Lebed cafe, Sivtsev Vrazhek 3/18	203-1283		
Benham Int'l, Inc. (c/o Mosmontazhspetsstroi),			
Saymonovskiy pr. 5/2	203-6060	203-7051	
Benetton, GUM, 2nd line, 1st fl.	926-3420		
Hotel Moskva, ul.Okhotny Ryad 2	924-2734		
ul. Arbat 13			
Benninger AG, B. Starodanilovskiy p. 5, #434	954-0634		612366
Benxon Worldwide	205-1416	241-4771	
Bering Air	373-9664		
Beriozka, Krasnokholmskaya nab. 5/9	272-0474		
Luzhnetskiy pr. 12	246-2742		
Rossiya Hotel	298-3620		
ul. Fersmana 5	124-5024		
Beriozka Cinema, Martenovskaya ul. 25	302-0362		
Berlitz, Sovintsentr, Mezhdunarodnaya Hotel 1	253-8223		
Berner Ross Ltd., Blagoveshchenskiy p. 3A	299-4837	299-4837	
Berosil JV (Australia), ul. B. Maslovka 21	212-8482	212-8202	
Berstorff Machinenbau,			
see Herman Berstorff Machinenbau GmbH			
Bestinfo, Inc., ul. Dovzhenko 12, k. 1, office 165	143-7511	938-2123	
Bet JV (UK), ul. Profsoyuznaya 86	334-2474		
BET Trading Associates Limited	203-5303		
Betatron, Inc., Park Place, Leninskiy prosp. 113, #713	956-5055		
Bezopasnost Joint Stock Company,			
see Security Joint Stock Company			
BFG Moskau, Kamergerskiy per 5/6, kv. 35	292-4839	200-0215	413955
BHP, Leninskiy prosp. 2	239-1629	954-5395	414834
Bicar, ul. Vavilova 15	135-7189	135-7429	
Bierstube, Pekin Hotel, 13th floor	209-4240		
Big Business Center, Leninskiy prosp. 2, 9th floor	239-1021	954-5395	
Big Village Leisure Company, Ltd., The,			
ul. Tverskaya 15/2, #208	244-9432	152-0159	
Bingo Club Gabriela, ul. Pravdy 1	214-0787		
Biocard Health Center JV (Belgium),			
3rd Cherepkovskaya ul. 15a	149-0533	415-2962	411355
BioChimMak JV (Austria),			
GSP-3 Leninskiye Gory MGU	939-2421	939-0997	411483
Biological Sciences Journal,			
Vorobiniye Gory, ul. Mendeleeva, MGU	939-3326		
Biology Museum (Timiryazev Museum of Biology),			
M. Gruzinskaya ul. 15	252-0749		
Biplan JV (Spain), M. Tryokhsvyatitelskiy p. 4/6	297-7069	925-1679	
Birusinka Cinema, Bulatnikovskaya ul. 9	383-8292		

First things first.

The first thing most people do when they pick up a phone directory is look up an address they know (usually their own) and check to see if it is listed correctly (or at all). If you find your address to be incorrectly listed or missing, please let us know by fax (1-802-223-6105) or mail (address on page 2). We will correct the error for subsequent publications.

| --- | --- | --- | --- |
BiSko JV (UK), ul. Bakhrushina 20	235-8254	235-1225	
Bison Bahre & Greten, ul. Mytnaya 1, Office 29	230-0665	230-2375	413295
Bistro, Leninskiy prosp. 37			
Bistro Restaurant, Hotel Baltschug	230-6500	230-6502	414873
Bistro-Nedelya cafe, Oktyabrskaya ul. 18	288-9398		
Bitsa Horseback Riding Complex,			
Balaklavskiy prosp. 35	318-6820		
Biznes i Pravo, Denezhny p. 12, 2nd floor	241-5078	241-6368	
Bizness Journal, ul. Zatsepa 43b	208-8440	207-8189	
Blackwood Apt. Rentals, Kotelnicheskaya nab. 1	387-7356		
Blaupunkt, ul. Mytnaya 3, #4	230-6080	230-6081	
BMT Courier Service,			
Hotel Mezhdunarodnaya 2, #940	271-2609	271-9242	413725
BNL, see Banca Nazionale Del Lavoro			
BNP, see Banque Nationale de Paris			
Boat tours,			
from South River boat station to Serebriany Bor	118-7811		
from Ustinskiy Most (near Rossiya) to Kolomenskoye	118-7811		
from Ustinskiy Most (near Rossiya) to Krylatskoye	118-7811		
Bochako GmbH,			
Krasnopresnenskaya nab. 12, Office 1407	253-2260	230-2685	413271
Boge Larsen Oy AB, ul. Konyushkovskaya 28, kv. 6	253-9671	253-9213	413575
Boliden Allis, Krasnopresnenskaya nab. 12, Office 901	253-2970	253-2971	413491
Bollus JV, Skakovaya ul. 32	945-2824	945-6369	
Bolshaya Rossiyskaya Entsiklopedia Publishers,			
Pokrovskiy bul. 8	297-7483		
Bolshoy Theater, Teatralnaya pl. 1	292-9986		
Bombay Restaurant, Rublyovskoye sh. 91	141-5504		
Bominflot, Mamonovskiy p. 4, Office 5	200-0284	209-6588	413123
Bonita, Leninskiy prosp. 91	132-5474		
Book Boutique, 1st Kadashevskiy p. 12	231-1020		
Book Chamber Intl. (Switz.), ul. Ostozhenka 2	202-6911		
Booking for Voskresensskoe Hotel /Savoy/,			
Rozhdestvenka 3	929-8569	230-2186	
Bookkeeping Journal (BukhUchyot),			
ul. Sadovaya-Triumfalnaya 4/10	299-8670	299-2012	
Books and Prints, ul. Prechistenka 31	203-9262		
Books, Moskniga, Hotel Mezhdunarodnaya	253-2376		
ul. Tverskaya 18	200-0146		
Denezhny p. 8	241-9587		
Bordiga Art-Image JV (Italy), ul. Tverskaya 29A	249-6007	200-2211	411030
Borland, Okruzhnoy prosp. 19	366-4298	366-4637	
Borodino Bar, Aerostar Hotel	155-5030		
Borodino JV (UK), Kutuzovskiy pr. 2	249-6774	249-6774	
Borodino Panorama, Kutuzovskiy prosp. 38	148-1967		
Bosch, see Robert Bosch AG			
Bosch Auto Parts Store,			
Petrovskiy Passazh, 1st fl. (See Passazh)			
Boston Globe, Smolenskaya nab. 2A, kv. 106	244-0406	415-2937	
Botanical Gardens, Botanicheskaya 4, metro VDNKh			
Botany 500, GUM, 1st line, 2nd fl.	926-3215		
Botkin Clinic, 2nd Botkinskiy pr. 5, k. 5	945-0033		

	Phone	Fax	Telex
Boyarskiy Zal Restaurant,			
Hotel Metropol, 4th floor, Teatralny pr. 1/4	927-6089		
Boys and Girls, Sadko Arcade (Expocenter)	253-9588	973-2158	
BR-Soviet International JV, Ogorodny pr. 16	218-2345		
Bradley's of London, ul. Stary Arbat 4	291-7067		
Brasserie Restaurant, Olympic Penta Hotel	971-6101	230-2597	
Bremco Exporters, Rublyovskoye sh. 26, k. 1, kv. 56-57	415-2902	415-2914	413622
Brest Cinema, Yartsevskaya ul. 21	141-6448		
Brezhnev's hunting dacha	203-4820		
Bricom, Hotel Mezhdunarodnaya II, room 940	253-2115	253-9374	413197
Bridges (USA), prosp. Mira 146, kv. 116	282-6909	283-0939	
Brigita (Germany), Kutuzovskiy prosp. 9, kv. 5	243-7895		
Bristol-Myers Squibb,			
1st Krasnogvardeyskiy prosp. 25b (Hotel Soyuz), #233	256-4044	259-9578	414468
British Airways,			
Krasnopresnenskaya nab. 12, Office 1905	253-2492	230-2261	413197
Sheremetevo 2 Airport	578-2923		
British American Tobacco Co. Ltd. (BAT Co. Ltd.),			
B. Strochenovskiy p. 22/25, floor 1, office 102	230-6140	230-6148	413523
British Broadcasting Corporation,			
ul. Sadovaya-Samotechnaya 12/24, kv. 9	200-0245	200-0296	413498
British Club, Kutuzovskiy prosp. 7/4			
British Council Resource Center,			
Nikoloyamskaya ul. 1, 2nd floor, Foreign Lit. Library	297-7733		
British Gas, Radisson-Slavyanskaya Hotel, office 7051	941-8782	941-8780	
British Petroleum, ul. Malaya Ordynka 7	230-6200	230-6206	
British Siberian Coal Company,			
Korovinskoye sh., Pullman Iris Hotel	906-0068	488-8070	
British Women's Club, The	199-6907		
British-Russia Chamber of Commerce,			
Krasnopresnenskaya nab. 12, Office 1904	253-2554	230-2358	413523
Broadway and Company, Kutuzovskiy prosp. 13	243-2575		
Brok Invest Service, Nikitskaya, B. ul. 60/3	291-4017	202-9095	
Brown & Williamson Tobacco Corp.,			
B. Strochenovskiy p. 22/25, floor 1, office 102	230-6130	230-6148	413523
Brown Bear Bar,			
Sadko Arcade (Expocenter), Krasnogvardeiskiy prosp. 1	255-2742		
Brown, John, PLC, see John Brown			
Bruel and Kjaer Export A/S,			
Leninskiy prosp. 63/2, room 2321	135-9003		
BSK Medical (England),			
ul. B. Cheremushkinskaya 25, k. 40	127-0832	127-0830	
BT-Master JV (Switz.), Petrovskiy p. 6	200-6896		
Budapest Cinema, ul. Leskova 14	407-2783		
Budapest Hotel, Petrovskiye linii 2/18	921-1060		
Budapest Restaurant	924-4283		
Budget Rent-a-Car, ul. Novoryazanskaya 28	262-2876	262-1325	
Budimpex, Milyutinskiy p. 9	208-0636	925-3788	414361
Buhler AG and GmbH,			
ul. Timiryazevskaya 1, k. B, kv. 411	211-0947	211-0933	413749
Bukharest hotel, see Baltschug hotel			
Bukinist, ul. Arbat 9			
ul. Maroseyka 8			

ul. Pushechnaya 4

Bulgarian Civil Airlines, see Balkan Air

Bulgarian Orthodox Services,

	Phone	Fax	Telex
Uspenskaya Church, Goncharnaya ul. 29	271-0124		
Bulgarian Tourist Information, Kuznetskiy Most 1/8	292-3125		414560
Bull S.A., ul. Konyushkovskaya 28, kv. 4	253-9713	253-9281	413574
Bulletin of Foreign Commercial Information,			
ul. Pudovkina 4	143-0478		
Bulletin of Legis. Acts of Ministries and Government			
Departments, Zemlyanoy val 38/40	297-8583		
Bulvar Yana Rainisa Exhibition Center,			
bul. Yana Rainisa 19	493-1467		
Bunker Club, ul. Trifonovskaya 56	278-7043		
Burda Moden JV (FRG), ul. Pushechnaya 3	230-2815	230-2292	411941
Showroom, ul. Generala Belova 18	399-1460		
Bureau Francis Lefebvre, Nikitskaya, B. ul. 22, kv. 18	202-1170	975-2665	
Burevestnik Cinema, Serpukhovskaya pl. 3a	236-3136		
Burger Queen, Nikitskiy bul. 25	291-3262		
Burmasch Oil (Deutschland) Kastrol GmBH,			
ul. Obrucheva 4, k. 2, entrance 1	936-4193	936-4204	414300
Business and Banks Newspaper,			
ul. Dekabristov 10, k. 1	907-8210		
ul. Timura Frunze 8/5	245-3509	245-0226	
Business Center of Pekin Hotel,			
Pekin Hotel, ul. B. Sadovaya 1/5	209-3323	200-1420	
Business Consulting Agency, Leninskiy prosp. 36	248-3360		
Business Contact, ul. Khokhovka 31, k. 2	331-9555	310-7005	
Business Furniture International (BFI),			
ul. D. Ulyanova 4/1	135-2105	135-0505	
Business in Russia, bul. Tverskoi 10	202-9466	202-6553	
Business International	128-0961		
Business Man Journal (Izdatelskiy Dom			
Kommersant), ul. Vrubelya 4	943-9705	943-9705	
Business MN, ul. Tverskaya 16/2	200-0851	209-0100	
Business Tour, Hotel Mezhdunarodnaya 2, office 701	253-2940	253-9072	413697
Business Week, Kutuzovskiy prosp. 9, k. 2, kv. 122	243-6600	230-2512	413155
Butek Narodny Concern, Yartsevskaya ul. 30	149-3200	149-0903	
BWR Casing Corp.,			
Krasnopresnenskaya nab.12, Mezhdunarodnaya-2, #233	253-2233	253-9388	
Byelorusskiy Train Station, Tverskaya zastava 7	973-8464		
Bykovo Airport	155-0922		

C

	Phone	Fax	Telex
C&P&S Technical Center, Chelonikhinskaya nab. 18	259-8818		
C-E International Inc., ul. Profsoyuznaya 23	120-3030	120-4490	
C. Itoh & Co., LTD.,			
Krasnopresnenskaya nab. 12, Office 602-605	253-8339	230-2224	413381
C.C.I. Capital Contracts International Ltd.,			
ul. Spartakovskaya 6A	267-3783	265-4308	
Cable News Network (CNN),			
Kutuzovskiy prosp. 7/4, kv. 256-8	233-7975	233-6133	411047

	Phone	Fax	Telex
Cadence Inc., Smolenskiy bul. 4	135-0080	246-7955	
Cadwell Resources Limited, 1st Radiatorskaya 5	150-7658	159-2390	
Cafe Berlin, Hotel Baltschug	230-6500	230-6502	414873
Cafe Confectionery, Hotel Metropol, Teatralny pr. 1/4	927-6122		
Cafe Mozart, Palace Hotel, ul. Tverskaya 19	956-3152		
Cafe Mziuri, ul. Arbat 42	241-0313		
Cafe Taiga, Aerostar Hotel	155-5030		
Cafe Vienna,			
Sovintsentr, Mezhdunarodnaya Hotel I, Atrium	253-2491		
Cafe Viru, ul. Ostozhenka 50	246-6107		
Caffe Gelateria, prosp. Mira 58	280-9679		
California Cleaners	497-0005	493-5271	
California Microelectronic Systems, Inc.,			
Khoroshevskoye sh. 4, floor 2	316-6130	230-2101	
California Trading Company, Litovskiy bul. 5/10-32	427-0140	427-0140	
Camco, Krasnopresnenskaya nab. 12, office 1340	253-1575	253-1340	413523
Canada-Russia Business Council,			
Novy Arbat 21, suite 712	291-3292	290-3898	
Canadian Broadcasting Corporation,			
Gruzinskiy p. 3, kv. 163	250-5264		413149
Canadian Business Council, Tabaskiy p. 8	157-7619		
Canadian Club, Starokonyushenny p. 23			
Canadian Television,			
Rublyovskoye sh. 36, k. 2, kv. 287-288	415-4280	415-2957	
Canadian Tribune, Smolenskaya nab. 5, kv. 9	244-7332		413066
Cannon Associates, Bogoslovskiy p. 7, kv. 40	956-3050	956-3049	
Capricorne International,			
Simferopolskiy Blvd. 7A, #15,16	113-2933	310-7095	
Capstone Ltd., Kutuzovskiy prosp. 2/1, office 728	243-2559	243-2559	411654
Carat Russia, ul. Sheremetevskaya 2	971-0302	971-6986	
Caravella JV (France), Leninskiy prosp. 90/2	131-8185		
CARE Deutschland, ul. Petrovka 22	227-1312	227-1312	
CARE USA, prosp. Vernadskovo 41, #801	431-2660	432-8672	
Cargill Enterprises, Inc.,			
Radisson-Slavyansksya Hotel, #3006	941-8278	941-8260	650452
Cargo International Services, Ltd.,			
Radisson-Slavyanskaya Hotel, 6th floor	941-8880	941-8880	
Cariplo, Saimonovskiy p. 7, 3rd fl.	202-3652	202-3652	413899
Carl Schenk AG,			
Krasnopresnenskaya nab. 12, Office 1502	253-2458	253-9908	413646
Carlisle Syntec Systems, ul. Neglinnaya 17	200-3736	200-4495	
Carpigiana, Hotel Mezhdunarodnaya			
Cascade Airlines, Trubnaya pl. 20/2	208-2090	200-6884	
Casino Aleksander Blok,			
Krasnopresnenskaya nab. 12, docking	255-9284	253-9578	
Casino Arbat, Novy Arbat 29	291-1172		
Casino Bombay, Rublyovskoye sh. 91	141-5504	141-5502	
Casino Club Fortuna, Hotel Mezhdunarodnaya, 2nd fl.	253-2236		
Casino Club N, Leninskiy prosp. 88	131-1603		
Casino Gabriela, Hotel Intourist, Tverskaya ul. 3/5	203-9608		
Casino Moscow,			
Leningradskaya Hotel, ul. Kalanchovskaya 21/40	975-1967		
Casino Okhotny Ryad, Hotel Moskva			

	Phone	Fax	Telex
Casino Portture, Hotel Mezhdunarodnaya	252-3440		
Casino Ralina, ul. B. Yushunskaya 1a, Hotel Sevastopol	318-6474	318-2309	
Casino Riga, Volgogradskoye sh. 54	179-2350		
Casino Savoy Club, Hotel Savoy, 2nd fl.	929-8500		
Casino Tars, Hotel Ukraina	243-3004		
Casino U Arkadia, Spartakovskaya pl. 1/2	261-8040		
Casino Valery, pl. Indira Gandi 1	939-9611		
CASOV, Hotel Mezhdunarodnaya 2	253-1830		
Castle Foods GMBH, Hotel Mezhdunarodnaya 2, #506	253-2506	253-2086	
Castol Glob (England), Nakhimovskiy pr. 32	129-2900	129-2900	
CAT Software Ltd.	209-7256		
Cat Theater, Kutuzovskiy prosp. 25	249-2907		
Cate & Friends, Dmitrovka M. ul. 15	209-9814	209-1398	
Caterpillar Overseas S.A., Pokrovskiy bul. 4/17, kv. 13	207-1007	230-2777	413202
Catherine Mamet Real Estate Agency,			
Tverskoy bul. 25	291-1941	202-0449	
Catholic Services, see Roman Catholic Services			
CBS Radio, ul. Sadovaya-Samotechnaya 12/24, kv. 38	100-2992		
CECA S.A., see Elf Aquitaine			
Cedok (Czech Travel Bureau),			
Tverskaya-Yamskaya ul.4. 33/39	258-8932	258-9922	414442
CEKA, Mamonovskiy p. 4, kv. 4a	299-6206	200-2258	413519
Cenerentola, Novosushchevskaya ul. 26	972-1450		
Centaur Shop, Smolenskaya pl. 8, Hotel Belgrade 2	248-2828		
Center 'Energozvetmet', ul. Krutitskaya 9 stroyenie 1	276-4905	276-2390	
Center for Intensive Language Training	291-3727		
Center for Scientific-Technical Exchange JV (US),			
Nakhimovskiy prosp. 3	129-0744	310-7015	411076
Center for Soviet American Dialog, prosp. Mira 36	280-4166		
Center for Study of Russian JV (FRG),			
2nd Minaevskiy p. 2	258-9101		411798
Center-South, ul. Verkhnyaya Doroga 1, 16th fl.	976-1112	976-1112	
Central Bank of Russia, ul. Neglinnaya 12	928-9922	921-6465	
ul. Zhitnaya 12	237-5145	237-5055	412312
Central Chess Club, Gogolevskiy bul. 14	291-0641		
Central Children's Theater, Teatralnaya pl. 2/7	292-0069		
Central Exhibition Hall (Manezh), Manezhnaya pl. 1	202-9304		
Central House of Art Workers,			
Kuznetskiy Most metro	921-9744		
Central House of Artists, Krymskiy val 10	238-9843		
Central House of Tourism, see Tsentralny Dom Turista			
Central Lenin Museum, pl. Revolyutsii 2	295-4808		
Central News Service and New Age,			
ul. Pravdy 7/9, kv. 35	213-7209		413248
Central Polytechnic Libr., Polytechnicheskiy prosp. 2	928-6465		
Central Post Office, ul. Myasnitskaya 26/2	928-6311		
Central Puppet Theater, ul. Sadovaya-Samotechnaya 3	299-3310		
Central Revolution Museum, ul. Tverskaya 21	299-5217		
Central Telegraph, Telegrams	927-2002		
ul. Tverskaya 7	924-9004		
CentreCanadSovstroy JV, Leninskiy prosp. 42			
Centrocredit Commercial Bank,			
2nd Kolobovskiy p. 9/2	299-6090	299-9576	

	Phone	Fax	Telex
Cerasi and Company,			
Hotel Mezhdunarodnaya II, kv. 1601	253-1601		
Ceylon Tea, Leninskiy prosp. 2, floor 3, office 22	239-1788	239-1132	414834
CEZAM, Zvonarskiy p. 7 str.1	255-6148		
Cezar's, Radisson-Slavyanskaya Hotel	941-8398		
CFF, see Compagnie Francaise des Ferralles			
CGM/Unitramp, see Compagnie Generale Maritime			
Chadbourne, Parke, Hedman & Union of Advocates,			
Maxim Gorkiy nab. 38	231-1064	233-5298	
Chaika JV, Prechistenskaya nab. 3/5	202-3461		
Chaika Sports Complex, Turchaninov p. 1/3	246-1344		
Chaika Tennis Courts, Korobeynikov p. 1/2	202-0474		
Chalyapin Bar, Hotel Metropol	927-6113		
Cham-MEI JV, ul. Energeticheskaya 8	362-6821	361-1620	411610
Chamber Music Theater, Leningradskiy prosp. 71	198-7204		
Champagne Bar, Hotel Baltschug	230-6500	230-6502	414873
Chance JV (FRG), ul. Butlerova 24B	334-2470	334-2560	
Channel 4, ul. Marksistskaya 1, k. 1, kv. 45-46	270-6688	274-0004	413543
Charles Jourdan, Sadko Arcade (Expocenter)	253-9592	973-2185	
Charodeika, Novy Arbat 17	290-5339		
Charter Boat Tours,			
from Northern river station to Ikshinskoye Reserv.	459-7476		
Chase Manhattan Bank N.A.,			
Krasnopresnenskaya nab. 12, Office 1709	253-2865	230-2174	413912
Chastnaya Zhizn, see Private Life			
Chekhov Museum, ul. Sadovaya-Kudrinskaya 6	291-6154		
Chekhov's Theater,			
see Moscow Theater of the Arts (Old)			
Chelek Agroplast JV filial (Chelek JV),			
1й Parkovaya ul. 12, k. 1	165-9243		
Chelek Agroplast JV filial (Intercross JV),			
B. Sukharevskiy p. 21	207-0101	200-0294	
Chelek JV (Denmark), ul. Raskovoy 4	257-0810	258-0921	411172
Chelovek (Man) Journal, Maronovskiy p. 26	238-2300		
Chelovek Studio Theater, Skatertny p. 23a	291-1656		
Chemical Goods Exchange	281-9258		
Chemimetal	227-4039	227-4038	413499
Chemimpex Pvt. Ltd, ul. Mytnaya 1, 7th fl.	230-0832	230-0521	413001
Chemos JV (Finland), ul. Petrovka 17, str. 10	119-5968		
Chempion, ul. Myasnitskaya 13	927-2319		
Cheppel JV (Finland), ul. Tverskaya 55, str. 1, kv. 2	250-1319	292-6511	
Cheremushki Cinema, ul. Garibaldi 21	120-9003		
Cheromushkinskiy Bread Kombinat	315-3810		
Cherry Casino,			
Metelitsa Entertainment Complex, ul. Novy Arbat 21	291-1170		
Cherus, Profsoyuznaya ul. 130, k. 3, kv. 217	338-1225	427-6544	
Chetek, ul. Varvarka 15	206-5735	206-2847	
Chevron Overseas Co., ul. Dostoevskovo 23	974-1067	974-1066	413792
Chicago Tribune, Kutuzovskiy prosp. 7/4, kv. 138	243-9593	253-9012	413436
Chicken Grill, Sadko Arcade (Expocenter)	255-2638	973-2185	
Chico, Detskiy Mir, 4th floor			
Children's Fund, Armyanskiy p. 11/2	925-1376		
Children's Music Theater, prosp. Vernadskovo 5	930-7021		

	Phone	Fax	Telex
Chilewich International Corp., Kursovoy p. 9, kv. 2	203-5192	200-1215	413211
Chillinger Vika JV (Austria), Uglovoy p. 2/120	972-4231	274-8420	
Chimmashexport, Protopovskiy p. 25	288-3690		411032
Chinar Exports Ltd.,			
Krasnopresnenskaya nab. 12, Room 1404B	253-2196		413998
Chips & Technology Inc., Vorotnikovskiy p. 7, str.2	200-0007	299-1162	
Chis Ital,			
Krasnopresnenskaya nab. 12, Mezh-II, office 804	253-2804	253-9460	
Cho Hung Bank,			
Olympic Penta Hotel, Olympiyskiy prosp. 18/1	971-6101	230-2597	
Chopsticks, Tumba Golf Course, ul. Dovzhenko 1	147-7368		
Chori Co. Ltd., Dmitrovka B. ul. 9, kv. 9	292-4841	200-0249	413407
Chosonminhang (N. Korean Airways),			
ul. Mosfilmovskaya 72	143-6307		413636
Sheremetevo 2 Airport	578-7580		
Christian Dior, GUM, 1st line	926-3430		
Sovintsentr, Mezhdunarodnaya Hotel 1	253-9297		
ul. Tverskaya 4	292-0722		
Christian Science Monitor,			
ul. Sadovaya-Samotechnaya 12/24, kv. 53	200-2546	956-3030	413423
Christian Scientist Church	928-7370		
Christmas Films JV, ul. Kibalchina 4/6	286-3011		
Christmas JV (US), Dolgorukovskaya ul. 23a	251-8844	251-8844	
Chrysler Corp., See McDermott International			
Chubb, B. Strochenovskiy p. 22/25, floor 1, office 102	230-6136	230-6124	413523
Chunichi Shimnun & Tokyo Shimbun,			
Kutuzovskiy prosp. 9, kv. 25	243-1671	230-6888	413388
Church of Jesus Christ of Latter Day Saints	240-6332		
Church of Saint George, ul. Varvarka 12	298-3872		
Church of the Trinity in Nikitniki,			
Nikitnikov p. 3	298-5018		
CIBA Corning Diagnostics Ltd., Palashevskiy B. p.15	973-2121	203-4808	413377
CIBA-Geigy AG, Pokrovskiy bul. 4/17, kv. 37	227-0022	230-2666	413133
CIC-Union Europeenne, l'ntl ET CIE.,			
Krasnopresnenskaya nab. 12, Office 609	253-1182	230-2104	413375
Cifal, Tryokhprudny p. 11/13, kv. 4	299-2272	200-1232	413037
Cinebridge JV (USA), ul. S. Eisensteina 8	181-6200	181-6201	411841
Cinema Service, Ltd., ul. Akademika Koroleva 8/1	216-8162	216-8162	
Circus (New) on Lenin Hills, prosp. Vernadskovo 7	930-2815		
Circus (Old), Tsvetnoy bul. 13	200-0668		
Circus-Europe JV (France),			
3rd Frunzenskaya ul. 10, kv. 88	424-8004		411230
CIS Direct Mail, P.O. Box 85	229-7883	202-7510	612287
Citibank, M. Poryvaevoi ul. 7, #622	207-2679		
Citizen Democracy Corps,			
ul. Spiridonovka 22/2, kv. 36	290-6948	290-0822	
City Express 2B	946-1368		
City Looks Hair Salon, ul. Pokrovka 2/1 str. 1	928-7084		
Claude Litz, GUM, 1st line, 2nd fl.	925-1227		
Clear Water	247-1945	201-4154	
Cleopatra JV (Egypt), ul. 1st Tverskaya-Yamskaya 46b	250-8813	938-8038	411030
Clifford Chance, Palashevskiy B. p. 15a	973-2415	973-2336	413777

	Phone	Fax	Telex
Clivedon Property Services,			
1st Tverskaya-Yamskaya 13, #79	250-0152	250-9780	
Smolenskiy bul. 22/17, #2	134-0862	248-6778	
Club Golden Ostap, Shmitovskiy pr. 3	259-4795		
Club Kachalova-27 JV, Nikitskaya M. ul. 27	202-5611	202-1213	411153
Club na Taganka, ul. Verkhnyaya Radishchevskaya 19	272-7320		
Club Royale, Begovaya ul. 22	945-1410		
Cluster JV (Finland), B. Tryokhsvyatitelskiy p. 3/12	925-1085	925-1085	
CNN, see Cable News Network			
Co-op Trade Japan Ltd., B. Gnezdnikovskiy p. 7	200-2535	200-4293	
Co-Star JV (US), Valdayskiy pr. 16	457-8186		411474
Coats Viyella PLC, ul. Chaplygina 1a	921-0419	202-0249	411775
Cobra Bank, M. Gnezdnikovskiy p. 9 str. 4	229-0028	229-0028	
Coca-Cola Co., Gazetny p. 17/9			
Coca-Cola Refreshment Moscow,			
Nikopeskovskiy B. p. 15, k. 2, floor 3	241-9921	241-2807	
Coe & Clerici Trading, 4th Dobryninskiy p. 6/9, office 4	237-6892	230-2683	413281
Coexcafe, Rublyovskoye sh. 36, k. 2, kv. 241/243	415-5109	415-2956	
Coffee House (Pizza Pazza),			
Sadko Arcade (Expocenter)	940-4071	973-2185	
Cogolo S.r.L., ul. Timiryazevskaya 1	257-8814	200-3223	413603
Cole-Parmer International,			
Krasnopresnenskaya nab. 12, TsMT, office 1150	253-1720	253-9310	
Colgate-Palmolive,			
Moscow Region, Krasnogorskiy region, Gorky-6, #2	418-4854	418-4854	
Colognia Supermarket, ul. B. Sadovaya 5/1	209-6591	250-9741	413597
Columb JV (Panama),			
ul. 4th Tverskaya-Yamskaya 13, kv. 9	251-9817	973-2049	125267
Columbia Alumni Association	252-2451		
Columbia Broadcasting System,			
ul. Sadovaya-Samotechnaya 12/24, kv. 38	200-2992	299-2631	413435
Colve Austria, Leninskiy prosp. 49	135-8210		
ul. Delegatskaya 16/1, ent. 0	281-8447	281-8447	
Combellga, Mytnaya 3, ent.2, 14 fl.	239-1149	239-1474	
Kutuzovskiy prosp. 9, kor. 2, #64	244-9158	243-3375	
Combustion Engineering International Inc.,			
Leningradskiy prosp. 47	158-6401	157-6279	
Comecon,			
see International Organization of Economic Cooperation			
Comef S.A., ul. Mytnaya 1, Office 24	230-0022	230-2712	413046
Comfortobuv JV (Austria), Elektrozavodskaya ul. 46	963-4100		
Commercial Bank of International Integration,			
Olympiyskiy prosp. 32	284-0630	284-0630	
Commercial Herald, Kolpachny p. 7	227-2232	206-8401	
Commersant, Kiosk	202-9951		
Commersant Information Center, ul. Vrubelya 4	943-9710	943-9784	
Commersant Publishing House, ul. Vrubelya 4	943-9771	943-9705	
Commerzbank Aktiengesellschaft,			
Mamonovskiy p. 4, kv. 9	209-6440	200-0246	413274
Commission of the European Community,			
Astkakhovskiy p. 2/10	220-4658	220-4654	413786

Committee for
  Antimonopoly Policy, prosp. Vernadskovo 41 — 434-8466 — 434-8466
  Coal Industry, Novy Arbat 23, k. 2 — 202-7923
  Cooperation of CIS States — 925-9051
  Culture (Export of Cultural Objects of value),
    ul. Neglinnaya 8, room 29 — 921-3258
  Food Industry, Orlikov p. 3 — 204-4110
  Geology and Use of Subsoil, ul. B. Gruzinskaya 4/6 — 254-6824
  Security and Cooperation in Europe,
    ul. Prechistenka 3 — 203-6271
  Trade, Myasnitskaya ul. 47 — 207-7501
  Water Resources, Orlikov p. 3 — 207-6706

Name	Phone	Fax	Telex
Committee on UNESCO Affairs, ul. Vozdvizhenka 9	290-0853	202-1083	411595
Commodity-Credit Partnership	271-0730	271-1372	
Comont U.K., Krasnopresnenskaya nab. 12, office 720	253-2720	253-1250	
Compagnie Generale de Geophysique,			
ul. Mytnaya 1, Office 28	230-2071	230-2663	413568
Compagnie Generale Maritime,			
Serpukhovskiy val 8, kv. 201	232-4835	230-2296	413100
Companie European de Petrol (SEP),			
Dmitrovka B. ul. 9, kv. 8-8a	229-4311	220-2233	413182
Complete Ltd., Krzhizhanovskovo ul. 24/35, kor. 4	125-7041	125-7210	
Complex Systems Co., Ltd., ul. Kerchenskaya 1, kor. 3	121-3102	122-2151	
Comptrade Marketing PTE,			
VVTs, bldg. 8, prosp. Mira 120	181-0495	181-0495	
Computer Aided Technology JV (Switz.),			
Krutitskiy val 3, k. 2	276-4714	274-0097	
Computer Automated Systems JV (UK),			
Studencheskaya ul. 39, k. 2	200-4671		
Computer Center Moscow,			
Pervy Krasnoselskiy p. 7/9, kor. 4	264-7669		
ul. B. Yakimanka 31	238-1223		
Computer Exchange SM	236-9613		
Computer Partner JV (Austria), ul. Kievskaya 21	144-2274		
Computer Support Services Moscow (CSS),			
Bryanskaya ul. 9	240-0544	240-0493	
Computer Systems and Technology JV (US),			
ul. Pokrovka 10	924-5969	923-0748	412166
Computer World Moscow	181-9303	188-5476	414819
Computerland, Chekhova ul. 5	200-4171	209-0580	
Kutuzovskiy prosp. 8	243-7882	243-7848	
Leninskiy prospect 146, Dom Turista	434-9758		
Verkhnyaya Radishevskaya ul. 14/2	298-1102		
Computerland Training System Development,			
ul. Ostrovityanova 1	434-2192	434-6183	
Comstar Business Center,			
ul. Petrovka 10 (Passage), Room 301	924-0892	975-2319	
Comstar JV (UK), 3rd Tverskaya-Yamskaya ul. 39/5	250-1730	200-3283	414708
Conagra, Radisson-Slavyanskaya Hotel, #721-735	941-8883		
Concern Mairan, Hotel Belgrade, room 1827	248-7270		
Concert Hall in the Church of Pokrova v Filyakh,			
Novozavodskaya 6	148-4552		
Concert JV, ul. Neglinnaya 15		288-9588	411124

	Phone	Fax	Telex
Concord JV (US), ul. Smolenskaya 10			
Concord Night Club, ul. Lavochkina 32	454-6155		
Coneco, Mezhdunarodnaya II, room 439	253-1353		
Congress of Business Circles of Russia, Novy Arbat 21	291-3409	291-3710	
Connect International JV (US), ul. B. Filevskaya, 37/17	248-7273	144-0558	
Conoco International Petroleum Co.,			
Palashevskiy B. p. 13/2	973-3101	973-2311	413778
Conservatory, Nikitskaya, B. ul. 13	229-8183		
Consortium JV, Nikitskaya M. ul. 27	202-5611	200-1213	411153
Constanta JV (FRG),			
Rublyovskoye sh. 26, korp. 1, kv. 305	254-4087	415-4080	
Construction Exhibition, Frunzenskaya nab. 30	242-8968		
Construction Marketing and Trading Inc.,			
Novolesnaya ul. 18, k. 1, kv. 84	972-4662	173-5713	
ConsultAmerica, ul. Krasnokholmskaya 1/15, office 73	271-2580	230-2101	413205
Consulting Construction Company JV,			
Golovinskoye sh. 12	331-3055		
Contact, Novaya Basmannaya ul. 37	261-0990	261-3747	
Contact JV (Lichtenstein), ul. Pyatnitskaya 73	230-8908	230-2345	
Contemporary Art Center, ul. B. Yakimanka 6	238-9666		
Continental Airlines, Kolokolnikov p. 11	925-1291	924-9120	
Continental Restaurant,			
Sovintsentr, Hotel Mezhdunarodnaya 1	253-1934		
Continentalinvest JV (France),			
VVTs Expo Center, prosp. Mira 120	181-1377	181-4133	411418
Control Data Corporation,			
Krasnopresnenskaya nab. 12, Office 1704A	253-8379	253-9004	413311
Convent, Sukharevskaya pl.	234-5678	234-5678	411700
Conversion Concern, 4th Sokolnicheskaya ul. 1	268-6643	268-2744	
Convertla, Pokrovskiy bul. 4/17, kv. 17	207-3470	298-4490	413065
Cooper Industries Inc., Mamonovskiy p. 4, kv. 12	209-6520	200-0207	413376
Coopers and Lybrand, ul. Shchepkina 6	288-9801	284-5273	413258
Copechim France, Pokrovskiy bul. 4/17	208-7642	200-2243	413157
Copex, Milyutinskiy p. 9	208-0643	208-0643	
Copia Moscow, Pechatnikov p. 26	208-4007		
Copy Shop, Petrovskiy Passazh, 1st fl.	923-6055		
Copyrus, ul. Vavilova 11/19	235-1475		
Corinth JV, ul. Usacheva 11	246-8473	247-3421	
Corning Inc., Rublyovskoye sh. 26, corpus 1, office 31	415-4016	415-4018	
Corona JV (Germany), B. Gruzinskaya 4/6, str.2	254-0401	253-9484	411117
Corporate Forwarding, ul. Festivalnaya 28	454-1345	458-4492	
Correo Espanole (El)/El Pueblo Vasco,			
Rublyovskoye sh. 26, k. 1, kv. 229	415-2919		
Corriere Della Sere, Kutuzovskiy prosp. 9, kv. 15	243-1309	243-5276	413456
Cosmos Hotel, prosp. Mira 150	217-8680		411488
Dubrava Restaurant	217-0495		
Indoor Pool	217-1183		
Intourist Car Rental	215-6191		
Intourservice	215-9391		
Jindo Rus	217-0025		
Vesti Shop	217-1194		
Costar Corp., ul. Pogodinskaya 10	163-3641	304-1334	
Coudert Brothers, Staraya Basmannaya ul. 14	262-2744	262-2351	413310

Counsel for Trade and Economic Cooperation
(CIS-USA), Nab. Shevchenko 3 — 243-5470 — 230-2467
Cox Newspapers, ul. D. Ulyanova 16, build. 2, room 264 — 124-0183
Credit Bank Moscow, B. Ordynka 51 — 253-1430
   Gospitalnaya ul. 16 — 263-2638 — 263-0728
Credit Lyonnais, Pokrovskiy bul. 4/17, kv. 18 — 207-6489 — 230-2288 — 413228
Credit Lyonnais Russie (Moscow branch),
   ul. Ulianovskaya 15, 1st floor — 221-7520 — 221-7519
Credit Suisse, Palashevskiy B. p. 15/1 — 973-2413 — 973-2414 — 413775
Creditanstalt, Krasnopresnenskaya nab. 12, Office 1108 — 253-2752 — 253-2852 — 413556
Credito Italiano, Pokrovskiy bul. 4/17, kv. 40 — 207-0389 — 230-2724 — 413266
Credobank – Main office, Leontyevskiy p. 10 — 229-2252 — 925-8074
   Sadovnicheskaya ul. 15/2 — 220-3435 — 975-2154 — 412308
Croatia Airlines, Kutuzovskiy prosp. 13, #10-13 — 233-6797 — 243-1115 — 413771
Crokus International JV (US), ul. Grimau 10a — 126-2635 — 310-2140
Crosna Space Communications, Presnenskiy val 27 — 253-8603 — 253-3930 — 113768
CSA, Czechoslovak Airlines, 2nd Brestskaya 21/27 — 250-4571
   Sheremetevo 2 Airport — 578-2704
CSS, see Computer Support Services
Cubana de Avacion, Koroviy val 7, sect. 5 — 238-0223
   Sheremetevo 2 Airport — 578-2704
Cuddington Business Agency, ul. Kuusinena 9-26 — 956-2230 — 956-2231
Cultural Initiative Foundation, B. Kozlov p. — 928-4632 — 288-9512
Culture and Heritage JV, see Kultura i Naslediye JV
Cummins Engine Co. Inc.,
   Krasnopresnenskaya nab. 12, Office 2006 — 253-8379 — 253-9004 — 413311
Curtains Company, The, Kutuzovskiy prosp. 74, kv. 27 — 243-6102
Customs Committee of the Russian Federation,
   Komsomolskaya pl. 1A — 975-3289 — 975-4823
Cvosna — 253-1972 — 253-7530

D

D'Arcy Masius Benton and Bowler, Tverskoy bul. 13 — 200-7286 — 200-6937 — 411943
DAB Beer Bar, Belgrade Hotel, ul. Smolenskaya 8 — 248-2684
Daewoo, Nikitskaya M. ul. 27 — 202-8142 — 202-7797 — 411153
Dagens Industri, Kutuzovskiy prosp. 14, kv. 14 — 243-0036 — 243-0036 — 413382
Dagens Nyheter, Kutuzovskiy prosp. 13, kv. 95 — 243-1759 — 230-2589 — 413280
Daily Express, ul. D. Ulyanova 16 k. 2 apt. 304 — 124-1119
Daily Telegraph,
   ul. Sadovaya-Samotechnaya 12/24, kv. 25 — 299-0628 — 229-7437 — 413429
Daimler-Benz Akziengesellschaft,
   Park Place, Leninskiy prosp. 113/1 — 956-5055 — 256-5183 — 413346
Daksi, Kholmogorskaya 1, k. 33 — 182-5526 — 182-5526 — 411800
Daksin Petroleum International Ltd.,
   Kutuzovskiy prosp. 13, kv. 131-132 — 243-5876 — 243-9563 — 413154
Dalkon Trading JV, ul. Sadovaya-Kudrinskaya 19, kv. 17 — 254-6179
Dallas Morning News, Rublyovskoye sh. 26, kv. 109 — 415-4244
Danata, Radisson-Slavyanskaya Hotel — 941-8028
Daniele & C S.p.A. Buttrio, ul. 2nd Baumanskaya 9/23 — 267-9936 — 975-2049 — 413665
Danieli, ul. 2nd Baumanskaya 9/23 — 261-7386 — 261-7386 — 411580
Danilov Hotel, Danilovskiy Monastery, B. Stary Danilov p. — 954-0503

	Phone	Fax	Telex
Danilovskiy Monastery Restaurant, Danilovskiy val 22	954-0566		
Danish Radio, ul. Sadovaya-Samotechnaya 12/24, kv. 64	200-0770	200-2200	413351
Danish Remont Trading, ul. Strominka 20	268-2889	269-4498	
Danish TV, Kutuzovskiy prosp. 7/4, kv. 130-131	243-5165	253-9179	413365
Danone, ul. Tverskaya 4	292-0512		
Dansk Industri Syndikat A/S, see DISA Technologies			
Dartland International,			
Park Place, Leninskiy prosp. 113, Bldg. E, #320	956-5790	956-5690	
ul. Nikolskaya 5/1, 2nd fl.	923-4745		
Vtoroy Minaevskiy pr. 2, Bldg. 2, k. 7			
Daru Handelsgesellschaft mbH, Hotel Soyuz II, kv. 3	253-9594	253-9571	413625
Darwin Museum, M. Pirogovskaya ul. 1	246-6470		
DAS JV (Italy), ul. Nametkina 106			
Data Press Service (Pergamon Press PLC),			
Leninskiy prosp. 45, entr. 15, office 426	135-1164	230-2010	413199
Dateline International, Inc, 3rd Golutvinskiy p. 2	233-3972	450-3205	
Daval, Glazovskiy p. 7, kv. 3	203-6161		413165
Davy Corporation,			
Krasnopresnenskaya nab. 12, Office 703b	253-1263	253-9861	413070
De Beers Centenary Ltd., ul. Tverskaya 22, 3rd floor	209-3327	230-6169	
Decor Espana, Varshavskoye sh. 46	111-5201	111-5201	
Decorative Art of Russia Journal,			
ul. Tverskaya 9, entr. 6	229-1910	229-2760	
Def JV (US), Yakimanskaya nab. 10/2	230-1553		
DEG	253-2552	333-3340	
Delfin, Leninskaya Sloboda 26	275-0003	274-0044	
Delhi Restaurant, ul. Krasnopresnenskaya 23b	255-0492		413561
Delo i Pravo Magazine, ul. Yablochkova 5	210-4030	210-6112	
Deloitte & Touche, 2nd Samotyochny p. 1/23	281-5520	971-6419	612134
Delovaya Rossiya Bank, Klenovy bul. 3	112-1310		
Strastnoy bul. 8	200-1465	200-2453	412750
Delovaya Volna Radio Company	217-9162		
Delovie Lyudi, ul. Profsoyuznaya 73	330-1568		414741
Delphin JV (FRG), Leninskaya Sloboda 26	275-1130	243-6714	414804
Delphin-Service JV Filial, ul. Trofimova 1/17	279-0829	277-5212	114726
Delta Airlines, Krasnopresnenskaya nab. 12, Office 1102a	253-2658		413089
US Embassy Ticket Office	253-9871		
Sheremetevo 2 Airport	578-2738		413089
Delta Consulting Medical,			
Berezhkovskaya nab. 12, pod. 15	245-9999		212257
Delta Express Service JV (France),			
Sheremetevo 2 Airport	208-7419		
Delta Industrieberatung GmbH, Kursovoy p. 9, 4th fl.	201-2018	200-1242	413021
Demag AG, see Mannesmann AG			
Deminex, Degtyarny p. 15, P.B. 121	299-9142	200-4888	412384
Demos JV (Switz.), Mosfilmovskaya ul. 25	143-4892		
Den norske Bank, Dmitrovka B. ul. 5/6, kv. 34	292-0338	200-0237	413286
Dengi i Kredit, see Finance and Credit Journal			
Dental Clinic, The, Pullman Iris Hotel	488-8279		
Dental-Beker JV (FRG), Kuznetskiy Most 9/10	923-5322	924-9601	4114789
Dentsu Inc., Radisson-Slavyanskaya Hotel	941-8112	941-8111	
Depark JV (Brazil), ul. Sovkhoznaya 10	357-0180	207-5859	411672
Depars JV (Argentina), Ilovayskaya ul. 10	357-0241	207-5859	411672

	Phone	Fax	Telex
Department of Forestry, Arkhangelskiy p. 1	208-0101		
Department of General Automobile Industry, Kuznetskiy most 21/5	921-2510		
Department of Metallurgy, Slavyanskaya pl. 2/5	220-8180		
Department of Textile Industry, Tverskaya-Yamskaya ul. 1/3	200-5688		
Dernieres Nouvelles D'Alsace (Les), see Le Figaro			
Desta JV (Austria), B. Ochakovskaya 15a	430-6880	430-7862	411927
Detective Theater, see Moscow Detective Theater			
Detskiy Mir (Children's World), Teatralny pr. 5	927-2007		
Deutsche BA, Sovintsentr, Mezhdunarodnaya Hotel I, #1905	253-2492	230-2261	413771
Deutsche Babcock, Mamonovskiy p. 6, kv. 7	209-2837	200-0222	413226
Deutsche Bank AG, ul. Ostozhenka 23	201-2988	200-1227	413073
Deutsche Genossenschaftsbank, Hotel Intourist, room 2009	203-1621	200-2224	411823
Deutsche Presse Agentur (DPA), Kutuzovskiy prosp. 7/4, kv. 210	243-9790	243-8092	413122
Deutsche-Roschtoff Handel GmBH, Leninskiy prosp. 95a	132-5400	132-5400	414303
Devro Ltd., Kadashevskaya Nab. 6/1	236-5446	230-2190	
Dewald, Jerome W. & Assoc., see Jerome W. Wald & Assoc.			
DG Bank, see Deutsche Genossenschaftsbank			
DHL Worldwide Express Mail, 1st p. Chernyshevskovo 3	956-1000	971-2218	205113
Express Centers:			
Mezhdunarodnaya Hotel, ent. 4, rm. 902	253-1194		
Olympic Penta Hotel	971-6101		
Radisson Slavyanskaya Hotel, Int'l Press Center	941-8621		
Di Pace SRL, ul. Fedotovoy 6, kv 5	241-1743	241-1743	411432
Di Style, Petrovskiy Passazh, ul. Petrovka 10, 2nd fl.	292-4056		
Diadora Sporting Goods, Petrovskiy Passazh, 2nd fl.			
Diag International JV (Switz.), Volzhskiy bul. 114a, k. 9	179-3597	179-5213	
Diagraf JV Filial (UK), B. Tulskaya ul. 52	234-0021	230-2029	
Dialekt, ul. Novozavodskaya 27, kom. 27	145-8956		
Dialog Bank, Staropanskiy p. 4	921-9104	923-6556	
Radisson-Slavyanskaya Hotel, 1st fl.	941-8434	941-8424	
Dialog Data Bank	932-5610	932-6300	
Dialog International Inc., ul. Ryabinovaya 28a	448-3786	446-1592	
Dialog JV (US), ul. Spartakovskaya 13	932-4762	265-5714	411498
Dialog Magazine, ul. Pravdy 24	257-2691		
Diamex Studio JV Filial (FRG), Volzhskiy bul. 114a, k. 9	179-3045		
Diana, ul. Mytnaya 74	230-3614		
Diana JV (Japan)	298-5800		
Diana JV Filial (Japan), ul. Dubininskaya 27	235-4916		
Diaplus JV (Switz.), Nauchny pr. 8	332-6440	302-6557	
Diario-16/Cambio-16/El Observodor, ul. Sr. Pereyaslavskaya 14, kv. 86-87	280-0298		
Die Bierstube Restaurant, Olympic Penta Hotel, Olympiyskiy prosp. 18/1	971-6101		
Digital Equipment Corp. (DEC), Krasnopresnenskaya nab.12, TsMT, office 803	253-2550	253-2995	
Dileon, Rublyovskoye sh. 36, k. 2	415-4904	415-4924	

	Phone	Fax	Telex
Dina International, ul. Akad. Pilyugina 14, k. 3, kv. 953	936-2011	936-2700	413550
Dinaelektronik JV (FRG), ul. Sadovniki 4	111-4255	200-5822	412272
Dinamika JV, Tsvetnoy bul. 26	200-6651	230-3090	411389
Dinamo Sports Palace, ul. Lavochkina 32	453-6501		
Dinamo Stadium Gym, Leningradskiy prosp. 36	212-7092		
Dinamo Swimming Pool, Leningradskiy prosp. 36	212-8483		
Diners Club	284-4873		
Diomides Inc., ul. Bryanskaya 12, kv. 128	240-6430	240-6430	
Dipace Arredamenti s.r.l.,			
Krasnopresnenskaya nab. 12, Office 321	253-2321	253-2498	411432
Diplomat Auto Service, ul. Kievskaya 8	249-9197	240-0553	
Diplomat Food Store, ul. B. Gruzinskaya 63	251-2589		
Diplomatic Polyclinic, 4th Dobryninskiy p. 4	237-8338		
Drugstore	237-5335		
Direct Net Telecommunications,			
Novy Arbat 36, Room 2834	290-9541	290-8056	
Directory Assistance	09		
DISA Technologies,			
prosp. Vernadskovo 9/10, kv. 635-8	131-3393	938-2117	413079
Discovery JV (FRG), ul. Sadovaya-Samotechnaya 3	230-2392	230-2392	411730
Distrade Ltd., Boyarskiy p.4	925-4192	921-3539	
Diversified Business Moscow JV, Nikitskaya, B. ul. 47	132-3492	230-2571	411700
Djamirco JV, ul. Pyatnitskaya 22, str.2			
DL Lota, ul. Solyanka 9 str.1	924-5010	923-2937	
DMB&B Moscow, See D'Arcy Masius, et al			
Dmitrovskiy customs point	587-3391		
DMM JV (Italy), Novocheremushkinskaya 58	120-8590	120-4244	411688
Do It Yourself, Sadko Arcade (Expocenter)	253-9588	973-2185	
Doall Co., Kursovoy p. 9, office 2	203-5192	200-1215	
Doctors Without Borders,			
Dokuchayev p. 10, kv. 841-843	207-4593	207-4618	
Dom Biruni JV (Jordan), ul. Rozhdestvenka 12	924-7220		412157
Dom Khudozhnikov (House of Artists),			
Krymskiy val 10	238-9634		
Dom Knigi, ul. Novy Arbat 26			
Dom Mebeli, Leninskiy prosp. 101	432-2986		
Dom Modi, prosp. Mira 55			
Dom na Tverskoy cafe, ul. Gotvalda 12	251-8419		
Dom Uchonikh (House of Scientists),			
ul. Prechistenka 16	201-4555		
Domino Print Shop, B. Vatin p. 4	227-3125		
Domodedovo Airport	234-8656		
Domus Construction, ul. Rossalimo 4	246-9258		
Don Quixote Restaurant, Pokrovskiy bul. 4/17	297-4757	245-0223	
Dona, 2nd Tverskaya-Yamskaya 54	251-0245		
Donau-Bank AG, Wien,			
1st Krasnogvardeyskiy pr., Exh. Complex, Pav. 2	256-7444	253-9483	413599
Donna, Sadko Arcade (Expocenter)	253-9588	973-2158	
Dorin Electronics, Khimkiy, Spartakovskaya 12	571-8108	571-8108	
Dostoyevskiy House Museum, ul. Dostoyevskovo 2	281-1085		
Dovesgate International/Russian Express,			
2nd Obydenskiy p. 14	202-5732	202-5745	
Dow Chemical Company, Pokrovskiy bul. 4/17, kv. 9	297-0074	230-2933	413217

	Phone	Fax	Telex
Dow Elanco, Nikitskaya, B. ul. 26, office 54	200-4597	200-4257	
Dowell Chlumberger,			
Nikoloyamskaya ul. 51, k. 2, fllor 2	274-0131	272-2711	
Dragun GmbH, Rublyovskoye sh. 36, k. 2, kv. 212	415-4296	415-2959	413587
Drama Theater on Malaya Bronnaya, M. Bronnaya 4	290-4093		
Dresdner Bank AG,			
Krasnopresnenskaya nab. 12, Office 1708	253-2681		413183
Dresser Engineering JV (US), Okhotny ryad 18, k. 8	202-5866		
Dresser Industries, Inc., Glazovskiy p. 7, kv. 16/17	203-7924	200-1225	413337
Dresser Marketing KDC, Leninskiy prosp. 113, kv. 1-315	956-5412		413337
Drevko JV, B. Sergiyevskiy p. 18	925-2736		
DRG International, Inc.,			
Krasnopresnenskaya nab. 12, TsMT, office 508	253-1904	253-1082	
DRI, PO Box 15	396-0853	292-6511	
DRT Inaudit, 2nd Samotyochny p. 1/23	281-5520	971-6419	612134
Drug Store, Sadko Arcade (Expocenter)	253-9592	973-2185	
Druzhba, Luzhnetskaya nab. 10	201-1655	201-1658	
Druzhba Cinema, ul. Waltera Ulbrikhta 16/1	943-4182		
Druzhba Hotel, prosp. Vernadskovo 53	432-9629		
Druzhba Narodov, Povarskaya ul. 52	202-5203		
Druzhba Restaurant, prosp. Vernadskovo 53	432-9939		
Druzhba Tennis Courts, Luzhnetskaya Nab. 10	201-1780		
Druzhba Trading House, Voznesenskiy p., 1	229-6603	229-1193	
Druzhba-Filia JV (Cyprus), prosp. Vernadskovo 53	431-7812	924-5021	412170
Dubrava Restaurant, Hotel Kosmos	217-0495		
Dukhan Shavo Restaurant, Karamyshevskaya nab. 58	197-1975		
DUMEZ (Societe),			
ul. B. Dorogomilovskaya 14, k. 1, kv. 39	243-3948	243-5264	413315
Dun & Bradstreet Russia, Bumazhny pr. 14	250-2025	250-4898	
Dupont, see E.I. Dupont De Nemours and Co.			
Durov Corner, ul. Durova 4	281-2914		
Dusseldorfer Messegesellschaft M.B. H. Nowea,			
Hotel Soyuz II	256-7395	230-2505	413509
Duval Khinchuk Ljanders, ul. B. Ordynka 61, str. 2	238-1744	200-3203	
'24' Newspaper, Tverskoy bul. 10-12	292-3609		
Dyen i Noch Restaurant, Kolomenskiy pr. 12	112-5092		
Dzhangiri, ul. Skakovaya 9, #432	945-2679	945-2765	
Dzhuna JV (FRG), ul. Lyusinovskaya 12	238-4101		
Dzintars, Pushkinskaya pl. 12			

E

	Phone	Fax	Telex
E.I. Du Pont De Nemours & Co., Inc.,			
Palashevskiy B. p. 13/2	973-1001	973-2440	413778
East Consult, Ltd., ul. Rozhdestvenka 12	924-1233	925-8523	
East-West Creative Association, Voznesenskiy p. 9	229-6901	200-4249	411417
East-West Project JV (Belgium),			
ul. Shcherbakovskaya 40/42	369-5987		
Eastern Express Publishing and Commercial Assn.,			
ul. Sadovaya-Kudrinskaya 9	244-8820	292-3690	
EastLight Art JV (Austria),			
B. Ovchinnikovskiy p. 20, K-104	299-5957		

	Phone	Fax	Telex
Echo of the Planet (Ekho Planety) - weekly,			
Tverskoy bul. 10-12	202-6748	290-6645	
Echo-Trends JV (US), Sivtsev Vrazhek p. 24, k. 2	241-9547	241-9539	
Echomed JV, Perevedenovskiy p. 4, str.3	261-4149	267-8143	
Echomin JV, Zvenigorodskoye sh. 9			
Echor JV, ul. Kedrova 8, k. 1	125-5282		
Echosintez JV, ul. Krupskoy 4, korp.1	200-2289	200-2289	
Eclipse JV (UK), prosp. Vernadskovo 95, k. 3, kv. 122	433-1507	433-1507	
Ecoenergetika JV (US), GSP Leninskiy prosp. 19	234-0005	234-4250	
Ecomedpol, Ltd., ul. Pekhotnaya 3	196-1974	943-0046	
Economic Daily, Kutuzovskiy prosp. 14, kv. 99	243-3739		
Economics and Life Journal, see Ekonomika i Zhizn			
Economika Publishers, Berezhkovskaya nab. 6	240-4877		
Economist, The, ul. Akad. Koroleva 4, k. 2, kv. 78	215-2574	215-2574	
Economy and Law Journal, ul. Dmitrovskaya 9, str. 8	292-0700	292-0700	
Econotech, Sredne-Kislovskiy p. 3, str. 1A	229-6916	229-5582	
Eczacibasi Drug Store, Arkhangelskiy p. 5 str. 4	923-3615	921-2709	612246
ul. Maroseyka 2/15	928-9189		
Eden International, ul. Novy Arbat 21, 8th fl.	291-4392	291-4585	
Edland JV (Austria), Balaklavskiy prosp. 1	316-0181	316-0511	411418
EFE Agency, ul. Sadovaya-Samotechnaya 12/24, kv. 23	200-1532	200-0219	413114
Egli AG, see Joseph Agli AG			
Egyptair, Sovintsentr, Mezhdunarodnaya Hotel, #831	253-2831		
Ehlsid JV, Leningradskoye sh. 18	150-9775		
EKA Corporation, Kursovoy p. 9, Office 6	202-1441	200-1259	413176
Ekhsso JV, 2nd Brestskaya ul. 31	254-3974		
Ekonomicheskaya Gazeta, Bumazhny pr. 14	212-2389	200-2297	
Ekonomika i Zhizn, Bumazhny pr. 14	212-2385	200-2297	
Ekoplast JV, Dmitrovskoye sh. 102a	483-7500		
Eksimer JV (US), sh. Entuziastov 8	246-6151	246-2211	
Eksimer, Leninskiy prosp. 76a	930-7193	930-7192	
Ekstra Newspaper, Kutuzovskiy prosp. 9, k. 2	243-6718	243-6718	413420
El Rincon Espanol Restaurant,			
Hotel Moskva, Okhotny Ryad, 7	292-2893		
El-Trol JV, Leninskiy prosp. 99	434-5253	434-5253	
Elba JV (US), ul. Rokotova 1/12, pom. 120	425-2724	425-2625	41332
Elbim bank, 2nd Tverskaya-Yamskaya 15	251-0334		
Krasnopresnenskaya nab. 12, pod 3, #1707	253-2693	253-2694	
Sheremetevo 2 Airport, Office 646	578-2708		413973
Krasnopresnenskaya nab. 12, room 1707	253-1200	253-9410	
Elbrus Cinema, Kavkazskiy bul. 17	321-1796		
Elders Australia and New Zealand,			
see Sovenz New Zealand			
Electrical Communication Journal,			
Kuznetskiy Most 20/6	921-0913	924-5290	
Electronics and Engineering JV (Lichtenstein),			
Podkopayevskiy p. 7, str. 2, kv. 16	227-1449	237-2635	414357
Eleftherotypia, ul. B. Pereyaslavskaya 7, kv. 41	280-5441		413931
Elegant Logic, Inc., ul. 1st Tverskaya-Yamskaya 2/1	251-7289	250-9815	
Eleks International Corporation, M. Sukharevskiy 9	208-2109		
Elektrobank, Voznesenskiy p. 20, str. 2	229-2279	924-3811	
Elektrofarfor, sh. Entuziastov 17	273-7896	291-4281	411003
Elektroimport, Tryokhprudny p. 11/13, 2nd fl.	299-6682	200-0234	413452

	Phone	Fax	Telex
Elektrointorg, ul. Usiyevicha 24/2	155-4026		
Elektromatik JV (Austria), ul. B. Semenovskaya 49	369-2893		
Elektronika, Leninskiy prosp. 99	134-9009		
Elektronika Research Inst., prosp. Vernadskovo 39	432-9223		411668
Elektroninvest JV, ul. M. Kaluzhskaya 8	315-3574		
Elektronmatik JV (Austria), ul. B. Semyonovskaya 49	369-7911	369-7911	
Elektronorgteknika, Nikitskaya, B. ul. 24	205-0033	205-3901	411385
Elektrontex JV (Bulgaria), Shukhova 14	236-4695		
Elektroprivod, Gazetny p. 5	229-6110	291-5932	
Elend JV (Italy), Leningradskoye sh. 18			
Elex Vest, M. Sukharevskiy p. 9A	208-4190	208-6676	411622
Elf Aquitaine, ul. Bolshaya Nikitskaya 47	291-8412	200-0258	413519
Elf Lub, see Elf Aquitaine			
Eli Lilly & Co., M. Mogiltsevskiy p. 3	241-4819	241-6799	413685
Eliada JV (Cyprus), Krymskiy val 9	237-0973	237-0710	
Elite, ul. Krzhizhanovskovo 24/35, korp. 3	124-5941		
Elite Flora, B. Gruzinskaya 32	254-3992	254-2810	
Elkat JV (Finland), 2nd Kabelnaya ul. 2	361-4393	247-0058	
Elkom JV, ul. Dorozhnaya 38	921-0888	921-0442	411700
Elmako JV, Starokonyushenny p. 6	201-7602	201-7357	411418
Elogar JV, ul. Novaya Basmannaya 23a	261-5764	202-9056	
Eloks JV (France), Nikolskaya ul. 17	928-7614	921-2040	111122
Elpav JV, ul. Petrovka 26	200-4151		
Elsa Moda Italia, ul. 60 Let Oktyabr 2	135-4085		
Eltech JV (Austria), Sofiyskaya nab. 30	214-7811	214-7803	414727
Eltemek, ul. B. Spasskaya 1/2	208-2837	208-2745	411003
Elza, ul. Elektrozavodskaya 21	369-3078	963-9765	411589
Emanuelle, Hotel Moskva, Teatralnaya pl. entr.	924-3776		
Embassy of			
Afghanistan, Sverchkov p. 3/2	928-5044	924-0478	413270
ANC (Mission), ul. Konyushkovskaya 28, kv. 9	252-3295		413583
Algeria, Krapivinskiy p. 1a	200-6642		413273
Angola, ul. Olaf Palme 6	143-6531		143402
Commercial Office	143-6335		
Argentina, ul. Sadovaya-Triumfalnaya 4/10	299-0367		413259
Armenia, Armyanskiy p. 2	924-1269	928-1556	
Australia, Kropotkinskiy p. 13	956-6070	230-2606	413474
Austria, Starokonyushenny p. 1	201-7317	230-2365	413398
Commercial Office	201-7308	230-2365	413399
Azerbaidzhan, Leontyevskiy p. 16	202-4730		
Bangladesh, Zemledelcheskiy p. 6	246-7900	248-3185	413196
Belarus, ul. Maroseyka 17/6	924-7031	928-6403	
Belgium, ul. M. Molchanovka 7	203-0531	291-6005	413471
Benin, Uspenskiy p. 4a	299-2360	200-0226	413645
Bolivia, Lopukhinskiy p. 5	201-2508		413356
Brazil, Nikitskaya, B. ul. 54	290-4022		413476
Bulgaria, ul. Mosfilmovskaya 66	147-9022		
Commercial Office	147-9007		
Burkina Faso, ul. Meshchanskaya 17	971-0620		413284
Burma, see Embassy of Union of Myanmar			
Burundi, Uspenskiy p. 7	299-7200		413316
Cambodia, Starokonyushenny p. 16	201-4736	201-7668	413261
Commercial Office	132-7074		413987

	Phone	Fax	Telex
Cameroon, Povarskaya ul. 40	290-6549		413445
Canada, Starokonyushenny p. 23	241-5882	241-4400	413401
Cape Verde, B. Spasskaya 9	208-0856		413929
Chad, Rublyovskoye sh. 26/1, kv. 21	415-4139		413623
China, ul. Druzhby 6	143-1544		413981
Columbia, ul. Burdenko 20	248-3042	248-3025	413206
Congo, Kropotkinskiy p. 12	246-0234		413487
Costa Rica, Rublyovskoye sh. 26, kv. 58-59	415-4042		413963
Cuba, ul. Mosfilmovskaya 40	147-4312		
Commercial Office	290-6230		
Cyprus, Nikitskaya, B. ul. 51	290-2154	200-1254	413477
Czech and Slovak Republic, ul. Yuliusa Fuchika 12/14	251-0540		
Commercial Office	250-8403		
Denmark, Prechistenskiy p. 9	201-7860	201-7860	413378
Commercial Office	201-7860	201-7860	413378
Ecuador, Gorokhovskiy p. 12	261-5544	216-2739	413174
Egypt, Skatertny p. 25	291-6283	291-4609	413276
Commercial Office	243-0363	230-2114	413200
Equatorial Guinea, Kuznetskiy prosp. 7/4, k. 5, kv. 37	243-9611		
Estonia, Kalashny p. 8	290-3178		
Ethiopia, Orlovo-Davydovskiy p. 6	230-2036		413980
Finland, Kropotkinskiy p. 15/17	246-4027	230-2721	413405
France, Yakimanka B., ul. 45	236-0003	230-2169	413290
Commercial Office	237-8740		413325
Gabon, Denezhny p. 16	241-0080	241-1585	413245
Georgia, Nozhovy p. 6	291-6602		
Germany, Mosfilmovskaya ul. 56	956-1080	938-2354	413411
Commercial Office		938-2356	413412
Ghana, Skatertny p. 14	202-1870		413175
Greece, Leontyevskiy p. 4	290-2274	200-1252	413472
Commercial Office	290-4753		
Guinea, Pomerantsev p. 6	201-3601		413404
Guinea-Bissau, ul. B. Ordynka 35	231-7928		413055
Guyana, 2nd Kazachiy p. 7	230-0013		413071
Hungary, ul. Mosfilmovskaya 62	143-8611	143-4625	414428
Commercial Office	252-0001		
Iceland, Khlebny p. 28	290-4742	200-1264	413181
India, ul. Vorontsovo pole 6-8	297-0820		413409
Indonesia, ul. Novokuznetskaya 12	231-9549	230-2213	413444
Iran, Pokrovskiy bul. 7	227-5788		413493
Iraq, ul. Pogodinskaya 22	246-4061	230-2922	413184
Economic Bureau	246-4061		
Ireland, Grokholskiy p. 5	288-4101		413204
Commercial Office	280-6500		413512
Israel, B. Ordynka 56	230-6700	238-1346	413628
Italy, Denezhny p. 5	241-1533	253-9289	413453
Commercial Office	248-3152		
Ivory Coast, Molochny p. 9/14	201-2400		413091
Jamaica, Koroviy val 7, kv. 70-71	237-2320		413358
Japan, Kalashny p. 12	291-8500		413141
Jordan, Mamonovskiy p. 3	299-9564	299-4354	413447
Kazakhstan, Chistoprudny bul. 3a	208-9852	208-2650	
Kenya, ul. B. Ordynka 70	237-3462	230-2340	413495

	Phone	Fax	Telex
Kirgizistan, ul. B. Ordynka 64	237-4882	237-4452	
Korea (North), ul. Mosfilmovskaya 72	143-6249		413272
Commercial Office	143-6241		413279
Korea (South), ul. Gubinka 14	938-2802		
Kuwait, 3rd Neopalimovskiy p. 13/5	248-5001	230-2423	413353
Laos, ul. B. Ordynka 18/1	233-2035		413101
Commercial Office	231-2862		
Latvia, ul. Chaplygina 3	923-6666	923-9295	
Lebanon, ul. Sadovaya-Samotechnaya 14	200-0022	200-3222	413120
Libya, ul. Mosfilmovskaya 38	143-0354	143-7644	143443
Lithuania, Borisoglebskiy p. 10	291-2643		
Luxembourg, Khruschevskiy p.3	202-2171	200-5243	413131
Madagascar, Kursovoy p. 5	290-0214		413370
Malaysia, ul. Mosfilmovskaya 50	147-1514	147-1526	413478
Mali, ul. Novokuznetskaya 11	231-0655		413396
Malta, Koroviy val 7, kv. 219	237-1939	237-2158	413919
Mauritania, ul. B. Ordynka 66	237-3792		413439
Mexico, Lyovshinskiy B. p. 4	201-4848	230-2042	413125
Moldova, Kuznetskiy Most 18	928-5405		
Mongolia, Borisoglebskiy p. 11	290-6792		
Commercial Office	229-5407		
Morocco, Prechistenskiy p. 8	201-7395	230-2067	413446
Mozambique, ul. Gilyarovskovo 20	284-4007		413369
Myanmar (Burma), Nikitskaya, B. ul. 41	291-0534	291-0163	413403
Namibia, ul. Konyushkovskaya 28, kv. 10	252-2471	253-9610	413567
Nepal, 2nd Neopalimovskiy p. 14/7	244-0215		413292
Netherlands, Kalashny p. 6	291-2999	200-5264	413442
New Zealand, ul. Povarskaya 44	956-3579	956-3583	413187
Nicaragua, ul. Mosfilmovskaya 50, k. 1	938-2701		413264
Niger, Kursovoy p. 7/31	290-0101	200-4251	413180
Nigeria, Nikitskaya M. ul. 13	290-3783		413489
Norway, Povarskaya ul. 7	290-3872	200-1221	413488
Commercial Office	202-3484		413563
Oman, p. Obukha 6	928-6418	975-2174	411432
Pakistan, ul. Sadovaya-Kudrinskaya 17	250-3991		413194
Palestine, Kropotkinskiy p. 26	201-4340		413126
Peru, Smolenskiy bul. 22/14, kv. 15	248-7738		413400
Commercial Office	246-6836		
Philippines, Karmanitskiy p. 6	241-0563	230-2534	413156
Poland, ul. Klimashkina 4	255-0017	254-2286	414362
Commercial Office	254-3421		
Portugal, Botanicheskiy p. 1	230-2435	280-3134	413254
Qatar, Koroviy val 7, kv. 197-8	230-1577	230-2240	413728
Romania, ul. Mosfilmovskaya 64	143-0424		
Rwanda, ul. B. Ordynka 72	237-4626		413213
Senegal, ul. Donskaya 12	236-2040		413438
Sierra Leone, Rzhevskiy M. p. 4	203-6200		413461
Singapore, p. Kammenoy slobody 5	241-3702	230-2937	413128
Somalia, Spasopeskovskaya pl. 8	241-8624		413164
Spain, Nikitskaya, B. ul. 50/8	202-2161	200-1230	413220
Commercial Office	202-7772	200-1226	413900
Sri Lanka, ul. Shchepkina 24	288-1651		413140
Sudan, Povarskaya ul. 9	290-3993		413448

	Phone	Fax	Telex
Sweden, ul. Mosfilmovskaya 60	956-1200	956-1202	413410
Switzerland, Ogorodny slobody p. 2/5	925-5322	200-1728	413418
Syria, Mansurovskiy p. 4	203-1521		413145
Tadzhikistan, Skatertny p. 19	290-6102	290-0609	
Tanzania, ul. Pyatnitskaya 33	231-8146	230-2968	413352
Thailand, Yeropkinskiy p. 3	201-4893		413309
Togo, Granatny p. 1	290-6599		413967
Tunisia, Nikitskaya M. ul. 28/1	291-2858		413449
Turkey, Vadkovskiy p. 7/37	972-6500	200-2223	413731
Commercial Office	972-6500	200-2223	413148
Turkmenistan, Filippovskiy p. 22	291-6636	291-0935	
Uganda, Mamonovskiy p. 5	251-0060		413473
Ukraine, Leontyevskiy p. 18	229-6475		
United Arab Emirates, ul. Olaf Palme 4	147-6286		413547
United Kingdom, Sofiyskaya nab. 14	230-6333	233-3563	413341
Commercial Office	956-6052	249-4636	413314
United States of America, Novinskiy bul. 19/23	252-2451	255-9965	413160
Commercial Office, Novinskiy bul. 15	255-4848	230-2101	413205
Uruguay, Lomonosovskiy prosp. 38	143-0401	938-2045	413238
Uzbekistan, Pogorelskiy p. 12	230-0076		
Venezuela, ul. Yermolova 13/15	299-9621	200-0248	413119
Vietnam, Commercial Office	250-4852		
Yemen, 2nd Neopalimovskiy p. 6	246-1814		413214
Yugoslavia, ul. Mosfilmovskaya 46	147-4106		
Commercial office, INA Commerce,			
Krasnopresnenskaya nab. 12, office 107	253-1253	253-1270	414451
Zaire, Prechistenskiy p. 10	201-7673	201-7948	413479
Zambia, prosp. Mira 52a	288-5001		413462
Zimbabwe, Serpov p. 6	248-4367	230-2497	413029
Emergency Towing Service, Ryazanskiy p. 13	267-0113		
Varshavskoye sh. 91	380-2101		
Emerson Electric Co., VVTs, Technopark, Bldg. 4, #45	181-7312	181-7347	
Emery Worldwide, see Inservice			
Emita JV (Italy), ul. Mytnaya 1, kv.31	238-9714	230-2093	413507
EMS Garantpost, Varshavskoye sh. 37	117-8560	230-2719	
Ener JV (US), Bryusov p. 8/10, k. 2			
Energobigmach JV, ul. Oktyabrskaya 5, str. 8			
Energomashexport, Protopopovskiy p. 25A	288-8456	288-7990	411965
Enervek JV (Greece), Potapovskiy p. 5, str. 3	927-5506	230-2898	411776
Engelhard, ul. Tverskaya 22A, 5th floor	209-3388	209-3368	
Engineering VO- Investment Center JV,			
ul. Nametkina 10a	172-9710	172-9708	
Engraving Shop, TsUM, 1st fl.			
Engraving Shop, ul. Petrovka 8	928-2954		
ENI - Ente Nazionale Idrocarburi,			
Staropimenovskiy p. 13	973-0552	973-0563	413136
ENICO, Krasnopresnenskaya nab. 12, Office 2009	253-2066	253-9070	414440
Enims, 5th Donskoy pr. 21b	234-2300		411928
Enix JV (India), Kirovogradskaya 11	315-3904		
ENKA, ul. Yelanskovo 2	248-5042	288-9521	4133379
Enka Pazarlam, ul. Petrovka 12	928-8547	288-9521	413379
Ensy Gallery, Mir Exhibition Hall, prosp. Mira 14	208-1403		
Entertainment World, GUM Dept. Store, 3rd line	926-3454		

	Phone	Fax	Telex
Enthusiast JV (Bulgaria), Vspolny p. 4	203-3706	200-2216	
Entourage Beauty Salon,			
Radisson-Slavyanskaya Hotel, main lobby	941-8157		
Entuziast Cinema, ul. Vishnyakovskaya 18	373-5000		
Epek JV (FRG), ul. Myasnitskaya 18	928-5655	975-2095	414816
Epsilon JV (India), Leninskiy prosp. 53	132-5917		411479
Epson, see Seiko Epson Corporation			
Equestrian Center, Balaklavskiy prosp. 33	318-0581		
ERLAN, Leninskiy prosp. 57	135-8245	135-8245	
ul. Ozernaya 46	437-3701	437-2910	
Erma International JV (UK), Rublyovskoye sh. 28, k. 3	415-5207	415-2973	
Ermitage Theater, Karetny ryad 3	209-6742		
Ernst & Young, Podsosenskiy p. 20/12	297-3121	297-3607	612130
Erten JV (France), 5th Donskoy pr. 21b	230-2991	230-2991	
Esa Seppanen Consulting Ltd.,			
Dmitrovka B. ul. 21/7, #6	200-3388		
ESAB AB Sweden, ul. Usacheva 35	245-5735	245-5070	413913
Escada, GUM, 1st line, 2nd fl.	926-3231		
Esme JV (Greece), ul. Skakovaya 17	945-5161	945-5071	
Esso-Gutzeit Oy, see Valmet Oy			
Essor Carpets, Leninskiy prosp. 85	134-0531	134-0531	
Estafeta Cinema, ul. Timiryazevskaya 17	211-3553		
Estee Lauder, Plotnikov p. 12	244-7235	230-2060	
GUM, 1st line, 1st fl.	921-7064		
Petrovskiy Passazh	923-6057		
Estee Lauder A.G., Lachen,			
Petrovskiye linii, 2/18 Hotel Budapest Room 321	923-6057	975-2301	411662
Esteti JV (Italy), ul. Verkhnyaya Radishchevskaya 9A	297-7297		
Estina Mir, Ltd., ul. Profsoyuznaya	420-9775	434-7429	
Estrada Theater, Bersenevskaya nab. 20/2	230-0444		
ETA, Hotel Orlyonok, ul. Kosygina 15, #1206	939-8906		
Etex Ligne Reguliere, Pokrovskiy bul. 4/17, kv. 1	297-4835	230-2277	413326
Ethiopian Airlines, Sheremetevo 2 Airport, Office 641	578-2717		
Etienne Aigner, Petrovskiy Passazh, 1st fl. (See Passazh)			
ETPM, ul. Dorogomilovskaya 54, kv. 39	243-3948	243-4241	413315
Eurasia Global, ul. Baumanskaya 43/1, 5th fl., rm 505	261-1392	261-4035	
Eurasia TV, ul. Lesnaya 63/43	250-1248	973-1216	
Eureka JV, ul. Narodnovo Opolcheniya 38 k. 2	943-0893	943-0993	
Eurintrade S.A., Glazovskiy p. 7, kv. 10-11	202-8511	253-9502	413163
Eurocard/Mastercard	284-4794		
Eurodeal JV (Luxemburg), Gorokhovskiy p. 19	265-3908	975-2234	412817
Eurofinance Commercial Bank, Vspolny p. 5, str. 1	202-4902	204-9593	614446
Euroimpex SrL, Kursovoy p. 9, Office 1	202-1858	200-1245	413535
Euroline JV, Volgogradskiy prosp. 139	175-2450	172-1927	
Euromedical Emergency Service	432-1616		
Euronet, 2nd Skotoprogonnaya ul. 35	278-0029		
Euronet & Telecom, ul. 2nd Brestskaya 41	200-0628	200-0628	
Euronetics, ul. Dubininskaya 65	235-2251	235-1665	
Euronews Moscow, B. Tishinskiy p. 2-19	254-9049	230-2298	
Europ Assistance, Berezhkovskaya nab. 12, pod. 15	240-9999	230-2432	413945
Europaeishes Reiseburo GmbH, ul. B. Spasskaya 12	280-6438	280-6066	414306
Europalette JV (FRG), ul. Vavilova 9a	135-1726		

	Phone	Fax	Telex
Europcar, Novaya pl. 14	923-9749	923-1783	414730
Hotel Mezhdunarodnaya 1	253-1369		
Hotel Novotel, K 339	578-9407		
Krasnaya Presnya ul. 23B	255-9190		
Olympic Penta Hotel	971-6101		
Pullman Iris Hotel	488-8000		
Sheremetevo 2 Airport	578-3878		
Europe Enery Environment, Mironovkiy p. 26	238-2188		
Europe JV (Switzerland), ul. Staraya Basmannaya 15a	131-1579	200-2278	
Europe Plus JV, ul. Akad. Koroleva 19	215-9938	217-8986	
European Medical Center, Gruzinskiy p. 3	253-0703		
European Paints and Wallpaper Shop, Ul. Vavilova 55	125-3479	124-6461	
European Trading Ltd.,			
Krasnopresnenskaya nab. 12, TsMT, office 937	253-2937	253-9006	
Europmin, Krasnopresnenskaya nab. 12, Office 1221	253-2146	253-2147	
Eurosam Express Drycleaning,			
ul. Krasnopresnenskaya 11/3	259-4157	131-0402	
Eurosov Petroleum Ltd., Kuznetskiy Most 17, str. 4	921-9438	921-5019	612243
Eurospan Human Resources,			
ul. Baumanskaya 43/1, 5th fl., suite 106	261-5228	261-4035	
Eurostron JV (France), ul. Luganskaya 4, k. 1	322-4757	292-5611	
Evangelischer Pressedienste (EPD),			
Kutuzovskiy prosp. 7/4, kv. 301	243-4046		
Eve Fashion, Petrovskiy Passazh, 2nd fl.			
Evik JV, ul. Mikhalkovskaya 34	456-5156	453-6004	
Evko JV (FRG), ul. Vyborgskaya 16	150-2684	150-9935	
Evricom JV, ul. Lva Tolstovo 5/1	271-1702		
Evroalliance, prosp. Vernadskovo 14	133-9620	432-9681	
Evroeknopak, B. Sadovaya 5/1, Pekin Hotel, #1001	209-3816	209-2142	
Evromin C.A., Kuznetskiy Most 3	921-6303	924-7596	413810
Evropeyskiy Restaurant, Hotel Metropol	927-6039		
Ewald Budde, Krasnopresnenskaya nab. 12, Office 1247	253-1763		
Excelsior, Gruzinskiy p. 3, kv. 266	250-4165	250-4167	413013
Exchange Herald (Birzhevie Vedemosti),			
B. Ordynka 7, office 5	231-2653	233-3863	
Exchange, The, Radisson-Slavyanskaya Hotel	941-8333		
Excimer, Leninskiy prosp. 76	939-0692	930-7193	
Excimer Computers, ul. Ivana Babushkina 24A	125-7001	125-7868	
Exhibition Hall of Moscow Artists' Trade Union,			
ul. M. Gruzinskaya 28	253-7355		
Exhibition Hall of the Academy of Arts,			
ul. Prechistenka 21	201-3704		
Exhibition Hall of the Union of Artists,			
ul. Tverskaya 25/9	299-2289		
Krutitskiy val 3	276-5483		
ul. 1st Tverskaya-Yamskaya 46b	250-1412		
ul. Kuznetskiy Most 20	928-1844		
ul. Usiyevicha 13	151-2441		
ul. Vavilova 65	125-6809		
Exotic-Tour JV (France), Zemlyanoy val 57	227-0412		
Expertek JV (US), Nakhimovskiy prosp. 32	129-1633		
Expo-Consta JV (Finland), 1st Krasnogvardeyskiy pr. 1	255-2536	253-9513	411865
Expocenter, Sokolnicheskiy val. 1a	268-1340	288-9537	

	Phone	Fax	Telex
Exporters' Assn. of Russia, Nikitskaya, B. ul. 22/7	202-7089		
Exportkhleb, Smolenskaya-Sennaya pl. 32/34	244-4701	253-9069	411145
Exportles, Trubnikovskiy p. 19	291-6116	200-1219	411299
Exportsamotsveti, ul. Narodnovo Opolcheniya 29/1	197-5401		
Exposhop Cash & Carry, Krsnopresnenskaya nab. 14	256-5571		
Supermarket	259-4017		
Expovestrans JV (FRG), 1st Krasnogvardeyskiy pr. 12	256-7323	256-5571	411591
Express Credit Comm. Bank, 3rd Pryadilnaya ul. 3	367-2979	367-2979	
Express Dry Cleaners, ul. Polbina 6	259-4157	292-6511	
Express Mail Service (USA), Varshavskoye sh. 37	114-4613		
Express Motors, ul. Alabyana 12	198-0034	198-9991	
Express Taxi	254-6590		
Express-Boyd	203-2675		
Expressen, ul. B. Dorogomilovskaya 14, kv. 66	243-7232		

F

	Phone	Fax	Telex
F & C Trade Corporation, ul. Oktyabrskaya 7	281-2964	284-4577	612362
Service Department, ul. Oktyabrskaya 7	556-6877		
F. Hoffmann-La Roche LTD, Mamonovskiy p. 4, kv. 13	209-6808	200-4275	413090
F.I. Realty, ul. Yaroslavskaya 8, k. 3	217-6042	217-6047	
FAB Club, pr. Zhukova 4	195-1031		
Fabela Groupe International, ul. 2nd Brestskaya 41	200-0628		
Fabeg JV (FRG), ul. Dobroslobodskaya 7/1, str. 4, kv. 33	267-6962	200-2216	411700
Face to Face Quasar Company Ltd.	288-2822		411630
Fairn & Swanson Ltd., Olympiyskiy prosp. 18	288-1512	288-1512	
Sovintsentr, Mezhdunarodnaya Hotel I, 1st fl.	253-9408	253-9383	
Fakel Cinema, sh. Entuziastov 15/16	362-1168		
Fakt, Khoroshevskoye sh. 41	299-0004	941-0900	411712
Falcon Express, ul. Shukhova 17/3	954-0223	954-8596	
Falkon JV (US), Kutuzovskiy prosp. 2/1, Hotel Ukraina	243-3256	200-2171	411172
Fambris JV (UK),			
ul. Zoi i Alexandra Kosmedemyyanskikh 31	159-6356	159-6356	
Famiglia Cristiana, Kutuzovskiy prosp. 14, kv. 50	243-1932	243-4116	413064
Fantest, ul. Plekhanova 17/1	368-4769	369-1065	
Farkhad cafe, B. Marfinskaya 4	218-4136		
Farmakon Drugstore, ul. Tverskaya 4	292-0843		
FATA European Group SrL, Koroviy val 7, Office 6	236-2141	230-2477	413916
Faxon, ul. Kuusinena 21b	987-7431	943-0089	411925
Fazis-Moscow JV Filial (FRG),			
ul. Sadovaya-Triumfalnaya 12	200-2792	253-9316	411169
Federal Express,			
Krasnopresnenskaya nab. 12, fl. 1, Ent. 3	253-1641	253-1066	911559
Fedulov Gallery, ul. Pervaya Tverskaya Yamskaya 18	250-2774		
Fel Funk - Electronic Labor, Koroviy val 7, kv. 100	238-9995	230-2824	413017
Femida	258-5487	250-5384	
Femker JV, ul. Dubininskaya 83/4	928-2492		
Fer-Chip JV (Singapore), M. Karetny p. 4			
Ferado Trade Co., ul. Ryabinovaya 39/2	242-0765	448-9733	
Ferguson Hollis, ul. Shchepkina 6	288-9801	971-6958	
Ferrostaal, see MAN AG, Munchen			
Fersam AG, B. Starodanilovskiy p. 5	952-7598		

	Phone	Fax	Telex
Festo-Didactic JV (Austria), 2nd Baumanskaya ul. 5	261-9036	267-4984	
Fexima, ul. Sadovaya-Samotechnaya 4a	923-8001	200-2280	413186
Fias, Leninskiy prosp. 72/12A	131-9968	930-5292	
Fiat, Tryokhprudny p. 11/13, 2nd fl.	299-0229	200-0289	413458
Fidimage JV (US), Nikitskaya, B. ul. 19	291-4536		
Fiesta Air, Inc., Olimpiyskiy p. 15/2, kv. 54	511-1403		
Fifth Floor Studio (Na Pyatom Etazhe),			
Kostomarovskiy p. 3	297-6564		
Filyevskiy Park Video Arcade, Filyevskiy Park			
Finance and Credit Journal, ul. Neglinnaya 12	921-5286	925-9024	
Finances in Russia, ul. Tverskaya 22B	299-4333		
Financial and Business News, Khoroshevsloye sh. 4	945-4569		
Financial Times, Kutuzovskiy prosp. 14, kv. 8	230-2267	243-0077	413300
Finansovaya Gazeta, ul. Krzhizhanovskovo 14	124-3802		
Finansy i Statistika Publishers, ul. Pokrovka 7	925-4709		
Finatec S.A.,			
Krasnopresnenskaya nab. 12, Office 2001-2002a	253-7183	253-9904	413920
Fininvest, Nikitskiy bul. 8	203-2355	291-5550	
Finistbank, Kutuzovskiy prosp. 26 str. 3	249-0256		
Finmeccanica Group, ul. Mytnaya 1, kv. 33	230-1110	230-2769	413233
Finn-Stroy Oy, Koroviy val 7, Office 10	237-1250	230-2202	413950
Finnair, Kamergerskiy p. 6	292-8788	200-1288	413902
Sheremetevo 2 Airport	578-2718		
Finnair Cargo, Sheremetevo 2 Airport	578-2718		413902
Finnart JV (Finland), Petrovsko-Razumovskiy pr. 17	214-5277	214-7730	
Finnboard, see Finnpap-Finnbumaga			
Finncell, see Finnpap-Finnbumaga			
Finnish Radio & TV, Koroviy val 7, kv. 122	237-1047	230-2876	413054
Finnish School, Kropotkinskiy p. 15/17	246-4027	230-2721	413405
Finnish-Russian Chamber of Commerce,			
Pokrovskiy bul. 4/17, kv. 2	925-9001	230-2711	413406
Finnpap-Finnbunaga, Pokrovskiy bul. 4/17, k. 4a	227-0022	200-3293	413976
Finprogetti, see Programma 2000			
Finpromerchant, see Programma 2000			
Finsider, see ILVA/Finsider			
Fire (Emergency Assistance)	01		
Firestone, Duncan & Associates,			
ul. B. Polyanka 28/1, 4th fl., Ste 295	237-5657	238-5306	
First Gallery, The, Strastnoy bul. 7	299-0498		
First Republic, Miusskaya pl. 7, 3rd floor, rooms 330/331	251-7939	251-7939	
First Russian Real Estate Corp., Shyolkovskoye sh. 2	165-5511	284-4358	412440
First Trading Consortium Limited,			
Gogolevskiy bul. 31	291-1663	290-0132	
Firta Partia, prosp. 60-letiya Oktyabrya, 9	135-6072	135-4330	
Firvet, ul. Krutitskaya 9/1 kv. 32	276-4136	276-4136	
Fisherman's Harbor, ul. 1st Tverskaya-Yamskaya 46A	251-3379	250-1302	
Service, Krasnobogatyrskaya 79	963-8780		
Fisons Instruments, Denezhny p. 7	241-6217	230-2414	
Fisons Pharmaceuticals,			
B. Strochenovskiy p.22/25, 1-st floor, office 102	230-6172	230-6124	
Fitil Cinema, Frunzenskaya nab. 12	245-0438		
Flakt Suomen Puhallintehdas Oy,			
Mamonovskiy p. 4, kv. 3	209-3726	200-0253	413483

	Phone	Fax	Telex
Flamingo Hotel, see Inflotel			
Flamingo JV Filial, ul. Sushchyovskiy val 50	289-2566		
Flash Telecomm, see Sovamer Trading Company			
Flat Finders, Kutuzovskiy prosp. 4/2, #328	413-9301	413-9301	
Flax Union JV, Rublyovskoye sh. 36, k. 2			
Fleet Street International Ltd.,			
Novy Arbat 36, kv. 1335-1336	290-8527	290-9436	
Flora JV (Austria), ul. Vavilova 15	209-8855		411045
Flower Shop, Leningradskiy prosp. 74	151-2283		
Novy Arbat 23	203-0321		
ul. Tverskaya 16	229-0468		
Novy Arbat 15	203-0204		
prosp. Mira 74	281-6281		
Flowers Shop, Petrovskiy Passazh, 1st fl.			
Flying Mouse Cabaret, see Lyetuchaya Mysh Cabaret			
FMC Corporation, Gruzinskiy p. 3, kv. 201-202	254-4119	200-2291	
Fobit Car Rental, 1st Dorozhny pr. 3a	315-0134		
Foliant	202-9505	202-2413	
Fonetiks, Semyonovskaya nab. 2/1	360-0874	360-6317	911508
Fonon International JV, ul. Buzheninova 16	963-0180	288-9598	412243
Food & Toy Processing JV (Australia),			
Aviatsionny p. 8	152-1800	151-1359	
Food Line Supermarket, Krasnaya Presnya ul. 23	252-6591	253-4666	
Food Orders Store, Biryulevskaya ul. 37	326-4477		
Foodland, Sadko Arcade (Expocenter)	256-2213	973-2185	
Foodmark, B. Starodanilovskiy p. 5	954-0730		
ForbesProgress JV (USA), ul. Malogvardeyskaya 41	140-1970	140-0562	
Ford Motor Company, ul. Gorbunova 14	447-3804		
ul. Marx-Engelsa 8	203-9237		
Foreign Commercial Info. Bulletin,			
ul. Pudovkina 4	143-0458	147-4300	664411
Foreign Correspondents' Association,			
International Press Center & Club	941-8746	941-8761	
Foreign Literature Journal, ul. Pyatnitskaya 41	233-5147	233-5147	
Foreign Literature Library, Nikoloyamskaya ul. 1	227-8810		
Foremost Progress JV (Canada),			
Staraya Basmannaya ul. 20, str. 8	261-3530	261-3632	411255
Forepost Information Service, ul. Skhodnenskaya 26	555-5510	420-2459	
Form & Technik, Hotel Mezhdunarodnaya 2, #506	253-2506	253-2086	
Formula Information Technologies Center,			
N. Kiselny p. 5	925-6897	432-9294	
Fort Info Int•rn'l Trading, ul. Baumanskaya 56/17	261-5164	265-5512	
Forto, ul. Mytnaya 11	236-4467	230-2912	
Fortuna JV (Spain), Milyutinskiy p. 13/1	925-3679	230-2387	411211
Forum Cinema, ul. Sadovaya-Sukharevskaya 14	208-2220		
Forward International, Teatralny pr. 5	926-2765	925-8130	
Fotopro JV (FRG), 2nd Smolenskiy p. 2/3	241-0861		
Foundation for Economic Development of Russia,			
M. Gnezdnikovskiy p. 4	229-9558		
Framatome, Mamonovskiy p. 4, kv. 4	209-2838	243-7262	413285
Francaise (La), Pullman Iris Hotel	488-8000		
Franco-Russian Chamber of Commerce,			
Pokrovskiy bul. 4/17, kv. 3	297-9092	230-2277	413326

	Phone	Fax	Telex
Franco-Serra Italia, ul. Tverskaya 1			
Frankfurter Algemeine Zeitung,			
Kutuzovskiy prosp. 7/4, k. 5, kv. 28	243-5388		413313
Franki Gritop JV (Italy), ul. B. Cheremushkinskaya 19b	126-3506	200-4212	
Free Way, ul. Baumanskaya 32/6	265-2963		
French Bread Bakery, Lazarevskiy pr. 4			
ul. Generala Glagoleva 30			
French Church of St. Louis (Catholic),			
ul. M. Lubyanka 12	925-2034		
French Cultural Center,			
Nikoloyamskaya ul. 1, 2nd floor, Foreign Lit. Library			
French School, Spasonalivkovskiy p. 12/16	237-4636		
Frezenius JV (FRG), Kolomenskiy pr. 4	118-8347	288-9567	
Friedman & Rose, 1st Baltiyskiy p. 6/21, k. 1, 3rd fl.	151-8092		
Fritz Companies, Grokholskiy p. 19/27	284-4791	284-5422	
Froesch K.G., Kutuzovskiy prosp. 7/4 kv. 115	243-1930	356-2059	413847
Frost, ul. Kuntsevskaya 4/1	417-9400		
Fryazinskiy customs point	734-59		
FTI JV, Chapayevskiy p. 14	157-0672	157-0672	
Fuji Center,			
Mezhdunarodnaya Hotel I, Krasnopresnenskaya nab. 12	253-2914	253-1450	
Fuji Film, Stoleshnikov p. 5/20	229-0100		
Fuji Film Center, Novy Arbat 25	203-7307		
Fuji TV, ul. B. Dorogomilovskaya 14, kv. 86	230-2514	230-2349	413198
Future Technology, ul. Festivalnaya 22	453-4204		
Fyodorov's Institute, see Mikrokhirugiya Glaza			

G

	Phone	Fax	Telex
G.K. Etno JV (Hong Kong), ul. Ulyanova 4, k. 1	335-0267		
Gaber Gazanlangen GmBH,			
prosp. vernadskovo 103, k. 1, kv. 4	434-1626	434-1579	414351
Gabi's Drugstore, Hotel Mezhdunarodnaya 2	253-7692		
Gadfly, Ltd., The, Novoshukinskaya 3-21	193-5096	292-6511	
Gaia International Women's Center, Khlebny p. 2/3	135-3207	200-1207	411089
Gala-Disk JV (FRG), Mozhayskoye sh. 5	443-7805	443-8644	413017
Gala-Kameron JV (UK), Zemlyanoy val 54	297-2381		
Galaktika Agency, ul. Metallurgov 23/13 kv. 56	304-1968	304-1968	
Galaxy Restaurant and Pub,			
Selskokhozyaystvennaya prosp. 2	181-2169		
Galerie Du Vin, Kutuzovskiy prosp. 1/7	243-0365		
Galeries Lafayette, GUM, 1st line, 1st fl.	926-3457		
Galika AG, Krasnopresnenskaya nab., Office 717	253-2717	253-9160	
Galla, Kozikhinskiy B. p. 7, #2	202-3002	202-3002	
Galla International, B. Filevskaya 14-2, kv. 11	145-4821	145-0634	
Gallery, ul. Malaya Gruzinskaya 28	253-7505		
Gallery 1.0, ul. Bolshaya Yakomanks 2/6	238-6905		
GAM-Impianti SA,			
Krasnopresnenskaya nab., Office 1447	253-1777	253-9703	
Gamos JV (US), ul. B. Yakimanka 7/8	230-1208	253-9703	411691
Garant, ul. Krzhizanovskaya 14/1	129-0154		
Garanti Bank, Krasnopresnenskaya nab. 12, rm. 1425	253-1589		

Garden Bar, Hotel Intourist Lobby

	Phone	Fax	Telex
Garden Ring Supermarket, B. Sadovaya 1	209-1572		
Leninskiy prosp. 146, Dom Turistov	956-5458		
ul. Serafimovicha 2	230-0718		
Garmonia JV (India), ul. Petrovka 25	200-6375	230-2057	411653
Garvard Brokk Society, ul. Myasnitskaya 26	262-4682	262-4682	
Gas Alsin, Pokrovskiy bul. 4/17, kv. 21	207-6573	230-2688	413115
Gas Industry Journal, ul. Stroiteley 8, build. 1	930-0695	133-0070	
Gazkro JV, ul. Verkhnyaya Radishchevskaya 17	272-1600	271-1029	
Gazprom Concern, M. Stroiteley ul. 8 korp. 1	133-1300		
Gazprombank, ul. Stroiteley 8	133-4610	133-6689	111823
GE-CGR Medical Systems,			
Krasnopresnenskaya nab. 12, office 1542	253-1542	253-9402	413904
Gebr. Helbig MOS-Auto GmbH,			
Krasnaya Presnaya, Krasnogvardeyskiy 1.pr. 12	255-2551	255-2552	
Gebr. v.d. Berg Moving and Storage	140-6571		
GEC Alsthom, Pokrovskiy bul. 4/17, kv. 21	207-7002	230-2688	413115
Gemeenschappelijke Pers Dienst (GPD),			
Rublyovskoye sh. 36, kv. 239	415-4312	415-4309	
Gemini Management Group, ul. Pudovkina 4a	147-1127		
General Electric Co., Pokrovskiy bul. 4/17, kv 20	297-2995	230-2882	413236
General Motors - Moscow,			
Krasnopresnenskaya nab. 12, office 1004B	253-2577	253-2585	
General Resources International (GRI),			
ul. Vavilova 15	124-8070	124-5001	
Generale Bank,			
Krasnopresnenskaya nab. 12, Office 1705-1706	253-7572	253-9778	413904
Genser, VVTs, bldg. 1, prosp. Mira 120	187-2781	187-7133	
Geo, Kutuzovskiy prosp. 7/4, kv. 314	230-2748		
Geokor JV (Thailand), Teterinskiy p. 12/2	297-5514		
Geonora JV (FRG), ul. Sovetskoy Armii 6	288-9190	288-9291	411700
Georam JV, Leninskiye Gory, MGU, Geography Faculty	939-3772	939-0126	
Georgian Cultural Center, ul. Arbat 42			
Geoservice Operation (represented by Framatom),			
Mamonovskiy p. 4, kv. 4	209-2838	243-7262	413285
Geosoft JV (Austria), Podsosenskiy p. 26, k. 1,2	256-2610	230-2390	414455
Geotim JV (Germany), ul. Miklukho-Maklaya 23	433-6265	956-5016	
Gerate und Reglerwerk, Leipzig GmbH,			
Leninskiy prosp. 95a	132-5347	132-5347	414500
German Bakery, Pyatnitskaya ul. 29			
German Evangelical Church Services,			
German Embassy Mosfilmovskaya ul. 56	238-1324		
German Red Cross	126-0021	126-4787	
Germes Concern, Komsomolskiy prosp. 24	245-0228	907-2566	
Gewika Autoservice GMBH, ul. Kotlyakovskaya 3a	113-7803	113-3848	
Gewika Industrieanlagen GmbH,			
Dmitrovka B. ul. 9, kv. 10	292-1784	292-6840	413162
GGK Moscow	250-0196	315-3274	
Ghtumya, ul. Mytnaya 1, Office 21	230-0465	230-0467	413049
Gibson, Dunn & Crutcher, Kazenny M. p. 10, kv 6	297-3784	297-3784	
Gildemeister AG,			
Krasnopresnenskaya nab. 12, Office 1501	253-5968	253-9908	413995
Giminey Foodstore, ul. B. Yakimanka 22	238-6262	299-1450	

	Phone	Fax	Telex
Ginseng salon, ul. Pokrovka 32	227-1641		
Giza S.p.A., ul. Vorotnikovskiy p. 11	229-5607	229-2116	413208
Glarus, TsUM, 4th fl.	292-4786		
Glasnet, ul. Yaroslavskaya 8/3, #216	207-0704	207-0889	
Glavk Ltd.	120-9568		
Glavmosstroi, Tverskaya ul. 2/6	921-0056	200-3212	
GlavUPDK, ul. Prechistenka 20	201-2326		
Accommodation Department	201-2398		
Appliance Repair	202-2865		
Atelier, ul. B. Pereyaslavskaya 7	280-2763		
Gas Coupons	240-9680		
Home Service	201-2706		
Legal Department	563-8850		
Office Equipt. Repair	143-1502		
Phone Repair	202-2706		
Printing, Kursovoy p. 1/1	203-2294		
Supply Depot, ul. Durova 32	288-1263		
Tailor	280-5451		
Travel and Tickets	202-2725		
Glaxo Eastern Europe Ltd.,			
Kadashevskaya nab.6/1, 6-th floor			
Glazur cafe, Smolenskiy bul. 12	248-4438		
Glinka Concert Hall, ul. Fadeyeva 4	251-1066		
Glinka Museum Hall, ul. Fadeyeva 4	972-3237		
Global Development Services,			
ul. Petrovka 20/1, 1st floor	200-3588	200-3446	
Global Edge-Moscow, Gorokhovskiy p. 18, str 2	267-1850	267-5218	
Global Properties, Tryokhprudny p. 11/13, 5th fl., #61	299-3759	209-9642	
Global USA, ul. Usacheva 35	245-5657	246 8917	111554
Global Village, Olympic Village 8-105, 11th floor	430-0142		
Global-System JV, ul. B. Serpukhovskaya 5			
Globaltest JV (US), Nagornaya ul. 24/9, kv. 2	127-6677	253-9771	413996
Globe and Mail of Canada,			
Kutuzovskiy prosp. 7/4, kv. 60	243-1362	243-1464	413044
GMM Trust Financial Services BV	253-9205		
Gnesin Institute Opera Studio, Povarskaya ul. 30/36	290-6737		
Goethe Institute Moscow, Leninskiy prosp. 95a	936-2457	936-2232	
Gogol Theater, ul. Kazakova 8a	261-5528		
Golden Dragon na Ordynke Restaurant,			
B. Ordynka 59	231-9251		
Golden Dragon Restaurant, ul. Plyushchikha 64	248-3602		
Golden Horseshoe Club, Leningradskiy prosp. 32	214-8070		
Golden Lady, Detskiy Mir, 4th floor			
Golden Lion JV, ul. Letchika Babushkina 26			
Golden Lotus Restaurant,			
Expocenter, 1st Krasnogvardeyskiy pr. 12	255-2510		
Golden Ostap Restaurant, Shmitovskiy pr. 3	259-4795		
Golden Star Trading Company,			
Krasnopresnenskaya nab. 12, Office 703a	253-1265	253-9180	413541
Goldstar Co., Ltd., Khlebny p. 19, 4th fl.	291-7430	202-5211	
Goldstar East West Mktg. Inc., Dmitrovka M. ul. 6	299-5732	299-3842	
Golf Course, see Tumba Golf Course			

	Phone	Fax	Telex
Golodetz, M (Overseas) Ltd.,			
Mamonovskiy p. 4, Office 11	299-2883	200-0227	413344
Golubka, ul. Garibaldi 11, #76	134-0295		
Good Luck JV (Holland), Izmaylovskoye sh. 69a	166-0363		
Gorizont Cinema, Komsomolskiy prosp. 21/10	245-3143		
Gorkiy House Museum, Nikitskaya M. ul. 6/2	290-0535		
Gorkiy Museum of Literature, Povarskaya ul. 25a	290-5130		
Gorkiy Park Enterprises JV (UK),			
Krymskiy val 9, Gorkiy Park, Zelony teatr	232-5385	237-3435	
Gorkom Grafikov, see Moscow Graphic Arts Society			
Gorkiy Park, Krimskiy val 9, metro Park Kultury			
Goskomstat Information Center,			
see Gosstatistika Information Center			
Gosstatistika Information Center, ul. Myasnitskaya 39	207-4681		
Gotabanken, Pokrovskiy bul. 4/17, kv. 4	207-3429	230-2456	413188
Gourmet Restaurant, Hotel Baltschug	230-6500	230-6502	414873
Government of the Russian Federation			
(Admin. Info.), Staraya pl. 4	925-3581		
Grafica M, ul. B. Kommunisticheskaya 23	272-0069	272-4682	
Gran,			
Volgogradskiy prosp. 46/15, 3d fl. (House of Culture)	179-8422	179-8422	
Grant Clothing Store, Petrovskiy Passazh, 2nd fl.			
Grat JV (FRG), ul. Kastanayevskaya 8	145-2123		
Greatis, ul. Nagornaya 31, 4th Bld	127-5940	127-0522	
Greek Restaurant, Inflotel, Krasnopresnenskaya N12	255-9284		
Greenfield JV (Malta), Raushskaya nab. 4	318-2218	975-2165	
Greenpeace, ul. Dolgorukovskaya 21	258-3950	251-9088	
Greentec (MGU), Nikitskaya, B. ul. 31	291-0510	291-0145	
Grig, ul. Verkhnyaya Krasnoselskaya 3	264-4298	264-2274	
Griphon Travel, Hotel Ukraine, Rm. 743	243-2595	243-3002	
Grundig, ul. Obratsova 17	956-3409	956-3407	412191
GRW Leipzig, see Geraete und Reglerwerk, Leipzig GmbH			
GT&E, see Sovintel			
Guangming Daily, Kutuzovskiy prosp. 7/4, kv. 146	243-1779		413086
Guardian, The, Gruzinskiy p. 3, kv. 75-76	254-4354	230-6432	413945
Guelman Gallery, ul. B. Yakimanka 2/6	238-8492		
GUM, Krasnaya pl. 3 (Red Square)	921-5763	975-2581	412179
Alberto Beski, 3rd line, 1st fl.	926-3246		
Arrow, 1st line, 1st fl.	926-3474		
Benetton, 2nd line, 1st fl.	926-3420		
Botany 500, 1st line, 2nd fl.	926-3215		
Christian Dior, 1st line	926-3430		
Claude Litz, 1st line, 2nd fl.	925-1227		
Entertainment World, 3rd line	926-3454		
Escada, 1st line, 2nd fl.	926-3231		
Estee Lauder, 1st line, 1st fl.	921-7064		
Galeries Lafayette, 1st line, 1st fl.	926-3457		
GUM Flower Market, 2nd line, 1st fl.	926-3346		
Gumir, 1st floor	926-3250		
Gzhel Store, 2nd line, 1st fl.			
JVC, 1st line, 1st fl.	923-8200		
Karstadt, 1st line, 1st fl.	926-3229		
Karstadt Sports, 1st line, 1st fl.	926-3326		

	Phone	Fax	Telex
Karstadt-Kids, 1st line, 2nd fl.	956-3556		
L'Oreal, 2nd line, 1st fl. (see GUM)			
Lakme, 2nd line, 1st fl.	926-3370		
Lego, 2nd line, 1st fl.	926-3264		
Maksimilian, 2nd line, 2nd fl.	926-3304		
Polaroid Studio Express, 3rd line			
Red Square Business Center, 1st line, 2nd fl.	921-0911	921-4609	
Roditi, 3rd line, 1st fl.	921-1529		
Rosenberg & Lenhart, 1st line, 1st fl.			
Rostik's, 3rd line, 2nd fl.	921-1529		
Salamander, 1st line, 2nd fl.			
Samsonite, 1st line, 2nd fl.	926-3466		
Sharp, 3rd line, 1st fl.	926-3455		
Sizai, 2nd line, 1st fl.	926-3412		
Souvenirs, 2nd line, 1st fl.			
Steilmann, 1st line, 2nd fl.			
Stolichny Bank, 2nd line, 1st fl.			
Tefal, 1st line, 1st fl.	926-3463		
Yakovlev & Co., 1st line, 2nd fl.			
Yves Rocher, 2nd line, 1st fl.	926-3408		
Gumir, GUM, 1st floor	926-3250		
Gummerus Publications, ul. Alabyana 10, kv. 347	198-6138		413094
Guria cafe, Komsomolskiy prosp. 7/3	246-0378		
Guta Bank, ul. Dolgorukovskaya 5	251-0105	250-0780	
Gutehoffnungshutte, see Man AG			
Gypsy Theater 'Romen', Leningradskiy prosp. 32/2	250-7353		
Gzhel Store, GUM, 2nd line, 1st fl.			
Radisson-Slavyanskaya Hotel	941-8928		
Sovintsentr, Mezhdunarodnaya Hotel I, 1st fl.	253-2359		

H

	Phone	Fax	Telex
H.G.S. JV (Austria), ul. Gilyarovskovo 10	281-7445	975-2559	
Haagsche Courant, ZOP, AVRO,			
ul. Marksistskaya 1, kv. 1	270-1539	270-1615	413544
Hadler International Ltd., ul. Donskaya 6	236-2310		
HAKA Corporation, see EKA Corporation			
Halliburton Company, Grokholskiy p. 19-27	288-9966	288-9646	
Hamilton Standard, Pokrovskiy bul. 4/17, k. 3, office 5	208-9714	230-2713	
Hankkija, see Novera			
Hanoi Cinema, Litovskiy bul. 7	425-6101		
Hanoi Restaurant, prosp. 60-letiya Oktyabrya 20/21	125-6001		
Hantarex S.U., ul. Obrucheva 36	334-2974	420-2250	412160
Hantarex Vek, M. Gnezdnikovskiy p. 2/4	229-8819	420-2250	412160
Hanver JV, ul. Simonovskiy val 12	274-5466		
Hanzetat, Dmitrovka M. ul. 2, office 509	299-7225		
Hard Rock Cafe, see Viktoria (Hard Rock Cafe) cafe			
Hard Soft, ul. Butyrskiy val 24	258-8256		
Harrisburg, Inc., Lyusinovskaya ul. 72	236-3717		
Harvard Alumni Association	962-4464		
Hash House Harriers	280-5493		
Havana Cinema, ul. Sheremetevskaya 6	281-9464		

	Phone	Fax	Telex
Havana Restaurant, Leninskiy prosp. 88	131-0091		
Heinrich Klingenberg International Moving,			
prosp. Vernadskovo 103, k. 1, kv. 49	434-2414	434-2414	413770
Helsingin Sanomat,			
ul. 26th Bakinskikh-Komissarov 9, kv. 6	434-3685	230-2421	413053
Hemaks, Krutitskiy val 3, k. 2, kv. 105	276-9792	276-9520	413440
Hermitage, Karetny ryad 3, Hermitage Theater	299-9774		
Savoy Hotel	929-8577		
Hertz Car Rental, Leninskiy prosp. 152	434-5332		
Sheremetevo 2 Airport	578-7532		
Hewlett Packard, VVTs, bldg. 2, prosp. Mira 120	181-8002		
Hewlett Packard Co., Pokrovskiy bul. 4/17, office 12	923-5001	230-2611	
Heydemann Shaw Ltd., ul. Chaplygina 1a	921-0419	202-0249	
High-Tech Stroi JV, 2nd Zachatyevskiy p. 2, str. 18	201-4839		
Hill International,			
Sovintsentr, Mezhdunarodnaya Hotel 1, #1329	253-1329		
Hilti, ul. Krasina 9	254-0751	254-8304	
Hines Interests,			
Park Place, Leninskiy prosp. 113/1, #E100	956-5051	956-5058	
Hippodrome, ul. Begovaya 22	945-4516		
Historical Museum, Krasnaya pl. 1/2	928-8452		
History of Moscow Museum, Novaya pl. 12	924-8490		
Hitachi, Krasnopresnenskaya nab. 12, Office 2004	253-5960	253-1854	
Hoechst Pharma, Tryokhprudny p. 11/13	299-8285	200-2206	413138
Hokkaido Shimbun, Kutuzovskiy prosp. 9, kv. 24	243-6998	243-0784	
Hol'N One Donuts	975-3392		
Holding Center, Shyolkovskoye sh. 7	241-5014	462-0906	
Hollming, Kursovoy p. 9, Office 6	202-1441	200-1259	413176
Holographic Systems, Inc., ul. Novokuznetskaya 17/19	233-2724	231-0426	
Hom Clothing Store, Petrovskiy Passazh, 1st fl.			
Homatek JV (FRG), ul. Ordzhonikidze 11	234-9869	230-2227	411025
Home Sweet Home, Kutuzovskiy prosp. 14, #155	255-4659		
Honeywell Inc., Tryokhprudny p. 11/13, 3rd fl.	299-6543	200-0252	413255
Hope Industries Inc.,			
Krasnopresnenskaya nab.12, #1046	253-1715	253-9181	
Hopf Catering, Krasnogvardeyskiy pr. 1	259-5384	973-2185	
Horse-breeding Museum, Timiryazevskaya ul. 44	216-1003		
Hotel Mezhdunarodnaya, see Mezhdunarodnaya Hotel			
House of Journalists, Zubovskiy bul. 8a	203-3644	291-2174	
House of Trade Unions (Kolonny Zal),			
Dmitrovka B. ul. 1	292-0178		
House Service Ltd., Nikopeskovskiy B. p. 7	241-7402	241-7402	
Houston Instrument, ul. Dovzhenko 12, k. 1, office 165	143-7511	938-2123	
Houston Peterbilt Inc., B. Starodanilovskiy p. 5	954-0719		
Hughes Network Systems/General Motors Corp.,			
Krasnopresnenskaya nab. 12, Office 10041	253-2577	253-2585	612208
Huhtamaki Oy, ul. Mytnaya 1, kv. 15	230-0443	230-2245	413993
Humbolt-Zab Zementanlagenbau GmbH,			
ul. Kalanchevskaya 6/2, k. 1, floor 4	262-8299	975-1915	413704
Hungarian Chamber of Commerce,			
Krasnopresnenskaya nab.12, Mezhdunarodnaya 2 kv. 91	253-2921	252-0930	
Hungarian School, ul. Olaf Palme 5, k. 2	143-6057		
Hungexpo, Povarskaya ul. 21	291-1845	202-8241	414328

Hunstman-Aeromar JV, Sheremetevo 2 Airport, K-340 578-3132 578-2714
Hunter Douglas Europe B.V.,
   Stary Petrovsko-Razumovskiy pr. 2 212-5112 213-5354 413677
Huolintakeskus Oy, Staraya Basmanaya 18, office 37-38 261-9440 261-6414 412228
Hurriyet, Kutuzovskiy prosp. 7/4, kv. 151 243-1489
Hypo Bank, B. Gnezdnikovskiy p. 7, 4th fl. 200-4627 200-4295 413675
Hyundai, Krasnopresnenskaya nab. 12, Office 1809 253-1683 253-1682 413698
Hyundai Motors, Krasnopresnenskaya nab. 12, #1809A 253-1683 253-1682 413698
HZZ-Moskau, see Humbolt-Zab Zementanlagenbau GmbH

I

I-Kub-K JV (US), Bryusov p. 2a 229-9862 229-9860 411809
I.M.S. Corp. JV (USA), ul. Svobody 8/4 491-8412
I.V.K. International, Main Office: Hotel Intourist 203-9439 203-9355
   2nd Pugachevskaya ul. 10, k. 1 161-2954
IAN, see ITAR (Novosti Information Agency)
Iarus JV, Granatny p. 3 290-3294 290-2886
Iberia Airlines, Kuznetskiy Most 3 921-9293 230-2242
   Sheremetevo 2 Airport 578-2791 578-2789
Iberia Restaurant, ul. Rozhdestvenka 5, str. 2 928-2672 928-2672
Ibis JV (UK), ul. Rozhdestvenka 11 923-4632   411488
IBM Corporation, Pokrovskiy bul. 4/17, kv 6 207-5597 230-2733 413232
IBM Russia, ul. Bakrushina 18 235-6602 235-4849 413232
Ibris JV (Brazil) 921-2683
Ibusz (Hungarian Travel Company),
   Staropimenovskiy p. 5 299-7402 299-8876 414400
ICD Group Inc., M. Kozikhinskiy p. 4, #2 299-3443 200-2220 413648
ICF/ EKO, Novoalekseevska 20A 283-3015 286-4591
ICL, see International Computers Limited
IDM, Mercator Corporation, Nab. Shevchenko 3 243-1404 243-9777 412100
IEB, ul. Studencheskaya 5 249-2910
IHI, see Ishikawajima-Harima Heavy Industries
III (Information, Research & Publishing Int'l),
   prosp. Vernadskovo 84 436-0758
Ikarus-Cooperation JV (Hungary), Kropotkinskiy p. 7 245-2300 230-2469 414336
Ikon JV (UK), ul. Moskovrechye 31, k. 2 362-8774 230-2574
IKON, KRO (Radio & TV), TROUW,
   Leninskiy prosp. 45, kv. 427 135-1172 230-2010 413304
Ikoni, ul. Arbat 34
Ikpa JV (Finland), ul. Tverskaya 23 326-0886 253-9794 411238
Il Giorno, Kutuzovskiy prosp. 13, kv. 43 243-1550 243-1550 413664
Il Manifestu, ul. Vavilova 85, kv. 57 134-9312   413268
Il Sole/24 Ore, Rublyovskoye sh. 26, k. 1, kv. 7 415-4034 415-2910 413634
Ildent, 10 Letiya Oktyabrya ul. 2 245-4078
Illuzion Cinema, Kotelnicheskaya nab. 1/15 227-4339
ILM Handleskontor GmbH & CO KG,
   Podkopayevskiy p. 9, str. 2 297-6839 230-2302 414357
ILVA/Finsider, ul. Mytnaya 1, kv. 32-33 230-1110 230-2769 413233
Image, ul. Petrovka 26/104 925-6021 925-8508
Image Publishers, Khoroshevskoye sh. 4 945-4569 954-5375

	Phone	Fax	Telex
Imatran Voima OY, Mamonovskiy p. 4, kv. l	209-6856	200-1277	413247
IMAX Show International JV (US), Tryokhgorny val 6	205-7279	205-7438	
IMM-Bivest JV (UK), ul. Seleznevskaya 13	258-8602	258-6802	
IMO JV (FRG), Yakimanskaya nab. 10/2	238-9021		
Imperial Bank, Sadovnicheskaya ul. 63, str. 7	237-6601	237-7717	412093
Imperial Chemicals Industries PLC (ICI),			
B. Strochenovskiy p. 22/25	230-6111	230-6119	413241
Imperial Restaurant, Gagarinskiy p. 9/5	291-6063		
Imporleste Representacoes, S.A.,			
ul. B. Ordynka 50, kv. 3-4	233-8597	230-2814	416222
Impulse-Apparat JV (Korea), Vspolny p. 13	290-4269	290-4269	412201
In Vino Restaurant, Ukraine Hotel, 3rd floor	243-2316		
In-Consult Ltd. (UK), ul. Snezhnaya 27, k. 1, office 109	180-4317	180-4317	
INA Commerce, p. Obukha 8	297-3455	297-2773	414451
Inatours	253-1529		
Inaudit, ul. Konyushkovskaya 28	253-9505	253-9293	612142
Inbio JV (FRG), ul. B. Kommunisticheskaya 27	271-1269	253-9310	411432
Inbor-Induro JV (FRG),			
Rublyovskoye sh. 44, k. 2, kv. 294	413-0359		414756
Incar, ul. Marksa-Engelsa 8	202-4917	203-4080	
Incomtrade, ul. Kulakova 22	944-9793	944-9793	
Incomtrade JV, Podsosenskiy p. 28	113-2157	310-7016	
Independence, Selskokhozyastvenny prosp. 2. 6	181-5149	181-0157	411686
Independent Radio News,			
ul. Akad. Koroleva 4, k. 2, kv. 19-20	215-1147	215-1147	
Independent Television News,			
ul. Marksistskaya 1, kv. 47-48	270-6688	274-0004	413543
Independent Theater Union, see Arlekin, Inc.			
Independent, The, ul. D. Ulyanova 16, bldg. 2, rm 421	124-2612	124-0712	413526
Independiente (El), Rublyovskoye sh. 26, k. 1, kv. 294	415-4138	415-2936	413630
Indian School, Dorogomilovskaya 32	240-6437	240-6439	
Indonesian School, Novokuznetskaya 12	231-9549		
Induro, Krasnopresnenskaya nab. 12, Office 807	253-2807	253-1577	
Industriale Export, ul. Mosfilmovskaya 64	143-0422	143-0449	414360
Industrie Pirelli SpA,			
Krasnopresnenskaya nab. 12, Office 1003	253-2568		413023
Industrieberatung Wilkening,			
ul. B. Molchanovka 34, bdg. 2	291-4735	200-2263	411775
Industry Service Bank, Miusskaya pl., 7	251-6004	956-1611	
Ineko JV (US), ul. Kalibrovskaya 22a	281-4622		
Inex JV (Japan), Hotel Orlyonok, room 514-515	939-8016	253-9506	413593
Infa-Otel JV (Finland), ul. Rozhdestvenka 3	928-9169	230-2186	411620
Infatel JV (Japan), ul. Tverskaya 7	201-9174	292-0616	414793
Inflotel, Krasnopresnenskaya nab. 12, docking	255-9278		
Info-Global JV (FRG), Tikhvinskiy p. 10/12	241-3228		
Infocom JV (Finland), Teterenskiy p. 10	915-5093	915-7158	
Inforcom Express, Petrovskiy p. 5, stroyeniye 7, kv.26	925-4433	975-2679	
Inform-Pravo JV, ul. Druzhby 10/32	143-6771	938-2120	411734
Informatic, Kozikhinskiy B. p. 7, str. 2	202-8501	882-0212	
Informatika NPC JV, ul. Skhodnenskaya 6	497-6378	497-7200	
Information Computer Enterprise JV (US),			
VVTs, bldg. 4, prosp. Mira 120	187-9331	187-8830	411665

	Phone	Fax	Telex
Information Moscow,			
Leninskiy prosp. 45, ent 15, kv 426	135-1164	230-2010	413199
Information on City Phone Numbers	927-0009		
Informbank Agency, ul. Timura Frunze 8/5	245-0213	245-0213	
Informcom, Merzlyakovskiy p. 8	925-6644	925-2679	
Informinvest JV (Switz.), ul. M. Bronnaya 28/2	299-0587	334-1921	412196
Informlitsenzreklama JV (FRG),			
Leninskiy prosp. 146, office 1901	438-8100	230-2818	411670
Informpravo JV, Neglinnaya ul. 29/14, bldg. 3	200-2775	208-2151	
Informprogress JV (US), ul. Kosygina 15	939-8412	939-8241	
InformVES, Ovchinnikovskaya nab. 18/1	220-1606		
ING Bank, see Inter-Alpha Group of Banks			
Ingersoll-Rand Company,			
Krasnopresnenskaya nab. 12, Office 1101	253-7151	253-9075	413969
Ingosstrakh Insurance Company, ul. Pyatnitskaya 12	231-1677	230-2518	411144
Inko Ltd. JV (Finland), Novy Arbat 16	290-6922	200-1209	411286
Inkom Bank			
Central Division, Sibirskiy pr. 2, k. 2	270-9290		
Arkhangelskiy p. 12/8	923-3709		
ul. Nametkina 14, k. 1	332-0699	331-8833	412345
Inkom JV, Zubovskiy bul. 3	299-4937	299-4937	414754
Inkomeks JV, ul. Myasnitskaya 45	921-1085	200-2258	
Inkompex JV (Austria), ul. Krivorozhskaya 33	113-2025	310-7016	
Inmart, ul. Rabochaya 63, #1026	270-3054	270-3054	413630
Inmet JV (Switz.), Tsvetnoy bul. 16	200-2779	253-9904	413920
InNis JV (Japan), ul. B. Ordynka 32	238-3077	200-3207	414883
Mozhayskoye sh. 165	599-9222		
Innovation Land Bank, Nakhimovskiy prosp. 32, rm 605	129-1211		
Innovation, Info., Intellect & Communication,			
Bryusov p. 2a	229-4668	229-3237	411809
Inntel, ul. Nemchinova 12	211-0983	211-0983	
Inostrannaya Kniga, Nikitskaya M. ul. 16	290-4082		
Inpred, Krasnopresnenskaya nab. 12	253-7075	253-9913	411486
Inpribor JV (Austria), ul. Koshtoyantsa 1A	432-0975	938-2239	
Inprogress JV, p. Kammenoy slobody 2/1, office 3	241-1690	241-5927	
Inrosspreus JV (FRG), ul. Skakovaya 17	945-5030	253-9001	
Inrosvet JV (Spain), ul. Udaltsova 67a	133-8528	288-9522	411466
Inservice Courier, ul. Mayakovskaya 17/7	203-9945	200-1295	411044
Insigdat JV, prosp. Mira 4a			
Insplast JV (FRG), Perovskiy pr. 35			
Institute of Bioorganic Chemistry,			
ul. Miklukho-Maklaya 16/10	335-1800		
Inst. of Diagnostic Systems, Shchukinskaya ul. 12, k. 1	190-7772	190-7828	
Inst. of Organized Markets Research, ul. Kazakova 8a	262-8988		
Instituto Bancario San Paolo di Torino,			
ul. Mosfilmovskaya 54	143-6021	938-2144	413854
Insurance Company IMKO,			
ul. Yartsevskaya 30, kom. 1105-1106	141-3396	149-9774	
Inta JV (Spain), ul. Novoalekseyevskaya 16	283-5718	288-9522	411466
Intark JV (FRG), Sechenovskiy p. 6, str. 1	273-2361		
Intarkor International JV (FRG),			
Nizhniy Taganskiy tupik 11, str. 2	272-7733		
Intekkom JV (Finland), ul. Usiyevicha 22	272-7640		

	Phone	Fax	Telex
Intekkom JV (Switz.), sh. Entuziastov 5	277-4060	277-4162	411024
Inteko JV (Austria), ul. Lesnaya 41	258-6787	258-4411	411072
Intel Corp., ul. Kremenchugskaya 6/7	443-9785	445-9606	
Intelligent Technologies, Baltiyskaya ul. 14	155-4450		
Intelmas JV (FRG), ul. Prechistenka 37, str. 2	231-7596		
Inter Aks JV, Volzhskiy bul. 114a, k. 9	179-3045		
Inter MTD JV, Seliverstov p. 8	208-2880	233-1711	
Inter Oceanic Factors Agency Inc.,			
Protopovskiy p. 16, kv. 38	280-8731		413277
Inter Techno Corporation,			
Stary Petrovsko-Razumovskiy pr. 6/8-3, kv. 76	214-9801	214-1842	
Inter-Alpha Group of Banks, The,			
ul. Skakovaya 3, 2nd fl.	945-2479	945-2501	
Inter-Republican Universal Trade Exchange	208-6681		
Interagra, Dmitrovka B. ul. 9, kv. 8	292-3036	230-2233	413182
Interagrokompleks JV (Austria), Mozhayskoye sh. 24	449-5840		
Interagrosystems JV (FRG),			
ul. Yartsevskaya 30, kom. 1107	141-3396		
Interagrotex JV (Sweden), ul. Pryanishnikova 31	976-4616	973-2217	411624
Interalpha, ul. Voykova 2	151-1168	245-6473	
InterArt Bazar, Serpukhovskiy val 24, kor.2	952-3008		
Interartbazaar JV (British/Russian),			
Serpukhovskiy val 24, kor 2	952-3008	954-2300	
Interastro JV (Hungary), ul. Profsoyuznaya 32/34			
Interatlantic JV, ul. Izhorskaya 7	486-4778		
InterAvto M	297-0003		
Interavtocom JV (Italy), Volgogradskiy prosp. 42	179-5367	274-0049	411333
Interbeton BV, ul. Lyusinovskaya 53/12, #17	237-6895	230-2265	
Interbite JV (Cyprus), Pugovishnikov p. 11/8	246-7397	246-9662	
Interbook JV (Yugoslavia), 2nd Smolenskiy p. 1/4	241-6399	241-6379	411871
Interbusinesstour, Molodyozhnaya Hotel, #1520	210-9438	200-3285	
Intercar Minishop (and offices), ul. Pilyugina 14, k. 3	936-2469		
Intercar Moscow 189, B. Sadovaya 5/1	200-5200	250-9741	414002
Intercinema Agency, ul. Druzhninikovskaya 15	255-9052	973-2029	
Intercity Communications Agency (ICA),			
ul. Klary Tsetkin 11, Kor. 1	450-6788	450-6800	
Interclub Moscow JV (FRG), ul. Begovaya 22, kv. 1	481-7772		
Intercom JV (Austria), Leningradskiy prosp. 63	157-3040	157-3446	
Interconcepts, Inc., ul. Dovzhenko 12, k. 1, office 165	143-7511	938-2123	413610
Intercontact Agroservice JV (Holland),			
ul. B. Filevskaya 37, k. 1	144-0588		411311
Intercoop, Krasnopresnenskaya nab. 12, Office 1517	253-1517	253-9173	
Intercross JV, see Chelek Agroplast JV filial			
Intercross Trading Corporation, Zubovskiy bul. 4	201-8837	230-2170	411323
Interdean AG, Rublyovskoye sh. 36, k. 2, kv. 212	415-4296	415-2959	413587
Interdepartmental Council for Foreign Advertising,			
Bolshaya Ordynka 7 str. 2	231-8428		
Interdesign JV, Dokuchaev p. 2	200-4254	200-4254	411672
Interdialekt, Glazovskiy p. 1, 2nd flr.	241-6307	241-9970	
Interdum Corporation JV, ul. Im. Kurchatova 182	190-5171		411594
Interexpert JV, Berezhkovskaya nab. 6	240-5883	240-4869	
Interexpo,			
Krasnopresnenskaya nab. 12, Office 1335 Mezh II	253-1335	253-9067	413649

	Phone	Fax	Telex
Interexpressia JV (Switz.), ul. Neglinnaya 27/2/26	299-5894		
Interface JV, ul. Klimashkina 9	253-3453		411429
Interfax, 1st Tverskaya-Yamskaya ul. 2, floor 3	250-9203	250-9727	
Interferma JV, ul. Timura Frunze 34, Ship Vermont	243-7855	200-3220	
Interflug, ul. B. Spasskaya 12	280-7233		
Intergeomodel JV, see PPS-Intergeomodel JV			
Intergorizont, Stoleshnikov p. 11	928-4515	921-8924	411838
Intergrafservice JV (FRG), Sushchyovskiy val 49	289-7253		414777
Intergraph Corp., Frunzenskaya nab. 8, kv. 47	246-6328		
Intergraph Graphic Systems,			
ul. Bakhrushina 20, Room 401	235-4652	235-6028	
Interguide Tour Agency, pr. Yakushina 3, #52	903-5303		
Interimpex-Engineering JV,			
ul. Novocheremushkinskaya 60, k. 2	332-6931	420-2002	
Interimpulse JV, prosp. Mira 114b	287-2022	287-2022	
Interinformset JV (Australia), ul. Tverskaya 5/6	203-7571	200-4256	411666
Interinvest JV, Mozhayskoye sh. 41	443-1835		
Interkeramika JV (Finland), ul. Ozernaya 48	430-7770	430-9000	
Interkholod JV, ul. Kostyakova 12	210-3601		411581
Interkinofototekhnika JV (Switzerland),			
Leningradskiy prosp. 47, Nikfi	157-2923	157-2374	
Interkom JV (Bulgaria), prosp. Vernadskovo 4	490-3721		411088
Interkontakt JV, Novinskiy bul. 11	255-4613	243-5126	41172
Interkoop JV (Italy), p. Gorkovo 3/1	127-5695	310-7057	
Interkor JV (Austria), Yauzskaya ul. 10	297-0809		
Interkous JV, Sukharevskaya pl. 6, str. 2	250-8993		
Interkovent JV (Sweden), Nikoloyamskaya ul. 38/23	227-0700		411700
InterLazerLeasing JV (UK),			
Nikitskaya B. ul. 22/26, rooms 2C 9	231-4870	230-2309	
Interling JV (US), sh. Entuziastov 62	305-0239		
Interlink JV (FRG), ul. Narodnovo Opolcheniya 34	946-8711	943-0087	610101
Interlink JV (Sweden), ul. Izhorskaya 7	486-2696	486-4748	
Intermarket, Degtyarny p. 5	299-7968	299-7968	
Patriarshiy B. p., 12	291-7655	291-7655	
Intermebel JV, ul. Litvina-Sedova 9/26	259-6933	256-2972	
Intermechanika JV (Hong Kong),			
Lomonosovskiy prosp. 24	939-3262	939-0186	411483
Intermed, ul. Durova 26, floor 4, kor. 1 & 6	971-2836		
Intermed JV (FRG) Head Office, Sukharevskaya pl. 5/1	928-5757	208-1738	
Intermedbio-IMB JV (US), Leninskiy prosp. 156	434-1020	434-1020	411649
Intermedia International S.r.L.,			
Begovaya alleya 11, k. 629	945-2764	946-1100	
Intermedservice JV (Switzerland),			
Hotel Intourist, rooms 2030-2031	203-8631	200-0282	411271
Intermedtest JV (Switz.), Abrikosovskiy p. 1	248-5317	292-6511	
Intermet Engineering JV (US), Leninskiy prosp. 24	238-3536	236-8043	414751
Intermetod JV, Frunzenskaya nab. 30	242-8881		413832
InterMicro, ul. Nizhnyaya Krasnoselskaya 39	267-3210		
Internal Affairs with Moscow City Council,			
Main Department, ul. Petrovka 38	200-8342		
Int'l Assoc. of Sport Clubs (Lokomotiv),			
Okhotny ryad 7	262-9215	262-8935	

	Phone	Fax	Telex
Int'l Association of Business Cooperation,			
Shelepikhinskoye sh. 11, kv. 64	259-6788		
Int'l Bank of Economic Cooperation,			
ul. Mashi Poryvayevoy 11	975-3861	975-2202	411391
Int'l Baptist Fellowship,			
Druzhinnikovskaya ul. 15, 5th fl., #6	150-3293		
International Business Service (IBS),			
1st Tverskoy-Yamskoy p. 18/3, #326	956-1525	251-5447	
Int'l Center for Better Health (Aezop), PO Box #27	252-3316	252-3316	
International Center for Children's Health	236-2594	230-1436	
Int'l Center for Small Enterprise Development,			
MGU, Humanities Faculty, k. 2, k. 473	939-3555	939-0877	
International Christian Assembly,			
Lenin Children's Library, Kaluzhskaya pl.	138-8293		
International Committee of the Red Cross,			
Smolenskaya Nab. 5/13, kv.125	241-5160	241-6012	
International Committee of Youth Organizations,			
ul. Maroseyka 7/8	206-8542	206-8173	
International Company Services Ltd.,			
ul. Sadovaya-Spasskaya 19, str.1	975-3096	975-4604	
Int'l Compensations Exchange, ul. Sretenka 19	207-1622		
Int'l Computers Ltd. (ICL), ul. Vavilova 83, kv. 5	134-9549	134-6423	413074
International Cultural Enterprises	159-2700		
International Distillers & Vintners Ltd. (IDV),			
Krasnopresnenskaya nab. 12, TsMT, office 540	253-2540	253-2540	
International Exch. of Information and Telecom,			
Leningradskiy prosp. 80/2	158-7492	230-2819	411127
International Exchange of Intellectural Property,			
Staraya pl. 10/4			
International Exchange of Secondary Resources,			
B. Matrosskiy p. 1/1	269-0211		
International Exhibition Complex, see Expocenter			
International Federation of Peace and Consensus,			
prosp. Mira 36	280-0850		
Int'l Found. for the Survival and Dev. of Humanity,			
Denezhny p. 9/5	241-8243		
International Fund 'Conversion',			
B. Molchanovka 23, kv.38	291-3929	202-7942	
International Fund of Goodwill and Health,			
ul. Pokrovka 22-1	297-4999		
International Information Service JV (Italy),			
ul. Sivashskaya 4/2	110-5702		411195
International Interest Group, Inc.,			
ul. Sadovaya-Samotechnaya 9, kv. 34	979-7065	292-6511	
Int'l Investment Bank, ul. Mashi Poryvayevoy 7	975-4008	975-2070	411394
Int'l Medical Center JV, ul. Vorontsovo pole 14	297-1453		
International Monetary Fund (IMF), Novy Arbat 36	290-7133		
International Moscow Bank, Kamergerskiy p. 6	292-9632		
International Moscow Bank JV, ul. Plyushchikha 37	246-2567		411174
International Moscow Radio, ul. Pyatnitskaya 25	233-7934	230-2828	411136
International Network Connections,			
ul. Profsoyuznaya 61, office 326	334-8249	330-3576	
Int'l Pharmacie in UPDK, Gruzinskiy p. 3, kor. 2	254-4946		

	Phone	Fax	Telex
International Post Office, Varshavskoye sh. 37	114-4584		
Int'l Press Center & Club, Radisson-Slavyanskaya Hotel	941-8621	941-8659	
International Processing Systems (IPS)	209-6095		
Int'l Relations Publishers, ul. Sadovaya-Spasskaya 20	207-6793	200-2204	
International Science Foundation (Soros)	939-1092		
International Shipping Lines, Novy Arbat 21	291-9331		
International Sports Exchange, Luzhnetskaya Nab. 8	201-1994	248-0366	
International Women's Club, c/o US Embassy	253-2508		
InterOccidental, Izmailovskoye sh. 44	367-9645	366-0175	
Interoceanic Shipping and Oil Inc.,			
Protopovskiy p. 16, kv. 37	280-6692	973-3875	
Interoko Drug Store, Petrovskiy Passazh, 2nd fl., 1st line	292-3451		
Interoko JV (FRG), Frunzenskaya nab. 30	242-8941		
Interolimp JV (FRG), Staropanskiy p. 1/5	928-3381	923-3545	411791
Interperevod, Sadovaya-Kudrinskaya 11	252-7388	200-2250	
Interperiodika JV (US), Profsoyuznaya ul. 90	336-0066	336-0666	
Interplastica, Hotel Leningradskaya, room 439	975-5328	230-2234	
Interpravo JV (Austria), Kholodilny p. 3	232-5922		
Interprint JV (Bulgaria), Butikovskiy p. 12	291-9597		
Interproekt JV (Italy), Novoslobodskaya ul. 58	258-9700	973-2003	
Interprogress JV, Miklukho-Maklaya 55a	241-7911		
Interprokom JV (FRG), Savvinskaya nab. 25	246-1105	247-1052	111541
Interros FTO	207-1275	207-2229	
Interscrap JV (US), ul. Ostozhenka 26	299-8648	943-0052	413094
Interservice JV (FRG), Shlyuzovaya nab. 6	235-1347	230-2157	
Intershelf, JP Kenny (UK), Kozhevnicheskaya ul. 11	235-9693	230-2301	411782
Intershtrikhkod JV (UK), Strastnoy bul. 8	229-1933	229-3511	411871
Intersignal JV (US), Profsoyuznaya ul. 82	330-6528	333-1088	
Intersoft JV (US), Lomonosovskiy prosp. 18	930-5570	310-7050	411853
Intersoyuz JV (FRG), Pushkinskaya pl. 5	209-3755	230-2330	111121
Intersputnik, 2nd Smolenskiy p. 1/4	244-0333	253-9906	411288
Interstroy Service Division	972-0232	972-0232	411700
Interstroy Standard JV, ul. Krzhizhanovskovo 13	124-3768		
Interstroykompleks JV, ul. Sadovaya-Sukharevskaya 2/34	925-2184		
Intersurdo JV (Sweden), Seliverstov p. 8	208-2821		
Intertechnologia JV Filial, Michurinskiy pr. 1	939-3262		
Intertes, ul. Narodnovo Opolcheniya 34	947-8560		
Intertest JV (US), Tsevtnoi bul. 28 str. 2	208-1951	200-3276	
Intertex JV, Nab. Novikova-Priboya 9, k. 2	197-9195	273-1937	412176
Intertop JV (New Zealand), Tsvetnoy bul. 21, str. 8	200-3009	200-3341	
Intertorg, Inc., Gruzinskiy p. 3, kv. 63-64	254-3162	253-9771	413996
Intertrade JV (Belgium), ul. Kuznetskiy Most 19	925-9469	975-2358	
Intertrest JV (US), Sadovnicheskaya nab. 1/15	233-0626		
Interunity JV (UK, Panama), Novinskiy bul. 20a	202-2107	200-2201	413932
Interrural JV (Switzerland), ul. Tverskaya 9a, str.7	229-6688	973-2083	414807
Intervils JV (Australia), ul. Gorbunova 3	449-7783		
Interyunis JV (Austria), ul. Myasnitskaya 24, str. 3-4	923-5604	923-5604	911557
Intex-90, Leningradskiy prosp. 63	157-3317	157-3196	
Intourconsult JV (Austria), Kronshtadtskiy bul. 43a	454-3071	454-3071	
Intourguideservice, Milyutinskiy p. 13/1	923-8575	924-8481	
Intourist, Mokhovaya ul. 13	292-2365	200-1243	411211
Intourist Car Rental, Hotel Kosmos	215-6191		

	Phone	Fax	Telex
Intourist Hotel, ul. Tverskaya 3/5	203-4008		411823
Casino Gabriela	203-9608		
Jindo Rus	203-9742		
Nefertiti	203-1589		
Patio Bar	203-4008		
Santa Lucia Bar	203-1632		
Intourist Information	203-6962		
Intourist Moscow, Stoleshnikov p. 11	923-5763	928-4813	411331
Intourservice, Hotel Kosmos	215-9391		
Hotel Mezhdunarodnaya	255-6803		
Hotel Rossiya	298-1173		
Nikitskiy p. 4a	203-9898	200-1243	411211
Intourservice			
Car Rental, ul. Varvarka 6 hotel 'Rossiya'	298-5853		
Central Excursion Bureau, ul. Tverskaya 1	292-5133	203-6962	
Intourtrans, ul. Petrovka 15/13	927-1181	921-1996	411449
Intourtransavto, ul. Petrovka 15	928-8614		
Intraco, ul. Timiryazevskaya 1/3	979-6895	210-0012	413686
Intrada, ul. M. Pirogovskaya 1a	256-4570	246-5766	
Showroom, Okhotny ryad 2, first floor	925-9336		
Intrakon, N. Kiselny p. 5	200-6921		
Intravel, ul. Vavilova 55	124-5888		411488
Intur-Kone JV (Finland), ul. 26 Bakinskikh Komissarov 9	434-5219	434-7064	
Invemo JV, ul. Bakhrushina 28			
Investaudit, M. Golovin p. 8	231-8122	211-2377	
Investronic Holland b.v., Hotel Pekin, room 1103	200-5219	200-4222	413297
Invex, Hotel Mezhdunarodnaya 2, #742	253-2742		411654
Invino JV (FRG), Kutuzovskiy prosp. 2/1 hotel 'Ukraina'	243-2444	243-3282	
Invipo JV (FRG), ul. B. Molchanovka 34, str. 2	291-4713	200-2263	411775
Inyurcolleguia, ul. Tverskaya 5	203-6864	200-5247	411811
Inzhener Ltd., prosp. Mira 20, kor. 2	288-7177	280-1508	
Inzhmebel JV (FRG), 2nd ul. Marinoy Roshchi 22	971-4288	961-6372	
Inzhplast GmBH JV (Germany), Perovskiy pr. 35	273-7388	273-2958	
Ipatco, ul. Petrovka 15, office 19-20	924-5893	200-1228	413310
IPCO Group, Leninskiy prosp. 64A	930-3640	930-3374	412432
IPS Theater Box Office,			
Hotel Metropol, Teatralny pr. 1/4	927-6728	927-6729	413597
Iraqi Airways, ul. Pyatnitskaya 37	231-2974		
Sheremetevo 2 Airport	578-2707		
IREX - Int'l Research and Exchange Board,			
Khlebny p. 8, 4th fl.	290-6233	202-4449	
Irik JV (Cyprus), ul. Gasheka 12, k. 7, kv. 51	250-9563	973-2188	412004
Iris Car Rental, Pullman Iris Hotel	488-8106		
Iris JV (France), Beskudnikovskiy bul. 59a	905-4381	485-5954	411856
Irish Bar, Sheremyetevo 2 Airport, Duty Free Zone	578-6878		
Irish Times, ul. Marksistskaya 1, k. 1, kv. 57-58	274-0051	274-0397	413537
IRSOTR, Serpukhovskiy val 8, kv. 69-70	952-4975		413566
Ishikawajima-Harima Heavy Industries Co., Inc.,			
ul. Mytnaya 1. Office 7	230-1032	230-2756	413087
Iskra	312-1205		
Iskra Cinema, ul. Kostyakova 10	216-2724		
Iskra Industry Co., Ltd., Pokrovskiy bul. 4/17, kv. 30	298-5014		413239

Iskusstvo i Elektronika (Arts & Electronics) JV (US),
ul. Gotvalda 10 — 251-0131 — 200-2232
Island Jeep Eagle/Chrysler Corp. — 147-8610 — 335-8869
Issko JV (FRG) — 152-5916 — — 411432
Istok JV (India), Romanov p. 2, bul. 4-5 — 924-7434 — 923-8484 — 411778
Istok-K Computer Network — 245-5165
Istros JV (Syria), Mamonovskiy p. 10 — 207-4406 — 291-0608
IT Club, ul. Novaya Basmannaya 4/6/342 — 262-1027 — 262-1027
IT Comercio Internacional, SA,
see Imporleste Representacoes
ITA (Novosti Telegraph Agency), Zubovskiy bul. 4 — 201-2424 — 201-2119 — 411321
Ital-moda, Leninskiy prosp. 41/1
Italgrani, Krasnopresnenskaya nab. 12, Office 1006b — 253-8347 — 253-8276 — 413076
Italia Restaurant/Bar, ul. Arbat 49 — 241-4342
Italian Bakery, ul. B. Polyanka 30
Italian School, ul. Lobachevskovo 38 — 431-4966
Italian-Russian Chamber of Commerce,
Denezhny p. 7 — 241-6517 — 230-2414 — 413171
Italimpex, ul. Mytnaya 1, office 16 — 230-0787 — 230-2696 — 413237
Italimpianti, ul. Mytnaya 1, kv. 31 — 238-9714 — 230-2093 — 413507
Italiya - Stil, ul. Kasaktina 1A — 187-9625 — 187-9625
Italsovmont JV (Italy), see Italimpianti
ITC, see Inter Techno Corportion
Iteko JV (Switz.), 2nd Frunzenskaya ul. 10 — 242-0323 — 242-8898
Items Warehouse and Storage, B. Cherkasskiy p. 4 — 924-6495 — 928-8054
ITM JV (India), ul. Dovatora 12, k. 2 — 247-0938
Itoman & Co., LTD., ul. Mytnaya 1, 2nd fl. — 230-2605 — 237-1306 — 413085
ITTM JV (Canada),
Krasnopresnenskaya nab. 12, Office 736 — 253-1666 — 253-2736
IVK SYSTEMS, ul. Dubininskaya 96 — 955-6519 — 958-0603
Izdatbank, ul. Petrovka 26 — 200-6869 — 200-6869
Izdatelstvo Slog, Chistoprudny bul. 8 — 928-9429 — 925-4274
Izmailovo Concert Hall, Izmaylovskoye sh. 71 — 166-7844
Izmailovo JV (Canada), Izmaylovskoye sh. 71 — 166-0165 — 166-2563
Izmailovo Tourist Complex, Izmaylovskoye sh. 69A — 166-0109
    Jever Stube — 166-3490
    Kings Casino — 166-6735
Izmailovskiy Park,
Narodny prosp. 17, metro Izmailovskiy Park
Izophleks JV (UK), ul. Shuchinskaya 12, k. 1 — 190-7826 — 943-0026
Izvestiya, Pushkinskaya pl. 5 — 209-9100
Izvestiya-Burda JV (FRG), Pushkinskaya pl. 5 — 200-3462 — 230-2303

J

J K Enterprises Ltd., ul. B. Spasskaya 15 — 207-2931 — 208-8302 — 413621
J.A.T. Ltd., Sushchyovskiy val 5 — 973-0757 — 973-0761
Jack's Sandwiches — 281-3536
Jacko's Piano Bar,
Leningradskaya Hotel, ul Kalanchovskaya 21/40 — 975-1967
Jacob Hohermuth AG,
B. Starodanilovskiy p. 5, Danilovskiy Complex, #33 — 954-0624 — 956-0624 — 612366

	Phone	Fax	Telex
Jahn International, VVTs, bldg. 6, prosp. Mira 120	188-4361		
JAL, Japan Air Lines, Kuznetskiy Most 3	921-6448		413111
Sheremetevo 2 Airport	578-2942		413922
Jamestown Foundation	208-9512	208-9512	
Janayugom, ul. Akad. Anokhina 30, k. 4, kv. 854	430-4517		
Japan Sea Corporation, ul. Mytnaya 1, 2nd fl.	237-2349	230-2790	413907
Japan Trade Representation,			
Krasnopresnenskaya Nab. 12, #1905	253-2482		
Japan-Russian Trade Association,			
ul. Mytnaya 1, floor 2	237-2465	230-2648	
Japanese School, Leninskiy prosp. 78	131-8733		
JAT Yugoslav Airlines, Kuznetskiy Most 3	921-2846		
Sheremetevo Airport	578-2724		
Jazz Club, Kuznetskiy Most Metro	921-9744		
JB Electronics Supplies Ltd. (UK),			
Krasnopresnenskaya nab. 12, TsMT, office 1109	253-1109	253-1109	
Jerome W. Dewald & Assoc.,			
Leningradskiy prosp. 52, kv.10	308-4713	308-4713	413205
Jetta	307-8351	307-2703	
Jever Pilsner, Detskiy Mir, 4th floor			
Jever Stube, Hotel Izmailovo, corpus D	166-3490		
Jever-Bistro, Rossiya Hotel, East entrance	298-2923		
Jewish Drama Studio Theater, Varshavskoye sh. 71	110-3758		
Jewish Music Theater, Taganskaya pl. 12	272-4924		
Jewish Services,			
Maria Roshcha Synagogue,2nd Veshlavtzev p.5a			
Jewish Synagogue (choral), ul. Akhipova 10	923-9697		
Jewish Youth Cultural Ctr. Tkhiya, ul. B. Tulskaya 44	234-5297		
Jiji Press, ul. Sadovaya-Samotechnaya 12/24, kv. 21	200-1017	200-0231	413137
Jindo Rus, Hotel Intourist	203-9742	227-1013	412130
Hotel Kosmos, prosp. Mira 150	217-0025		
JJ International, ul. Fuchika 17/19	250-4150	250-4150	414480
John Brown PLC, Pokrovskiy bul. 4/17, kv. 27	207-3269	230-2315	413419
John Nurminen Oy, ul. B. Ochakovskaya 15a	430-7861	430-7521	411927
Johnson & Johnson Ltd., ul. Krzhizhanovskovo 18, kor 2	125-0052	125-2239	413857
Joint Stock Service Company,			
B. Gnezdnikovskiy p. 10, Suite 108	229-2618	229-4058	
Joint Way JV (US), ul. Timiryazevskaya 4/12	216-8223	216-8627	
Jones Development Group, ul. Tverskaya 6, #97	229-7201	229-2717	
Josef Schmitter, Hotel Mezhdunarodnaya II, room 1207	253-1207	253-9361	411432
Journal de Geneve (Le), ul. B. Spasskaya 12, kv. 30-2	230-2464		
Journal of Commerce/Knight-Ridder,			
ul. Karetny ryad 10/5, kv. 43	299-1174	200-2216	
Journalists' Union Photocenter,			
see Photocenter of the Journalists' Union			
JSR Holdings Company Ltd.,			
B. Strochenovskiy p. 22/25	236-1237	202-4359	
Julius Meinl Supermarket, Leninskiy prosp. 146	438-3444	434-9065	
Jump,			
Luzhniki Sports Complex, Universalny Sportivny Zal	247-0343		
Jump Joint Stock Company,			
ul. Novocheremushkinskaya 60, k. 2	331-2170	420-2002	

	Phone	Fax	Telex
Jurakon International Agency JV,			
1st Khoroshevskiy pr. 14, k. 3, kv. 86	946-0838	946-0838	411700
Just Subs, Kutuzovskiy prosp. 22	243-0109		
JVC, GUM, 1st line, 1st fl.	923-8200		
Leninskiy prosp. 60	137-2025		
Jyllands Posten, Rublyovskoye sh. 26, k. 1, kv. 117	415-2925		413553

K

	Phone	Fax	Telex
K & S Fruits and Vegetables, Leninskiy prosp. 42	938-7986	930-6637	
K-Boutiques, Aerostar Hotel	155-5030		
Pullman Iris Hotel	488-8100	290-4556	
Kabelbel JV (Austria), ul. Belomorskaya 26	458-3486		
Kairin Co. Ltd., ul. 2nd Baumanskaya 9/23 - 18	261-6336	265-7095	
Kaleva Travel Agency Ltd., Intourist Hotel, Room 801	203-6108		
Kalinka Stockmann, see Stockmann			
Kalinka Tekseks, ul. Profsoyuznaya 15	129-7711		
Kamernaya Tsena Theater, Zemlyanoy val 64	297-3718		
Kami Corp., Bolshaya Kommunisticheskaya ul. 11	272-4963	271-0984	
Kamir Advertising Agency, ul. Goncharova 17a	219-0101	976-5275	
Kamneft JV (FRG), ul. Narodnovo Opolcheniya 40, k. 3	192-8057	492-8059	114444
Kamos JV (Poland), Okhotny ryad 18	203-2505	292-6511	411429
Kan, ul. Solyanskaya 8A	300-8721		
Kanematsu Corp, Krasnopresnenskaya nab. 12, 1508	253-2488	253-9907	413480
Kansallis, Osaki, Pankki, Pokrovskiy bul. 4/17, kv. 4	207-3429	230-2456	413188
Kansan Uutiset, ul. B. Cherkizovskaya 5a, kv. 12	168-2524	168-2526	413095
Karabakh Restaurant, ul. Lipetskaya 52	329-7100		
Karavan, ul. Zoologicheskaya 1	285-8584	285-8584	
Karina Restaurant, Solyanskiy pr. 1/3	924-0369		
Karo, Pushkinskaya pl. 2	229-0003		
Karstadt, GUM, 1st line, 1st fl.	926-3229		
Sports, GUM, 1st line, 1st fl.	926-3326		
Kids, GUM, 1st line, 2nd fl.	956-3556		
Kashtan Restaurant, Taganskaya ul. 40/42	272-6242		
Kastilia JV (Spain), Ozerkovskaya nab. 26			
Kaufmann's Handel-Maatschappij N.V.,			
Stary Petrovsko-Razumovskiy pr. 2	212-2341	213-5354	413677
Kaukomarkkinat Oy, Pokrovskiy bul. 4/17, kv. 10	207-4144	298-4490	413278
Kazakhstan Cinema, Leninskiy prosp. 105	433-4165		
Kazanskiy Train Station, Komsomolskaya pl. 2	266-2843		
Kemira Oy, Koroviy val 7, kv. 12	236-0519	230-2354	413918
Keptstowe Freight Services Ltd. (UK), sh. Frezer 17	170-4101	170-4550	
Keram-Optic Systems JV, ul. Vavilova 38	135-0387		
Kerch Cinema, ul. Biryulevskaya 17	326-1666		
Khamoyun, ul. Tverskaya 22, Hotel Minsk, room 548/648	299-1548	299-1548	
Kharis Corporation, ul. I. Franko 147	444-4137	443-1575	
Khaskoi Int., Novinskiy bul. 5	241-5935	241-5884	
Khelar Aasar, Leninskiy prosp. 148, kv. 138	434-4051	434-4052	413946
Khemocomplex, Krasnopresnenskaya nab. 12, Mezh-II	255-0487	252-3589	414422
Khemol, Krasnopresnenskaya nab. 12, Mezh-II	252-6378	252-1173	414422
Khepos Ido, ul. Fuchika 17/19	250-4725	250-4725	414480
Khimbank, ul. Myasnitskaya 20	928-9188	927-7701	412771

	Phone	Fax	Telex
Khimimport, Mosfilmovskaya ul. 52	147-1419		414345
Khimvak, ul. Ryabinovaya 8, #209	362-1740		
Khleb Rossiyi, ul. Petra Romanova 16	279-1517	279-5477	
Khram Luny Restaurant, Koslovskiy B. p. 1	291-0401		
Khrustal, ul. Tverskaya 15			
Khudozhestvenny Cinema, Arbatskaya pl. 14	291-9624		
Kiev Cinema, Kutuzovskiy prosp. 30/32	249-3864		
Kievskaya Hotel, Kiyevskaya ul. 2	240-1444		
Kievskiy Train Station, pl. Kiyevskovo Vokzala	262-6230	251-7190	
Kings Casino, Izmailovo Hotel, Beta Bldg	166-6735		
Kino Centre, ul. Druzhinnikovskaya 15	205-3001		
Kinokom JV, ul. Lesnaya 27	251-7189		411700
Kinotsentr, Druzhinnikovskaya ul. 15			
Kira JV, ul. Spiridonovka 22/2	202-6019	200-1269	
Kirgizia Cinema, Zelyony pr. 81	301-4246		
Kishinev Cinema, ul. Yunykh Lenintsev 12	179-3747		
Kissen (Germany), Glazovskiy p. 7	241-6867	230-2264	413227
Kiteksim JV (Poland), ul. Fadeyeva 1	299-3157	253-9794	411238
Klein, Schanzlin & Becker AG,			
Krasnopresnenskaya nab. 12, Office 1502	253-2456	253-9908	413646
Klemm, Petrovskiy Passazh, 2nd fl.	921-3915		
Klever Corporation, P.O. Box 745	297-5628	227-2039	
Klinchayan Brokerage Company	378-0768		
Klingenberg, prosp. Vernadskovo 103, kor 1, kv. 48	434-2414	434-2414	413770
Klinskiy customs point/Zelenogradskiy	535-1793		
KLM Royal Dutch Airlines,			
Krasnopresnenskaya nab. 12, Office 1307	253-2150	230-2304	
Sheremetevo 2 Airport	578-2762		
Cargo, Sheremetyevo 2 Cargo Terminal	578-4541	578-4542	
Klockner & Co., AG, Pokrovskiy bul. 4/17, k. 3	208-9942	230-2516	413296
Klockner-Humbolt-Deutz AG,			
ul. Kalanchevskaya 6/2, k. 1, 4th fl.	975-1902	975-1915	413704
Klodiks JV (China), Profsoyuznaya ul. 65	334-9211	334-9110	411899
Klont JV, Leninskiy prosp. 55	135-9581		
Kloos-Niitavtoprom-Avtosvarka JV,			
prosp. Andropova 22/30	118-7092	118-3555	412158
Kniga Bookshops, see K-Boutiques			
Kniga i Biznes, ul. 1st Tverskaya-Yamskaya 22	251-6003		
Kniga Printshop JV (Canada),			
ul. 1st Tverskaya-Yamskaya 50	251-1210	230-2207	411871
Knizhnaya Palata, Oktyabrskaya ul. 4, str. 2	288-9238		
Knizhnoye Obozreniye, Sushchyovskiy val 64	281-6266		
Knizhny Znak, see Book Boutique			
Knowledge Express Inc., ul. Alabyana 12	198-0034	198-9991	
Kobe Steel LTD,			
Krasnopresnenskaya nab. 12, Office 806-808	253-2806	253-2648	413632
Kobelco, see Kobe Steel LTD			
Kobus JV, MGU, 2nd Uchebny, k. au406-407	939-1028	939-2914	
Kodak Express, Detskiy Mir, 4th floor			
Leningradskiy prosp. 74	151-0826		
ul. Tverskaya 25	299-5483		
Kodak Film Developing, Hotel Mezhdunarodnaya	253-1643		

	Phone	Fax	Telex
Kodak Film Shop, Komsomolskiy prosp. 25	245-1594		
Petrovskiy Passage, ul. Petrovka 4	928-5468		
Kodak Ltd., ul. Listyeva 3	958-0504	954-0305	
Kodak One Hour Store, Americom Business Center	941-8941		
Kokusai Koeki Co., LTD,			
Krasnopresnenskaya 12, Office 1102	253-7612	253-9694	413022
Kolkhida cafe, ul. Sadovaya-Samotechnaya 6, stroen. 2	299-6757		
Kolnish/Bonner Rundschau,			
Kutuzovskiy prosp. 14, kv. 102	243-1189	243-9941	413319
Kolomenskiy customs point	344-25		
Kolomenskoye, Proletarskiy pr.	115-2309		
Kolomenskoye Museum, prosp. Andropova 39	115-2713		
Koloss, ul. Shvernika 14/1	126-0208	126-5625	
Komatsu LTD,			
Krasnopresnenskaya nab. 12, Office 1503-1504	253-7550	253-9773	413975
Kombi's Deli, prosp. Mira 46/48	280-6402		
ul. Tverskaya-Yamskaya 2	251-2578		
Komed JV (US), ul. Pravdy 7/9	214-3260	200-0209	411267
Komel JV (FRG), 1st Cheremushkinskiy pr. 5	230-1568	200-2217	411700
Kometika CLK JV (UK), Leningradskoye sh. 46	251-9249		
Komipex JV (Switzerland), ul. Rustaveli 15			
Kommercheskiy Vestnik, see Commercial Herald			
Kommisioni, ul. Tverskaya-Yamskaya 16			
Kompania Yever Stube Rossia JV,			
Studencheskaya ul. 30 kv. 2	200-4671		
Kompar JV (Austria), ul. 1905 goda 10	259-4171		
Kompat JV (FRG), Lubyanskiy pr. 5	923-6173	200-2203	411693
Kompleks Inc. JV, ul. Durova 36	921-2829	200-2265	
Komplektimport V/O Rosvneshtorg,			
Barrikadnaya ul. 8/5	254-8050	253-9576	411060
Kompro JV (UK), ul. Ordzhonikidze 3	234-6370		
Komsomolskaya Pravda, ul. Pravdy 24	257-2701	200-2293	
Komsomolyets Cinema, Dmitrovskoye sh. 49	488-6946		
Komtek JV (Singapore), ul. Kosmonavta Volkova 16	202-7171	943-0072	411080
Komtorgbank, ul. Myasnitskaya 47	207-7096		
Komvek JV (Yugoslavia), Volokolamskoye sh. 1	158-0633	158-9743	
Kone, see NOKO			
Konfort JV (India), Leninskiy prosp. 36	246-4868	246-4969	411432
Konica (Tokyo Boeki), ul. Leninskaya Sloboda 9	275-1674	275-2775	
Konica Complex (Fort), ul. Malaya Pereyaslavskaya 7/12	284-4396	279-0506	
Konica Copiers	277-3819	200-5254	
Kontinent Bank, ul. Gostinichnaya 9, k. 4	482-1654	482-1923	
Kontinent JV (China), Kadashevskaya Nab. 12	441-7041		
Kontrakt JV Filial, Sirenevy bul. 2	166-1381	166-4945	
Kontur JV (Finland), prosp. Mira 188	187-1976		
Konversbank, ul. B. Ordynka 24/26	239-2028	233-2540	911951
Koopbank Tsentrpotrebsoyuza, B. Cherkasskiy p. 15	923-2790		
Kopris and M JV (Lichtenstein), ul. Tamanskaya 2a	943-0095	934-0096	
Kor-United JV, Starokonyushenny p. 5/14	242-1454		
Korall JV (FRG), Kutuzovskiy prosp. 9, k. 9, kv. 113	243-6728	243-6718	413420
Korea House, Volgogradskiy prosp. 26	270-1300		
Korean Air (South Korea), Hotel Cosmos, room 1629	217-1627	578-2729	
Sheremetevo 2 Airport	578-2728	578-2729	

	Phone	Fax	Telex
Korean Airways (North Korea), see Chosinminhang			
Korolyov House Museum, 6th Ostankinskiy p. 2/28	283-8197		
Korona, ul. Geroyev Panfilovtsev 20	496-6375		
Korsar Airlines, pl. Suvorova 1	281-7452	281-7452	
Kosmonaut Museum, prosp. Mira, Space Monument			
Kosmos Cafe/ Bar, ul. Tverskaya 4	292-6544		
Kosmos Cinema, prosp. Mira 109	283-5636		
Kosmos TV, ul. Akad. Koroleva 15	282-3360	216-4034	
Kotra, Hotel Mezhdunarodnaya II, room 747	253-1569	253-1698	413657
Kozikhinskiy cafe, see Moskovskiye Zori cafe			
KP-Emag JV (FRG), ul. Butlerova 17	330-2574	330-2676	411017
KPA	123-5364	926-0786	
KPMG Moscow, ul. Novaya Basmannaya 37, 3rd flr.	261-7173	261-7305	
Krafts Technologies JV (US/FRG), ul. Vavilova 13	923-1150	924-5114	411630
Kramis JV (Spain), ul. Tikhvinskaya 1/13	972-6846	972-6848	411069
Krasnaya Gorka, ul. Podelskikh 6, build. 2, room 106	381-2746		
Krasnaya Presnya Cinema, ul. Mantulinskaya 5	256-6566		
Krasnaya Presnya Museum, Bolshevitskaya ul. 4	252-3035		
Krasnaya Zvezda, Khoroshevskoye sh. 38	941-2158		
Krasnopresnenskiy baths, Stolyarny p. 7			
Krasny Proletary, M. Kaluzhskaya 15	330-9882		
Kremlin Palace of Congresses, Kremlin	926-7901		
Krestyanka, Bumazhny pr. 14	212-2063	212-1353	
Kristal Motors, ul. Tverskaya 29/3	209-6596	292-4504	
TsUM, ul. Petrovka 2, 1st fl.	292-2347	292-4504	
Krokodil, Bumazhny pr. 14	257-3114		
Krone-Iskra JV (FRG), pl. Kurchatova	196-7213	196-9933	
Kropex JV, ul. Prechistenka 36/21	203-1738	200-3217	
Kropotkinskaya 36 cafe, ul. Prechistenka 36	201-7500		
KrossPak, 4th Parkovaya ul. 12, k. 1	165-9243	200-0294	
Krouni JV, ul. Narodnovo Opolcheniya 10, k. 2, kv. 46	238-3409	230-2406	411610
Krovtekh (US), ul. Neglinnaya 17	200-4555	310-7024	411191
Krugovaya Panorama Cinema, VVTs, prosp. Mira 120	181-9525		
Krugozor, Pyatnitskaya ul. 25	231-2902		
Krupp GmbH, Krasnopresnenskaya nab. 12, Office 1304	253-2074	230-2835	413941
Krylatskoye Olympic Sports Ctr, Krylatskaya ul. 10	140-7369		
KSB Pumpen, see Klein, Schanzlin & Becker AG			
Kudesnitsa, Nikitskaya, B. ul. 37	291-2111		
Kuilong cafe, Litovskiy bul. 7	425-1001		
Kultura, Novoslobodskaya 73	285-7802		
Kultura i Naslediye JV, Vspolny p. 14	290-3338		
Kuntsevo Cinema, ul. Ivana Franko 14	444-0115		
Kurskiy Train Station, pl. Kurskovo Vokzala			
Kurt Hans Simon, ul. Akad. Pilyugina 14, #3	936-2003		
Kurt Mitterfermer,			
Krasnopresnenskaya nab. 12, room 1150	253-2880	253-9310	
Kuskovo (Ceramics Museum), ul. Yunosti 2	370-0160		
Kutuzov Hut, Kutuzovskiy prosp. 38	148-1967		
Kutuzovskiy 9, Kutuzovskiy prosp. 9	243-7501		
Kuzminki Hotel, Volzhskiy bul. 114a, k. 9	179-0879		
Kuznetskiy Most Clothing Store, Kuznetskiy Most 10	921-6971	923-2458	
Kuznetskiy Most JV (Italy), Kuznetskiy Most 10	928-5525	923-2458	
Kvant, Leninskiy prosp. 1	238-4993	238-4993	

SCOTT–EUROPEAN CORPORATION

FOR 20 YEARS, SPECIALISTS IN SALES AND MARKETING IN RUSSIA AND THE COMMONWEALTH, WITH A MOSCOW STAFF OF OVER 50 PROFESSIONALS, HEADQUARTERED IN THE WORLD TRADE CENTER, MOSCOW

SERVICES OFFERED

MANUFACTURER'S REPRESENTATIVE

We have traditionally provided representation and consultation services to a wide range of Western manufacturers.

HOSPITAL/MEDICAL EQUIPMENT & PHARMACEUTICALS SUPPLIER

We act as distributor, dealer or agent for a wide range of medical/hospital equipment and pharmaceuticals. We can plan and supply a complete, multi-disciplinary hospital. We also supply individual units of equipment and various supplies to clinics and hospitals across the Commonwealth. We own and operate a Russian company which provides high-quality technical service to medical devices of any manufacturer.

CONSTRUCTION, MINING, AND OILFIELD EQUIPMENT SUPPLIER

We own and operate one of the first successful dealerships for construction equipment in Russia. We act as sales agent and distributor for a wide range of equipment for the oilfields and the open-cast mines.

INVESTMENT ADVISING/INVESTMENT MANAGEMENT

We are one of the few Western firms to successfully master the complexities of working within local joint-ventures. We offer to share our experience and knowledge of the market to assist in finding suitable investment targets and partners in manufacturing ventures.

In the CIS:
12 Krasnopresneneskaya nab. Suite 502
Rosinpred
Moscow 123610
Ph. (095) 253-1094 • Fax (095) 253-9382
Telex 411813 REPR SU

In the United States:
58 East State Street
Montpelier
Vermont 05602 USA
Ph. (802) 223-0262 • Fax (802) 223-0265
Telex 5101011983

6 easy ways to make doing business in Moscow well worth the trip.

❶

Fax Service-Globus your Moscow itinerary,
language requirements and visa support needs

❷

Let Service-Globus make or confirm
your hotel reservations

❸

Step off the plane and be greeted by an
experienced Service-Globus interpreter

❹

Check out a free copy of the Business Survival Guide
while your personal Service-Globus driver
delivers you to your hotel or meeting

❺

Get right to work in well-equipped
meeting sites pre-arranged by Service-Globus
to meet all your requirements

❻

Say goodbye at the airport
to your Service-Globus interpreter
after a productive, hassle-free stay

Call for information about our *very* reasonable rates.

MOSCOW 109004 BOLSHAYA KOMMUNISTICHESKAYA 1/5
7(095) 298-6146   FAX 7(095) 298-6149

SHEREMETYEVO AIRPORT OFFICES
7(095) 578-7534   FAX 7(095)578-4650

	Phone	Fax	Telex
Kvorri Master-Lamas JV, ul. Platovskaya 4	240-4347		
Kyodo News Service, Kutuzovskiy prosp. 14, kv. 13	230-2367	253-9774	413382
Kyoho Tsusho Kaisha, LTD,			
Krasnopresnenskaya nab. 12, Office 1007	253-2587	230-2312	413147

L

	Phone	Fax	Telex
L'Evenement Du Jeudi, Kutuzovskiy prosp. 7/4, kv. 304	243-7050		41330
L'Humanite', ul. Alabyana 10, kv. 192	943-0055		413307
L'Oreal, GUM, 2nd line, 1st fl. (see GUM)			
Petrovskiy Passazh, 1st fl. (see Passazh)			
L'Unita, ul. Pravdy 7/9, kv. 11	214-4259	253-9278	413490
La Cipolla D'oro, ul. Gilyarovskovo 39	281-9498		
La Pantera, prosp. 60-Letiya Oktyabrya 12	126-8510		
La Victoria Clothing Store, Petrovskiy Passazh, 2nd fl.			
Labomed GmbH	253-2142		
Labtam Limited, Hotel Mezhdunarodnaya II, rm 1547	253-1778	253-9285	
Lada Export, Otkrytoye sh. 48a	168-2828	168-2715	414902
Ladoga Cinema, ul. Shirokaya 12	479-5856		
Lakme, GUM, 2nd line, 1st fl.	926-3370		
Lal JV (Sweden), ul. B. Kommunisticheskaya 23	272-0069	272-4684	411738
LAL, Lithuanian Airlines, B. Rzhevskiy p. 7	203-6730	230-9155	
Lamport Co. Ltd., ul. Prechistenka 40	246-6845	246-7446	
Land Rover, B. Starodanilovskiy p. 5	954-0624		
Service, ul. Dubininskaya 55	235-6580		
Landinform, Sibirskiy pr. 2/2	249-0779		
Lando JV (Syria), Leninskiy prosp. 146, (CTH) rm 1001	438-5866		411823
Lanit JV, ul. Sivashskaya 4, k. 2	110 5752	119 0001	111195
Large International, ul. Profsoyuznaya 102a	335-0500	420-2088	
Larsen Oy, see Borge Larsen Oy AB			
Lasagne cafe, Pyatnitskaya ul. 40	231-1085		
Latham & Watkins,			
Park Place, Leninskiy prosp. 113/1, #C200	956-5555	956-5556	
Lavalin International Inc.,			
Krasnopresnenskaya nab. 12, office 608-609	253-1182	253-1181	413752
Lavash Bakery, B. Sadovaya 3, k. 6	251-7888		
LB International Trade Services	200-5224		
Le Cafe Francais, Pullman Iris Hotel	488-8000		
Le Chalet Restaurant, Korobeynikov p., 1/2	202-2611		
Le Figaro, ul. B. Spasskaya 12, kv. 32	230-2464	230-2465	413323
Le Monti, TsUM, 4th fl.	292-4057		
VVTs, prosp. Mira 120	188-6474	187-9817	
Le Romanoff, Hotel Baltschug	230-6500		
Le Soir, ul. B. Spasskaya 12, kv. 10	280-0380		
Le Stelle Del Pescatore, ul. Pushechnaya 7/5	924-2058		
Leboeuf, Lamb, Leiby & MacRae,			
Novy Arbat 36, City Administration Bldg., 14th fl.	290-9000	290-9009	413205
Lefortovskiy Commercial Bank, Lefortovskiy Val, 16a	362-4053	361-0602	111828
Legal information by phone	946-2550		
Lego, GUM, 2nd line, 1st fl.	926-3264		
TsUM, 3rd fl.	923-7704		
Legstroininvest, ul. Novaya Basmannaya 24/1	267-7987		417316

| --- | --- | --- | --- |
Lemos JV, prosp. Mira, VVTs	181-9931	188-6356	
Lenin Funeral Train, Paveletskaya pl. 1	235-2898		
Lenin Library, see Russian State Library			
Lenin Museum in Gorkiy (Gorkiy Leninskiye)	136-2334		
Lenin Stadium, Luzhniki	246-5515		
Swimming Pool, Luzhniki	201-0764		
Leningrad Cinema, ul. Novopeschanaya 12	157-6014		
Leningrad Train Station, Komsomolskaya pl. 3	262-4281		
Leningradskaya Hotel, ul. Kalanchevskaya 21/40	975-3032		411659
Vesta Car Rental	248-2657		
Jacko's Piano Bar	975-1967		
Casino Moscow	975-1967		
Lenkom Theater, Dmitrovka M. ul. 6	299-0708		
Les Champs Elysees Restaurant, Pullman Iris Hotel	488-8000		
Lesinvest, Ltd. JV (Switz.), ul. Ilyinka 15	206-0318	975-2165	
Lesnaya Skazka, ul. Vvedenskovo 11a	334-7334		
Lesniye Dali Hotel, Rublyovskoye sh., 29th km	592-3628	215-1861	
Levi Strauss Ltd., Sovintsentr, Mezhdunarodnaya Hotel 1	253-1265		
Levi Strauss Store, Stoleshnikov p. 9			
Lewisohn & Marshall, Dmitrovka M. ul. 31/22, office 8	299-2101	956-3271	
Lexica JV (Syria), Dmitrovka B. ul. 23/8	229-0534	972-4426	411796
LG Associates, B. Spasskaya ul. 12, kv. 49-50	280-0426	230-2992	612205
Lianozovo Club Courts,			
Lianozovskiy Park, ul. Uglicheskaya 13/2	909-3011		
Liberation, ul. Gilyarovskovo 8, kv. 69	288-9533	288-9533	413652
Liberty, B. Sadovaya 5, Hotel Peking, room 401	209-4601	209-4601;	
Library of the Inst. for Sci. Info. on Social Sciences,			
Nakhimovskiy pr. 28/21/21	128-8881	420-2261	
Libre Belgique, Krutitskiy val 3, k. 2, kv. 137	276-9974	276-9976	413332
Libyan Arab Airlines, Koroviy val 7, ent. 2	237-2976	237-3095	413606
Sheremetevo 2 Airport	578-2730		
Liebherr-Holding GmbH, Mamonovskiy p. 6, kv. 10	209-6679	200-0235	413372
Lignacon GmbH, Hotel Mezhdunarodnaya 2, rm 1050	256-7268	253-1711	
Liko-Raduga JV (Japan), see Auto Sun			
Line JV (Canada), ul. Rimskovo-Korsakova 3	281-9892	975-2027	411815
Linea-M, B. Starodanilovskiy p. 6	235-0402	235-1676	
Lingua	390-1250		
Lingvotekhnika JV (Bulgaria), Kargopolskaya 17	402-8984		
Liniya-Poligraf Advertising Firm, ul. Sovkhoznaya 2	351-6173		
Link JV (Switz.), ul. Shcherbakovskaya 40/42	369-2643	369-5947	411205
Linkful International Ltd., Abrikosovskiy p. 1a	248-1877	230-2753	
Linklaters & Paines, prosp. Vernadskovo 82, office 107	956-5566	956-5567	
Liron JV (Sweden), ul. Sretenka 20	207-0003	207-0008	
Lis's, Olympic Stadium, Olympiyskiy Prosp.	288-4027		
Liskun Museum, see Animal Husbandry Museum			
Literary Gazette International JV (US),			
Kostyanskiy p. 13	208-8594	200-0238	411294
Literary Museum, ul. Petrovka 28	221-3857		
Literaturnaya Gazeta, Tsvetnoy bul. 30	924-1168	200-3272	411294
Litmond Trade House and INCO, Ltd.,			
ul. Solyanka 1/2, str. 1	928-8186	975-2372	412370
Litpharm JV (Switzerland), ul. Chernyakhovskovo 4	155-7722	444-5730	
Litsenzintorg, Minskaya ul. 11	145-1111	142-5902	411415

	Phone	Fax	Telex
Litsom k Litsu, see Face to Face			
Little Rome, Kutuzovskiy prosp. 18	243-0080		
Litva Cinema, Lomonosovskiy prosp. 29/8	147-2282		
Litwin, Koroviy val 7, kv. 168, bureau 7	238-4922	230-2930	413210
Lloyds Bank PLC,			
Krasnopresnenskaya nab. 12, Office 1808	253-8174		413057
Lobby Bar, Radisson-Slavyanskaya Hotel	941-8411		
Lobster Grill, Hotel Metropol, Teatralny pr. 1/4	927-6739		
Locarus, prosp. Vernadskovo 7	430-5219	430-5995	
Logimix, Leningradskiy prosp. 37, k. 5	155-5880	155-6322	
LogoVaz, ul. Volgina 6A	330-3231		
LogoVaz JV (Switzerland), ul. Prechistenka 17/8, str. 2	203-1724	200-4224	412182
Lokomotiv Hotel, ul. B. Cherkizovskaya 125a	161-8133		
Lokus, TsUM, 2nd fl.	941-3523		
Lomonosov Restaurant,			
Palace Hotel, ul. Tverskaya-Yamskaya 19	256-3152		
Lomos Finance & Credit Consortium JV (Finland),			
ul. Tverskaya 23, str.2	299-6519	253-9794	411238
Lonrho Eastern Europe, ul. Malaya Polyanka 2/3, str.7	238-0311	238-1561	
Lord, Day & Lord Barrett Smith, Ltd.,			
ul. Vavilova 72/13, kv. 33	134-8293	134-8293	411700
Los Angeles Times,			
ul. Sadovaya-Samotechnaya 12/24, kv. 37	200-0204	299-2304	413421
LOT Polish Airlines, Koroviy val 7, Office 5	238-0003		
Sheremetevo 2 Airport	578-2706		
Lotintorg JV (Lichtenstein), Savvinskaya nab. 3	247-4859	943-0096	412148
Lotus Development Russia, 2nd Frunzenskaya ul. 8	242-8929	242-5046	
Love Fashions, ul. B. Yakimanka 26	237-4114		
LTW International, ul. B. Ordynka 14	233-1038	231-9342	
Lubimex Holland B.V., Glazovskiy p. 7, kv. 1	241-0414	230-2115	413948
Luch Concert Hall, Varshavskoye sh. 71	110-3758		
Luchnik, ul. Maroseyka 6/8	928-0056		
Lucky-Goldstar, Palashevskiy B. p. 9	299-8777	975-2163	413753
Lufthansa Airlines,			
Olympic Penta Hotel Olympiyskiy prosp. 18/1	975-2501	971-6784	413608
Sheremetevo 2 Airport	578-3151	578-2771	413078
Cargo, Sheremetevo 2 Cargo Terminal	578-6758	578-9276	
Luge Anlagenbau-Hemnitz GmBH,			
Leninskiy prosp. 95a	132-5583	310-7066	
Luna Trading Inc., Krutitskiy val 3, k. 2, kv. 97	276-4906	276-4890	413179
Lunacharskiy House Museum, Denezhny p. 9/5	241-0877		
Lurgi GmbH Frankfurt/Main, Koroviy val 7, Office 9	230-2324	236-7275	413097
LUX, ul. Pelshe 4	437-6438		
Lux Bar, Petrovskiy Passazh, 2nd fl. (See Passazh)			
Lux Supermarket, Olympic Village, Michurinskiy prosp. 4	932-1000	938-2164	
Luzhniki Tennis Courts, Luzhnetskaya nab, 10	201-1655		
Lyetuchaya Mysh Cabaret, B. Gnezdnikovskiy p. 3	930-7021		

Where in St. Petersburg

Featuring St. Petersburg's first yellow pages, only white pages and best city street map! See info at the back of this book.

M

	Phone	Fax	Telex
M & M Ferrous America, Ltd., Koroviy val, kv. 174	238-7363	238-7363	413660
M & S, ul. Ostozhenka 42	291-3232		
M & S Clothing Store (Oltes),			
1st Tverskaya-Yamskaya ul. 11	250-5032		
ul. B. Gruzinskaya 39	253-8298		
ul. Pushechnaya 4	921-4907		
M & S Electronics Store (Oltes), Strastnoy bul. 7	229-7641		
M & S Store, ul. Pushechnaya 7	921-3045		
M & T Chimie, see Elf Aquitaine			
M BIS, ul. Goncharova 6	218-0860	210-6587	
M J Exports LTD, Hotel Mezhdunarodnaya II, rm 441	253-2441	253-9475	413584
M-I, Leninskiy prosp. 24/4	203-5103		
M. & D. Gertner K.G., ul. Mytnaya 1, 3rd floor, 5-6	230-1010	230-0987	413173
M. Leader, Leningradskiy prosp. 39	157-8345		
Maar, ul. Rusakovskaya 23A	264-9977		
Mac Shop, ul. Pokrovka 43	297-4987		
MacArthur Foundation	290-5088	290-6870	
Machmir Perevod, 2nd Frunzenskaya 8	242-5441	230-2851	
MacLean's Magazine, Kutuzovskiy prosp. 13, kv. 128	243-9604	243-7901	413585
Macleod Dixon, 7th M. Levshinkiy 3	201-4073	201-7424	
Madjess JV (Lebanon), Milyutinskiy p. 3-31	205-6150	205-6152	
Magazin del Mondo, Ukraine Hotel, 8th floor	243-4682		
Magra, Dmitrovka B. ul. 9, kv. 19	292-5142	230-2388	413152
Magro, B. Dorogomilovskaya ul. 8, kv. 165	243-6623	243-6623	413578
MagSoft, Michurinskiy prosp. 3	430-0001	938-2221	
Main Dept for Special Construction, ul. B. Ordynka 22	233-5251		
Mainichi, Kutuzovskiy prosp. 7/4, kv. 1	253-9005	230-2484	413390
Maksimilian, GUM, 2nd line, 2nd fl.	926-3304		
Malbranc, Krasnopresnenskaya nab. 12, Office 1009	253-5145	230-2783	413190
Malcolm Maclaine, Dmitrovka M. ul. 31/22, office 8	299-2101	956-3271	
Male Fashion (Muzhskaya Moda),			
1st Tverskaya-Yamskaya 26	251-1294		
Malev Hungarian Airlines, Kamergerskiy p. 6	292-0434		414489
Maly Theater, Teatralnaya pl. 1/6	924-4083	924-4084	
Filial, ul. B. Ordynka 69	237-6420	237-6422	
Malysh Grupo Libro Int'l JV, see MGL International			
MAN AG, Munchen, Mamonovskiy p. 4, kv. 7	209-6674	200-0205	413185
Man and Law (Chelovek i Zakon) Journal,			
Olympiyskiy prosp. 22	281-6995	281-3821	
Manager Service JV (Denmark), Frunzenskaya nab. 30	242-8927	242-8973	414737
Manakey Global, Inc., Parusny pr. 32/9	193-1804	908-8673	
Manezh, see Central Exhibition Hall			
Manhattan Express, Hotel Rossiya	298-5355		
Manila Restaurant, The, ul. Vavilova 81	132-0055	938-2285	
Mannesmann AG, ul. B. Dorogomilovskaya 14, kv. 28-31	243-0791	230-2306	413172
Mannheimer Swartling, Pokrovskiy bul. 4/17, apt. 35	207-6008	230-2544	413201
Mantigo JV, ul. Novocheremushkinskaya 60, k. 2	274-0048	240-2002	
Manusonik JV Filial, ul. Perekopskaya 9A	122-3336		
Manvik JV, ul. Krzhizhanovskovo 14, k. 2	124-3531	125-1753	411237
Manyam & Associates, Inc., Parusny pr. 32/9	193-1804	908-8673	

	Phone	Fax	Telex
MAPA, Koroviy val 7, Office 220	230-2034	230-2055	413965
Marathon Oil Company, St. Basmannaya ul. 14	262-1189	262-2907	
Marc Largo, ul. Myasnitskaya 40/1 kom. 264	921-5234	921-8150	
Marc Rich & Co. AG,			
Krasnopresnenskaya nab. 12, office 1604	253-2100	253-2095	413793
Marchi-Intensiv, ul. Rozhdestvenka 11	928-1269	921-1240	
Marco Polo Presnaya Hotel, Spiridonevskiy p. 9	202-0381	230-2704	414748
Marex, Severnoye Chertanovo 7, k. 5, kv. 50	318-2739	200-2216	411700
Margarita cafe, M. Bronnaya 28	299-6534		
Mari JV (Austria), ul. Kapitsy 34	429-1500		
Maria Information, Butyrskiy val 24	251-7766	973-3987	
Maria-Trazer JV (Italy), ul. Baumanskaya 57	265-0180		
Marine Liner Services, ul. Petrovka 20/1	925-9433	230-2397	414747
Marine Resources Company International,			
Hotel Budapest, room 201	921-7971	200-1214	413052
Marine Transport & Trade Co., Plotnikov p. 12	241-3593	244-7235	
Market Knowledge Inc., ul. Pudovkina 4	143-0418	147-4300	
Marketing Information Center JV (Finland),			
Kolpachny p. 7	924-7941	923-2856	
Marketing Research and Consulting JV,			
ul. Tverskaya 16/2	941-0900	200-0267	411712
Marposs S.p.A., Tryokhprudny p. 11/13	299-0932	200-0234	413938
Mars Cinema, Beskudnikovo ul. Inzhenernaya 1	901-0588		
Mars Gallery, M. Filevskaya ul. 32	146-2029	253-9794	411283
Marubeni Corporation,			
Krasnopresnenskaya nab. 12, Office 1908	253-1817	230-2731	413391
Mary Kay Cosmetics, 3rd Samotechny p. 3, Floor 1	974-1000		
Mascot International Corp., ul. Ivana Franko 4	146-1725	146-3217	
Mashinoexport, ul. Mosfilmovskaya 35	147-1542	938-2116	411207
Mashinoimport, ul. Mosfilmovskaya 35	143-8927	938-2116	411242
Mashintorg-Lida, ul. Stavropolskaya 70, kv. 99	351-5459		
Mashpriborintorg, ul. Smolenskaya-Sennaya 32/34	244-2775		
Massage Russkaya Amerika, Luzhnetskaya nab. 10	201-1680		
Master Ltd., ul. Marksa-Engelsa 15, kv. 5	202-3715		
Mateko JV, ul. Novo-Basmannaya 10	299-1909	253-9098	
Matimport S.A., ul. Snezhanaya 16, build. 2	180-6253	189-0772	
Matsushita Electric Industrial Co., LTD,			
Hotel Mezhdunarodnaya 2, room 1047	255-6983	253-9013	
MAXA Cash and Carry, Silikatny proezd 13	583-6502	583-9801	
Mayak, ul. Pogodinskaya 4	248-0022		
Mayak Hotel, ul. B. Filevskaya 25	142-2384		
Mayakovskiy House Museum, Lubyanskiy pr. 3/6	921-6607		
Mayakovskiy Theater, Nikitskaya, B. ul. 19	925-3070		
Filial, Pushkarev p. 21	208-3312		
Mayekawa Kawasho Corp., ul. Mytnaya 1, kv. 8	230-0132	230-2112	413118
Mayers International (Hong Kong),			
Frunzenskaya nab. 30, pavil. 15, level 3	242-8946	498-5813	
MB, ul. Pokrovka 12	924-5133	925-3920	
MBL International East Inc. Computerland,			
Leninskiy prosp. 14b	438-9538	438-9538	
MBM JV, Tikhoretskiy bul. 1	358-7228	358-1167	414789
MBTS Dry Cleaning, ul. Volgina 6	335-6192	331-0511	412264
MCBE Company, Ltd, B. Gnezdnikovskiy p. 10	229-5810	305-8769	

	Phone	Fax	Telex
McCall Tours	201-5895	201-5289	
McCann-Erickson Advertising Ltd.,			
1st Volkhonskiy p. 10	299-1056	299-5503	
McDermott International, Inc.,			
ul. Petrovka 15, kv. 19-20	924-5893	200-2237	413329
McDonald's, ul. B. Bronnaya 29	200-1655	241-4200	
ul. Arbat 50/52	241-3681		
Gazetny p. 15	956-9818		
Delivery, ul. B. Bronnaya 29	200-1655		
McDonald's Office Center,			
Nikopeskovskiy B. p. 15, str.2	241-4146	241-4200	
McHugh International, M. Bronnaya ul. 19A	203-5679		
B. Pirogovskaya ul. 9a, str. 2	246-7700	245-3807	
MCM, Olimpiyskiy prosp. 18	288-7788	288-7666	
MD-Seis JV, ul. Narodnovo Opolcheniya 38/3	192-8087	943-1105	
Mebinvest JV (USA), Vlasyevskiy M. p. 7a, kv. 4	554-8972	244-0749	
Mechta Cinema, Kashirskoye sh. 42/2	324-8577		
Medchoice Moscow JV, ul. Shchukinskaya 1	193-8654	292-6511	
Medecho JV, Shyolkovskoye sh. 29	462-1281	462-0104	411424
Medexport, ul. Kakhovka 31	331-8200	311-8988	411247
Medialink JV (Finland),			
Olympic Village, Michurinskiy prosp. 3	437-5951	437-5951	411424
Medical International JV (US), ul. Zhuravleva 2/8-1	213-6678		
Medicine Information Technology JV,			
ul. Sadovaya-Kudrinskaya 5 '	135-3027	310-7050	
Medicine Man, The, ul. Chernyakhovskovo 4	155-7080	151-4506	
MediClub, Profsoyuznaya ul. 65, Ste. 380	956-5081	956-5082	
Medigrant JV (India), Abrikosovskiy p. 2	248-0926	230-2480	
Meditrade Ltd., ul. Petrovka 23/10, str. 5, office 13	200-5219	956-3040	
Meditsinskaya Tekhnika	290-1256		
Medrex Instruments JV (US), Leninskiy prosp. 113	434-4438		
Medservice, Trifonovskaya ul. 61, kv. 65	288-5875	284-5149	
Medstar, Lomonosovskiy prosp. 43, 2-nd floor	143-6076		
Medtech JV, Simferopolskiy bul. 8	113-2351	113-2633	
Medtik, Pushkarev p. 7	208-5339	255-1922	
Medtrade JV, 2nd Troitskiy p. 6a			
Medusa Bar, The,			
M.S. Alexander Blok (Inflotel)	255-9284		
Mega-Inter, B. Dorogomilovskaya ul. 8	240-0331	202-7628	
Megapolis Express, ul. M. Lubyanka 16	925-1473	921-7427	
Megasoft	576-2400	576-2400	
Mei-hua Restaurant, ul. Rusakovskaya 2/1, str. 1	264-9574		
Mekhatron JV, ul. Pyatnitskaya 48	231-0730		412824
Mekong Restaurant, Litovskiy bul. 7	425-1111		
Melan, Leninskiy prosp. 45	137-6819	137-6525	
Melar JV (Sweden), ul. Pyatnitskaya 48	231-0730		411576
Melodia, Novy Arbat 22	291-1421		
Memorial Cosmonaut Museum,			
Alleya Kosmonavtov (VVTs)	283-1837		
Menatep, Manezhnaya pl. 7	202-8556	923-5931	
Menatep Commercial			
Innovation Bank, Kolpachny p. 4	963-6013	923-5931	412323
Menatep Financial Corporation, ul. Dubininskaya 17a	235-1681	235-3615	

	Phone	Fax	Telex
Menatep Real Estate, pl. Suvorova 1, pod. 3	971-7958	258-1993	
Menonsovpolygraph JV (India), ul. Nikitinskaya 5a	165-0265	165-5865	412213
Mercantile Oy, ul. Mytnaya 1, Office 21	230-0465		413049
Mercator Corp., Nab. Shevchenko 3a	243-6628	243-1661	
Mercedes-Benz AG, prosp. Vernadskovo 9/10, kv. 602	131-3448	230-2522	413346
Merck, Sharp & Dohme,			
Radisson-Slavyanskaya Hotel, office 3013, 3014	941-8275	941-8276	
Mercury Garments Industries, Kursovoy p. 9, Office 3	203-1851	230-2540	413522
Merian Publishers, Kutuzovskiy prosp. 14, kv. 122	243-2218		
Merichem Co., Leningradskiy prosp. 36	212-7482	214-9829	
Meridian Air Co, Ltd.,			
c/o Argus Trading, ul. Skakovaya 9, 4th fl.	945-2778	945-2765	
Mercator,			
Moscow Commercial Club, B. Kommunisticheskaya 2A	274-0081		
Merkury	207-3139	208-8855	
Merloni Finanziaria S.p.A., Mamonovskiy p. 6, kv. 1	209-6840	200-0236	413215
Messaggero, Kutuzovskiy prosp. 7/4, k. 5, kv. 34	243-0658		413457
Messe-Reisen Falk, Vsevologskiy p. 3, stroyeniye 1	201-2149		
Messemagazin Int'l, Leningradskiy prosp. 28, kv. 122	212-9033		413986
Metal Hammer, Obydenskiy p. 14	202-5747		
Metallgesellschaft AG,			
Leninskiy prosp. 95a, kv. 601-603	132-5855	310-7066	413328
Metapress Agency, 4th Tverskaya-Yamskaya ul. 4	972-6453	972-6250	
Metelitsa Moscow, Novy Arbat 21	291-1130		
Meteor Cinema, ul. Svobody 10	491-1397		
Meteor Personnel, ul. Pyatnitskaya 20., str.3	231-6174	239-1402	
Metmashikoss JV, Ryazanskiy prosp. 8a	171-0247	274-0023	
Metorg GmbH and Co. KG,			
Hotel Mezhdunarodnaya II, room 1233	253-1233	253-9384	
Metropol Hotel, Teatralny pr. 1/4	927-6000	927-6010	
Artists' Bar	927-6159		
Boyarskiy Zal Restaurant	927-6089		
Business Center	927-6090	927-6010	
Cafe Confectionery	927-6122		
Evropeysky Restaurant	927-6039		
Health Club	927-6148		
IPS Theater Box Office	927-6728	927-6729	
Lobster Grill	927-6739		
Metropol Restaurant	927-6000		
Metropol Salon	927-6024		
Olga Co., Ltd.	927-6139	975-2336	
Shalyapin Bar	927-6113		
Teatro Mediterraneo	927-6739		
Metroreklama JV (FRG), prosp. Mira 41	288-0309		
Metros JV (FRG), prosp. Mira 41	288-0588	288-0791	
Mexican Television, ul. Akad. Koroleva 4, k. 2, kv. 212	286-4411	283-4333	
Meyer & Zinger,			
Krasnopresnenskaya nab. 12, Mezhdunarodnaya-II, 542	253-2542	253-9712	413098
Mezhbirzhevaya Torgovaya Kompaniya,			
see AsA Interexchange Trading Company			
Mezhdunarodnaya Hotel, Krasnopresnenskaya nab. 12			
Hotel I	253-2382		411446
Hotel II	253-2760		411432

	Phone	Fax	Telex
Baginskiy Fashion	253-2697		
Bookstore	253-2376		
Business Club	253-1792		
Cafe Vienna	253-2491		
Carpigiana			
Casino Club Fortuna	253-2236		
Casino Portture	252-3440		
Continental Restaurant	253-1934		
Christian Dior	253-9297		
Dry Cleaning	253-2776		
Europcar	253-1369		
Fairn & Swanson Ltd.	253-9408		
Fuji Center	253-2914		
Gabi's Drugstore	253-7692		
Gzhel Store	253-2359		
Indoor Pool	255-6691		
Intourservice	255-6803		
Kodak Film Developing	253-1643		
Levi Strauss Ltd.	253-1265		
Modus Vivendi			
Red Lion Pub	253-2283		
Rus	253-1785		
Sakura Restaurant	253-2894		
Salon	953-2378		
Service Bureau	253-2762		
Supermarket	253-1389		
Tino Fontana Restaurant	253-2241		
VideoForce	253-7708		
Xerox Copy Center	205-6903		
Mezhdunarodnaya Kniga, ul. B. Yakimanka 39	238-4600		
Mezhdunarodnaya Prodovolstvennaya Birzha,			
see International Food Exchange			
Mezhdunarodnaya Zhizn, Gorokhovskiy p. 14	265-3781		
Mezhdunarodnye Otnosheniya,			
see International Relations Publishers			
Mezhnumismatika JV (FRG), Dmitrovka B. ul. 9	292-0177	200-0270	411717
MGL International JV (Spain), ul. Davydkovskaya 5	443-0654		411700
MGL Corporation, ul. Timura Frunze, Suites 14, 15	246-8529	146-8034	
MGPO Tourist, Izmailovskoye sh. 71, k. V, 4th flr.	166-2036	166-5018	
MGU (Moscow State University),			
Vorobyoviye Gory			
Mokhovaya 8,9	939-1000		
Mia Shoe, Tikhvinskiy p. 1/50			
MIAT Mongolian Airlines, Spasopeskovskiy p. 7/1	241-0754		
Sheremetevo 2 Airport	578-2759		
Michael Paris, ul. Druzhinikovskaya 11A	255-9140	252-0984	
Micorsam International Corp.,			
ul. Verkhnyaya Radischevskaya 1	227-1184	479-7026	
MicroAge Computers, Balaklavskiy prosp. 3	316-2111	316-2118	
Microcomputersystem JV (FRG), Dmitrovka B. ul. 32	229-4491		
Microdin, Volokolomtsoye sh. 13	158-5271		
Micrograf-Moscow JV Filial, Tokmakov p. 14	261-1911		
Micron Co., ul. Dovzhenko 12, k. 1, #165	143-7511	938-2123	

	Phone	Fax	Telex
Microsoft, Leningradskiy prosp. 80	158-1112	158-8181	
Middle East News Agency (MENA),			
Sokolnicheskiy val 24, k. 2, kv. 176	264-8276	288-9527	
Midland Montagu,			
Krasnopresnenskaya nab. 12, Office 1305	253-2144	230-2003	413108
Mikrodin, ul. Novozavodskaya 18	145-8966	145-9563	
Mikrokhirurgiya Glaza, Beskudnikovskiy bul. 59a	484-8120	485-5954	411856
Mikromed-Moscow JV Filial, ul. Timiryazevskaya 1	211-1722	211-1724	411267
Milan, Leninskiy prosp. 45	137-6514	137-6525	
Milbank, Tweed, Hadley & McCloy, ul. Pokrovka 28	975-2524	975-2524	
Milbari JV, ul. Yuzhnoportovaya 7A	279-2813	975-2683	
Milena Inform JV Filial (Italy),			
Hotel Intourist, Tverskaya ul. 3/5, room 1320	203-1774	975-2026	
Millioner, Tryokhprudny p.8, kv.4	202-7287		
Milliyet, ul. Donskaya 18/7, kv. 136	236-2483	236-1344	
Milo JV (Italy), ul. Krasnobogatyrskaya 2	168-1728		
Miloserdie, ul. Admirala Makarova 15	452-4190		
Mineralimpex, Krasnopresnenskaya nab. 12, Mezh-II	255-5530	255-1162	414422
Mineralogy Museum (Fersman Mus. of Min'ology),			
Leninskiy prosp. 18, k. 2	232-0067	232-6667	
Minerma JV (Luxemburg), ul. B. Ordynka 49, k. 1	233-5992	230-2465	
Ministry of			
Agriculture, Orlikov p. 1/11	207-4243	288-3580	411021
Automobile and Farm Machinery Manufacturing,			
Kuznetskiy Most 21/5	925-1132		
Automobile Roads, ul. Bochkova 4	287-3600		
Automobile Transport,			
ul. Sadovaya-Samotechnaya 10	200-0809		
Aviation Industry, Ulanskiy p. 16	207-0025		
Civil Aviation, Leningradskiy prosp. 37	155-5009		412297
Cargo Transport Division			411969
Civil Construction,			
see Rosgrazhdanrekonstruktsiya Concern			
Communications, ul. Tverskaya 5	292-1075		
Construction Materials Indust,			
ul. Krzhizhanovskovo 13	124-3177		
Construction for the Oil and Gas Ind.,			
ul. Zhitnaya 14	238-5000		
Construction in the North and Western Reg.,			
ul. Stroiteley 8, k. 2	930-4229	930-4119	
Construction in the Southern Region,			
ul. Petrovka 14	200-4535		
Culture, Kitaygorodskiy pr. 7	925-1195		
ul. Arbat 35	241-0709		411290
Russian State Library, ul. Vozdvizhenka 3	203-1419		
Defense, Krasnopresnenskaya nab. 2	296-3955		
Ecology & Natural Resources,			
ul. Bolshaya Gruzinskaya 4/6	254-7683	943-0013	
Economics, Okhotny ryad 1	292-9139		
Education, Chistoprudny bul. 6	924-8468		
Electronic Industry, Kitaygorodskiy pr. 7	220-6744		
Electrotechnical Ind. and Eqpt, Gazetny p. 5	229-7154		

	Phone	Fax	Telex
Finance (Committee on Foreign Investments),			
Okhotny ryad 1	292-7800		
Foreign Affairs, ul. Smolenskaya-Sennaya 32/34	244-4314	244-1969	
Foreign Companies Accreditation Department	244-4125		
Protocol Department	244-2987		
Visa Department	244-2459	244-3068	
Foreign Economic Relations,			
ul. Smolenskaya-Sennaya 32/34	220-1350		
Fuel and Power Industry, Kitaygorodskiy pr. 7	220-5200	206-8107	
Health Care, Rakhmanovskiy p. 3	928-4478		
Heavy Automobile Industry, Nizhniy Kislovskiy p. 5	203-0437		
Industry, ul. Tverskaya 33	209-8222		
Internal Affairs, ul. Zhitnaya 19	239-6500		
Law, Karetny B. p. 10a	209-6055		
Light Industry, see Roslegprom Association			
Local Industries, see Rossoyuzmestprom			
Machinery and Equipment,			
see State Joint Stock Assoc. for Mach. and Equip.			
Maritime Shipping, ul. Rozhdestvenka 1/4	926-1000		
Medical Industry, Kamergerskiy p. 2	292-9623		
Nuclear Power Industry, ul. B. Ordynka 24/26	239-4908		
Press and Mass Media, Strastnoy bul. 5	229-3353	200-2281	
Public Services, ul. Shabolovka 4	236-4482		
Leontyevskiy p. 7	290-1638		
Radio Industry, ul. Myasnitskaya 35	207-9842		
Residential Buildings, ul. Myasnitskaya 13	924-6734		
River Transport, see Rosrechflot Concern			
Security, ul. Myasnitskaya 1	224-5097	224-5217	
Ship Building, ul. Sadovaya-Kudrinskaya 11	255-0941		
Trade and Material Resources, Orlikov p. 5	204-0178		
Transport, ul. Sadovaya-Samotechnaya 10	200-0803		
Transport Construction, ul. Sadovaya-Spasskaya 21	262-9901		
Minneftegasprom, see Rosneft			
Minsk Cinema, Mozhayskoye sh. 54	447-0200		
Minsk Hotel, ul. Tverskaya 22	299-1300	299-1529	
Mir Cinema, Tsvetnoy bul. 11	200-1695		
Mir Hotel, B. Devyatinskiy p. 9	290-9519		
Mirbis JV (Italy), ul. Zatsepa 41	237-8277	237-3430	
Mission of the Israeli Fed. of Chambers of Comm.,			
Krasnopresnenskaya nab.12, Office 809	253-2809		
MIT Alumni Association	242-4701		
Mitranss JV, Tsvetnoy bul. 21	200-2870	200-3071	412202
Mitsubishi Corporation,			
Krasnopresnenskaya nab. 12, Office 702-710	253-1278	230-9673	413387
Mitsubishi Heavy Industries, LTD,			
B. Gnezdnikovskiy p. 7, 2nd fl.	200-2551	200-6373	
Mitsui & Co., LTD,			
Krasnopresnenskaya nab. 12, Office 1804	253-1592	253-9273	413395
Mivaro JV (Italy), Lubyanskiy pr. 25	928-1869		
MKhAT, see Moscow Theater of the Arts			
MKS Plus JV, ul. Pionerskaya 12	190-5427	944-7471	
MKT-Inter JV, ul. Akad. Koroleva, k. 2	215-2292	225-2056	
MKTS-Hertel JV (FRG), ul. Polkovaya 13	289-7385	971-6200	

	Phone	Fax	Telex
MM & M, ul. Spartakovskaya 6A	267-4559	975-2024	
MM International JV (Spain),			
bul. Matrosa Zheleznyaka 23, k. 2, pom. 3	450-9160	450-9160	
MMC Union LTD, Profsoyuznaya ul. 93A	336-4900	330-7933	411679
Moag JV (Sweden), ul. Lesnaya 59	251-2535		
Mobil Oil Company Limited,			
Novovorotnikovskiy p. 4/1	973-2379	973-2378	411633
Mobile Oil Osterreich AG,			
Krasnopresnenskaya nab. 12, office 504-507	253-1000	253-1040	
Mobile Ventures Inc., Novovorotnikovskiy p. 4/1	973-3687	973-2378	412622
Moda, Frunzenskaya Nab. 44	242-3102		
Moda JV, ul. Tikhvinskaya 1/13, str. 2	258-9738	972-4426	411796
Moda-Plast JV, B. Cherkasskiy p. 15	924-1620	924-1721	411127
Moden JV (Italy), ul. Vodnikov 2	190-4788		141719
Modern Ross JV, ul. Nikitinskaya 1a	165-1356	292-6511	
Modus Vivendi,			
Sovintsentr, Mezhdunarodnaya Hotel I, 1st fl.			
Modus Vivendi Press Agency, Romanov p. 5	299-0502	230-2297	411795
MOES, see Int'l Organ. of Economic Cooperation			
MOL, MOL-ADEL, ul. Krasnaya Presnya 1/7	252-1271	252-2095	414340
Molkom JV (FRG), ul. Verkhnyaya Radishchevskaya 12	227-8535	200-3279	414731
Molodaya Gvardiya Publishers, Sushchyovskiy 21	972-2200	972-0582	411261
Molodyozhnaya Hotel, Dmitrovskoye sh. 27	210-9311		
Molodyozhny Cinema, ul. Lyublinskaya 11	177-9010		
Monde (Le), Kutuzovskiy prosp. 13, kv. 3	243-7242	230-2942	413367
Monde Diplomatique (Le),			
Rublyovskoye sh. 26, k. 1, kv. 221-222	415-2912		
Mongolian Airlines, see MIAT Mongolian Airlines			
Monolit JV (Denmark), ul. Yunosti 5/1	374-7877	374-7131	
Monsanto Company, Volkov p. 19	255-0001	255-5001	413314
Montana, B. Cherkasskiy p. 15	923-8271	921-4184	
Novy Arbat 21	203-5103		
Montana Coffee Traders, ul. Marksistskaya 1/1	271-9280	271-9280	
Monte Dei Paschi di Siena,			
Krasnopresnenskaya nab. 12, Office 1105-1106a	253-2677	253-9087	413092
Montedison, Koroviy val 7, Office 1	237-2622	230-2032	413460
Montreal Bread Bakery, ul. Shipok			
Moosh cafe, ul. Oktyabrskaya 2/4	284-3670		
Morbank, B. Koptevskiy pr. 6	151-5674	151-5674	411197
Morgan Grenfell & Co. Ltd,			
B. Strochenovskiy p. 22/25, office 101	230-6154	230-6156	413860
Morikawa Shoji Kaisha LTD, Glazovskiy p. 7, kv. 18	203-0041	200-1273	413283
Morozko, ul. Kedrova 7a			
ul. Lva Tolstovo 2	246-0504		
Morsea, ul. B. Pereyaslavskaya 15, kv. 1-2	280-9654	230-2841	413102
Morsvyazsputnik, Novoslobodskaya 14/19	258-7045	253-9910	411197
Mosad, ul. Oktyabrskaya 58	219-3128		
Mosbank, ul. Obrucheva 34/62	333-9070	420-2262	
Mosbudproekt JV (Poland), ul. Smolnaya 34a	459-8338	459-8338	911532
Mosbusinessbank, Kuznetskiy Most 15	921-8582	224-0490	411864
Mosc-American Real Estate, Nizhegorodskaya ul. 3/23	278-4947	292-6511	
Moscom Paging	199-0300	203-9603	
Moscomissiontorg, Bolshoi Cherkasskiy p. 2/10	923-1444		

	Phone	Fax	Telex
MosComputerTrade JV (US),			
ul. Novokuznetskaya 17/19	231-0426		411386
Moscow Artists' House Hall, Kuznetskiy Most 11	925-4264		
Moscow Ballet Theater, ul. Skakovaya 3	251-3221		
Moscow Bird JV (US), Kutuzovskiy prosp. 17	243-9796		
Moscow Bombay, Glinishchevskiy p. 3	292-9731	292-9778	
Moscow Book World, ul. Myasnitskaya 6			
Moscow Boston International Ltd.,			
Novobasmannaya ul. 13/2 str. 3	267-1302	267-2233	
Moscow Business (Moskovskiy Bizness) Mag. JV,			
Zubovskiy bul. 4	201-7475	230-2667	411323
Moscow Business Journal (Face to Face),			
5th pr. Marinoy Roschy 15a	284-4374	971-6886	411630
Moscow Business Telephone Guide,			
Khoroshevskoye sh. 4	316-6130	946-1925	
Moscow Cash and Carry Mozhaisk,			
ul. 20-ovo Yanvarya 20, Mozhaisk	238-24104	936-2203	911607
Moscow Catering Company, B. Kalitnikovskaya 36	270-5197	278-7488	
Moscow Cellular Communications,			
Vorontsovskaya ul. 18/20	271-3749	271-9460	
Moscow Center for Scientific-Technical Info.,			
Lubyanskiy pr. 5	928-6605		
Moscow Central Address Information Bureau,			
Krasnoproletarskaya 10	258-2820		
Moscow Central Customs (Rostrans),			
4th ul. Marinoy Roshchy 12	971-1178	971-0105	
Moscow Central Industrial Bank of Russia,			
ul. Zhitnaya 12	230-7962		
Moscow Central Real Estate Exchange, Frolov p. 1	924-0330	924-5082	
Moscow Central Stock Exchange,			
Romanov p. 5, kv. 37	229-7635		
Moscow Chamber of Commerce, M. Dmitrovka ul. 13	299-7612		
Moscow Christian Center,			
October Theater, ul. Novy Arbat	344-9067		
Moscow City Council			
Exec. Comm. ul. Tverskaya 13	229-5431		
Interagency Commission	202-2782		
Council Planning Comm., Leontyevskiy p. 24	925-3123		
Moscow City Orgkomitet, Nikitskaya, B. ul. 12	203-2655	291-6773	
Moscow City Sports Committee, Milyutinskiy p. 18	200-2264	200-2264	
Moscow City Telephone Network, Degtyarny p. 6	299-2885	200-3208	
Moscow Commercial Club,			
ul. B. Kommunisticheskaya 2A	274-0081	274-0080	
Moscow Commodity Exchange,			
VVTs, bldg. 4, prosp. Mira 120	187-8614	188-9601	
Energy Dept.	187-8505		
Moscow Conservatory, Nikitskaya, B. ul. 13	229-7412		
Moscow Consulting Center JV, Kolokolnikov p. 22/19	207-1441	253-1601	
Moscow Country Club,			
Krasnogorskiy District, Makhabino	561-2977	563-8635	
Moscow Credit Bank, Orlikov per 7	204-0562		
Moscow Detective Theater, ul. B. Lubyanka 13	222-5213		
Moscow Diplomatic Transport Svc. JV (Sweden)	434-0160		

	Phone	Fax	Telex
Moscow Duty Free, Sheremetevo 2 Airport	578-9089	230-2351	411954
Moscow Engineering-Construction Institute JV,			
Yaroslavskoye sh. 26	183-4692		
Moscow Enterprises Inc.	291-3944	299-8147	
Moscow Fair JV, Sokolnicheskiy val 1, pavilion 4	269-3076	268-0891	412802
Moscow Fashion Club, ul. Vavilova 69	134-3425	134-1311	
Moscow Finance Group, ul. Kedrova 15	129-6700	240-6915	
Moscow Guardian, ul. Vrubelya 4	943-9738	943-9796	
Moscow Hill Night Club, Trubnaya pl. 4	208-4637	299-7922	
Moscow House of Charity	925-3042	200-2265	
Moscow Industrial Bank	952-7408	952-5927	
Moscow Institute for the Economy (MINKh),			
Stremyanny p. 28	237-8508		
Moscow Interbank Currency Exchange (MICE),			
Zubovskiy bul. 4, #6026	201-2817	230-2271	
Moscow Inter'l Agricultural Exch., ul. Koroleva 15	283-3693		
Moscow International Bank, Dmitrovka B. ul. 5/6	292-8371	975-2214	412284
Moscow International Peace Marathon JV (US),			
Milyutinskiy p. 18	924-0824	200-2264	
Moscow Int'l Stock Exchange, ul. Neglinnaya 23	238-3632		
Moscow Kennan Project, Vspolny p. 16, kv. 38	299-6875		
Moscow Labor Department, ul. Pyatnitskaya 2	233-4643		
Moscow Laundry Service	480-9452		
Moscow Legal Advice Center,			
M. Poluyaroslavskiy per 3/5	227-1248	975-2416	
Moscow Legal Collegium, Dmitrovka B. ul. 9, str. 6	229-9033		
Moscow Legis International JV,			
see Computer Systems and Technology			
Moscow Lobster & Fish Co.,			
Krasnopresnenskaya nab. 12, m/s Alexander Blok	255-9279	255-9279	
Moscow Management International,			
Petrovskiy bul. 25	924-7416	200-5241	
Moscow Mayor's Office, ul. Tverskaya 13	292-7238	280-8554	
Moscow Medical Center, ul. Mosfilmovskaya 31a	432-1616	143-3612	
Moscow Medical International Centre JV (FRG),			
ul. Vorontsovo pole 14	297-1848		
Moscow Messengers, ul. B. Polyanka 28/295	238-5308	238-5306	
Moscow Metro Museum, Sportivnaya metro	222-7309		
Moscow Municipal Trade House, Dmitrovka M. ul. 2	299-5213	229-0962	411655
Moscow News, ul. Tverskaya 16/2	200-2010	209-1728	
Moscow Non-Ferrous Metals Exchange,			
ul. Gorbunova 20	449-7783		
Moscow Oil Exchange	233-8981		
Moscow Oil Refinery, Kursovoy p. 9	172-7674	200-2018	
Moscow Outdoor Swimming Pool,			
Prechistenskaya nab. 38	202-4725		
Moscow Parachute Club	111-3315	111-4475	
Moscow Patriarchate, Chistoprudny p. 5	201-3416		
External Dept, Danilovskiy val 22	235-0708		
Moscow Patriarchy Publishing House,			
Pogodinskaya 20	246-9848		
Moscow Periodicals, Voznesenskiy p. 20, build. 4	202-8180		
Moscow Pizza JV (USA), Kutuzovskiy prosp. 43	243-9964	243-1994	

	Phone	Fax	Telex
Moscow Project Management JV (USA),			
B. Pereyaslavskaya 50	280-3435	280-9005	411660
Moscow Protestant Chaplaincy, ul. Olaf Palme 5, kor 2	143-3562		
Moscow Puppet Theater, Spartakovskaya ul. 26	261-2197		
Moscow Rent-a-Phone, Novotel Hotel, #718	578-7252	578-2765	
Moscow Rotary Club	284-7896		
Moscow Social Union for the Disabled, Romanov p. 2	203-7936		
Moscow State University, see MGU			
Moscow Theater of the Arts – New, Tverskoy bul. 22	203-8744		
Old, Kamergerskiy p. 3	229-0443		
filial, Petrovskiy p. 3	229-9631		
Museum, Kamergerskiy p. 3a	229-0080		
Moscow Times,			
ul. Pravdy 24, entr. 3, floor 8, #821/822/835	257-3628	257-2569	
Advertising	257-2574	257-2569	
Moscow Tourist Club, Sadovaya-Kudrinskaya 4	203-1094		
Moscow Trade House, Dmitrovka M. ul. 2	299-1333	299-5676	
Moscow Trade Union Sport Consulting JV (FRG),			
Bobrov p. 6	925-5290		
Moscow Trading House, Dmitrovka M. ul. 2	299-4460	229-0962	411655
Moscow Tribune, Leninskiy prosp. 45, kv. 426	135-1114	230-2010	
Moscow Trust Bank, ul. Novaya Basmannaya 14	262-7767	262-9744	
Moscow Univ. Students Theater, Nikitskaya, B. ul. 1	203-6876		
Moscow Volvo Rentals, see MTDS JV			
Moscow Wood JV (Australia), ul. Udaltsova 22a	131-0560		
Moscow X-Service, ul. Mytnaya 18, entrance 2	238-6634	230-2459	
Moscow Youth Theater, Sadovskiy p. 10	299-5360		
Moscow-Ashok Company JV, ul. Krasnaya Presnya 23b	200-4153		
Moscow-Bilifeld Machine Building JV (FRG),			
2nd Irtyshskiy pr. 4/6	462-0150	462-0152	411681
Moscow-Carroll JV (UK), Presnenskiy val 1/5	238-0635		
Moscow-Color JV (Belgium), Okhotny ryad 7	262-9215		
Moscow-McDonalds JV (Canada), ul. B. Bronnaya 29	299-1811	934-2183	411770
Moscow-Milan System JV (Italy), Leninskiy prosp. 6	151-5416		
Moscow-Tours JV, Kalanchevskaya ul. 21/40	975-1850		
Mosdam JV, Vorontsovskiy Park 5	936-0014		
Moseniko-Invest JV (Switz.), see ENIKO			
Mosenka JV, Tsvetnoy bul. 25/3	291-3952	202-7512	
Mosgorspravka, ul. Tverskaya 7	292-5381		
Mosimedia JV (France), Kalashny p. 14	925-3476	975-2322	413182
Mosinterkon, ul. Lavochkina 44, kv.4	455-4782	455-4467	
MosJohnStroy JV, Tverskaya pl. 2/6	921-0056	200-3212	
Moskapstroi, ul. Tverskaya 23/12	299-4224		
Moskniga Books, see Books, Moskniga			
Moskompeksim JV (Switz.),			
ul. 1st Tverskaya-Yamskaya 37a	251-3376		
Moskovskaya Pravda Newspaper, ul. 1905 goda 7	259-8233		
Moskovskaya Pravda Publisher, ul. 1905 goda 7	256-9294		
Moskovskaya Regionalnaya Birzha Privatizatsii,			
see Moscow Regional Privatization Exchange			
Moskovskaya Tsentralnaya Birzha Nedvizhlmosti,			
see Moscow Central Real Estate Exchange			

Moskovskiy Mezhdunarodny Bank,
see Moscow International Bank

	Phone	Fax	Telex
Moskovskiy Rabochiy, Chistoprudny bul. 8A	921-0735	924-1454	
Moskovskiye Zori cafe, M. Kozikhinskiy p. 11	299-5725		
Moskovsksaya Yarmarka JV (FRG),			
Sokolnicheskiy val 1	268-0183		
Moskva Cinema, Triumfalnaya pl. 2	251-7222		
Moskva Electronics Store, Kutuzovskiy prosp. 31			
Moskva Hotel, Okhotny Ryad 7	292-1100		
Benetton	924-2734		
Casino Okhotny Ryad			
El Rincon Espanol Restaurant	292-2893		
Emanuelle	924-3776		
Moskva Restaurant	292-6227	292-9217	
Okhotny Ryad	924-6500		
Paradise Restaurant and Bar	292-2073		
Tamada Duty Free Shop	292-2874		
Transaero Airlines	292-7513		
Zolotaya Roza	292-1194		
Moskvich, Volgogradskiy prosp. 42	276-8200		
Mosreaktiv, Krivokolenny p. 12	928-3446	925-6619	
Mosrent Car Rental, Zemledelcheskiy per 14/17, str. 2	248-3607	248-0251	411762
Mosrentservice JV (FRG), ul. Krasnobogatyrskaya 79	963-9145	162-1675	414766
Sheremetevo 2 Airport	963-9173		
Mosrestoranservice, M. Palashevskiy p. 7	299-0161		
Mossoviet Cinema, Preobrazhenskaya pl. 4/2	963-0332		
Mossoviet Theater, B. Sadovaya 16	299-2035		
Sivtsev Vrazhek 44	241-0225		
Small stage, Khamovnicheskiy val 2	242-1707		
Mosspetsmontazhi, Sadovnicheskaya ul. 20	231-1357	270-6360	
Mosstroybank, Dmitrovka M. ul. 21/18	209-4157	299-6405	207892
Mosstroyeconombank, ul. Vavilova 81	132-2897	132-2893	
Most Bank, ul. Novy Arbat 36	202-9239	203-2976	411135
Most JV (Japan), Sretenskiy tupik 1/34	208-1206	434-1020	
Mosta Clinic, Bolshoy Cherkasskiy P.15, 2-nd floor	927-0765	925-3558	
MosTransEurope, Butyrskiy val 22, kom. 48/49	973-0076	975-2027	411815
Mosvart JV (Austria), Leningradskoye sh. 16	156-7525	930-1033	417343
Mosven JV, ul. Tverskaya 10	241-7580	244-7234	
Mosvneshinform, Krasnopresnenskaya nab. 1/2	205-1423	205-7873	412151
Moszhilproekt-2, 2nd Brestskaya ul. 5	200-0060		
Moulinex, Koroviy val 7, #74	238-3479	230-6103	413875
Moveable Feasts	309-0449		
Mozhayskaya Hotel, Mozhayskoye sh. 165	447-3434		
Mozhayskiy Disco, Mozhayskoye sh. 163	447-3294		
MPO Biomash	159-3030		
MPS, see Monte Dei Paschi di Siena			
Mr. Tillani's Hong Kong Fashions,			
ul. Oktyabrskaya 105, kor. 2 (Hotel Good Luck)	289-4575	289-9968	
MS-Group JV (US), Pyatnitskaya ul. 43	231-0759	231-6262	
MSF (Belgium)	207-4618	207-4619	
MTDS Moscow Volvo Rentals, Leninskiy prosp. 152	434-5332		
ul. Gorbunova 14	448-9531	448-6728	412343
MTS JV (France), B. Serpukhovskaya 14/13, str. 8	236-4631	230-2900	911615

	Phone	Fax	Telex
Multidesign JV (FRG), ul. Gilyarovskovo 17	284-3718		
Multiservice JV, ul. B. Polyanka 50	238-1032		
Multivision, Inc., ul. Bolshaya Yakimanka 24	230-7813	230-7813	
Mundo (El), Sadovnicheskaya ul. 21, kv. 48	231-5330		
Museum of Applied Folk Art, Delegatskaya ul. 5	221-0139		
Museum of Folk Art, Leontyevskiy p. 7	291-8718		
Museum of Oriental Art, Nikitskiy bul. 12a	291-9614		
Museum of the Defense of Moscow,			
Michurinskiy prosp. 3	437-3616		
Museum of the Mininstry of the Interior,			
Seleznevskaya ul. 11	258-0659		
Museum of the October Revolution,			
see Museum of Russian Revolutions			
Music Museum (Glinka Museum of Music Culture),			
ul. Fadeyeva 4	972-3237		
Musical Comedy Theater (Operetta Theater),			
Dmitrovka B. ul. 6	292-0405	292-2425	
Musika Publishers, Neglinnaya ul. 14	923-0497	925-6949	
Mypharm, ul. Nikolayeva 4, kv. 35	205-0624	205-1194	
Mysl JV Filial, Lubyanskiy pr. 4	298-3723		
MZhL Corporation, ul. Timura Frunze 18 kv. 15	245-3034	246-8034	

N

	Phone	Fax	Telex
N.H.K. TV & Radio, Afanasyevskiy B. p. 7	291-8566	291-8820	413393
N.V. Philips' Gloeilampenfabrieken,			
ul. Mytnaya 1, Office 18	230-0410	230-0410	413961
Na Sretenke, Turgenevskaya pl. 2/4	928-7444		
Nabisco Brands Inc., see RJR-Nabisco			
Nagornaya Gallery, ul. Remizova 10	123-6569		
Naidunia, Zemlyanoy val 52, kv. 158	227-8897		413320
Nalco Chemical Company,			
Hotel Mezhdunarodnaya 2, room 732	255-6807	253-2732	411432
Nargiz cafe, Lebedyanskaya 22, k. 4	329-7187		
Nashe Naslediye (Our Heritage),			
1st Neopalimovskiy p. 4	244-0106	253-9390	
Nataly Flora Service, ul. Krasina 7	255-9480		
Nataly Flora Service JV, ul. B. Kamenshchiki 6	271-3003		
National Broadcasting Company (US),			
Gruzinskiy p. 3, kv. 217-220	230-2675		413428
National Committee of the Int'l Council of Museums,			
p. Sivtsev-Vrazhek 30	241-7210	241-4623	
National Hotel, Okhotny ryad 14/1	203-6539		
National Instruments, prosp. Mira 186, str. 2	286-2438	286-2438	
National Iranian Steel Corporation, ul. B. Spasskaya	280-3360		
National Market Research Institute, ul. Pudovkina 4	143-8664	143-0271	
National Public Radio, ul. D. Ulyanova 16, kv. 195	124-0261	124-0261	
National Publishers' Association	921-6088		
National Westminster Bank PLC,			
Pokrovskiy bul. 4/17, kv. 33	207-5739	230-2244	413258
Nature and Man (Priroda i Chelovek) Journal,			
ul. Marshala Rybalka 8	194-0577		

	Phone	Fax	Telex
Nauka i Zhizn, ul. Myasnitskaya 24	928-5866	200-2259	
Nauka Publishers, ul. Profsoyuznaya 90	334-7610	420-2220	411612
Nauka v Rossii, Maronovskiy p. 26	238-1555		
Nedelya, Pushkinskaya pl. 5	200-3479		
Nefertiti, Hotel Intourist, 11th fl.	203-1589		
Nefte-Interoko JV, ul. Pivchenkova 1/3	144-7577	938-2033	411432
Neftegazstroybank, ul. Zhitnaya 14	239-1159	238-5677	412346
Neftekhimbank, ul. Gilyarovskovo 31	284-8838		
Neftekhimexport, ul. Shchepkina 28	284-8614		
Nefto Agip JV (Italy), B. Cherkasskiy p. 7, k. D	930-7973		414838
Leningradskoye sh. 63	457-2013	458-4957	
Neglinka, Kuznetskiy Most 9/10	924-0660		
Negrelli, Nikoloyamskaya ul. 15	111-5407	111-7710	
Nemetskaya Sloboda Restaurant, ul. Baumanskaya 23	267-4476		
Nemirovich-Danchenko House Museum,			
Glinishchevskiy p. 5/7	209-5391		
Nensel JV (Turkey), Vernadskovo prosp. 41	431-0554	434-8322	
Neo-Shag Gallery, Petrovskiye liniye 1/20	200-0562	200-0562	
Neptune Hotel, ul. Ibragimova 30	369-6383		
Neptune JV (Sweden), Nikitskaya M. ul. 27	291-9296	200-3246	
Nest International Ltd.	921-5100		
Neste Oy, Pokrovskiy bul. 4/17, kv. 38	207-7473	207-7693	413067
Netherlands Press Association,			
see Gemeenschapperijke Pers Dienst			
Neue Zuercher Zeitung, Kutuzovskiy prosp. 13, kv. 87	243-5139		413144
Neva Cinema, Belomorskaya ul. 16a	457-4221		
Nevka, Volokolamskoye sh. 15	943-4152	943-4197	
New Drama Theater, ul. Prokhodchikov 2	182-0347		
New Information Technology JV (Bulgaria),			
B. Savvinskiy p. 14	248-4148	943-0072	411080
New York Journal of Commerce,			
Kutuzovskiy prosp. 14, kv. 5	243-0032		
New York Motors Corp., ul. Pererva 19	348-7301	357-2801	
New York Times,			
ul. Sadovaya-Samotechnaya 12/24, kv. 56	973-2052	200-0240	413431
Newbridge Soviet Telecom JV, Voznesenskiy p. 12	299-2935	200-4233	
NewEurope Int'l, ul. Smolenskaya 10, ent. 4, kv. 125	241-3463	241-3463	
News Agency of Sweden, Norway, Denmark &			
Finland, Kutuzovskiy prosp. 7/4, kv. 196	243-0674		413469
News Pub, ul. Petrovka 18	921-1585		
News-Burda Advertising-Information Service JV,			
Pushkinskaya pl. 5	209-3674	230-2303	411121
Newstar, ul. Tverskaya 6, Suite 65	292-5057	292-5097	413205
Newsweek, Kutuzovskiy prosp. 9, kv. 78	243-1773	243-0788	413434
NGS Bank {answering machine}, ul. Zhitnaya 14	239-1508		
Niarmedik JV (UK), ul. Gamaley 18	190-6691		
Nichimen Corporation,			
Krasnopresnenskaya nab. 12, Office 1609	253-8224	230-2283	413985
Nick & Co., ul. Maroseyka 3/13	925-8513	206-8274	
Nidera Argentina S.A., Koroviy val 7, kv. 64	238-9146	230-2035	413932
Night Flight, ul. Tverskaya 17	229-4165		
Nihon Keizai Shimbun, Koroviy val 7, kv. 137	230-2782	230-2330	413389
Nilstar Co. Ltd., 1st pr. Marinoy Roschi 11, #606	515-1577		

	Phone	Fax	Telex
Nina Ricci, ul. Tverskaya 9	229-2967		
Nissho Iwai Corporation,			
Krasnopresnenskaya nab. 12, Office 908	253-1440	230-2325	413110
Nisso Boeki Co., LTD, ul. Gilyarovskovo 8, kv. 13-16	284-5381	281-9764	413169
Nit JV (FRG), ul. Sadovaya-Kudrinskaya, 5			
Nita, ul. Ostryakova 3	157-3421	157-3421	
Nofkoh, ul. B. Krasnoselskaya 15A	264-8318	264-7745	
Nokia, see NOKO			
NOKO, Chisty p. 11/7	241-0566	241-9327	413002
Nord JV, ul. B. Ordynka 39	231-6907		
Nord-Piligrim, ul. Pulkovskaya 6A, k. 4, room 201-202	459-1606	458-7576	
Nordbanken, Molochny p. 9/14, k. 3	201-3714	200-1289	413018
Nordick-Monolit JV, ul. Leytenanta Boyko 104	578-3701		
NordOst	201-2851		
Noris International Trading, Leningradskiy prosp. 33a	945-8504	945-8483	
Norman, Leninskiy prosp. 2, kv. 703-704	231-0346	239-1572	
Normos-JV (Norway), ul. Babayevskaya 4	280-5311	200-0259	413432
Norrskensflamman, ul. Sadovaya-Spasskaya 21, kv. 261	923-4525		413020
Norsk Hydro A.S., ul. Usacheva 35	245-5142	246-4948	
NORT, see Noviye Razrabotki i Technologiy			
North American Auto	137-4090		
North Korean Airways, see Chosonminhang			
North-Eastern Joint Stock Comm. Bank - Moscow Filial,			
prosp. Mira 9/18, str.1 , #18	207-7783	207-3168	613014
Northern River Boat Station, Leningradskoye sh. 51	459-7476		
Norton Rose, ul. Staraya Basmannaya 14	262-1803	262-1519	
Norvit JV (Israel), ul. Vuchechicha, 1a	211-5933	211-5938	
Norwegian Broadcasting Corporation,			
ul. Obrucheva 4, k. 2, kv. 145	936-2121	936-4344	413909
Norwegian, Swedish and Danish TV,			
Kutuzovskiy prosp. 7/4, kv. 130	243-5165	253-9179	413365
Notary, 3rd Novomikhalkovskiy pr. 5	154-0562		
Altufyevskoye sh. 24	401-3600		
Zlatoustinskiy B. p. 8	921-6941		
Beringov pr. 1	186-1756		
Bobrov p. 6, str. 3	928-4749		
bul. Yana Rainisa 1, k. 1	497-7807		
Dmitrovskoye sh. 149	483-0645		
Frunzenskaya nab. 44/2	242-5471		
Leningradskiy prosp. 14	214-1332		
Leningradskiy prosp. 75	158-5265		
Lyusinovskaya 41	237-1154		
M. Yakimanka 22	238-8701		
Marksistskiy p. 1/32	272-1218		
Mozhayskoye sh. 41	443-0694		
Nagorny bul. 14	123-6269		
Novomytishchi pr. 88, k. 3	581-0100		
Novy Arbat 23	205-2017		
Okskaya ul. 20, k. 2	177-5551		
Pervomayskaya 44/20	367-5042		
prosp. Olminskovo 3	282-0531		
prosp. Vernadskovo 127	438-7492		
Schyolkovskoye sh. 21 k. 2a	164-4804		

	Phone	Fax	Telex
ul. Berzarina 17, k. 2	946-8331		
ul. Bogdanova 42	435-8736		
ul. Dnepropetrovskaya 1	315-3864		
ul. Krasnodonskaya 2, k. 1	350-2636		
ul. Luganskaya 8	321-2938		
ul. Miklukho-Maklaya 20	335-0066		
ul. Miklukho-Maklaya 30	330-5851		
ul. Petrovka 23/10	200-6524		
ul. Plekhanova 28, k. 5	368-7186		
ul. Sergeya Makeyeva 8	259-1751		
ul. Soldatskaya 10	362-4390		
ul. Ustinova 2	413-1105		
Vorontsovskaya 30b	272-0164		
Zelenograd, 338b, kv. 74	535-1676		
Noty, ul. Neglinnaya 14	248-0153		
Nova Petroleum,			
Krasnopresnenskaya nab, 12, office 1617	253-1617	253-1617	
Novaplan, Staropetrovskiy pr. 11, k. 2	153-9461	153-9461	
Novasider, Tryokhprudny per 11/13, 2nd fl.	299-0932	200-0234	413452
Novator Cinema, Spartakovskaya pl. 1/2	261-9021		
Novaya Moskva JV (Canada), Milyutinskiy p. 4	928-6850	975-2237	
Novaya Zarya, ul. Pavla Andreyeva 23	236-7180		
Novick Link Corp.,, Leninskiy prosp. 122, kv. 117	431-6809	241-9859	
Novintech Concern, ul. Nezhinskaya 13	442-5792	441-1100	
Novintex JV (Bulgaria), M. Kommunisticheskaya 4	272-5666	272-0801	
Noviye Razrabotki i Technologiy, Leninskiye Gory	939-2494	371-0292	
Novodevichy Convent, Novodevichy p. 1	245-3268		
Novoexport, ul. Arkhitektora Vlasova 33	128-6859	128-1612	112212
Novorossiysk Cinema, ul. Pokrovka 47/24	297-6657		
Novort JSC, 4th Tverskaya-Yamskaya 21, str. 3	251-9151		412178
Novosibirsk-Seattle International	939-3741		
Novosti Information Agency, see ITAR			
Novosti Press Agency (APN), Zubovskiy bul. 4	201-2424	201-2119	411321
Novosti-Inform, Zubovskiy bul. 4, rm 5010	201-7193	230-2170	
Novotel Hotel, Sheremetevo 2 Airport	578-9401	578-2794	911620
Europcar	578-9407		
Lobby Bar, The	578-9407		
Piano Bar	578-9407		
Novoye Vremya (New Times), M. Putinkovskiy p. 1/2	229-8872	200-4223	411164
Novoye Vremya Hotel, ul. Avtozavodskaya 17, k. 1	274-4694	274-0031	
Novy Mir, M. Putinkovskiy p. 1/2	200-0829	209-7906	
Nowea, see Dusseldorfer Messegesellschaft			
NPO Polygrafmash- YAM Int'l Trading Ltd.,			
ul. Profsoyuznaya 57, rm 601	332-6420	334-2801	
NRC-Handelsblad, Krutitskiy val 3, k. 2, kv. 173	274-0008	2740059	
NTV, Kutuzovskiy prosp. 9, kv. 26	230-2389	253-9708	413109
Nuovo Pignone,			
Krasnopresnenskaya nab. 12. Office 1302	253-2084	230-2723	413940
Nurminen, see John Nurminen Oy			
Nutech Trading Ltd.,, prosp. Vernadskovo 41, kv. 502	437-6280	434-8455	413005
NY Dag, Protopovskiy p. 6, kv. 30	975-2011		413615

O

	Phone	Fax	Telex
O Salonen Oy, Koroviy val 7	238-3684	174-1500	
O-II Club, Sadovaya-Kudrinskaya 19			
O. Tabakov's Studio Theater, ul. Chaplygina 1a	928-9685	200-4241	
O.M.T. SpA, Hotel Volga, k. 4, room 147-148	280-3779	975-2023	
Oblastnoy Teatr Yunovo Zritelya, Prokhladnaya ul. 28	321-6277		
Obninsk, Vodolei International	357-7758	255-2225	
Oboronexport, Ovchinnikovskaya nab. 18/1	220-1752	233-1813	
Obraztsov Puppet Theater, see Central Puppet Theater			
Observador, El, ul. Sr. Pereyaslavskaya 14, kv. 87	280-0298		413570
Observer, The, ul. B. Spasskaya 12, kv. 28	230-2476	230-2476	
Occidental Petroleum Corporation,			
Krasnopresnenskaya nab. 12, Office 1409	253-2269	230-2641	413168
CIS, Grokholski p. 19/27	284-4791		
Ochakovo Taxi Service, ul. B. Ochakovskaya 47a	437-1564	430-0222	
October 19 Literary Salon, 1st Kazachiy p. 8	238-6489		
Odessa Cinema, ul. Kakhovka 21	122-3375		
Ofema, ul. Mytnaya 1	230-0621		413190
Office Club, ul. Ogrucheva 34/63	336-0550	334-9389	
Office Equipment, Petrovskiy Passazh (see Passazh)			
Offset Print Moscow,			
Krasnogvardeyskiy 1.pr., pavilion #2	259-7367		411485
Offset Printshop, Nagornaya ul. 20, k. 7	123-4477		
Ogilvy and Meisez, prosp. Vernadskovo 33	131-5743	138-3743	
Ogilvy & Mather, ul. Mytnaya 3, #3A	230-6606	230-6610	
Ogonyok, Bumazhny pr. 14	212-2269	943-0070	112349
Okanora Finance, ul. Sovetskoy Armii 6	288-9190	971-6807	
Okhotnik, ul. Tverskaya 10			
Okhotny Ryad, Moskva Hotel, 2 Okhotny Ryad	924-6500		
Oko JV (England), Vorontsovskiy p. 5/7	272-0882	271-2068	
Okobank, Koroviy val 7, Office 13a	230-1387	230-1386	413056
Oktrabrskaya Tovarnaya Stantsiya,			
Komsomolskaya pl.	975-4460		
Oktyabr Cinema, Novy Arbat 42	202-1111		
Oktyabr Concert Hall, Kalininskiy prosp. 42	291-2263		
Oktyabrskaya Hotel I, see President Hotel			
Oktyabrskaya Hotel II, see Arbat Hotel			
Olan	425-9322		
Olbi Diplomat, Petrovskiy Passazh, 2nd fl.			
Olbi Store, ul. D. Ulyanova 3	135-6567		
Old Believers, Rogozhskiy p. 29			
Olex Agency, Pokrovskiy 14/5	137-6469		
Olga Co., Ltd., Hotel Metropol, Teatralny pr. 1/4	927-6139	975-2336	
Oliks JV, ul. Profsoyuznaya 65	334-8751		411899
Olimp, ul. Krasnaya Presnya 23			
Olimp Restaurant, Luzhnetskaya nab.	201-0148		
Olivetti Synthesis	197-5283		
Olivier S.A., Mamonovskiy p. 6, kv. 5	209-6705	200-2256	413253
Olmed, ul. 3rd Kabelnaya 1	273-1775	273-1708	411700
Olmi Center, Olympiyskiy prosp. 18, ent. 5	288-2488	288-6766	
Olwis, Leninskiy prosp. 60/2	137-4660		

	Phone	Fax	Telex
Olympia JV (Japan), prosp. Mira 12	297-2968		
Olympic Complex Swimming Pool,			
Olympiyskiy prosp. 16	288-1333		
Olympic Penta Hotel, Olympiyskiy prosp. 18/1	971-6101	230-2597	411061
Bakery, The	971-6101		
Brasserie Restaurant	971-6101		
Business Center	971-6101	290-2597	
DHL Express Mail	971-6101		
Die Bierstube Restaurant	971-6101		
Europcar	971-6101		
Health Club	971-6101		
Lufthansa Airlines	975-2501	971-6784	413668
Olympic Bar	971-6101		
Olympic Boutique	971-6101		
Vienna cafe	971-6101		
Olympic Sports Complex, Olympiyskiy prosp. 16	288-3777		
Olympic Supermarket, Krasnaya Presnya 23	252-6591	253-4666	
Olympic Village Concert Hall, Michurinskiy prosp. 1	437-5650		
OMC, see Overseas Marketing Corporation Limited			
OMV AG, Krasnopresnenskaya nab. 12, Office 1004A	253-1480	255-1514	413437
Onegin Hall, Konstantine Stanislavskiy Museum,			
Leontyevskiy p. 6	299-2855		
Open Radio, Pyatnitskaya ul. 25	233-7640	233-6973	411137
Open World Association, ul. Petrovka 19, Bldg. 6, #3	923-9504	309-6000	
Opportunity, Radisson-Slavyanskaya Hotel	150-1308	230-2170	
Optic Moscow, ul. Arbat 30, bldg 2	241-1577	241-1577	
Optika, Kuznetskiy most 4	292-0573		
Optika Moscow Ctr JV (Finland), Frunzenskaya nab. 54	242-3650	242-3650	
Optimum Commercial Bank, Nakhimovskiy prosp. 31	238-0089	238-1343	612291
Optintorg – Car Sales, ul. Krzhizhanovskovo 16, k. 1	127-7011		
Optintorg – Electronics, ul. Krzhizhanovskovo 16, k. 1	124-8056	310-7074	411098
Orbita Bank, 2nd Spasonalivkovskiy p. 5-7	238-8720	230-0128	414768
Orbita Cinema, ul. Novinki 2	115-6580		
Orbita JV (Poland), ul. Tverskaya 50	250-0489	250-0489	411069
Orbita-Limosine Service JV, ul. Ryabinovaya 43a	447-0042	447-0042	
Orbita-Service, Krivorozhskaya ul. 33	113-4490	318-9881	
Ordynka, B. Ordynka 40	238-1322	238-1300	
Ordynka Restaurant, B. Ordynka 71/36	237-9905		
ORF (Radio & TV), Koroviy val 7, kv. 68	237-7134	230-2603	413159
Orgkomitet Joint Stock Co., Nikitskaya, B. ul. 12	202-1166	291-6773	
Orient, Nikoloshchepovskiy p. 1/9	241-1078		
Orient Co., Ltd., Hotel Mezhdunarodnaya II, rm 1001	253-1001	253-1538	413702
Oriental Art Museum, Nikitskiy bul. 12a	202-4555		
Oriental Excelsior Club, ul. Novy Arbat 21	291-1172	291-0045	
Orion Cinema, ul. Letchika Babushkina 26	470-5147		
Orlyonok Cinema, ul. Rusakovskaya 23	264-0729		
Orlyonok Hotel, ul. Kosygina 15	939-8853		
Orri Master-Lamas JV (Finland), ul. Platovskaya 4		240-4347	
Ortex, Litovskiy bul. 3a	427-1101	427-6410	131310
Ortcard Service Center, Tarusskaya ul. 8a	427-0101	425-4300	
Oscar Jacobson, ul. Nikolskaya 5/1	921-8333	921-8821	
Ost-West Handelsbank AG, Kamergerskiy p. 5/6	292-4839		
Ostafievo Estate Museum, Sherbinka, Moscow region	119-7300		

	Phone	Fax	Telex
Ostankino Hotel, ul. Botanicheskaya 29	219-2880		
Ostankino Museum (Museum of Serf Art),			
1st Ostankinskaya ul. 5	283-4575		
Oster and Company, Box 152	956-3300	956-3301	
Ostermann, ul. Sadovaya-Samotechnaya 5, kv. 21	292-5110	230-2142	413851
Ostrovskiy Museum (N.A. Ostrovskiy),			
ul. Tverskaya 14	209-1222		
Otema Glaza JV (Luxembourg), Lubyanskiy pr. 4	207-4548	207-8048	411630
Otis Elevator	245-8940		
Outokumpu Oy, see Kemira Oy			
Overseas Marketing Corporation Limited (OMC),			
Krasnopresnenskaya nab. 12, office 1405	253-1701	253-9487	413672
Oversize JV (Australia), Gruzinskiy val 16	205-0709		
OVK JV, Krasnopresnenskaya nab. 12, Office 704	203-9920		
OWEG GmbH, ul. Tverskaya 36, kv. 2-3	251-8950	230-2078	413252
Oy Esmi	238-5520	341-5018	
Oy Partek AB, ul. Mytnaya 1, kv. 15	230-0443	230-2245	413993
Oy Stockmann AB, see Stockmann			
Ozdorovlenie JV (FRG), M. Gruzinskaya 26	252-3950	200-6166	

P

	Phone	Fax	Telex
P.L. JV (Sweden), Peschany p. 1a	412-9551		
P.R. Lotus Trading GmbH,			
2nd Brestskaya ul. 5, Room 1	973-0602	973-2057	
PA Consulting Group, Smolenskiy bul. 24, str.2	248-7430	248-7430	
Pacific Union Investment Corp. JV (Panama),			
ul. 1st Dubrovskaya 1	276-4204	276-5039	411766
Painoanson Printing Svc, Staraya Basmannaya 18/1, #17	267-4130		
Pais (EI), Kutuzovskiy prosp. 14, kv. 107	243-7073	243-1394	413944
Pakistani School, ul. Sadovaya-Kudrinskaya 17	254-7201		
Palace Hotel, ul. Tverskaya Yamskaya 19	956-3152		
Anchor Restaurant	956-3152		
Cafe Mozart	956-3152		
Lomonosov Restaurant	256-3152		
Vienna Restaurant	956-3152		
Palace JV (Bulgaria)	923-2507		
Palace Night Club, Izmailovskaya pl. 1	165-0283		
Palace of the 16-17th Centuries in Zaryadye,			
ul. Varvarka 10	298-3235		
Palace of Water Sports, ul. Mironovskaya 27	369-7444		
Paleontology Museum, Leninskiy prosp. 16	234-2985		
Palet JV (Bulgaria), Grokholskiy p. 12a	265-5911		
Palmira Travel Ltd., ul. Vavilova 48, entr 5-a	135-1200	248-3805	412352
Palms & Company Investment Bank,			
Zelenograd, building 342-22	214-6504	925-9462	
Pan Fun Copiers, ul. Levchenko 1	943-4101	943-6216	
Panalpina, Gogolevskiy Blvd. 17, Ste. 205	202-1713	203-1814	612403
Panaramatour Travel Svcs., Leningradskiy prosp. 10	257-0533	257-0813	
Panasonic, ul. B. Polyanka 30	238-4122	238-4124	
Petrovskiy Passazh, 2nd fl.	923-7080		
VVTs, prosp. Mira 120	181-9263	181-9790	

	Phone	Fax	Telex
Panav-Moscow JV, ul. Marksa-Engelsa 8		202-6075	411135
Panda Catering	298-6565		
Panda Restaurant, Tverskoy bul. 3/5	298-6505		
Paninter JV, ul. Lyusinovskaya 40, str. 7/8	237-2755	237-4655	
Panoramatours Travel Svcs, ul. Levoberezhnaya 32	458-5786	458-5554	911548
Pantomime Theater (Mimiki i Zhesta),			
Izmaylovskiy bul. 39/41	163-8130		
Paradise Restaurant and Bar,			
Hotel Moskva, Okhotny Ryad 2	292-2073		
ParaGraph JV (US), Petrovskiy bul. 23	924-1781		
Paris Match, Leninskiy prosp. 13, kv. 73	237-3106		
Park Avenue, Volgogradskiy prosp. 18	276-1074	200-4224	
Park Place Moscow, Leninskiy prosp. 113/1	956-5050	434-5920	
Parker, Petrovskiy Passazh, 2nd fl. (see Passazh)			
Partek, see Oy Partek AB			
Party of Economic Freedom, Novaya pl. 3/4 str. 2	262-3619		
Pasilak, see APV-Pasilak			
Passazh, see Petrovskiy Passazh			
Passport to the USSR, Novy Arbat 15	202-2285	202-6917	
Pasta House, Sadko Arcade (Expocenter)	255-2638	973-2185	
Patio Bar, Intourist Hotel	203-4008		
Patio Pizza, Volkhonka ul. 13A	201-5000		
Patriarchi Dom, Kozikhinskiy B. p. 17, #20	299-5971	230-2101	
Patrick's, Petrovskiy Passazh, 1st fl.			
Patriot Cinema, ul. Salyama Adilya 4	199-3888		
Paurat, Hotel Mezhdunarodnaya II, room 1739	253-1739	253-9381	
Paveletskiy Train Station, Paveletskaya pl. 1	235-0522		
Pavlovo-Posadskiy customs point	44-751		
PB-Technic, ul. Dorogomilovskaya 8	240-9076	243-3933	
PDN Company, Radisson-Slavyanskaya Hotel, #3025	941-8489	941-8659	
PC Center Techno, ul. Pervomaiskaya 126	461-8775	461-3514	
PCB Tools JV (Switzerland), ul. B. Pionerskaya, 4			
Peja Chemie/Aussenhandel,			
Krasnopresnenskaya nab. 12, Office 1704	253-2163	253-2161	413036
Peja Holding N.V., Pokrovskiy bul. 4/17, kv. 39	297-5813	200-1279	413207
Pekin in Moscow JV, ul. B. Sadovaya 1/7	209-1387	209-1863	
Peking Hotel, ul. B. Sadovaya 1/5	209-3400	200-1420	411661
Bierstube	209-4240		
Business Center	209-3323		
Peking Restaurant	209-1815		
Pencil Group, Pokrovskiy bul. 4/17, kv. 25	230-2955		
Penta Business Center,			
Olympic Penta Hotel, Olympiyskiy prosp. 18/1	971-6101	290-2597	
Pepper, Hamilton & Scheetz, Grokholskiy p. 19/27	280-5279	280-5518	
Peppino Conte, Krasnopresnenskaya nab. 1/2	205-3115	205-3225	
Pepsi-Cola International, Kutuzovskiy prosp. 17	243-9428	243-4576	413527
Perekop Cinema, ul. Kalanchevskaya 33	280-4077		
Perestelf Hardware Store,			
Kosmodemyankich Zoi i Alexandra 17/2	450-0896	450-1283	
Perestroika JV (Finland), ul. Kosmonavtov 2/4			
Peresvetov 4 Gallery, Peresvetov p. 4	275-2228		
Perfect Technologies Ltd.	401-0163	401-0163	
Pergamos JV, Simonovskiy Pr, 5/2	203-7815		

	Phone	Fax	Telex
Perkin-Elmer Corp., Leninskiy prosp.31	955-4449	952-7514	
Personnel Agency International, Shchipovskiy p. 1. 20	237-3643	230-7060	
Perspektiva Kronomarsk, 1st Dubrovskaya ul. 1			411766
Perviy Torgoviy Bank, Olympiyskiy prosp. 26	284-3031	974-1327	
Pervomayskiy Cinema, ul. Pervomayskaya 93/20	465-7575		
Pescatore Restaurant, prosp. Mira 36	280-2406	280-3582	
Pet Holding, Dmitrovskoye sh. 108, Lianozovo Hotel	484-7022	484-6413	411228
Peter Justensen, 4th ul. Marinoy Roshchi 12	971-1178	971-1178	
Peter's Place, Zemlyanoy val 72	298-3248		
Peter's Shop, Zemlyanoy val 72	298-3248		
Petraco Oil Co.Ltd.,			
Kotelnicheskaya nab.1/15, corp.B-V, office 363	227-4288	200-2282	
Petroexport, ul. Mosfilmovskaya 64	143-0471		
Petrofina, Novy Arbat 36, office 1319-1327	290-8988	290-8585	
Petrovskiy Passage, ul. Petrovka 10	923-6055		
Avon Cosmetics Store, 1st fl.			
Bosch Auto Parts Store, 1st fl.			
Copy Shop, 1st fl.	923-6055		
Di Style	292-4056		
Diadora Sporting Goods, 2nd fl.			
Etienne Aigner, 1st fl.			
Estee Lauder	923-6057		
Eve Fashion, 2nd fl.			
Flowers Shop, 1st fl.	924-9532		
Grant Clothing Store, 2nd fl.			
Hom Clothing Store, 1st fl.			
Interoko Drug Store, 2nd fl.	292-3451		
Klemm, 2nd fl.	921-3915		
La Victoria Clothing Store, 2nd fl.			
L'Oreal, 1st fl.			
Lux Bar, 2nd fl.	292-4003		
Office Equipment, 1st fl.			
Olbi Diplomat, 2nd fl.	924-5902		
Panasonic, 2nd fl.	923-7080		
Parker, 2nd fl.			
Patrick's, 1st fl.			
Pioneer Electronics Store, 2nd fl.			
Print Shop, 1st fl.			
Red Line, 1st fl.			
Ristorante Belfiore	924-6469		
Rosso di Libiege			
Russian Style Souvenirs, 1st fl.			
Samsonite, 2nd fl.			
Sima Clothing Store, 2nd fl.			
Sony, 2nd fl.			
Sunbreeze Electronics			
Temkas Clothing Store, 2nd fl.			
Valentin Yudashkin Salon			
Vossen Clothing Store, 2nd fl.			
Wolfgang Held, 1st fl.			
Yamaha Pianos, 2nd fl.			
Petrovskiy Park Tennis Club 36,			
Leningradskiy prosp. 36	212-8351		

	Phone	Fax	Telex
Pettina Hamburgers, ul. Kosmonavtov 2/4	286-5217	286-5531	
Peugeot Moscow, Leninskiy prosp. 2, 9th floor	231-1442	954-5395	414834
Pfizer Int'l (USA), VVTs, bldg. 5, prosp. Mira 120	181-7510	181-7538	
PGD JV (US), ul. Amurskaya 44	165-4892	975-2098	411787
Phargo-Moskva, Nikitskiy bul. 25	290-4556	230-2207	
Pharma-Eks JV (Sri-Lanka), ul. B. Pirogovskaya, 2/6	248-5153		
Pharmacy Rossiskaya, ul. Novy Arbat 31	205-2135	205-7545	
Phen Khuan Restaurant, ul. Sretenka 23/25	208-0654		
Pheonix International Radiology Inc., pl. Suvorova 2	281-0661	281-1800	
Phibro Energy, Pokrovskiy bul. 4/17, kv. 22	207-6265	975-2686	413219
Philadelphia Inquirer, ul. B. Dorogomilovskaya 14, kv. 6	243-4697	230-2842	413954
Philip Morris Companies Inc., Palashevskiy B. p. 13/2	973-2432	973-2435	
Philips', see N.V. Philips' Gloeilampenfabriken			
Phillip Morris, Palashevskiy B. p. 13/2	973-2431	973-2435	
Corp. Service, Inc., B. Dmitrovka 10	923-5620	923-5700	
Philosophocal Sciences Journal,			
Leninskiy prosp. 8, rm 301	236-9728		
Phoenicia Investments Ltd., ul. Volgina 6	336-2533	331-0511	
Phoenix Company Lt JV, ul. Buzheninova, 16	963-0180	963-5137	412243
Phoenix Engineering, Kozikhinskiy B. p. 22, str. 1, fl. 5	299-4345	200-6675	
Phoenix International, Suvorovskaya pl. 2	974-1031	974-1030	
Phoenix Overseas Limited,			
Hotel Mezhdunarodnaya II, room 1450	253-1319	253-9998	413710
Phoenix Publishing JV (France), ul. Tverskaya 6 str. 7	229-1161	229-3946	
Photo-ITAR TASS, Bryanskaya ul. 7	243-3903		411220
Photocenter, Gogolevskiy bul. 8	290-4188		
Piano Bar, Novotel Hotel, Sheremetyevo-II	578-9407		
Pilenga Godo JV Filial, pr. Cherepanovykh 72 k. 1	482-5803		
Pilgrim Tours, 1st Kirpichny p. 16	369-0389	369-0389	
Pinguin Ice Cream, Leninskiy prosp. 37	954-6466		
Nikolskaya ul. 4/5	927-1726		
Pioneer Cinema, Kutuzovskiy prosp. 21	249-2816		
Pioneer Electronics Store,			
Petrovskiy Passazh, 2nd fl.			
Pirelli, see Industrie Pirelli SpA			
Pirit, Kolomenskiy pr. 1A	112-7210	112-7210	
Pizza Hut Restaurant, Kutuzovskiy prosp. 17	243-1727		
ul. Tverskaya 12	229-2013		
Take-out, Kutuzovskiy prosp. 17	243-1727		
Pizza JV (Canada), ul. Marksistskaya 1/1	272-3828		
Pizza Pazza, Sadko Arcade (Expocenter)	940-4071		
Planeta Cinema, ul. Nezhinskaya 11	441-8201		
Planeta Publishers, ul. Petrovka 8/11	923-0470	200-5246	411733
Planetarium, ul. Sadovaya-Kudrinskaya 5	254-1838		
Planshop, Krasnopresnenskaya nab. 12	253-2773		
Plast-Service JV, ul. Pyatnitskaya 46, str. 2	231-2441	230-2295	911617
Playschool, ul. Tverskaya 28	214-9406	214-9406	
Playschool Moscow, Leninskiy prosp. 83 kv. 5	131-2471		
PLE Pipeline Engineering GmbH,			
Hotel Mezhdunarodnaya II, room 1739	253-1739	253-9381	
Plexsys International, ul. Tverskaya 16/2, #508	292-2092	200-0628	
Po Dvorye Restaurant, ul. Maroseyka 9	923-8949		
Pobeda Cinema, ul. Abelmanovskaya 17a	270-0321		

	Phone	Fax	Telex
Pochtoviy customs point, Varshavskoye sh. 37A	114-4581		
Podium International JV, Samokatnaya ul. 3/8, k. A	362-1819	362-1819	411700
Podmoskovye Travel Assn, Kalanchevskaya ul. 4/2	975-9545		
Podolskiy customs point	30-375		
Pokrovka Restaurant, ul. Maroseyka 4	923-0282		
Polar International Limited, Komsomolskiy prosp. 42	242-2279	230-2574	411619
Polar Star JV, see Polyarnaya Zvezda JV			
Polarny Cinema, ul. Polyarnaya 9	477-0033		
Polaroid Shop, Leninskiy prosp. 70/11	930-9627	938-2158	
Polaroid Studio Express, 70 Leninskiy prosp.			
Dmitrovka B. ul. 14			
Dobrininskaya pl. 36/71			
GUM, 3rd line			
Komsomolskiy prosp. 7			
Leningradskiy prosp. 33			
Leningradskiy prosp. 71			
Leninskiy prosp. 150			
Pyatnitskaya ul. 28			
Serpukhovskiy val 14			
Teatralny pr., Detskiy Mir			
Ukrainskiy bul. 7			
ul. Novy Arbat 30/9			
Vetoshny p. 5/4			
Poligrafresursy, ul. Petrovka 26	921-1971	200-6308	207787
Poligran, Pakgauznoye sh. 1	153-1021	154-5046	
Polish Airlines, see LOT Polish Airlines			
Polish School, ul. Mosfilmovskaya 60	147-1354		
Politiken, Rublyovskoye sh. 26, k. 1, kv. 118-119	415-2961		
Politizdat Publishers, Myusskaya pl. 7	251-4594	200-2254	
Polsib JV Filial, ul. Mosfilmovskaya 54	147-6488		
Polskaya Gvozdika, Leninskiy prosp. 79	134-5416		
Polyglot, ul. Rybalko 13	194-7781	946-9779	
Polyot, Vorontsovskaya 35a	274-0013	274-0022	411989
Polyot Cinema, ul. Nelidovskaya 10	492-8125		
Polytechnical Museum, Novaya pl. 3/4	923-0756		
Polyus International JV, ul. Varvarka, 8b	298-3398	361-4497	
Pony Express, Komsomolskiy prosp. 42, #206	245-9447	956-6078	
Port Service Ltd., ul. Michurinskaya 31/1	973-1346	251-8119	
Posad JV, Lyalin p. 21, str. 2	297-8825	929-8652	414519
Post Int'l, Inc., Pushkin Square, Novoe Vremya building	209-3118	200-4223	
Postfactum News Agency, Khoroshevskoye sh. 41	195-1820	255-9340	411712
Postipankki, Molochny p. 9/14, str. 3	201-3714	200-1289	413018
Potel et Chabot Restaurant, B. Kommunisticheskaya 2A	271-0707	274-0080	
Mezhdunarodnaya Hotel	253-2760		
Povtornovo Filma Cinema, Nikitskaya, B. ul. 23	202-4942		
Praga Restaurant Bakery, Arbatskaya pl.	290-6256		
Prague Cinema, ul. Zdeneka Neeldy 1	945-4211		
Prague Restaurant, ul. Arbat 2	290-6171		
Pralin JV, Leninskiy prosp. 8/6	954-7428	237-4802	
Pratt & Whitney Co., Pokrovskiy bul. 4/17, k. 3, office 5	208-9714	230-2713	
Pravda, ul. Pravdy 24	251-7386		
Pravda Cinema, ul. Lyusinovskaya 67	237-3665		
Pravda Publishers, ul. Pravdy 24	257-5111	200-2295	417529

	Phone	Fax	Telex
Prefecture of the			
Central District, Marksistskaya ul. 24	292-1635		
Eastern District, Preobrazhenskaya pl. 9	161-9887		
North-Eastern District, prosp. Mira 18	281-4385		
North-Western District, ul. Svobody 13/2	490-4438		
Northern District, Timiryazevskaya ul. 27	976-1008		
South-Eastern District, Aviamotornaya ul. 10	362-4288		
South-Western Dist., Sevastopolskiy prosp. 28, k. 4	128-2722		
Southern District, Avtozavodskaya ul. 10	275-0636		
Western District, ul. Ivana Franko 12	443-4335		
Premier SV, ul. Shchepkina 60/2, entr. A	281-4726	281-6215	
Premier SV-Print, Yeropkinskiy p. 16	201-3926	281-6215	
Preng & Associates, ul. Lyusinovskaya 72, kv. 50	952-7421	952-7421	
Prensa y Diplomacia, Rublyovskoye sh. 26, k. 1, kv. 294	415-4138	415-2936	413630
Present JV (Italy), ul. Koroleva 5	930-4118	930-3919	
President Hotel, ul. B. Yakimanka 24	238-7303	230-2216	412438
Presidium of the Russian Supreme Soviet,			
Krasnopresnenskaya nab. 2	205-6847		
Press and Book Shop, Leninskiy prosp. 113/1	206-9207		
Press Club, Radisson-Slavyanskaya Hotel	941-8051	941-8659	
Press Trust of India SPK,			
ul. B. Pereyaslavskaya 7, kv. 133-134	280-2749		413319
Press-Contact JV (France),			
ul. Marshala Novikova 10/1, k. 9	193-4281	943-0005	
Delovie Lyudi Mag., Profsoyuznaya ul. 73	333-3340	330-1568	414741
Pressa Publishers, ul. Pravdy 24	257-2884		
Prestige Radio, Radisson-Slavyanskaya Hotel, #6034-5	941-8811	941-8484	
Preussag AG, 4th Dobryninskiy p. 6/9	237-7035	230-2527	413363
Price, Helbig & Co., GUM Business Center, Red Sq. 3	921-7853	921-4609	
Price Waterhouse, B. Strochenovskiy p. 22/25	230-6185	230-6186	413866
Pride Taxi Service	451-0858		
Prima JV (Italy), Pleteshkovskiy p. 22	261-2675	975-2050	911570
Primary Industries Ltd. (UK),			
Zoologicheskaya 10, 3-d floor	956-3416	956-3419	
Primula Pharmacy, Ukrainskiy bul. 5	243-5119		
Princeton Alumni Association	241-7086		
Print and Stamp Shop, ul. Festivalnaya 13			
Print Shop, Petrovskiy Passazh, 1st fl. (see Passazh)			
Prioritet JV (US), see PRIS			
Priroda, Kutuzovskiy prosp. 5/3	243-5528		
PRIS JV (US), 1st Troitskiy p. 12/2, str. 4	284-8920	288-9513	413590
Privatization Committee	928-6213	928-6213	
Processor, prosp. Mira, VVTs	181-9240	187-4117	
Proco 75 SA,			
ul. Kosygina 15, Orlyonok Hotel, office 423-425	939-8420	938-2114	
Procordia, Krasnopresnenskaya nab. 12, Office 903	253-2980	253-9086	413921
Procter & Gamble, Pullman Iris Office Bldg.	244-2986	244-3035	
Prodintorg, ul. Smolenskaya-Sennaya 32/34	244-2629	244-2629	411206
Production Testing Services, ul. Nikolayeva 4/53	205-0129	205-0129	
Proektsofin JV (Finland), Komsomolskiy prosp. 42	245-6015	230-2574	411619
Professional Recruiting Group, ul. Petrovka 24	200-7521	200-5493	
Profil, ul. Donskaya 18/7, kv. 112	236-1296		
Prognoinfo JV (Hungary), ul. Sretenka 20/2	207-0003	207-0008	

	Phone	Fax	Telex
Programma 2000, p. Sivtsev-Vrazhek 15/25, kv. 123	241-3290	253-9711	
Programming Systems for Agr.JV (Bulgaria),			
B. Tishinskiy p. 8	254-4497		411614
Progress Bookstore, Zubovskiy bul. 17	246-9078		
Progress Cinema, Lomonosovskiy prosp. 17	133-1664		
Progress Publishers, Zubovskiy bul. 17	246-9032	230-2403	411800
Progress Trading Co., LTD, ul. Mytnaya 1, Office 30	230-1075	230-2226	413394
Progressor, Nakhimovskiy pr. 27	316-6901		
Project HOPE, Smidskiy pr. 29, Detskaya Bolnitsa #9	259-7990	253-9585	
Prokop JV (France), Leontyevskiy p. 24		200-2265	
Promed JV, Promyshlenniy pr., Kooperativ 'Volga3'	148-5557	148-5557	
Promen JV, ul. Vavilova, 38			
Prompt International, ul. Mayakovskaya 17/7	203-9945		
Promstroybank, Tverskoy bul. 13	200-7373	200-6507	411943
Promsyryeimport, Novinskiy bul. 13	203-0577	203-6177	411152
Prospect JV, Lesnaya ul. 13, kv. 12			
Protestant Services, See Moscow Protestant Chaplaincy			
Protsentkombank, ul. Bakhrushina 13 str. 1	231-9083	230-2939	
Provincias (Las), Krutitskiy val 3, k. 2, kv. 95	276-7146	274-0010	
Public Notary, Bobrov p. 6	923-6281		
Pullman Catering Service, Korovinskoye sh. 10	488-8279	906-0105	
Pullman Iris Hotel, Korovinskoye sh. 10	488-8000	906-0105	413656
Art Zone Gallery	488-8267		
Business Center	488-8104	906-0105	
Dental Clinic, The	488-8279		
Europcar	488-8000		
Francaise (La)	488-8000		
Iris Car Rental	488-8106		
K-Boutiques	488-8100		
Le Cafe Francais	488-8000		
Les Champs Elysees Restaurant	488-8000		
Pullman Hairdressers	488-8101		
Pulse Soft, ul. Burdenko 12	245-0406	246-4496	
Puma, Sadovaya-Spasskaya 19	975-1992		
Puolimatka International, Koroviy val 7, Office 14	230-1388	230-2810	413040
Pushkin Drama Theater, Tverskoy bul. 23	203-4221		
Pushkin Museum, ul. Prechistenka 12/2	202-3293		
Pushkin Museum of Fine Art, Volkhonka ul. 12	203-7998		
Puteshestviye v SSSR, see Travel Journal			
Putnik JV (Venezuela),			
B. Strochenovskiy p. 22/25, str. 1	237-5902	236-4493	414724
PVK JV (Bolivia), ul. Tverskaya 23, str.2			
PX Post, ul. Kuusinena 9, kv. 26	956-2230	956-2231	

Q

	Phone	Fax	Telex
Quality Products,			
B. Gnezdnikovskiy p. 10, floor 10, Room 2	229-8290	229-8487	
Que Pasa, see Dan News Agency			
Queen of Saba, ul. Tverskaya 9	229-2068		
Queen-Mosmebel JV (Egypt), ul. Garibaldi 26	128-7835	299-5676	412275
Queens, ul. Nizhegorodskaya 8	272-6680		

	Phone	Fax	Telex
Quelle Catalogue Sales, ul. B. Molchanovka 34, str 2	291-4735	200-2263	411775
Quest Automation PLC, Koroviy val 7, Office 4	236-2135	230-2488	413905
Quest Realty, Smolenskaya nab. 5/13, Suite 157	244-0527		
Quinta, B. Cherkasskiy p. 4, str. 1	923-1403	288-9501	
Quorum JV (US), ul. Yelanskovo 2	248-6822		

R

	Phone	Fax	Telex
R-Style, Simferopolskiy Proezd 5	316-9646		
R.C.B. Product Int'l JV (US), prosp. Mira 5, kv. 29a			
Rabotnitsa, Bumazhny pr. 14, 10th fl.	212-2039		
Racal Electronics PLC (UK),			
B. Strochenovskiy p.22/25, 1-st floor, office 102	230-6136	230-6124	
Radamer/Intourist JV, see Radisson Slavyanskaya Hotel			
Radial, B. Gruzinskaya ul. 20	254-1344	254-1344	
Radio 7, ul. Demyana Bednovo 24	946-6864	946-6456	
Radio Communications & Computers, PO Box 666	220-2818	230-1107	
Radio Communications International Corp. (RCI),			
VVTs, Transport Pavilion, prosp. Mira	181-6552	974-6039	
Radio Evropa Plus, ul. Akad. Koroleva 19	215-9938	217-8986	
Radio Maximum	200-1088		
Radio Nacional de Espana, Krutitskiy val 3, k. 2, kv. 93	276-6865	274-0006	
Radio Peking, ul. B. Pereyaslavskaya 7, kv. 105	280-8687		
Radio Rocks	116-4374	118-0974	
Radio Suisse Romande/Schweitzer Radio,			
Gruzinskiy p. 3, kv. 212	230-2443		413336
Radio-France & Television Francaise 1,			
Gruzinskiy p. 3, kv. 223	250-3122	253-9294	413322
Radioexport, ul. Myasnitskaya 35	923-7949	923-7941	411386
Radiotelevisione Italiana (RAI),			
prosp. Mira 74, kv. 160	280-7689	280-8289	413218
Radiotovary, prosp. Mira 27	280-3047		
Radisson Slavyanskaya Hotel, Berezhkovskaya nab. 2	941-8020	240-6915	612309
Amadeus Cafe	941-8333		
American Trade Center	941-8815	941-8376	
Americom Business Center	941-8427	941-8376	
Cezar's	941-8398		
Danata	941-8028		
Dialog Bank	941-8434	941-8424	
Entourage Beauty Salon	941-8157		
Exchange, The	941-8333		
Gzhel Store	941-8928		
International Press Center & Club	941-8621	941-8659	
Lobby Bar	941-8411		
Press Club	941-8051		
Skandia Restaurant	941-8020		
Slavyanskaya Health Club	941-8027		
Swimming Pool	941-8027		
Trussardi	941-8397		
Raduga, Mantulinskaya 5, Mezhdunarodnaya-II office 1447	253-1777	253-9703	413482
Raduga Car Service, 1st Dorozhny pr. 3a	315-3736		
Raduga Publishers, Zubovskiy bul. 17	245-0151	230-2403	411826

	Phone	Fax	Telex
Raiffeisen Zentralbank Austria,			
1st Krasnogvardeiskiy p., pavilion 2	256-7444		
Raketto-SU JV (Italy), Sredne-Ovchinnikovskiy p. 8	216-0885	216-3617	
Ralston Purina Co., Gruzinskiy p. 3, office 197	254-9978	200-4277	
Ramax JV (Holland), ul. Kedrova 20, kv. 1	301-1610		
Ramenskiy customs point/ 'Kuntsevo'	417-1324		
Ramsey Furniture, Uldatsova ul. 85	931-9207	931-9277	
Ranibo Ltd. (UK), Berezhkovskaya nab.4, office 143	240-6377	240-7012	
Rank Xerox Limited,			
ul. B.Yushunskaya 1a, corp.2, 15-th floor	237-6842	230-2728	413139
Rantarin JV Filial, Orlikov p. 3	204-4814		
Raritet, ul. Arbat 31	241-2381		
Rasma JV (Belgium), ul. Lesnaya 43	250-8763	288-9577	411273
Rassvet Cinema,			
ul. Zoi i Alexandra Kosmodemyanskikh 23	450-0213		
RAU, see Russian American University			
Rauma-Repola Oy, Mamonovskiy p. 6, kv. 8	209-2817	200-0214	413223
Rautaruukki Oy, see Valmet Oy			
Razgulyai Restaurant, ul. Spartakovskaya 11	267-7613		
Raznoexport, Verkhnyaya Krasnoselskaya 15	264-5656	268-9539	411408
Raznoimport, Ovchinnikovskaya nab. 18/1	220-1849	200-3218	411118
Raznoservice Coop, Oltufyevskiy p. 8a	246-9587		41118 R
Razvitie JV Filial (Australia), ul. Tyoply Stan 11, k. 1	338-1680	338-2033	
RCMI, Inc. , Dmitrovka M. ul. 15	209-9814	209-1398	
Real American Clothing Store, Leninskiy prosp. 36	137-6960		
Real Estate, Nikitskiy bul. 5/1	290-1457		
Realta Sovietica, ul. Chernyakhovskovo 8a, kv. 19	152-8317		
Recovery Treatment Ctr (AA), ul. D. Ulyanova 37/3	129-4366		
Red Cross and Red Crescent,			
Cheremushinskiy prosp. 5, 2nd fl.	230-6620	230-6622	
Red Line, Petrovskiy Passazh, 1st fl. (see Passazh)			
Red Lion Pub, Sovintsentr, Mezhdunarodnaya Hotel 1	253-2283	253-1482	
Red Square Business Center, GUM, 1st line, 2nd fl	921-0911	921-4609	
Red Square Productions,			
Kotelnicheskaya nab. 1/15, kv. 39 floor 8	227-4484		
Red Zone, Leningradskiy prosp. 39, TsSKA Ice Palace	212-1676	280-1942	
Redaktor, ul. Fadeyeva 2, kv. 262	251-9647		
Reebok Russia, pl. Suvorova 1, ent 2, off 464	281-7969	258-1660	
Referat, Basmanny tupik 10/12	263-1855		
Reformiz JV (FRG), ul. B. Semenovskaya 42	369-0260	369-0505	412298
Regie Nationale Des Usines Renault,			
Glazovskiy p. 7, kv. 12	202-0360		413327
REI Adventures, 1st Kerpichny p. 17a	365-4563		
Reichhold Chemie GmbH,			
Hotel Mezhdunarodnaya II, room 1736	253-1736	253-9302	
Rekon JV (Finland), ul. Dolgorukovskaya 26	973-0920	973-2198	
Rektime JV (Japan), ul. Gavrikova 3/1m, str. 1, kv. 98	264-2799	972-6250	
REM, Yaroslavskoye sh. 13			
Remy Martin Piano Bar, Sadko Arcade (Expocenter)	940-4065		
Rena, Mosk. Obl. P/O Mosrentgen	339-6021		411050
Renault, see Regie Nationale Des Usines Renault			
Rendezvous-Khungun JV (Hungary),			
Frunzenskaya nab. 36/2	242-4178		

	Phone	Fax	Telex
Renlund Biurobin, Ordynka M. ul. 37-39	237-7612	230-2523	
Renlund M, Stolyarny p. 3	253-4173		
Renova JV, Kashirskiy pr., 21	110-4895	110-4895	
REP, TsUM, 2nd fl.	292-4484	292-7540	
Reports of the Russian Academy of Sciences,			
Profsoyuznaya ul. 90, room 301	334-7380		
Representation of Tourist's Committee of Bulgaria,			
• Kuznetskiy Most 1/8	292-7042		414560
Rep. of UNO in Russia, ul. Seleznevskaya 11a	284-3220	973-1960	
Reprocenter (Rank Xerox), Kutuzovskiy prosp. 22	243-1290		
Ukraine Hotel	243-3007		
ul. Fadeyeva 1	181-2994	288-9561	411860
Republica (La), Kutuzovskiy prosp. 14, kv. 12	243-6778		413485
Republican Computer Center, ul. Krzhizhanovskovo 6	129-8166		
Rerikh Museum, ul. Marksa-Engelsa 5	203-6419		
Research & Commercial Medical Center JV,			
Sukharevskaya pl. 3	207-1425	207-0533	
Research Institute, ul. Taldemskaya 2	483-8474		
Resource, ul. Vorontsovo pole 3	297-2271	297-5273	
Rest-Ital, Vorotnikovskiy p. 11	299-2116	200-0251	413466
Restaurant Baltschug, Hotel Baltschug	230-6500	230-6502	414873
Resurs-Bank, 3rd Parkovaya ul. 24	306-7855		
Retatorg, Hotel Mezhdunarodnaya 2, room 826	253-9191	253-2825	411813
Retour Business Center, Savyolevskiy p. 6	202-7610	230-2535	
Reuters PLC, ul. Sadovaya-Samotechnaya 121	200-3948	200-2879	413342
Revertex Sales Ltd. (UK), Dmitrovka M. ul. 31/22, #8	299-2101	956-3271	
Reynolds International Inc., Leninskiy prosp. 2, floor 9	239-1028	954-5395	
Rheinische Post, Leninskiy prosp. 45, kv. 490	135-1358		413195
Rhone-Poulenc SA, ul. Mytnaya 1, Office 9	230-0232	230-20082	413117
RIA, see Russian Information Agency			
Riga Cinema, ul. Botanicheskaya 39	482-2360		
Rigas, Vtoroy Krestovskiy p. 79	281-1821		
Riglich Dina Market, Velozavodskaya ul. 3/2	275-6986		
Rikon JV, ul. B. Molchanovka 23	291-8000	291-8000	
Rimag Co., ul. Varvarka 15	206-3474	206-3067	
Rimos Pharma, Kashirskoye sh. 24	324-9624	324-9140	
Rimpex, Dmitrovka M. ul. 16	299-4012	973-2132	
RINAKO, see Russian Investment Joint Stock Company			
Rinako, Boss, Novaya Ploschad 3/4	262-4499		
Rinata Travel, ul. Zamarenova 5	252-3814	252-0263	
Ring Excel Technologies Group JV (Canada),			
1st Khoroshevskiy pr. 10, k. 2, podyezd 5	945-6128	200-2217	411700
Rio-Tinto Zinc Corporation (RTZ Corporation),			
B. Strochenovskiy p.22/25, office 102	230-6137	230-6176	
Ripol Publishing, ul. 1905 goda 3	259-7775	259-7775	
Ristorante Belfiore, Petrovskiy Passazh, ul. Petrovka 10	924-6469		
RITM Trading House, ul. Sadovaya-Spasskaya 19/2	262-1311	975-1297	
River Boat Tickets, Leningradskiy prosp. 1	257-7109		
Rizhskiy Train Station, Rizhskiy pl.	266-9535		
Rizospastis, ul. Krasnaya Presnya 23, kv. 178	252-2963		413153
RJR-Nabisco, Mytnaya ul. 1, entr. 1, floor 5, office 10	238-6085	230-1364	
Road Technologie Sam JV, ul. B. Pionerskaya 4			
Robert Bosch GMBH, ul. Mytnaya 4	230-6082	230-6081	413598

	Phone	Fax	Telex
Robin Hood Restaurant, ul. B. Gruzinskaya 42	254-0738		
Roche, see F. Hoffmann-La Roche LTD			
Rock and Jazz Laboratory, Staropanskiy p. 1/5	923-1604		
Rockall Ltd., Sofiyskaya nab. 35, office 5	238-9211	230-6077	
Rockwell International Corp.,			
B. Strochenovskiy p. 22/25, office 403	230-6010	230-6015	
Rodina	299-2096		
Rodina Cinema, Semyonovskaya pl. 5	369-1781		
Roditi, GUM, 3rd line, 1st fl.	921-1529		
Rolls-Royce of Moscow, ul. Mytnaya 11	237-7069	237-7681	
Rolls-Royce PLC, Mamonovskiy p. 4, kv. 12	209-6520	200-0207	413376
Roman Catholic Services,			
Kutuzovskiy prosp. 7/4, k. 5, kv. 42	243-9621		
Romanian Air Transport, ul. Mosfilmovskaya 64	143-2640	143-0449	578271
Sheremetevo 2 Airport	578-2716		
Romen Gypsy Theater, see Gypsy Theater Romen			
Romos JV, Staropanskiy p. 1/5	921-9392	200-3937	414745
Ronar Services Ltd., ul. Mytnaya 3, office 15	230-1853	230-7978	
Ros-Marketing JV (FRG), Lubyanskaya pl. 22	923-2045	921-6367	
Rosart Amorim JV (Portugal), Vorontsovskiy p. 5/7	272-3990		
Rosartson, 2nd Baumanskaya 9/23, Kor. 18	265-7094	265-7092	
Rosavtobirzha, see Russian Auto Exchange			
Rosavtoservis, Volgogradskiy prosp. 139	172-8781	172-6822	
Rosbiznessbank, Tryokhprudny p. 9	299-5771	299-0322	
Rosbri International Ltd. JV (UK), Garazhnaya ul. 6	366-8110	366-7877	412389
Rosenberg & Lenhart, GUM, 1st line, 1st fl.			
Rosenlew, see Imatran Voima Oy			
Rosfratex, Milyutinskiy p. 13/4	921-2557	921-2557	
Rosgosstrakh, Nastasinskiy p.3, k. 2	299-8945	200-4202	
Neglinnaya ul. 23	200-2995	200-5041	
Rosie O'Grady's, ul. Znamenka 9	203-9087	921-4660	
Rosinka, Leningradskiy prosp. 39	213-6661	213-7210	
Rosinkas, Sretenskiy bul. 1/4	928-3030		
Rosinter Teatr JV (USA), Strastnoy bul. 10	248-3540	230-2259	
Rosinterbank, Orlikov p. 3	204-4350	975-2459	411021
RosInterTeatr JV (USA), Strastnoy bul. 10	924-5496		411738
Roskomagenstvo, Yaroslavskoye sh. 5	182-2117	1889674	
Roslegprom Association, Zubovskiy bul. 2/39	246-3343		411621
Roslesbirzha, see Russian Forestry Exchange			
Rosneft, Sofiyskaya nab. 26/1	239-8800	239-8802	211512
Rosneftegazstroy Concern, Zhitnaya ul. 14	239-1005	238-7512	411979
Rospromstroybank, prosp. Mira 84	281-8936		
Rosrechflot Concern, ul. Petrovka 3/6	927-8373	927-8706	
Rosselkhozbank, ul. Neglinnaya 12	923-1032	921-7646	412301
Rossiya Cinema, Pushkinskaya pl. 2	229-2111		
Rossiya Concert Hall, Moskvoretskaya nab. 1	298-1124		
Rossiya Hotel, ul. Varvarka 6	298-5400		
Baskin Robbins	298-3594		
Beriozka	298-3620		
Intourservice	298-1173		
Intourservice Car Rental	298-5853		
Jever-Bistro	298-2923		
Manhattan Express	298-5355		

Corporate Forwarding
Your partner in the former USSR

Air Shipments
Daily Air consolidation to all major cities. From small parcels to Truckloads and full charter shipments.

Ocean Shipments
Our specialty is auto shipments.
Ocean containers, break bulk & LTL.
Weekly Express Service to all major points and ports.

Door to Door Service
Including pick up throughout the CIS, Baltics, USA, Europe, Hong Kong, Brazil, Mexico and other regions.

Storage
Bonded, high-security storage in Moscow, St. Petersburg, Tallinn, Riga, Odessa and other cities. Packing, sorting, distribution and on site-inspection.

Documentation
All air and ocean shipping documents, customs clearance. We submit letter of credit documentation to your bank.

Corporate Forwarding, Inc.
102 Southfield Ave.
Stamford Landing
Stamford, CT 06902 USA
ph. (203) 353-1441
fax (203) 353-1497
tlx 4961 4503 CORPFWDG

	Phone	Fax	Telex
Rossiya Restaurant	298-4133		
Tokyo Restaurant	298-5707		
Rossiya JV (USA), Neglinnaya ul. 6/2	924-4754		
Rossiya Restaurant, Hotel Rossiya	298-4133		
Rossiyanka Hotel, ul. Donskaya 1	238-0508		
Rossiyskoye Investitsionnoye Aktsionernoye			
Obshchestvo, see Russian Investment Joint Stock Company			
Rosskommunbank, ul. Myasnitskaya 13	290-6036	202-5070	
Rosso di Libiege, Petrovskiy Passazh, 2nd fl.			
Rossoyuzmestprom, ul. Krzhizhanovskovo 21/33	124-7642		
Rossteclo JV (FRG), ul. Kedrova 15	129-0909	129-1127	
Rostekhexport, Ovchinnikovskaya nab. 18/1	233-9081		
Rostik's, GUM, 3rd line, 2nd fl.	921-1529		
Rosvneshtorg, Barrikadnaya 8/5	255-1342	253-9576	411060
Rosvostokstroi, prosp. Vernadskovo 41	430-8809		
Rotel-Mikma JV (Switz.), M. Cherkizovskaya ul. 66	168-3796	975-2047	
Rotterdam Consult, Novy Arbat 16, #10	291-0677	291-0677	
Rovina Andorra, S.L., Balaklavskiy prosp. 5a	316-0590		
Rovstar JV, ul. Ilyinka 3/8,Strynie 1	925-0265		
Roy International Consultancy, Smolenskiy bul. 4, #11	246-4439	246-7955	411610
Royal Jordanian Air, Sheremetevo 2 Airport	578-2761		
Royal Zenith Hotel, Tamanskaya ul. 49 B	199-8001	199-8101	612623
Rozec Advertising Agency JV Filial,			
Sushchyovskiy val 50	289-0346	216-4714	
Rozec Car Rental, ul. Kulakova 20	233-2202		
Rozec JV, ul. Dovatora 13	245-4661		
RR Translations, B. Kondratyevskiy p. 4, kv. 168	254-9275	254-9275	
RT International Corp., ul. Kirova 13 str. 4	975-2610		
Rubens Gallery of Modern Art,			
Verkhnyaya Krasnoselskaya ul. 34	278-2584		
Rubicon International Ltd., ul. Letchika Babuskina 26	186-5301	470-8274	
Rubicon International Ltd. – Showroom,			
prosp. Andropova 22/30	186-5301		
Rubin Cinema, ul. Nizhegorodskaya 76	278-2584		
RUI a.r., see Apple Computer			
Rundfunk Nachrichten Agentur (RUFA),			
Leninskiy prosp. 148, kv. 117	938-2109	938-2185	413666
Rus, Sovintsentr, Mezhdunarodnaya Hotel I, 1st fl.	253-1785		
Rus Implant, 1st Tverskoy-Yamskoy p. 18/3	251-5369	251-5447	
Rus Restaurant,			
Krasnozvozdnaya 13, Saltykova Settlement	524-4202	524-2311	
Rus-Ellada JV (Greece), Banny p. 3a	284-3138		
Rus-H Supermarket, Novy Arbat 26 (Dom Knigi)			
Rusalochka (Little Mermaid) Restaurant,			
Smolenskiy bul. 12	248-4438		
Ruscan JV (Canada), Smolenskaya-Sennaya pl. 27/29	244-0568		
Ruscom, Presnenskiy val 19	252-0671	252-0785	
Rusganza JV (UK), see Intercontact Agroservice JV			
Rushmin Trust & Trade JV, ul. Dubininskaya, 17a			
Ruslan cafe, Vorontsovskaya 32/36	272-0632		
RusLan Shop, Smolenskaya-Sennaya pl. 27/29	244-0568		
Ruslit Publishers, Kutuzovskiy prosp. 1	243-4043		
RusOtel JV (US), Varshavskoye sh., 21st km	382-0586	382-2162	

	Phone	Fax	Telex
Russia, Government of, Information Department	206-4547		
Administration, Staraya pl. 4	206-5064	206-2431	
Council of Ministers, Krasnopresnenskaya nab. 2	205-5432		
Deputy Prime Minister, Staraya pl. 4	206-2171	206-3528	
First Deputy Prime Minister, Staraya pl. 4	206-2629	206-2183	
First Prime Minister, Staraya pl. 4	206-2629	206-2183	
Prime Minister, Kremlin	244-1886	206-3961	
Prime Minister's Administration,			
Government Information Service	205-4601		
Prime Minister's Admin., Information Department	928-3949		
Prime Minister's Administration, Staraya pl. 4	206-5064	206-2431	
Supreme Court (Criminal Division), ul. Ilyinka 3/7	925-2582		
(General Division), ul. Ilyinka 3/7	928-9766		
(Reception), ul. Ilyinka 3/7	921-3624		
Russian Academic Youth Theater, Teatralnaya pl. 2	292-6572		
Russian Academy of			
Arts, ul. Prechistenka 21	201-4031	201-7810	
Education, Pogodinskaya 8	245-1641		
Medical Sciences, ul. Solyanka 14	297-0504	297-0869	
Music, Nozhovy p. 1	290-6737		
Sciences, Leninskiy prosp. 14	234-2153		
Russian American University, Tverskoy bul. 7/2	496-4114		
Russian Archives Service, P.O. Box 27			
Russian Army Theater, Suvorovskaya pl. 2	281-5120		
Russian Bank for Foreign Trade, Kuznetskiy Most 16	921-3525	928-7262	
Russian Business Center, Staromonetny p. 33 kv. 2	238-8389		
Russian Business Monitor, Dynamovskaya ul. 1a	278-5485	276-5465	
Russian Club, Voznesenskiy p. 7	291-6965		
Russian Club of Young Millionaires,			
Leninskiy prosp. 45	137-0006	137-6525	
Russian Commerce Agency	246-4763		
Russian Commission for Humanitarian Assistance,			
ul. Vozdvizhenka 18	290-0903		
Russian Committee for			
Bread Products, ul. Krzhizhanovskovo 6	129-6436		
Fisheries, Rozhdestvenskiy bul. 12	923-7634		
Foreign Economic Relations,			
Ovchinnikovskaya nab. 18/1	220-1214		
Solidarity with Asia & Africa, ul. Prechistenka 10	202-4314	202-4258	
Veterans of War, Gogolevskiy bul. 4	202-5952		
Russian Commodity and Raw Materials Exchange,			
Novaya pl. 3/4	262-8080	262-5757	
Russian Credit Association, Leningradskoye sh. 84	452-1143	459-2047	
Russian Culture Guide, see Soviet Culture Guide			
Russian Enamel Miniatures	336-3444	335-8388	
Russian Federation Chamber of Commerce,			
ul. Ilyinka 6	924-5645		
Russian Fish Exchange, VVTs, prosp. Mira 120	181-0918		
Russian Forestry Exchange (Roslesbirzha),			
B. Kisselny p. 13/15	923-3350		
Russian Fur and Leather Commodity Exchange,			
Kolpachny p. 14	227-1013		
Russian Gov't Financial Academy, ul. Kibalchicha 1	283-7961		

	Phone	Fax	Telex
Russian Hall Restaurant, ul. Tverskaya 3	203-0150		
Russian Information Services,			
B. Kondratyevskiy p. 4, kor. 2, kv. 168	254-9275	254-9275	
Russian Int'l Cultural Fund, Gogolevskiy bul. 6	202-6984	200-1238	
Russian Investment and Joint Stock Company,			
Novaya pl. 3/4, entr. 6	936-0766	936-7545	
Russian Kompozitor Publishing Association,			
ul. Sadovaya-Triumfalnaya 14-12	209-2384		
Russian Language Studies Ctr JV, 2nd Minaevskiy p. 2	972-6200		411798
Russian Library Concert Hall, ul. Vozdvizhenka 3			
Russian Merchant Trade House 'Lan',			
B. Dekabrskaya ul. 6	253-4294	253-4294	
Russian Orthodox Patriarchate (Info. Center),			
ul. Pogodinskaya 20	245-2013		
Russian Petroleum Investor, Novy Arbat 19, kv. 828	203-9552	203-7821	
Russian Press Service Agency, Pitinkovskiy p. 1/2	209-7652	209-9612	
Russian Real Estate	244-2565	244-2556	
Russian Real Estate Exchange,			
see All Russian Real Estate Exchange JV			
Russian State Fuel Association,			
ul. Sadovaya-Chernogryazskaya 8	207-3370		
Russian State Library, ul. Vozdvizhenka 3	202-5790		
Russian Style Souvenirs, Petrovskiy Passazh, 1st fl.			
Russian Television and Radio, ul. Myasnitskaya 13, k. 4			
Russian Travel Monthly,			
B. Kondratyevskiy p. 4, kor. 2, kv. 168	254-9275	254-9275	
Russian-American Press and Information Center,			
Khlebny p. 2/3, West Wing	203-5724	203-6831	
Russian-European Insurance Co. (RESO),			
PO Box 33	238-0467	238-3578	
Russian-Italian Foundation, Michurinskiy prosp. 1	146-7001		
Russica Information Inc., Vinnitskaya ul. 4	932-4760	932-6300	
Russin & Vecchi,			
Danilov Hotel Complex, 5 Bol. Starodanilovskiy p.	954-0652	954-0653	
Russkaya Izba, Ilyinskoye Village	561-4244		
Russkaya Troyka, ul. Kosygina 15, Hotel Orlyonok	939-8683		
Russkiy Strakhovoy Bank, see Russian Trading Bank			
Russkiy Yazyk Publishers, Staropanskiy p. 1/5	928-3755	928-8906	411603
Russkoye Naslediye (Russian Heritage),			
1 st Neopalimovskiy p. 4	244-0106	253-9390	
Russkoye Voisko, see Fifth Floor Studio			
Russkiy Traktir Restaurant, ul. Arbat 44	241-9853		
RussLan JV (US), ul. Miklukho-Maklaya 21, blok 9	299-1549	299-1206	411640
Rutherfoord International	332-1623		
Rybcomflot JV, Rozhdestvenskiy bul. 9	925-8750		411208
Ryleeva 9 cafe, Gagarinskiy p. 9/5	291-6063		
Ryugen, ul. Malygina 9a	474-4433		
RZB: Raiffeisen Zentralbank Austria	256-7444		

S

	Phone	Fax	Telex
S & D Chemicals Ltd., B. Tishinskiy p. 43, office 30	253-5154	253-5154	
S.C. Inc. Freight Forwarders	229-1379	229-6689	
S3 Technologies JV (US), ul. Ferganskaya 25	377-0206		
Saab, Swedish Embassy	147-9009		
Saab Service, Volgogradskiy prosp. 177	379-6245		
Saaek JV (Finland), ul. Tverskaya 23	299-6519	253-9794	411238
SAAEK JV (US), ul. M. Bronnaya 26	202-3876		
Sab-Scray, Inc. JV (US), Romanov p. 2, k. 1	203-7631	203-6023	
Sabena Belgian World Airlines, Sheremetevo 2	578-2713		
Sabin Metal Corporation, ul. 1812 Goda 2, kv. 57	148-9116	148-9116	
Sacramento Bee, Povarskaya ul. 23a, kv. 3	291-6064		
Sadko, Kutuzovskiy prosp. 9	243-3730		
ul. B. Dorogomilovskaya 16	243-7501		
Sadko Arcade, Krasnogvardeyskiy pr. 1, Expocenter	259-5656	973-2185	
Beer House	940-4062		
Boys and Girls	253-9588		
Brown Bear Bar	255-2742		
Charles Jourdan	253-9592		
Chicken Grill	255-2638		
Coffee House (Pizza Pazza)	940-4071		
Do It Yourself	253-9588		
Donna	253-9588		
Drug Store	253-9592		
Foodland	256-2213		
Pasta House	255-2638		
Pizza Pazza	940-4071		
Remy Martin Piano Bar	940-4065		
Steak House	256-2206		
Swiss Bakery	940-4068		
Swiss Butchery	940-4068		
Swiss House Restaurant	940-4069		
Swiss Pastry Shop	253-9592		
Top Sport	253-9588		
Trattoria Restaurant	940-4066		
Wedgewood	253-9588		
Young Fashion	253-9592		
Sadko Distribution, Krasnogvardeyskiy pr., 1	255-2650	973-2185	
Sadovniki Gallery, ul. Akad. Millionshchikova 35	112-1161		
SAGMAR, ul. Sr. Pereyaslavskaya 14, kv. 111, 144	971-1726		413305
Sais JV (US), ul. Menogina 4	259-8261	292-6511	
Sako-200 JV, ul. Vavilova, 53, korp. 1			
Sakura, ul. Tverskaya 15	229-3709		
Sakura Restaurant, Hotel Mezhdunarodnaya	253-2894		
Salamander, GUM, 1st line, 2nd fl.			
Salans, Hertzfeld & Heilbronn, Gazetny p. 17/9	940-2944	940-2806	
Salentini, Dokuchayev p. 13	207-5607	292-6511	
ul. Tverskaya 37	973-3846		
Salma Service Center, Zelyony prosp. 2/19	306-0283		
Salomon Inc., see Philipp Brothers Inc.			
Salonen Oy, see O Salonen Oy			

	Phone	Fax	Telex
Salvation Army, Slavyanskaya pl. 4, str 1	213-8392	924-9169	
Salyut Cinema, ul. Kedrova 14, k. 3	125-0135		
Salyut Hotel, Leninskiy prosp. 158	438-6565		
Salzgitter AG, 4th Dobryninskiy p. 6/9, 4th fl.	237-7035	230-2527	413363
Saman JV (US), Ryazanskiy prosp. 99, k. 3	174-5754	273-8560	
Samer JV (Cyprus), Stremyanny p. 28	237-8351		
Sametko JV (UK), Rublyovskoye sh. 26, k. 1, kv. 305	415-4241	415-4080	412181
Samos JV (Poland), Komsomolskiy prosp. 7	202-5955		
Samsonite, GUM, 1st line, 2nd fl.	926-3466		
Petrovskiy Passazh, 2nd fl.			
Samsung Co., Ltd.,			
Krasnopresnenskaya nab. 12, Office 1104	253-2671	253-2670	413607
Samsung-Glavortsnab JV, Leninskiy prosp. 90/2	131-2288	248-0814	
Samtes JV, 2nd Kozhevnicheskiy p. 4/6	235-3674	235-5267	411602
Samuel M. Spiro & Associates	272-4101		
San Francisco in Moscow, Komsomolskiy prosp. 15	246-2142		
San Giacomo Furniture, Shyolkovskoye sh. 7	167-2527		
San Paolo, see Instituto Bancario San Paolo di Torino			
Sana Medical Center JV (France),			
ul. Nizhnyaya Pervomayskaya 65	464-1254	464-4563	412240
Sandoz A.G., Glazovskiy p. 7, kv. 4	203-1043	253-9511	413380
Sandunovskaya Sauna, Sandunovskiy p. 1a	925-4631		
Sandvik AB, ul. Usacheva 35	245-5770	245-1383	416913
Sankei Shimbun, ul. Sadovaya-Samotechnaya 12/24, kv. 6	200-2208	200-0220	413385
Sankyon Ltd., ul. Profsoyuznaya 23	120-5050	120-4157	411687
Sannibul JV, Tsvetnoy bul. 11	209-2639	200-1095	
Sanofi, see Elf Aquitaine			
Sanoma Publ'ns., ul. 26 Bakinskikh Komissarov 9, kv. 5	434-3685	230-2421	413053
Santa International JV (FRG), Dmitrovka M. ul. 8	200-2111	200-4208	
Santa Lucia Bar, Hotel Intourist, 3rd floor	203-1632		
Saor JV (Lebanon), sh. Entuziastov 36	273-4056		207348
SAP JV (US), 1st Vrazhskiy p. 4a	450-9391		
Sapporo Restaurant, prosp. Mira 12	207-8253		
Sarp JV (Austria), Patriarshiy B. p. 7	291-5989		
Sarpinservis, ul. Nikolskaya 5/1	923-1739		
SAS, see Scandinavian Airlines			
Satire Theater, B. Sadovaya 18	299-9042		
Satirikon Theater, Sheremetevskaya ul. 8	289-7844		
Satra Aerospace, Leningradskiy prosp. 45/5	157-3258	157-3616	
Satra Automotive, Tryokhprudny p. 11/13	299-9169	200-0250	413360
Satra Corporation, Tryokhprudny p. 11/13	299-9169	200-0250	413360
Sattarov & Co. Trading House,			
ul. M. Gruzinskaya 52/a-54	253-4269	255-9729	
Saturn Cinema, ul. Snezhnaya 18	180-4352		
Saturn-Comfort JV (Poland), ul. Shchipok 2	230-1088		41653 P
Saturn-Inmet, ul. Panfilova 20	198-4254		
SAV Entertain'mt JV (Canada), Olympiyskiy prosp. 16	288-1422	975-2003	411030
Savio, Krasnopresnenskaya nab. 12, Office 1302	253-2084	230-2723	413940
Savoy Club, ul. Dovzhenko 1, Tumba Golf Club	147-7368		
Savoy Hotel, ul. Rozhdestvenka 3	929-8500	230-2186	411620
Business Center	928-3780	230-2186	
Casino Savoy Club	929-8500		
Dry Cleaning	929-8693		

	Phone	Fax	Telex
Hermitage	929-8577		
Savoy Art Gallery	929-8660		
Savoy Restaurant	929-8600		
Travel Club	929-8559	928-3780	
Savva Car Land, ul. Energeticheskaya 6	362-7264	362-0703	
Savyolovskiy Train Station, pl. Savyolovskovo Vokzala	285-9000		
Sayani Cinema, ul. Sayanskaya 9	307-1864		
Sayani Hotel, Yaroslavskoye sh. 116, k. 2	183-1456		
Sayat-Nova cafe, ul. Yasnogorskaya 17, k. 1	426-9011		
SB EuroGroup JV (FRG), Trubnikovskiy p. 29/31	232-4787		
SB-Engineering JV (Sweden), Patriarshiy B. p. 3	204-7090	230-2940	207633
Sberegatelny Bank of Russia, ul. Seleznevskaya, 40	284-4043	281-9333	412487
Head Office	928-2620	928-2620	
Anadyrskiy prosp. 21	472-6786		
Astrakhanskiy p. 10\36	280-9616		
B. Andronievskaya 18/6	298-1152	298-1713	911555
B. Tulskaya ul. 2	236-3587		
Bakuninskaya ul. 48	265-4535		
Delegatskaya ul. 11	973-3657		
Dmitrovskoye sh. 64, kor. 2	487-5359		
Serpukhovskaya pl. 36	237-4261		
Leningradskoye sh. 84	452-5757		
Leninskiy prospect 64\2	137-2072		
Luganskaya ul. 5	322-3602		
Neglinnaya ul. 12	925-2075		
Nemanskiy pr. 9	942-3624		
Novaya ul. 10a	906-0750		
Novogirevskaya ul. 50	368-6533		
Olympiyskiy prosp. 10, k. 2	288-4678		
Profsoyuznaya ul. 20/9	125-0128		
Profsoyuznaya ul. 43 korp.2	331-3101		
Slavyanskiy bul. 3	445-1175		
Sredne-Pervomayskaya ul. 38/7	965-7555		
Leontyevskiy p. 14			
Trubnikovskiy p. 29/31	290-5477		
ul. Aviamotornaya 51	273-5248		
Dmitrovka M. ul. 15	299-9085		
ul. Chertanovskaya 32, k. 1	314-6111		
ul. Gvozdeva 7/4	272-2110		
ul. Lobachevskovo 2	432-9610		
ul. Obrucheva 28, k. 5	434-6605		
ul. Pyatidesatiletiya Oktyabrya 11	435-9652		
ul. Sovyetskoy Armii 17	289-1281		
ul. Stromynka 19	269-4433		
ul. Svobody 65	497-6609		
Volgogradskiy prosp. 1	276-3301		
Yunikh Lenintsev ul. 37	179-7179		
Zubovskiy bul. 13			
SBF Creative Union JV, ul. Druzhinnikovskaya 15	205-1392	205-2680	411070
SBS Business School	155-0789	155-0168	
Scan-Cargo, Institutskiy p. 2/1	200-1522		411310
Butovo	548-7144		411310

	Phone	Fax	Telex
Scandecor, Detskiy Mir, 4th floor			
Scandinavian Airlines, Kuznetskiy Most 3	925-4747	230-2142	413468
Sheremetevo 2 Airport	578-2727		413077
Scanflot-Scanior Design, ul. Biryuzovaya 19	194-8811		
Schenck, see Carl Schenck AG			
Schiess AG Lentjes AG,			
Krasnopresnenskaya nab. 12. Office 1502	253-2460		413646
Schreiber, see Ulrich Schreiber			
Schwing/Stetter Baumaschinen-Fabriken,			
Hotel Soyuz II, room 243	256-1930	253-9779	143722
Scientific & Technical Exchange Center JV,			
Nakhimovskiy prosp. 32	129-6491	310-7015	
Scientific Research Institute (VNIIKI), p. Granatny 4	290-3596	230-2598	
Scientific-Technological Engineering JV,			
Sechenovskiy p. 6	229-3937	200-3277	411354
SCM Center (Julius Meinl), Varshavskoye sh. 46	111-2200	111-7710	
SCOA Groupe, see Olivier S.A.			
Scorpio Cash & Carry, Berezhkovskaya nab. 8	240-2264		
Dubininskaya ul. 10	481-2400		
Zaporozhskaya ul. 1	449-7791		
Scorpio Trade Center, Kutuzovskiy pr. 17	207-9815	445-3920	
Scott-European Co.,			
Krasnopresnenskaya nab. 12, Office 501	253-1094	253-9382	411813
Scottish Equipment Suppliers LTD,			
Radisson-Slavyanskaya Hotel, #6028	941-8406	941-8407	
Screen JV, ul. Vasilyevskaya 13	251-3018	251-3641	411939
Scriabin Museum, Nikopeskovskiy B. p. 11	241-0303		
SDS	258-0149		
Seabeco Group, Hotel Mezhdunarodnaya 2, room 1647	255-6541	230-2821	413508
Seagram Co.	292-3191	292-7595	
SeaLand Service, Inc., ul. Petrovka 20/1	200-3588	200-3446	
Seawise, Karmanny p. 9	241-8770		
SEBA Spectrum JV, ul. Usacheva 35	245-5480	245-5070	411554
Secondex JV (UK), 2nd Botkinskiy pr. 5	259-4527	200-2216	
Security Formula, Kolpachny p. 7	925-6380	925-1607	613013
Sedgwick Russia Ltd., Park Place, Leninskiy prosp. 113/1	956-5055		
Sedmoye Nebo,			
Ostankino Tower, ul. Akademika Korolyova 15	282-2293		
Seeker (Iskatel), Novodmitrovskaya ul 5A	285-8884	285-8010	
Sefameks Soviet Export Film Ameks, Kalashny p. 14	290-6665	200-1256	411143
Segol, Ltd., Leningradskoye sh. #116	262-1452	292-6511	
Seibolt-Analit JV (Finland), Balaklavskiy prosp. 28B	318-9236	310-7067	
Seibu International Trading LTD,			
Krasnopresnenskaya nab. 12, Office 702a	253-1255	253-1259	413191
Seidel, Hotel Mezhdunarodnaya II, room 1142	253-1017		
Sekom JV, ul. Skladochnaya 6			
Selkhozpromexport, Ovchinnikovskaya nab. 18/1	220-1692	923-9364	411933
Selskaya Zhizn, ul. Pravdy 24	257-2963		
Semiramis JV (FRG), Oruzheyny p. 15, str. 1	972-1261	251-1889	
Seoul Plaza, Serpukhovskiy val 14	952-8254		
Separs JV, see Moscow Interregional Commercial Bank			
Sept JV, ul. Nametkina 10a	172-9708	331-4777	

	Phone	Fax	Telex
SER (Sociedad Espanola de Radiodifusion),			
Gruzinskiy p. 3, kv. 266	250-4165		413013
Serco JV (FRG), ul. 3rd Kabelnaya 1	200-3510		
Serebryany Slonyonok cafe, Bolotnikovskaya 52	121-2011		
Serebryany Vek, Teatralny pr. 3	926-1352		
Sergievo-Posadskiy customs point	447-51		
Serinter, Sadovnicheskaya ul. 77 k. 2	231-3094	233-2646	
Serpukhovskaya Zastava, see Diana			
Serpukhovskiy customs point	07-980		
Serso JV (FRG), Milyutinskiy p. 14	928-2381	928-3335	
Serveko JV (Switz.), ul. Marshala Biryuzova 1	229-7542	200-3214	412254
Service 11 (Sluzhba 11) Air Charter Agency,			
ul. Profsoyuznaya 98 korp.1 kv.294	330-7508	335-6320	411182
Service A.N. Dry Cleaning	248-1573		
Service Center Int'l JV (Austria), Noviy Arbat 17	203-7323	290-4519	
Service Exhibit, ul. Pokrovka 43, str. 1	925-7129	292-6511	411700
Service Globus (US), B. Kommunisticheskaya 1/5	298-6146	298-6149	
Sheremetevo 2 Airport	578-7534	578-4650	
Service Station No. 7, 2nd Selskokhozyaystvenny pr. 6	181-1374		
Service Vang JV (Austria), Komsomolskiy prosp. 1/1	112-3411	112-1380	
Service-Resource, ul. Aviamotornaya, 44	273-1733		
Servicenter International (Austria), Novy Arbat 25	203-7407	290-4519	911633
Servoimport, ul. Profsoyuznaya 88/20	335-4987	330-1555	
Setek JV (FRG), Volzhskiy bul. 19	178-8011	128-9723	411700
Seti JV (UK), Nikitskaya M. ul. 27	202-5611	200-1213	411153
Sevastopol Cinema, B. Cherkizovskaya 93	161-5301		
Sevastopol Hotel, ul. Yushunskaya 1a	318-2263		
Casino Ralina	318-6474		
Seventh Day Adventists, M. Tryokhsvyatitelskiy p. 3	297-0568		
Services	297-5167		
Sever Cinema, ul. Bazhova 9	181-2044		
Severnaya Hotel, ul. Sushchyovskiy val 50	289-6413		
Sevodnya Gallery, ul. Arbat 35	241-0209		
Sexton FOZD, 1st Baltiyskiy p. 6/21, corp. 2	237-5477		
Sezam JV, Shlyuzovaya nab. 8	183-5047	183-4374	
SFAO JV (France), Leningradskoye sh. 61a	459-7444	292-6511	411968
SFS JV (Finland), prosp. Andropova 1/2	118-0854		411700
SGS, see Societe Generale De Surveillance			
Shablen-Shop, Frunzenskaya nab. 30, pav. 12	242-8953	238-2033	
Shadow Theater, Izmaylovskiy bul. 60/10	465-6592		
Shaeffer Shop, see Interoko			
Shaines & McEachern, Michurinskiy prosp. 14A	437-6667	437-5422	
Shakovskaya House, Nikitskaya, B. ul. 19	201-6408		
Shalom Jewish Theater, Varshavskoye sh. 71	113-2753		
Shalyapin House Museum, Novinskiy bul. 25	444-0306		
Shamrock Bar, Arbat Irish House, ul. Novy Arbat 19	291-7641		
Sharp, GUM, 3rd line, 1st fl.	926-3455		
Sheldon Trading Co., ul. Krasnaya Presnya 6/2, office 10	252-3430	252-3430	
Shell International Petroleum Co., Ltd,			
Trubnikovskiy per 30a	956-6000	956-6010	612343
Sheremetevo 2 Airport	578-5614		
Sheremetevo Airport Business Center,			
see Telesource Business Center			

	Phone	Fax	Telex
Sheremetevo Customs Point, Sheremetevo 2 Airport	578-2120		
Sheremetevo Hotel, Sheremetevo 2 Airport	578-7663		
Shimadzu Europa GmbH, Hotel Belgrade, room 1805	248-2463		
Shkola Dramaticheskovo Isskustva, Povarskaya ul. 20	290-5888		
SHRM International,			
Korovinskoye sh. 10, Pullman Office Complex, Entr2	906-0991	906-0996	
Shtayelman, ul. B. Polyanka 30	238-4166		
Shuvalova House, Povarskaya ul. 30/1			
SI-Gruppa (India), Universitetskiy prosp. 9	930-6430		
SI-XXI JV (Italy), ul. Prechistenka 35-7	246-9632		
SIAG Food Store, ul. Tverskaya 22	299-1223	299-1223	
Siberian American Oil Co. JV,			
Krasnopresnenskaya nab. 12, Office 1026	253-1026	253-1491	
Sibir, Inc., Hotel Pekin, office 502	209-0902	209-4422	
Siderca, Kotelnicheskaya Nab. 1/15	227-4228		
Sidiamed, see Sidvim Aktiengesellschaft			
Sididmed JV (Switzerland), Michurinskiy prosp. 12, k. 2	932-5651	420-2016	411829
Sidvim Aktiengesellschaft,			
Hotel Mezhdunarodnaya II, room 1734	253-1734	253-1011	411446
Siemens, 1st Donskoy pr.2	237-6624	237-6614	414385
Siemens AG, ul. Dubininskaya 98	236-7500	236-6200	414783
Medtekhnika	235-1567	230-2864	414783
Service Hotline	236-4644		
SIF Television, Rublyovskoye sh. 26/1, k. 2, kv. 84	415-4209	415-2940	413638
Sigma-Trade JV (FRG), Hotel Budapest, room 533	928-6665	928-3374	411724
Sigulla JV (FRG), Aviamotornaya 4	362-6210		
Silicon Technology Corp., prosp. Vernadskovo 82	433-2575		
Silid, Rusakovskaya Nab.1	268-3318		
Sima Clothing Store, Petrovskiy Passazh, 2nd fl.			
Simon Engineering PLC,			
Krasnopresnenskaya Nab. 12, TsMT, office 438	253-1557	255-0504	
Simos JV, Skatertny p. 8	137-8007	137-8007	
Sims & Klein, ul. Tverskaya 36	251-8950	230-2078	413252
Sinergy International JV (US), Lopukhinskiy p. 3	248-8280	201-7444	
Sinion JV (Italy), ul. Ibragimova 15	366-4347	365-1065	
Sinko Light JV (Switz.), Golikovskiy p. 11	233-0686	230-2047	
Sintar, ul. Belomorskaya 26	455-9210	455-9210	
Sinti, Leninskiy prosp. 30	952-1343		
SIPA Press, ul. B. Spasskaya 12, kv. 3	975-2000		
Siprom JV, Pugovishnikov p. 11	246-9983	246-9662	
Siren, Novy Arbat 44	291-1225		
Sirena Bolshaya Spasskaya cafe,			
ul. B. Spasskaya (across from Hotel Volga)			
Sirin JV (Italy), Povarskaya ul. 4	202-2419		
Sisan JV, 60-Letiya Oktyabrya prosp. 9	135-4246	938-2209	411237
SISI, see Societa Di Iniziative Sovietico Italianeo			
Sitek JV (Lichtenstein), Pechatnikov p. 13	921-4223	200-4212	
Sitko JV, Starokonyushenny p. 47/27	291-0710		
Sizai, GUM, 2nd line, 1st fl.	926-3412		
Skadden, Arps, Slate, Meagher & Flom,			
Pleteshkovskiy p. 1	940-2304	267-0333	
Skandia Restaurant, Radisson-Slavyanskaya Hotel	941-8020		

	Phone	Fax	Telex
Skandinaviska Enskilda Banken,			
Dmitrovka B. ul. 5/6, kv. 34	292-0338	200-0237	413286
Skantek JV (Canada), Sechenovskiy p. 6	202-5818		
Skazka, Tovarishcheskiy p. 1	271-0998		
Skazka II Restaurant, Yaroslavskoye sh., 43rd km	584-3436		
Skif JV (France), 1st Krasnogvardeyskiy pr. 12	200-6919	229-1680	411055
Skiy, ul. Marksistskaya 1, k. 1 kv. 11	270-1426		413536
SKK Space Commerce Corporation JV,			
ul. Krasnoproletarskaya 9	972-4436	288-9583	411879
Skopbank, Mamonovskiy p. 4, kv. 2	209-6836	200-0259	413432
Skotoimport, Skatertny p. 8	291-7406		
Skurimpeks, ul. 1st Tverskaya-Yamskaya 28, kv. 88	250-1780	250-1780	414330
Skut Stamp Making, Protopovskiy p. 9	473-4109		
Skiy Line Ltd., ul. Geroyev Panfilovtzev 22, korp.1, kv.290	496-6013	496-1540	
Skytrump, Myusskaya pl. 6/5, 4th fl.	250-5555	250-5800	
Slami, Sadovaya-Triumfalnaya 14/12	209-2195	209-2194	
Slastyona Bakery, Krasnokazarmennaya 3	261-8626		
Slastyona i Moulen de la Galette JV,			
ul. Krasnokazarmennaya 3	261-8626	267-9726	
Slava Cinema, sh. Entuziastov 58	176-0417		
Slava Ltd., ul. Usacheva 62	245-5128	253-7947	
Slava Zaitsev, prosp. Mira 21	971-0547		
Slavinform JV (FRG), 12th Parkovaya ul. 5	463-0072	463-9872	
Slavyanskaya Radisson Hotel,			
see Radisson-Slavyanskaya Hotel			
Slavyanskiy Bazaar (reconstr.), ul. Nikolskaya 13	921-1872		
Sloboda JV, Seleznevskaya ul. 1	973-0719		
Sloveniyales	254-0587		
Slovo JV (UK), ul. B. Filevskaya 37/1	144-0562	144-0558	411311
Small Business Development Int'l Center JV,			
MGU, 2nd Gumanitarny k., kv. 473	939-3555		
Smena, Bumazhny pr. 14	212-1507		
Smeshannaya Company TIM JV, Gazetny p. 17/9	229-9310	229-9315	
Smirnoff, Pierre,			
Krasnopresnenskaya Nab. 12, TsMT, office 540	253-2540	253-2540	
Smith Corona, ul. Fadeyeva 1	253-9794	238-9533	411238
SmithKline Beecham PLC,			
B. Strochenovskiy p. 22/25, 1-st floor, office 102	230-6139	230-6146	
Smolenskaya Investment JV (France),			
Romanov p. 5, kv. 5	229-5510	200-5246	
SNAM, Staropimenovskiy p. 13	973-0566	073-0571	411948
SNC Radio Station (Stas Namin Ctr), Krymskiy val 9	191-1026		
SNIA BPD, Krasnopresnenskaya nab. 12, Office 1402	253-2179		413459
Sobesednik, Novoslobodskaya 73	285-4849		
Socialist Countries Insurance Joint Venture,			
ul. Pyatnitskaya 12	233-2668		
Societa Di Iniziative Sovietico Italiane,			
Oleny val 24, k. 2, kv. 146	161-3983	288-9572	413577
Societe Generale De Surveillance,			
Krasnopresnenskaya nab. 12, Office 1201	253-8293	253-9174	413481
Socimes SA, ul. Konyushkovskaya 28	255-9929	253-9601	
Socomext, Kutuzovskiy prosp. 7/4, kv. 127	243-7385	253-9011	413960
Sodeco, Kutuzovskiy prosp. 7/4, kv. 149	243-1554	243-1910	413275

	Phone	Fax	Telex
Sofi Courier Services JV (Finland),			
ul. Myasnitskaya 22, room 404	209-6207	928-6555	411787
Sofia Cinema, Sirenevy bul. 31	163-8320		
Sofinta JV (Finland), ul. Vesennyaya 14	265-5953	532-0997	
Sofis JV (Finland), Kuznetskiy Most 3, str. 2	292-2274		
Sofiteco SRL, Hotel Volga II, room 147-148	280-3779	975-2023	411672
Sofracop, Pokrovskiy bul. 4/17, k. 3, kv. 5	208-9714	230-2713	413324
Sofraplast JV (France), 2nd Nagatinskiy pr. 6	111-7110	111-7392	411711
SoftKomplex JV (Poland), Leninskiy prosp. 63/2, B-296	135-8509		
Software Technology, ul. M. Botanicheskaya 24-45	218-0302	195-2253	
Sogecred, Krasnopresnenskaya nab. 12, Office 1402	253-2179	253-9092	413459
Soglab JV (FRG), Shubinskiy p. 2/3	241-4870		
Soil Science and Agronomy Museum,			
Timiryazevskaya ul. 55	216-1619		
Sokhem, see Chimmashexport			
Sokolniki Exhibition Complex, Sokolniki Park	268-7151		
Sokolniki Park	268-5430		
Sokolnicheskiy Val, metro Sokolniki			
Sokolniki Sports Palace, Sokolnicheskiy val 1b	268-6958		
Sokro JV (FRG), ul. Vavilova 15	135-7525	310-7052	412215
SOLEAS, 1st Krasnogvardeyskiy pr. 12	256-7444		
Solidarnost Advertising Agency (Delovaya Sreda),			
B. Novodmitrovskaya ul. 14	256-9575		
Solidarnost Advertising Firm	222-0961		
Solnechnaya Polyana Resort	592-6064		
Solntsevo Cinema, ul. Bogdanova 19	435-2092		
Solyanka Art Gallery, ul. Solyanka 1/2	921-6332		
Sona Ventures Ltd. JV (Canada),			
Krasnopresnenskaya nab. 12, Office 1421	253-1421	230-2821	413508
Soniko JV (Japan), 1st Samotyochny p. 17a	925-1224	925-1224	
Soninfo JV, Gorodok Baumana	367-0772	166-0818	411892
Sony, Petrovskiy Passazh, 2nd fl. (see Passazh)			
Sony Europa Gmbh, B. Tishinskiy p. 38	205-3234	205-3932	
Soreal JV (France), Stupinskiy pr. 4a	384-0613	384-8670	411179
Sorice, ul. Petrovka 15/31, kv. 21	923-9549	230-2762	413116
Sorok Cheterie (44) cafe, Leningradskoye sh. 44	159-9951		
SOS Systems JV (Singapore),			
ul. Akad. Pilyugina 8, k. 1, podyezd 2	132-2677		
Sotrudnichestvo, ul. Rozhdestvenka 8, stroenie 2	923-6405		
Sotrudnichestvo Foreign Trade Assoc.,			
ul. Kievskaya 2, kv. 106	240-5252	230-2818	411670
South African Embassy, B. Strochenovskiy per 22/25	230-2152	230-7856	
Southam News, Kutuzovskiy prosp. 13/3, kv. 103	243-6708	243-3712	413538
Southern River Port, prosp. Andropova 11, k. 2	118-7811		
Souvenir, ul. Arbat 4			
Souvenir Trading JV (US), ul. Miklukho-Maklaya 37	335-1444		
Souvenirs, GUM, 2nd line, 1st fl.			
Sov It As JV, Nastasinskiy p. 3, k. 2	299-8406	299-7990	
SOV KRS JV, Oruzheyny p. 3	250-0630		
Sovagrital JV, Pekin Hotel, room 802	209-3816		
SovAm, see Marine Resources Company International			
Sovam Teleport, Bryusov p. 2a	229-3466	229-4121	411809
Sovamer Trading Company, Inc., ul. Koroleva 28, k. 1	482-2903	482-2910	

	Phone	Fax	Telex
Sovaminco JV, Nikitskaya, B. ul. 11/4 str. 2	229-3307	200-2289	
Quick Printing, Aviamotornaya 2, korp. 18	362-9081	362-1910	
Sovamit JV, Kompozitorskaya ul. 25/5	241-7580	244-7234	
Sovampex JV (US), Leningradskoye sh. 8/2, kv. 173	150-4744		
Sovaro JV, ul. Neglinnaya 14	923-0417	921-4986	
Sovautocapital, bul. Generala Karbusheva 8, str.1	212-8581	212-8581	
ul. Birysinka, 6	462-5120		
Sovbunker, Novoslobodskaya 14/19, str. 7	258-9122	288-9569	411134
Soveke JV (Finland), Tovarishcheskiy p. 19	204-8057		
Soveks JV, ul. 1st Karacharovskaya 8	175-9457		
Sovel JV (Cyprus), ul. Yablochkova 29 B/16	979-6319		
Sovelan Aroma JV (US),			
Rublyovskoye sh. 26, k. 1, kv. 43	415-4039	415-2911	113211
Sovelektro, ul. Sadovaya-Spasskaya 1/2	208-2837		411033
Sovenergo-MDI JV, Hotel Molodyozhnaya, room 2220	928-5844		414713
Sovengo JV (UK), Nikitskaya M. ul. 27	202-5611	202-1213	411153
Sovenz New Zealand, Leninskiy prosp. 83, k. 5, kv. 490	133-5740	230-2644	4131177
Sovetekavtomatika JV, ul. Gazoprovod 4	388-8588		
Sovetskaya Hotel JV (France),			
Leningradskiy prosp. 32/2	250-7255		411671
Sovetskaya Kultura, see Kultura			
Sovetskaya Rossiya Publishers, see Russkaya Kniga			
Sovetskaya Torgovlya Publishers,			
see Torgovaya Gazeta Publishers			
Sovetskiy Soyuz, see Voskresenie			
Sovetsko-Italyanskoye JV, ul. Dubininskaya 65	235-2251		
Sovexportfilm, Kalashny p. 14	290-5009		411143
Sovfinamtrans JV, ul. Krasnoprudnaya 26/1	262-3603	262-5346	
Sovfinechemie JV (FRG), 4th Likhachevskiy pr. 6	154-7091	943-0067	417622
Sovfinlift JV (Finland), 2nd Lykovskaya ul. 63	498-7951	498-7762	214151
Sovfintrade Joint Stock Co.,			
ul. B. Yushunskaya 1a, kv. 3	318-5787		
Sovfrakht, ul. Rozhdestvenka 1/4	926-1032	230-2640	411168
Sovhispan S.A., Novinskiy bul. 7/1	205-2008		413291
Soviet Children's Fund, see Children's Fund			
Soviet Committee of the Int Council of Museums,			
see National Committee of the Int Council of Museums			
Soviet Cultural Fund, see Russian Int'l Cultural Fund			
Soviet Culture Guide	157-3150		
Soviet Fund of Goodwill and Health,			
see International Fund of Goodwill and Health			
Soviet Peace Fund, ul. Prechistenka 10	202-4347		411489
Soviet Women's Committee,			
see Union of Women of Russia			
Soviet-American Gas and Oil Energy Resources JV,			
ul. Mayakovskovo 20	203-9264		411467
Soviet-American Joint Advertising Company,			
Mozhayskoye sh. 165	924-3821	230-2387	411211
Soviet-British Creative Cooperation JV,			
see East-West Creative Association			
Soviet-French Activity in Ocean JV (France),			
see SFAO JV			

	Phone	Fax	Telex
Soviet-Polish Informatics & Services Enterprise JV,			
ul. Yunnatov 18	212-8142		
Sovietskaya Entsiklopedia Publishers,			
see Bolshaya Rossiyskaya Entsiklopedia Publishers			
Sovietskaya Rossiya, see Pressa Publishers			
Sovietskiy Kompozitor Publishers,			
see Russian Kompozitor Publishing Association			
Sovietskiy Pisatel Publishers, Vorovskovo 11	202-8668		
Sovigco Export-Import JV Filial,			
Nagatinskaya nab. 16/3	118-3447		
Sovlmax JV (Canada), Lubyanskiy pr. 4	924-5549	921-5542	411630
Sovincenter,			
Mezhdunarodnaya Hotel I, Krasnopresnenskaya nab. 12	256-6303	253-2400	411486
Sovincenter Business Club,			
Mezhdunarodnaya Hotel I, 1st fl.	253-1792		
Sovincenter Car Rental, see Europcar			
Sovincenter Supermarket,			
Mezhdunarodnaya Hotel I, 1st fl.	253-1389		
Sovindata JV (India), Kuznetskiy Most 21/5	928-4197	200-2234	111115
Sovindtex JV (India), ul. Znamenka 11	246-4230		417227
Sovinfilm, see Soyuzkinoservice			
Sovingra JV, Babaevskaya ul. 1/8	268-4293		413104
Sovinpred JV (India), see Sefameks			
Sovinservice JV (Austria), Skatertny p. 4	290-2471	238-3345	411700
Sovinstandart, Novy Arbat 56	290-8780		
Sovintel JV (US), Dubovaya Roscha 25	215-6097	215-6888	
Sovinterarkhstroy JV (Italy),			
ul. 1st Tverskaya-Yamskaya 55	251-5392	253-9172	214525
Sovinteravtoservice, Institutskiy p. 2/1	299-7773	288-9575	411008
Sovinterluch JV (Bulgaria), ul. 3rd Kabelnaya 1	361-0560	290-3676	
Sovintertrade JV, see Radioexport			
Sovintervest JV (US), ul. B. Yakimanka 7/8	230-2038	230-2039	411691
Sovintex, 2nd Tverskaya-Yamskaya 6	251-5304		
Sovintkom Technologies JV (Switz.),			
Hotel Mezhdunarodnaya II, room 933	276-4722	253-9380	411432
Sovintrade Limited JV, Ukrainskiy bul. 8	443-7732		411386
Sovit-tours JV (Italy), ul. Angarskaya 15a	290-3270		
Sovitem JV (Italy), Dmitrovka M. ul. 27, str. 6a	257-1259	257-1588	
Sovitkom JV (Italy), Kuznetskiy Most 16	921-8625	928-7262	
SovJord JV (Jordan), Leninskiy prosp. 146	434-9739	420-2208	
Sovkabel, sh. Entuziastov 5	277-4028		
Sovkelme JV (Spain), ul. Ostozhenka 37	203-1266	248-0814	411287
Sovkhalidz JV (Kuwait), Leninskiy prosp. 52	137-3191	137-4769	411700
Sovkomflot, ul. Rozhdestvenka 1/4	926-1434	975-2637	411170
SovKuwait Engineering JV, Varshavskoye sh. 145	387-7204	310-7033	411006
Sovlaks, Kulakov p. 16	289-3407	344-7965	411664
Sovmara JV (Italy), ul. Initsiativnaya 9, k. 2	151-7347		
Sovmav JV, ul. Gavrikova 3/1, kv.98	367-3063	972-6250	411700
Sovmekhastoria, ul. Dorogomilovskaya 14	243-7672	243-7672	
Sovmestny Put JV (US), Timiryazevskaya 4/12	485-6266		
Sovmortrans, ul. Petrovka 20/1	925-0803	925-0857	414747
Sovmortrans JV, ul. Rozhdestvenka 1/4	926-1142	230-2640	411168
Sovo & Cie France, Smolenskiy bul. 22/14, kv. 9	248-7970	230-2211	413357

	Phone	Fax	Telex
Sovpak JV (Thailand), ul. 2nd Karacharovskaya 3	170-7110	171-5355	412192
Sovpoles JV, ul. Profsoyuznaya 43, k. 1	331-1433	332-6542	
Sovpolifin JV (Finland), Perovskoye sh. 7	174-2802		
Sovpolital JV (Italy), ul. Zelenodolskaya 3, k. 2	378-3356	378-3356	
Sovpoliuplas JV (Yugoslavia), Podkopayevskiy p. 4	297-5018	227-8914	
Sovremennik Publishers, Khoroshevskoye sh. 62	941-2992	941-3544	
Sovremennik Theater, Chistoprudny bul. 19a	921-1790		
Sovrybflot, Rozhdestvenskiy bul. 9	925-2639	230-2487	411208
Sovsaderm JV (Switz.), ul. Tatyany Makorovoy 18	239-3306	238-3553	412250
Sovtech JV (Australia), Leninskiy prosp. 45	137-6619		411784
Sovtrak JV, Zvyozdny bul. 17	287-0752		411008
Sovtransavto, Institutskiy p. 2/1 (Butovo)	971-3663		
Oktybraskaya ul. 2/4	292-8965	288-9558	4111251
Sovtransavto-Expeditsia, ul. B. Ochakovskaya 15a	548-7675		
Sovtransservice JV, ul. B. Ochakovskaya 15a	430-7867	430-7819	411927
Sovtranzit, Smolenskaya 34	244-3951	230-2850	411266
Sovventextile JV (Hungary), pr. Serebryankova 4	180-1002	180-0410	
Soyuz Hotel, ul. Levoberezhnaya 12	457-9004		
Soyuz II Hotel, 1st Krasnogvardeyskiy pr. 25b	259-3004		
Soyuz International JV, Tankovy pr. 4, k. 12	362-3227	230-2408	411662
Soyuz Marine Service JV (US), Gruzinskiy p. 3, kv. 63	254-3162	253-9771	413996
Soyuz Restaurant, Gospitalny val 22	360-7432		
Soyuzforinvest JV, 5th Monetchikovskiy p. 4/6, str. 1	233-8912	233-3540	411705
Soyuzgasexport, Leninskiy prosp. 20	230-2440	230-2410	411987
Soyuzgranpribor, see Elektroprivod			
Soyuzkarta, Volgogradskiy prosp. 45	177-4050		
Soyuzkhimexport, ul. Smolenskaya-Sennaya 32/34	244-2181		
Soyuzkinoservice, Skatertny p. 20	290-1000		
Soyuzkoopvneshtorg, Cherkasskiy p. 15	925-6822	230-2819	411127
Soyuzluchpribor, ul. 3rd Kabelnaya 1	237-1915		
Soyuzneftexport, ul. Smolenskaya-Sennaya 32/34	244-2291	244-2991	411148
Soyuzpatent, ul. Ilyinka 5/2	925-1661	230-2348	411431
Soyuzpechat, Bogoyavlenskiy p. 3	206-0709		
Soyuzplodimport, ul. Smolenskaya-Sennaya 32/34	244-2258	244-3636	411262
Soyuzpromexport, ul. Smolenskaya-Sennaya 32/34	253-9489	244-3793	411268
Soyuzpromimporttorg, prosp. Vernadskovo 25	131-5128		
Soyuzservice JV, Sokolnicheskiy Val, Dom 50, korp.2			
Soyuzvneshstroyimport, Tverskoy bul. 6	290-0684	973-2148	411434
Soyuzvneshtrans, Gogolevskiy bul. 17	203-1179		
Sozheks JV (Switz.), ul. Ilyinka 5/2	253-1913	921-5675	411883
Sozialdemokratische Pressedienste,			
Kutuzovskiy prosp. 14, kv. 151-152	230-2563		
Spain Commercial Office, Nikitskaya M. ul. 21	202-7772		
Spantek JV (US), Tatarskaya ul. 7, kv. 37	233-5019		411049
Spare Time In Moscow (Dosug v Moskve) Journal,			
ul. Myasnitskaya 24, room 77	925-0321		
Sparta JV (Australia), Tovarishcheskiy p. 25	272-7561	272-7561	
Spartak Yacht Club, c/o Savoy Hotel	929-8569		
Spate-Moscow JV (US), Ukraine Hotel	243-6550		
Spec Ltd., ul. Staraya Basmannaya 19	263-0200	200-4240	
Spectrum HDT JV (Canada), ul. Usacheva 35	261-7405	245-5070	411554
Spekfilm JV, Mosfilmovskaya 1			
Spektrum JV (UK), ul. Staraya Basmannaya 19	267-7529	200-4240	

	Phone	Fax	Telex
Spetzagrotrans JV, Volzhskiy bul. 3	179-9901	179-8500	
Spetzavtosentr, Kiyevskaya ul. 8	240-2092		
Sphera Theater, Karetny ryad 3	299-9645		
Spie Batignolles, ul. Mytnaya 1, kv. 14	230-0776	230-2647	413175
Spiegel (der), Krutitskiy val 3, k. 2, kv. 33, 36	274-0009	274-0003	413288
Spiro & Associates, see Samuel M. Spiro & Associates, Ltd.			
Sport Cinema, B. Pirogovskaya 53/55	246-1758		
Sport Hotel, Leninskiy prosp. 90/2	131-1191		
Sport Venture Moscow JV (FRG),			
Krasnopresnenskaya nab. 14	256-5078	259-7048	
Sportcenter Luzhniki JV (Austria),			
Luzhnetskaya nab. 24	201-1665		
Sportpromtex JV (FRG), ul. Ostozhenka 37	203-1577	203-1407	
Sports Palace, Luzhniki	201-0955		
Sprint International Communications Corp.,			
ul. Tverskaya 7, entrance 7	201-6890	923-2344	414750
Sprint JV (Luxembourg), Volgogradskiy prosp. 46B	178-6171	179-0038	414803
Sprint-Form JV (FRG), ul. Marksistskaya 22	277-0183	270-7602	
Spros Hotel JV (Switz.), Leninskiy prosp. 95/15	133-4393		414711
Sputnik Cinema, Soldatskaya ul. 15	361-4220		
Sputnik Hotel, Leninskiy prosp. 38	938-7096		
Sputnik Tourist Agency, M. Ivanovskiy p. 6, str. 2	925-9278	230-2787	411253
Ssha-Ekonomika, Politika, Ideologiya (USA),			
ul. Tverskaya 16/2			
St. Andrew's Church, Voznesenskiy p. 9	143-3562		
St. Basil's Cathedral, Red Square	928-3304		
St. George Street,			
Radisson-Slavyanskaya Hotel, Berezhovskaya nab. 2			
St. George's Church, ul. Varvarka 12	928-3872		
St. Vlasiy's Church Concert Hall, Gagarinskiy p. 20	299-5322		
Stamco Trading Company, LTD,			
ul. B. Dorogomilovskaya 14, k. 1, kv. 76	243-3837	230-2010	413669
Stampa (La), Kutuzovskiy prosp. 7/4, kv. 167	243-1751	230-2147	413455
Stanbet JV (US), Krymskiy val 9, Zelyony teatr	237-1089	237-3435	
Stanislavskiy & Nemirovich-Danchenko Musical Thtr,			
Dmitrovka B. ul. 17	229-8388		
Stanislavskiy Drama Theater, ul. Tverskaya 23	299-7224		
Stanislavskiy House Museum, Leontyevskiy p. 6	229-2855		
Stanislavskovo 2, Leontyevskiy p. 2	291-8689		
Stanko-Fanuk Service Limited JV (Japan),			
ul. Kalanchevskaya 31	208-5125	200-0275	111542
Stankoimport, ul. Obrucheva 34/63	333-5101	310-7021	411993
Stankovendt JV (FRG), ul. Sushchyovskiy val 5	289-2382	289-9541	
Star Progress, Frunzenskaya nab. 30, pav. 15	201-0692	230-2601	
Staraya Moskva Holding Company,			
N. Kiselny p. 19/10	923-3700		
Stariy Arbat, ul. Arbat 25	291-7101	202-4920	
Starkar JV (Finland), Bratsevskaya ul. 13	948-0211	948-0211	
Starlight JV, Khokhlovskiy p. 13	925-2844	975-2230	
Start JV (US), ul. Druzhinnikovskaya 15	205-2978	943-0022	411070
Startgroup JV, ul. Mantulinskaya 10		200-2216	411700
Stas Namin's, see Victoria Cafe			

	Phone	Fax	Telex
State Automobile Inspection (GAI),			
ul. Sadovaya-Samotechnaya I	923-5373		
State Bank of India, Pokrovskiy bul. 4/17, kv. 32	297-2190		413012
State Comm.for the Chemical and Oil Processing Ind.,			
ul. Gilyarovskovo 31	281-9479		
State Duma – International Department	290-7391		
State Joint Stock Assoc. for Mach. & Equipt.,			
ul. Tverskaya 20	209-5520		
State Taxation Service, ul. Neglinnaya 23	209-7341	200-4901	
Statfall, TsUM, 3rd fl.	954-0493	954-0492	
Statistica, Inc., ul. Skakovaya 9, 4th fl, kv. 22	945-3412	945-2765	
Statoil, ul. Malaya Ordynka 7	230-6200	230-6206	
Stavan-Engineering JV, ul. Elektrozavodskaya I			
Steak House, Sadko Arcade (Expocenter)	256-2206	973-2185	
Steepler Ltd., ul. Prechistenka 7	246-8192	246-7446	
Steepler Publisher Ltd., Bobrov p. 4	921-2381	928-8764	
Steilmann, GUM, 1st line, 2nd fl.			
Steklo Rosii, ul. Kedrova 15	129-0927	124-1600	
Steptoe and Johnson, 7th M. Levshinsky, #3	201-4073	201-7424	413205
Sterch Controls, ul. Lobachika 17/19			
Sterkh-Avtomazatsia JV (US), Tryokhprudny p. 11/13	299-2531	230-2600	413255
Stern Magazine, Kutuzovskiy prosp. 7/4, k. 5, kv. 15	243-3396	230-2950	413339
STET, Palashevskiy B. p. 11/1, 3rd floor	973-2478	973-2344	
Stetlan JV (FRG), Pokrovskiy bul. 8	297-5245		
STF-US JV, ul. Akad. Koroleva 12	217-9034	975-2073	
Stil	923-2318		
STN JV, Borisoglebskiy p. 8			
Stockmann			
Business to Business Trading, prosp. Mira 176	286-0292		
Fashion Store, Dolgorukovskaya ul. 2	258-2212		
Fashion and Business Store, Leninskiy prosp. 73/8	134-0386		
Grocery Store, Zatsepskiy val 4/8	233-2602		
Home Electronics and Car Supplies Store,			
ul. Lyusinovskaya 70/1	954-8234	952-6513	
Stoelck Aussenhandel AG,			
Hotel Mezhdunarodnaya II, room 438	253-1557	255-0504	411432
Stokmos JV, ul. Terekhova 13	244-7164	255-4018	412259
Stoleshniki cafe, Stoleshnikov p. 6	229-2050		
Stolichny Bank, GUM, 2nd line, 1st fl.			
ul. Pyatnitskaya 72	233-5892	237-2993	411913
Stolitsa Int'l Trade House, B. Filevskaya ul. 35	181-1500	181-0753	
STP (Systems Translation Programming, Inc.),			
ul. Tverskaya 12	229-8937	908-9000	
Strastnoy 7, Strastnoy bul 7	299-0498	200-1243	
Streif AG – Industrieanlagen, ul. Mytnaya 1, kv. 29	230-0754		413295
Strela Cinema, Smolenskaya-Sennaya pl. 23/35	244-0953		
Stroilesinvest, ul. Yablochkova 5	210-2832		
Stroydormashexport, Nikitskiy bul. 7	291-4931	202-9056	411063
Stroykomplektexport, Ovchinnikovskaya nab. 18/1	233-9512	230-2181	411397
Stroymaterialintorg, Kiyevskaya 19	243-7186		411887
Stroyservice JV (Austria), ul. Tverskaya 24/2	229-6590	229-9731	
Studio 777, ul. Eyzenshteyna 8	233-8998		

	Phone	Fax	Telex
Studio Theater on Spartakovskaya Pl., Spartakovskaya pl. 9-1	261-1030		
Studio Theater on Yugo Zapade, prosp. Vernadskovo 125	434-7483		
Study Company	237-4572		
Stupinskiy customs point	546-8681		
STW & Co., ul. Grimau 14	125-2055		
Success JV (USA), Kutuzovskiy prosp. 3	148-9966	292-6511	411700
Sudoexport, Novinskiy bul. 11	255-1813	200-2250	411116
Sudoimport, Uspenskiy p. 10	299-6549	209-1331	411272
Sueddeutsche Zeitung, Kutuzovskiy prosp. 7/4, k. 5, kv. 25	243-1166	200-1234	413334
Suiproekt JV (Yugoslavia), 3rd Tverskaya-Yamskaya 22	251-8247	241-4707	
Sulzer Brothers LTD, Kursovoy p. 9, Office 4	202-1717	200-1234	413526
Sumitomo Corporation, Krasnopresnenskaya nab. 12, Office 1203	253-2030	230-2664	413134
Summit Motors Moscow, Ltd., Sovintsentr, Mezhdunarodnaya Hotel I, #1202-1205	253-2280	253-1261	413134
Summit Systems, Vorotnykovskiy p. 7/2, 10	299-1162	299-1162	
Sunbreeze Electronics, Petrovskiy Passazh			
Sunday Express, Leninskiy prosp. 45, kv. 426	135-1164	230-2010	413199
Sunday News-Journal Union, see Voskresenye News-Journal Union			
Sunday Telegraph, see Daily Telegraph			
Sunday Tribune, ul. Sadovaya-Samotechnaya 12/24, kv. 72	200-2530		
Sunds Defibrator AB, Mamonovskiy p. 6/8	209-2817	200-0214	413223
Sunrise JV, 3rd Golutvinskiy p. 2			
Sunrise Limousines, ul. Zolotaya 11	366-4656	292-6511	
Super Nova, ul. Petrovka 2	292-9979	292-3868	
Supermarket Union, see Union Supermarket			
Supershop, Astrakhanskiy p. 5	280-2545		
Supply Side	238-5308	238-5306	
Supriz cafe, Medynskaya 5, k. 1	384-4400		
Susuman Gold Exchange, see Kolyma Susuman Gold Exchange			
SVAK, see North-Eastern Joint Stock Commercial Bank			
Svenska Dagbladet, Kutuzovskiy prosp. 9/2, kv. 119	243-6632		413193
Svenska Handelsbanken, Pokrovskiy bul. 4/17, kv. 35	207-6018	230-2544	413201
Svetoreklama JV, ul. Polyarnaya 13V	473-9266	473-5051	
Svetozor JV (US), Leninskiy prosp. 70/11		938-2158	
SVO Travel, Ltd., ul. Novy Arbat 15, 18th fl., #1820	202-2293	202-0420	
Svoboda Cinema, ul. Trofimova 17	279-2524		
Svobodnaya Mysl (Free Thought), ul. Marksa-Engelsa 5	203-0365		
SWAPO, see Embassy of Namibia			
Swatstroy JV (Canada), Dmitrovka B. ul. 10	921-4129	921-5059	
Swedbank, Mamonovskiy p. 4, kv. 2	209-6836	200-0259	413432
Swedish Furniture, Leninskiy prosp. 64	137-0291		
Swedish Radio, ul. Sadovaya-Samotechnaya 12/24, kv. 64	200-2200	200-2200	413351
Swedish School, Leninskiy prosp. 78	131-8766		
Swedish TV, Kutuzovskiy prosp. 7/4, kv. 130-131	243-5165	253-9179	413365
Sweet Way, ul. Tverskaya 12			
Swimming Pool of TsSKA, Leningradskiy prosp. 39	213-2583		

	Phone	Fax	Telex
Swiss Bakery, Sadko Arcade (Expocenter)	940-4068	973-2185	
Swiss Butchery, Sadko Arcade (Expocenter)	940-4068	973-2185	
Swiss Flora, Leninskiy prosp. 43	237-3942		
Swiss House Restaurant, Sadko Arcade (Expocenter)	940-4069	973-2185	
Swiss Pastry Shop, Sadko Arcade (Expocenter)	253-9592		
Swiss-Medical Interline, Hotel Intourist, room 2030	203-8631		
Swissair, Krasnopresnenskaya nab. 12, Office 2005	253-8988	253-1852	413417
Sheremetevo 2 Airport	578-2740		413030
Symantec	320-0733		
Symetrie Champagne Showroom, Leninskiy prosp. 85	134-0531		
Synagogue, see Jewish Synagogue			
Synergia JV (Italy), Stremyanny p. 28	237-8481		
Syntez Corporation JV, Kutuzovskiy prosp.30/32			
Syrian Arab Airlines, Koroviy val 7	237-1727		
Systems & Strategy, ul. Novoslobodskaya 36/1	973-1325		
Sytco, M. Bronnaya 26	209-6662		
Sytin Museum, Tverskaya 12, kv. 274	229-0755		

T

	Phone	Fax	Telex
TAAG, Angola Airlines, Koroviy val 7, #8	237-0010		
Sheremetevo 2 Airport	578-2773		
Tabakov's Studio Theater, see O. Tabakov's Studio Theater			
Tabani Corporation,			
Krasnopresnenskaya nab. 12, Office 1505	253-2462	253-9375	413524
Tadzhikistan Cinema, ul. Katukova 8	499-1511		
Taganka Bar, ul. Verkhnyaya Radishchevskaya 15	272-4351		
Taganka Drama and Comedy Theater,			
Zemlyanoy 76	272-6300		
Taganka II Supermarket, ul. Marksistskaya 1/1	272-2417		
Taganka JV (Austria), ul. Taganskaya 17-21	928-1614	253-9483	
Taganskaya 31/22 Gallery, Taganskaya ul. 31/22	278-5578		
Taiga JV (Switz.), Nikitskaya, B. ul. 46	290-5572		
Tairiku Trading Co., LTD, ul. Mytnaya 1, 2nd fl.	237-2060	230-2466	413058
Tais Sport JV, Luzhnetskaya nab. 10	201-1129		
Taki-Moscow, ul. Mnevniki 10	191-1377	943-0064	
Takt JV (Australia), Pushkarev p. 23/15	924-5080	924-9452	
Talisman cafe, ul. Shchepkina 1	208-9055		
Tallinn Cinema, Sevastopolskiy prosp. 33	127-9003		
Talus Corporation	255-9698		
Tamada Duty Free Shop, Hotel Moskva	292-2874		
Tamilas Limited, see M J Exports			
Tamko S.A., Kotelnicheskaya nab. 25/8, kv. 40	272-5897	274-0060	413333
Tanako JV, ul. M. Lubyanka 16	280-4447	975-2060	
Tangra MS (JV), Kutuzovskiy prosp. 14	243-7700		
Tansley Trading (TTL),			
Krasnopresnenskaya nab. 12, office 612	253-2612	253-2996	414523
Taroco Enterprises, Inc.,			
prosp. Mira POB 29, Moscow office VVC	974-6023	282-9197	
Tashkent Cinema, 1st Novokuzminskaya ul. 1	371-6587		
Task Optic, Goncharnaya ul. 12	921-0518	923-2961	
TASS Fotokhronika, ul. B. Dorogomilovskaya 12	243-3903		411220

	Phone	Fax	Telex
TASS News Agency, see ITAR			
Tavi JV, ul. Chaplygina 1a			
Taxi Reservations, 24 hours a day	927-0000		
9am - 6pm	227-0000		
9am - 6pm (Medvedkovo)	477-7068		
Tbilisi Cinema, ul. Novocheremushkinskaya 53a	120-9006		
Tchaikovskiy Concert Hall, Triumfalnaya pl. 4/31	299-3487		
Tea, Coffee and Other Colonial Wares, Khudozhestvenny pr. 2.			
Team Design, Americom Business Center	941-8389	240-6915	
Team Training Russia, ul. B. Spasskaya 10, #183	280-0018	956-3735	
Teatr Kinoaktyora (Filmactor Theater), Povarskaya ul. 33	290-5524		
Teatr Yunovo Zritelya, see Moscow Youth Theater			
Teatro Mediterraneo, Hotel Metropol, Teatralny pr. 1/4	927-6739		
Tebost JV (FRG), ul. Ostozhenka 30, str. 2	290-6139		
Tebowa, Hotel Mezhdunarodnaya II, room 1509	253-1509	253-9192	413624
Tech Trade JV (Sweden), prosp. Mira 186	283-5952	187-5847	
Techimex JV (Austria), Rybny p. 2			
Technik und Technologie, Krutitskiy val 3, kv. 105	276-9520		413440
Technip, see Technologie Progretti Lavori SpA			
Technische Beratung Schittko GmbH, Hotel Mezhdunarodnaya II, room 1226	253-1226	253-9170	411486
Technobridge JV, ul. Lukhovitskaya 5	180-3239	180-2480	411280
Technological & Marketing Centre JV, ul. Seleznevskaya 1/3, str. 1			411013
Technologie Progetti Lavori, Mamonovskiy p. 4, kv. 10	209-2839	200-0288	413235
Technology and Marketing Center, ul. Novoslobodskaya 10, str. 3	973-0719	973-3402	
Technology Ventures, Inc.	285-0600	285-0660	
Technopark Business Center, VVTs, prosp. Mira 120	188-7776	188-5665	414819
Technopolis Innovation Bank, Zelenograd k. 317a	534-1449	530-5537	
Technosoft JV (Italy), ul. Zverinetskaya 34/38	238-9679	230-2093	413507
Technotex USA Inc., Park Place, Leninskiy prosp. 113/1, #E307	956-5124	956-5402	
Techpetrol Trading, prosp. Vernadskovo 95, k. 3, kv. 32	434-0718	433-1507	612273
Teda JV (Yugoslavia), ul. Marksa-Engelsa 15	290-5061	290-5061	412189
Tefal, GUM, 1st line, 1st fl.	926-3463		
ul. Gilyarovskovo 57, office 401	284-1862	284-1213	412009
Tekhmashexport, ul. Mosfilmovskaya 35	206-9158	230-2363	411068
Tekhmashimport, Trubnikovskiy p. 19	248-8686	291-5808	411113
Tekhnobank, B. Gruzinskaya 56	254-4611	254-0855	
Tekhnoexport, Ovchinnikovskaya nab. 18/1	220-1782	230-2080	411338
Tekhnointorg, Pyatnitskaya ul. 64	233-0032	230-2642	411200
Tekhnokultura JV, ul. Arbat 35	248-2410		
Tekhnopromexport, Ovchinnikovskaya nab. 18/1	220-1523	233-3373	411158
Tekhnopromimport, Ovchinnikovskaya nab. 18/1	220-1218	230-2111	411233
Tekhnoservice JV, ul. Pervomayskaya 126	461-3514	461-3514	
Tekhnostroyexport, Ovchinnikovskaya nab. 18/1	220-1448		
Tekhpromexport, Ovchinnikovskaya nab. 18/1	220-1523	233-3373	411158
Tekhpromimport, Ovchinnikovskaya nab. 18/1	220-1505	230-2111	111874
Tekhsnabexport, Staromonetny p. 26	233-4846	230-2638	411328
Tekhvneshreklama, ul. B. Ordynka 7/2	231-8428		

	Phone	Fax	Telex
Tekhvneshtrans, see Technoexport			
Tekom JV (US), 1st Smolenskiy p. 9	241-0053	241-0109	
Tekotex JV (FRG), ul. Novo-Basmannaya 23, str. 1	265-3663	292-6511	
Tektron, ul. 2nd Vladimirskaya 31A	176-8911	377-2379	
Tekur JV (Australia), prosp. Vernadskovo 95	433-1507		612273
Teldico Communications, see Capricone Int'l S.P.R.L.			
Telebank Mezhdunarodny Kommercheski Bank, ul. Znamenka 13, str. 3	203-5397	290-6009	41231
Telecom Concern, 2nd Spasonalivkovskiy p. 6	230-2989	230-2765	414768
Telecommunication & Electronics, Novinskiy bul. 11	255-4792	252-5475	
Teledyne Industries International, Leningradskiy prosp. 55	943-9402	943-9403	
Telefonica Internacional, Rublyovskoye sh. 36, k. 2, kv. 241, 243	415-5109	415-2956	
Telekos JV (Holland), Dmitrovka M. ul. 5	209-7861	200-5253	
Teleset Service	166-9763	362-8070	
Telesource Business Center, Sheremetevo 2 Airport	578-4848	578-3838	
Temkas Clothing Store, Petrovskiy Passazh, 2nd fl.			
Temp Cinema, ul. Begovaya 5	946-0165		
Tempbank, Krutitskiy val 26	276-4141	276-3708	
Tennis International Corp., Paveletskaya nab. 4	235-7112	235-7126	
Tennis Shop, ul. Profsoyuza 18			
Tera, Ltd., Parushny pr. 32-9	193-1804		
Tereza JV, Strastnoy bul. 10		230-2258	
Termolik JV, 1st Institutskiy pr. 1	371-0125		
Terra Blok Sovetskiy Soyuz JV (Holland), ul. Zoi i Aleksandra Kosmodemyanskikh 26/21		943-0079	411085
Terrace Bar, Aerostar Hotel	155-5030		
Texaco Petroleum Development Company, ul. Novocheromushkinskaya 69	941-8704	332-5576	
Texas Timber Exporting, Inc., ul. Kuusinena 21b, office 410	198-7501	943-0089	
Textil Commerz, Leninskiy prosp. 95a	132-4110	936-2659	
Theater cafe, ul. Tverskaya 5			
Theater Salon Gallery, Tverskoy bul. 11			
Theater Tickets, see Box Office Theater Tickets			
Thermal-Spray-Tech GmbH, Perovskoye sh. 43	171-7628	309-5970	
Thermax Limited, ul. Mytnaya 1, Office 13	230-0276	230-2531	413011
Thomesto, ul. Mytnaya 1, kv. 19-20	230-0378	230-2366	413047
Thompson Publishing Group, Sadovaya-Spasskaya ul. 21	924-2298	924-2298	
Thomson Holidays	203-4025		
Thomson S.A., Pokrovskiy bul. 4/17, k. 3, kv. 6	208-9716	230-2355	413287
1001 Nights, Leninskiy prosp. 146	434-9739		
3M (MN Mining & Manufacturing), Samarskiy p. 3	288-9701	288-9792	
THY, Turkish Airlines, Kuznetskiy Most 1/8	292-5121		
Sheremetevo 2 Airport	578-2728		
Thyssen Vertretung Moskau, Glazovskiy p. 7, kv. 15	203-1938	230-2264	413306
Tiana Brokerage Firm	169-9171	230-2467	
Ticket Express, Novokonyushenny p. 9/2	244-7260	244-0213	
Ticket Office, 1st Krasnogvardeyskiy pr., pavilion 2, tower 3	256-7444		
Tiedonantaya, ul. Dostoyevskovo 1/21, kv. 9	288-9511		413569
Tierney & Associates, Kuznetskiy Most 19	928-5793	975-2495	

	Phone	Fax	Telex
Tifla JV, Petroverigskiy p. 4			
TIM Ltd. JV (Austria), Petroverigskiy p. 4	921-3622	928-2684	412170
Time Magazine, Kutuzovskiy prosp. 14, kv. 3-4	243-1511	243-3752	413433
Times of India, The, Frunzenskaya nab. 12, kv. 7	242-4440		413318
Times, The, ul. B. Dorogomilovskaya 14, kv. 78	230-2457		413010
Tino Fontana Restaurant,			
Hotel Mezhdunarodnaya, 3rd floor	253-2241		
Tip Top Mode, ul. Krasnaya Presnya 44	255-1498		
Tissa-Ogilvy and Mathers JV, prosp. Vernadskovo 33	131-5749	138-3743	414511
Titan JV (Austria), Goncharnaya ul. 16			
TM-Elektronika JV, ul. Kosmonavta Volkova ,12	150-4640		417603
TMG in Moscow JV, ul. Vavilova 81			
TNT Express Worldwide, 3rd Baltiyskiy p. 3	156-5771	151-2277	413984
Tokobank, ul. Mashi Poryvayevoy 7	204-9100	975-2578	41249
Tokyo Boeki LTD, Pokrovskiy bul. 4/17, kv. 24-5	298-3591	230-2855	413397
Tokyo Broadcasting System,			
Kutuzovskiy prosp. 9, kv. 20	243-9980	230-2528	413132
Tokyo Maruichi Shoji Co., LTD, ul. Mytnaya 1, 2nd fl.	237-3050	230-2037	413061
Tokyo Restaurant,			
Hotel Rossiya, Varvarka ul. 6, West block, 1st fl.	298-5707	230-2504	
Tolstoy House, ul. Lva Tolstovo 21	246-6112		
Tolstoy Museum, ul. Prechistenka 11	202-2190		
Toma JV (Belgium), Grokholskiy p. 32, k. 2	138-5019	133-5071	
Tomen Corporation,			
Krasnopresnenskaya 12, Office 1309	253-2154	253-9905	413170
Tomo JV (Canada), ul. Karetny ryad 5/10, str. 6	429-1377	404-1767	411661
TOO Dekorativny Kamen, Trifonovskaya ul. 61, str. 1	281-1857		
Top Sport, Sadko Arcade (Expocenter)	253-9588	973-2185	
Torgovlya Gazeta Publishers, ul. Varvarka 14	298-4848		
Toronto Star, ul. Vavilova 83, kv. 82	132-4856	133-6560	413513
Torrent Export Ltd., 1st Yamskovo-Polya ul. 19	250-5055	257-0464	
Toshiba Service Center, Maloafanasyevskiy p. 7	291-9210		
Toshiba Shop, ul. Kosmonautov 4	283-5613	283-5613	
Total, ul. Gilyarovskovo 65	284-5614	281-1114	414787
Tourist Hotel, ul. Selskokhozyaystvennaya 17/2	187-6018		
Tourist's Clinic, Gruzinskiy pr. 2	254-4396		
Tovnarbank, Novopeschanaya ul. 20	943-4102		
Toyota Tshusho Corporation, ul. Mytnaya 1	230-0943	230-2037	413596
TPL, see Tecnologie Progetti Lavori SpA			
Tracosa S.A., 4th Dobryninskiy p. 6/9	237-6065	230-2128	413470
Trade and Management, ul. Udaltsova 89/3, #765	931-4419	931-4419	
Trademetinvest JV (FRG), Ovchinnikovskaya nab. 18/1	220-1585	230-2203	411931
Train Info. Service (24 hrs), Komsomolskaya pl. 5	266-9000		
Train Ticket Delivery Service	262-8684		
Train Tickets by Phone	266-8333		
Traktoroexport, ul. Lesnaya 41	258-5934	288-9559	411273
Trans-Chemical Corporation,			
ul. B. Sadovaya 8A 'MGC'	209-9213	200-3271	412332
Trans-World Metals, B. Kharitonyevskiy p. 13a	207-2371	207-1142	
Transaero Airlines, Okhotny ryad 2 (Hotel Moskva)	292-7513		
Transcapital Bank, ul. Vorontsovskaya 27/35	272-5450	271-9306	412790
ul. Vorontsovskaya 27/35	272-0612	271-9306	412790
TransCargo, Putevoy pr. 3	901-1700	901-5195	414851

	Phone	Fax	Telex
Transcom JV (Austria), ul. Geroyev Panifilovtsev 24	250-0434		
Transimage JV (US), ul. Podolskikh Kursantov 3a	921-0955		
Transnautic Uberseeschiffahrtsagentur GmbH &			
Co. KG, Mamonovskiy p. 6, kv. 3	200-0292	200-0292	413925
Transstroi JSC, ul. Kalanchevskaya 2/1, #809	262-4807	971-5656	
TransSuper	177-1274	288-7781	
Trattoria Restaurant, Sadko Arcade (Expocenter)	940-4066	973-2185	
Travel Journal, 1st Brestskaya ul. 35	251-7711	251-6994	
Travellers Guest House,			
ul. Bolshaya Pereyaslavskaya 50, 10th Fl.	971-4059	280-7686	411700
TrekKingtour JV (FRG), ul. M. Yakimanka 2/1	230-7426	292-6511	411700
Trelleborg, Krasnopresnenskaya nab. 12, office 901	253-2970	253-2971	413491
Tremo JV (Italy), Taganskaya pl. 88, str. 1	272-0657		
TrenMos Bar, ul. Ostozhenka 1/9	202-5722		
Bistro, Ostozhenka ul. 1/9	202-5722		
TrenMos Restaurant, Komsomolskiy prosp. 21	245-1216		
Tretyakov Gallery (New), Krymskiy val 10	230-1116		
Tretyakov Gallery (Old), Lavrushinskiy p. 10	230-1116		
Tri-Mac, ul. Udaltsova 12	181-9738	181-0063	
Tribuna de Actualidad,			
ul. Akad. Koroleva 4, k. 2, kv. 69-70	215-2492	283-0657	
Trident International Ltd., Raushskaya Nab. 4/5	239-3046	230-7363	
Trifo Trading House, Hotel Mezhdunarodnaya 2, rm 649	253-9061	253-9406	
Trinity Graphics, ul. Serpukhovskaya 72, kv. 2	952-6484		
Trinity Motors, ul. Tverskaya 18	230-2535	200-2025	
Trio JV (UK), ul. Vyborgskaya 16	150-9934	150-9934	
Triza Agency, Sokolnicheskaya pl. 7	268-8701	268-8881	
Troika JV, Krasnopresnenskaya nab. 12, Office 1603	253-2255		411735
Tropinin Museum, Shchetininskiy p. 10	231-1799		
TROS, KRO (Radio & TV), Het Parool,			
ul. Marksistskaya 1, kv. 1	270-1539	274-0012	413544
Troyka Press Ltd., 1st Yamskaya ul. 8	289-1313	289-9287	411160
Trud Publishers, Nastasinskiy p. 4	299-3906	200-0124	
Trussardi, Radisson-Slavyanskaya Hotel	941-8397		
Trust	249-5252		
Tsakhkadzor cafe, ul. Lesnaya 15	251-0257		
Tsaritsino Hotel, Shipilovskiy prosp. 47/1	343-4343	343-4363	
Tsaritsyno JV, Shipilovskiy pr. 43, k. 1	343-4373	343-4363	
Tschelkovskiy customs point	435-82		
Tsentralnaya Hotel, ul. Tverskaya 10	229-8589		
Tsentralny Detskiy Kinoteatr, ul. Bakhrushina 25	233-4206		
Tsentralny Dom Sovetskoy Armii, Suvorovskaya pl. 2	281-5550		
Tsentralny Dom Turista (Cntrl House of Tourism),			
Leninskiy prosp. 146	434-2782	438-7756	
Tsentralny Dom Turista Concert Hall,			
Leninskiy prosp. 146	434-9492	438-7756	
Tsentralny Restaurant, ul. Tverskaya 10	229-0241		
Tsentrosoyuz Bank, B. Cherkasskiy p. 15	928-7683		
TsION and Public Onpinion Fund,			
see All Russian Exchange Bank			
Tsoukas Bros., Kutuzovskiy prosp. 18	243-3089	243-4338	
TsUM (Central Department Store), ul. Petrovka 2	292-7600		
Tudor S.A., ul. Konyushkovskaya 28, Office 4	253-9601		413572

	Phone	Fax	Telex
Tumanskiy Real Estate Co., Staropanskiy p. 4	921-8412	924-8942	
Tumba Golf Course (Finland), ul. Dovzhenko 1	147-8330	200-2264	611700
Business Center	147-5480	147-6252	
Turbotest JV (India), Aviamotornaya 2	267-1350	267-1350	411686
Turkish Airlines, see THY, Turkish Airlines			
TV Chanel '2x2', ul. Korolyova 12	215-6335	283-8814	
TV de Espana, Krutitskiy val 3, k. 2, kv. 130	276-4768	274-0053	413994
TV-Asahi, ul. Mytnaya 3, kv. 53	230-2831	230-6311	413107
TVK JV (Lichtenshtein), Bryusov p. 7, kv. 70/71	299-2176		
TWA, Radisson-Slavyanskaya Hotel, #5028	941-8146		
Twenty-First Century Devel.Commercial Bank,			
Volokolamskoye sh. 88, stroyeniye 8	250-9641	491-3771	
'24' Newspaper, Tverskoy bul. 10-12	292-3609		
Two Dmitriys and Co	381-1754	381-1754	
Tyazhpromexport, Ovchinnikovskaya nab. 18/1	220-1610	230-2203	411931
Tyumen Commodity and Stock Exchange	245-6265		

U

	Phone	Fax	Telex
U Babushki, ul. Bolshaya Ordynka 42	239-1484		
U Bankira Restaurant, Chasovaya 24/1	151-8681		
U Kamina cafe, ul. Pokrovka 32	297-0840		
U Margarity cafe, Gagarinskiy p. 9	291-6063		
U Nikitskikh Vorot, Nikitskaya, B. ul. 23	290-4883		
U Nikitskikh Vorot Studio Theater,			
Nikitskaya, B. ul. 23/9	291-8419		
Lebed Hall, Leningradskoye sh. 35	159-7844		
U Petra, see Peter's Place			
U Pirosmani cafe, Novodevichy pr. 4	247-1926		
U Yuzefa, ul. Dubininskaya 11/17	238-4646		
U.G.T., see Union, Gas & Technic GmbH			
U.K. Paints, Ltd, ul. Akad. Koroleva 4, k. 2, kv. 1-2	286-0790	282-4308	
U.S. East European Development, Inc.,			
Leninskiy prosp. 66	137-0003	133-4335	
U.S. West International, Inc.,			
Krasnopresenskaya nab. 12, Office 809	253-2058	253-2059	
U.S. Wheat Association, Olimpiyskiy prosp. 181			
U2 Family Superstore, ul. Bakuninskaya 32	265-2963		
Udarnik Cinema, ul. Serafimovicha 2	238-7664		
Ukraina Cinema, ul. Barklaya 9/2	145-6255		
Ukraina Hotel, Kutuzovskiy prosp. 2/1	243-2895		
Casino Tars	243-3004		
In Vino Restaurant	243-2316		
Magazin del Mondo	243-4682		
Reprocenter (Rank Xerox)	243-3007		
Ulan-Bator Cinema, ul. Grimau 12	126-2012		
Ulrich Schreiber	253-2704		
Umitec Exchange, ul. Profsoyuznaya 113, k. 3			
UN Information Center, Glazovskiy p. 4/16	241-2894	230-2138	413595
Underground Press Museum, Lesnaya ul. 55	251-2593		
UNESCO Assistance (Moscow Club),			
ul. Miklukho-Maklaya 22	330-6546		

Uni-Export Instruments LTD,
  Hotel Mezhdunarodnaya 2, room 1417 — 255-6609 — 253-1415 — 413338
Uniastrum Group, Suvorovskaya pl. 1 — 258-1665 — 258-1555
Unibank, Dmitrovka B. ul. 5/6 — 292-0338
Unibor JV (Cyprus), ul. Skladochnaya 6 — 289-0016 — 412271
Unicom JV (Yugoslavia), ul. Skladochnaya,6
Unicoop Japan, B. Gnezdnikovskiy p. 7, 2nd fl. — 200-2520 — 973-2024 — 413517
Unikombank, Khrustalny p. 1 — 925-3462 — 928-3836
Union Bank of Finland LTD,
  Dmitrovka B. ul. 5/6, kv. 34 — 292-0338 — 29236067 — 413286
Union Bank of Switzerland, Pokrovskiy bul. 4/17, kv. 4 — 207-3429 — 230-2456 — 413188
Union Carbide Corp., ul. Mytnaya 3, ent.1 — 230-7646 — 230-6104 — 413820
Union JV (Germany), Bernikov p. 2/6 — 227-2805 — 975-2303
Union JV (UK), ul. Chasovaya 24/1 — 155-7150 — 943-0075 — 411720
Union of Architects of the CIS, Granatny p. 3 — 290-3047 — 290-4384
Union of Architects of the RFSFR, Granatny p. 22 — 291-5578
Union of Cinematographers, Vasilyevskaya ul. 13 — 250-4114 — 200-4284 — 411939
Union of Composers of the RFSFR, Bryusov p. 8/10 — 229-5218
Union of Designers, Arbatskaya pl. 1/2, str. 3 — 202-4648
Union of Information and Management Centers,
  Kozhevnicheskaya ul. 3 — 253-1053 — 253-2481 — 411486
Union of Joint Stock Companies, Balakirevskiy p. 23 — 261-8293 — 292-6511
Union of Journalists, Zubovskiy bul. 4 — 201-4891
Union of Oil Producers, ul. Usacheva 35 — 245-5846
Union of Theater Workers,
  ul. Tverskaya 12, str. 7, kv. 228 — 209-2436
Union of Women of Russia, Glinishchevskiy p. 6 — 209-7433
Union of Writers, Komsomolskiy prosp. 13 — 246-4350
  ul. Povarskaya 52 — 291-6307 — 230-2716
Union Supermarket Cafe JV (Germany),
  Bernikov p. 2/6 — 227-2805 — 975-2303
Union, Gas & Technic GmbH — 248-2341 — 248-2032 — 413579
Unionchimstroy JV, Elokhovskiy p. 3 — 261-8685 — 261-8686
Unipharm JV (UK), Skatertny p. 13 — 202-5071
Unisat, Nikopeskovskiy B. p. 5 (off the Arbat)
Unisel Network, Leninskiy prosp. 85 — 134-0521 — 936-2371
Unison JV (US), ul. Maroseyka 7/8 — 411855
United Investments, Ltd., ul. Pomerantsev 8 — 203-8984 — 297-3607
United News of India, Michurinskiy prosp. 11, kv. 85 — 437-4360 — 413007
United Parcel Service, see UPS
United Press International,
  Kutuzovskiy prosp. 7/4, kv. 67 — 243-6829 — 413424
United Stone JV, ul. Pyatnitskaya 22, str.2
United Technologies, See Pratt & Whitney
United Way International, ul. Yaroslavskaya 8, k. 3 — 243-9726 — 243-9726
Unitek JV (Sweden), ul. Miklukho-Maklaya 18 — 330-7829 — 336-0993
Unitel Co., Ltd., ul. Mariny Raskovy 12 — 943-1506
Unitex JV, MGU — 939-5069 — 938-2136
Univermag, ul. Krasnoprudnaya 12
Universal American Trading Corp.,
  3rd Dobryninskiy p. 3/5-1 — 238-9984 — 113-8320
Universal Laser Service Ltd.,
  ul. Dolgorukovskaya 16, 3-d floor — 258-8153 — 972-6082

	Phone	Fax	Telex
Universal Telephone & Telecom. Systems, Inc.,			
Zelenograd, 3rd Zapadny pr. 13	534-7458	534-8174	
Universitetskaya Hotel, Michurinskiy prosp. 8/29	939-9731		
Univolt JV (Sweden), ul. Lobninskaya 21	483-4422		207080
Unsere Zeit, ul. Ivana Babushkina 3, kv. 284	310-7013		413414
UPDK, see GlavUPDK			
UPenn Alumni Association	241-1337		
Upjohn Company, Gazetny p. 17/9	956-9800	956-9801	612223
UPS Express Mail JV (Finland),			
B. Ochakovskaya ul. 15a	430-6373		411927
Ural Cinema, pl. Bela Kuna 1	462-5337		
Ural Hotel, ul. Pokrovka 40	297-4258		
US Embassy Day Care and Pre-School, US Embassy	252-2451		
US Impex Inc., Dmitrovskoye sh. 98	488-3102	488-0351	
US News & World Report, Leninskiy prosp. 36, kv. 53	938-2051	137-2593	413216
US Sprint, see Sprint Networks			
UTS Testesysteme	253-2422		
Uts-Umi-Test JV (FRG), M. Ivanovskiy p. 11/6, str. 1	924-8984	923-7071	411767
UUSI Suomi & MTV, ul. Narodnaya 13, kv. 34		274-0007	413130
UVIR, see Visa Registration Office for Foreigners			
UVL Plus, ul. Svobody 79	496-5163	490-7482	
Uzbekistan Restaurant, ul. Neglinnaya 29	924-6053		

V

	Phone	Fax	Telex
V. Spesivtsev's Experimental Studio Theater,			
ul. Rustaveli 19	218-2332	218-2332	
VAAP, see All Union Copyright Agency			
Vakhtangov Theater, ul. Arbat 26	241-0728		
Valentin Yudashkin Salon, Petrovskiy Passazh			
Valio, Koroviy val 7, Office 14		230-2810	413040
Valmet Oy, Pokrovskiy bul. 4/17, kv. 8 & 11	297-1176	230-2631	413257
Valtec Ltd., prosp. Mira 74, # 182, 183	280-1652	230-2726	413915
Van Vuuren BV, B. Danilovskiy p. 5	954-0723		
Vanguardia (La), Leninskiy prosp. 93, k. 2, kv. 66	938-2154	938-2167	413658
VAO 'Intourist' (Adventure Tours), ul. Mokhovaya 13	292-2791	200-0224	
Vareniki cafe, Rzevhskiy M. p. & Skatertny p.			
Varian Associates Inc., Borisoglebskiy p. 13	203-9920	291-1577	
Varioline Handelsgesellschaft mbH, Frezer sh. 17	170-3101	274-0057	413600
Varko JSK, ul. Lesnaya 45a	258-7502	258-7504	412116
Varshava Cinema, pl. Ganetskovo 1	156-8001		
Varshava I Hotel, Leninskiy prosp. 2	238-1970		
Varshava II Hotel, Kotelnicheskaya nab. 1/15	227-4078		
Vasinkraft JV, ul. Nikolskaya 19	928-8080	924-2307	411369
Vasnetsov House (A.M. Vasnetsov) Museum,			
Vasnetsova p. 13	208-9045		
VDNKh, see VVTs			
Vedomosti S'ezda Narod. Dep Ros Fed Verkh			
Sov RSFR, Krasnopresnenskaya nab. 2	205-6210		
VEEK JV, ul. Myasnitskaya 8	928-5560	921-7737	
VEK, LTD, Krasnopresnenskaya nab. 12, Office 1701	253-2842	253-2845	413968
Vektor Joint Stock Co., Bolshevistskiy prosp.	928-9953		

	Phone	Fax	Telex
Vektor SP Brokerage Firm, ul. Safonovskaya 17/43	415-7734	415-7635	
Velikaya Stena JV, Profsoyuznaya ul. , 5/9	125-1252	125-6971	
Vemo JV (Austria), 3rd Lyusinovskiy p. 3			
Vensta JV (Austria), ul. Vorontsovskaya 15/10	272-1848		411802
Vent-Inter JV (Finland), Nikolo-Yamskoy tupik 3	227-3537		
Vera Moda, Dmitrovka M. ul. 8	299-7448		
Vernadskiy Museum, ul. A.N. Kosygina 47a	137-0011		
Vernisage Theater, ul. Begovaya 5	946-0165		
Veronica TV, NOS TV & De Telegraaf,			
Rublyovskoye sh. 26, kv. 102-103	415-4064	415-2905	
Vessolink Paging Systems, Skakovaya ul. 32	945-2843	945-6452	
Vesta Car Rental, Leningradskaya Hotel, room 61	248-2657		
Vesta Taxi Service	447-5481		
Vesti Shop, Hotel Kosmos, prosp. Mira 150	217-1194		
Vestnik JV (Austria), ul. Arbat 54/2	241-8704	244-4160	411584
Veterinarian, ul. Yunnatov 16a	212-8076		
Via Montenapoleone, Kutuzovskiy prosp. 22	243-1250		
Videocomputer JV (FRG), Chistoprudny bul. 12	928-7883		
VideoForce, Koroviy val 7, ent 1	238-3136		
Mezhdunarodnaya Hotel, 1st floor, ul. Korovy val 7	253-7708		
Videoline JV (Switz.), 2nd Frunzenskaya ul. 10, k. 1	242-0110	245-7551	
Videoton, Grokholskiy p. 13	280-1648		414546
Vienna cafe, Olympic Penta, Olympiyskiy prosp. 18/1	971-6101		
Vienna Restaurant,			
Palace Hotel, ul. Tverskaya-Yamskaya 19	956-3152		
Vienna Trading House, Galarie, prosp. Mira 91 k. 1	287-2202	287-2202	
ViennaPlast (Austria), Kutuzovskiy prosp. 7/4-179	243-1525	243-1525	
Vietnam Airlines (Hang Khong Viet Nam),			
ul. Nikolskaya 17, #61	926-8378	928-4452	
Vigraf Studio, ul. Vavilova 24	238-4578	135-8949	
Viko, Sherbakovskaya 9	369-1757		
Viktoria (Hard Rock Cafe) cafe,			
Zelyony Theater, Krymskiy val 9	237-0709		
Viktoria JV (FRG), Leninskiy prosp. 90/2	202-9501	290-6497	411578
Viktoria Restaurant, prosp. Mira 78	971-0721		
Villa Peredelkino Hotel, 1st Chobatovskaya Alleya 2a	435-8184	435-1478	
Restaurant,	435-1478	435-1211	
Vima JV (Sweden), Koslovskiy B. p. 3/2	202-9106		
Vinson & Elkins, Povarskaya ul. 21	291-3156	200-0295	
VIP Center JV (Finland), Sadovnicheskaya ul. 77	233-2095	233-2095	
VIP JV (FRG), ul. Marksa-Engelsa 8	203-4331	200-5255	411135
Virginia-American Food Store, M. Bronnaya ul. 27/14	290-3531	924-8329	
Visa	284-4802		
Visa Reg. Off. for Foreigners (OVIR), ul. Pokrovka 42	924-9349		
Visit-Dialogue JV (US), ul. M. Bronnaya 23	202-3372		122205
Visnews Television, Gruzinskiy p. 3, kv. 219-220	253-9296	253-9295	413428
VIST JV (US), Tryokhprudny p. 4	200-3568	973-2025	
Vista JV (US), ul. Bakhrushina 28			
VIT Worldwide, Povarskaya ul. 21, 2nd fl., #14	291-1844	291-3758	414328
VITA, ul. Poklonnaya 6	249-7818	249-7818	
Vita-Commerce U.B. JV, Avtomobilny pr. 10	278-3456	274-4083	
Vitas Corp., ul. Rossolimo 4	246-9366	246-9543	413872
Vites, ul. Lesnaya 20/6	972-1755	298-9703	

	Phone	Fax	Telex
Vityaz Cinema, ul. Miklukho-Maklaya 27a	335-7192		
Vivat, Kolomenskiy pr. 1/1	112-1244	112-0254	
VIZA Bank, Gogolevskiy bul. 3/2	291-9514	230-2548	414763
Vladimir Restaurant, 5th Kotelnicheskiy p. 1	272-4566		
Vladivostok Cinema, ul. Lazo 3	309-1195		
Vltava cafe, Vasilyevskaya ul. 15/24	251-6898		
Vneshagro JV, Bobrov p. 4, str. 2	928-6974	928-2235	
Vneshconsult JV (Finland),			
VVTs, bldg. 4, prosp. Mira 120	181-4294	181-4133	411175
Vnesheconombank, Krasnopresnenskaya nab. 12	253-1799		
Serpukhovskiy val 8	292-8292		
ul. Plyushchikha 37	928-7116	207-0589	411174
Vnesheconomservis, ul. Ilyinka 6	259-3753		411431
Vneshiberika JV (Spain), ul. Fadeyeva 1	200-5205	200-5205	411238
Vneshmaltigraf JV, ul. Fadeyeva 1			
Vneshnaya Torgovlya (Foreign Trade) Magazine,			
Minskaya ul. 11	145-6894	145-5192	
Vneshposyltorg, Marksistskaya ul. 5	272-7222	274-0102	411250
Vneshpromtekhobmen, p. Vasnetsova 9	284-7241	284-7395	411181
Vneshstroyimport, Tverskoy bul. 6	220-3204	973-2148	411434
Vneshtekhnika, Starokonyushenny p. 6	201-7260	201-7357	411418
Vneshterminalkomplex, ul. Zenlyachkiy 3. str. 2			412190
Vneshtorgbank, Kuznetskiy Most 16	928-7116	925-3263	
Vneshtorgizdat Publishers, ul. Fadeyeva 1	250-5162	253-9794	411238
Vneshtorgreklama, ul. Kakhovka 31	331-8311	310-7005	411265
Vneshtradeinvest JV (Austria), ul. B. Yakimanka 7/8	238-9316	230-2039	411691
VNIKI, See National Market Research Institute			
Vnukovo Airport	234-8656		
Voaysh JV, Gorodok Baumana 3, k. 4			
VOCA, Boyarskiy p. 3	207-2000	924-3779	
Voerman W.W.R.S. Moscow,			
Novoyasenevskiy pr. 6, K. 1, Ap.68	425-8084	425-8084	
Voest-Alpine Aktiengesellschaft,			
Krasnopresnenskaya nab. 12, Office 1107	253-8540	230-2830	413016
Voice of America, Rublyovskoye sh. 26, kv. 134	415-4236	415-2950	413682
Vokrug Sveta (Around the World) Magazine,			
Novodmitrovskaya ul. 5a	285-8883	972-0582	
Volga Cinema, Dmitrovskoye sh. 133	485-5111		
Volga Hotel, Dokuchayev p. 10	280-7729		
Volga II Hotel, ul. B. Spasskaya 4	280-1364		
Volga Yacht Charter, ul. Maksimova 6, kv. 121	254-7998		
Volgograd Cinema, Ferganskaya ul. 17	371-6496		
Volkskrant (De), ul. Vishnevskovo 4, kv. 75	253-9796		413562
Volksstimme, prosp. Mira 68, kv. 24	971-3496		413999
Voltek JV,			
Kotelnicheskaya nab. 1/15, k. BV, podyezd 6, 357	276-7851	276-3066	414530
Volvo Auto Oy Ab	336-6565	336-6567	
Voprosy Economiki (Problems of Economics),			
Nakhimovskiy prosp. 27	129-0454	310-7001	
Vorlaufer, ul. Akad. Pilyugina 14, k. 3, kv. 958-959	936-2604	936-2160	
Voskhod Cinema, ul. Mikhailova 29, korp. 1	171-9983		
Voskhod Hotel, Altufyevskoye sh. 2	401-9822		
Voskreseniye, Petrovskiy p. 8	229-1419		

Voskresenskiy customs point — 2-26-03

Vossen Clothing Store, Petrovskiy Passazh, 2nd fl.

Vostochno-Evropeiskiy Investistionny Bank,
see East European Investment Bank

Vostok Bank, ul. Yaroslavskaya 4 — 217-6165 — 217-6163 — 411390

Vostok Cinema, pl. Akademika Kurchatova 1/1 — 196-4949

Vostokintorg, 1st Krasnogvardeyskiy pr. (Expocenter) — 205-6055 — 253-9275 — 411123

Votchina cafe, ul. Ostozhenka 18 — 203-7173

Votteler, see Theodor Votteler

Voyenno-Promyshlennaya Investitsionnaya Kompaniya,
see Military-Industrial Investment Company

Vozrozhdeniye Bank, Khrustalny per 1 — 921-4415 — 298-3045

VPIK, see Military-Industrial Investment Company

Vrbas, ul. Pushechnaya 4 — 925-7127 — 928-5182

Vremex, ul. Chasovaya 24/1 — 151-5511 — 943-0075 — 411720

Vremya, Pyatnitskaya ul. 62 — 233-5081 — 229-3511

Vstrecha cafe, ul. Gilyarovskovo 3 — 208-4597

Vstrecha Cinema, ul. Sadovaya-Chernogryazskaya 5/9 — 975-4389

**VVTs - All-Russian Exhibition Center
(former VDNKh)**, prosp. Mira 120 — 181-9332

Vyecherni Siluett, Taganskaya pl. 88 — 272-2280

Vympel Cinema, ul. Kominterna 8 — 472-3240

Vympel Fatex JV (UK),
Stary Petrovsko-Razumovskiy pr. 1/23 — 214-8149

Vysota Cinema, ul. Yunykh Lenintsev 52

W

Wackenhut, Sadovaya-Kudrinskaya ul. 21A — 254-0202 — 956-3256

Wako Koeki Co., LTD,
Hotel Mezhdunarodnaya II, room 1121 — 253-1676 — 253-9500 — 413347

Wall Street Journal, ul. B. Spasskaya 12, kv. 134 — 280-5049 — 280-5128 — 413299

Waltham Shopping Center, ul. Tverskaya 9 — 229-2869

Wang Computer Systems,
VVTs, bldg. 1, unit 17, prosp. Mira 120 — 263-9906

Wang-Service, Grubskovskaya nab. 3 — 261-4687

Wang/Management Data, Rubtsovskaya Nab.3 — 265-3708

Wartsila, Glazovskiy p. 7, kv. 13-14 — 230-2584 — 413371

Washington Film Assoc's, Leningradskoye sh. 8/170 — 150-5682 — 150-5682

Washington Post, Kutuzovskiy prosp. 7/4, kv. 2-3 — 243-1848 — 413430

Weather by phone — 975-9260

Weather forecast by phone — 975-9222

Wedgewood, Sadko Arcade (Expocenter) — 253-9588

Wega Aussenhandels GmbH, Hotel Budapest, rm 401 — 921-4461 — 411662

Weimos JV, ul. Kalanchevskaya 21/40, k. 201 — 975-4012

Wella, ul. Mayakovskovo 12 — 290-5137

Wellcome Foundation Ltd., ul. Dolgorukovskaya 21 — 973-3897 — 973-3685

Welt (Die), Kutuzovskiy prosp. 7/4, kv. 169 — 243-5286 — 413230

Wesak Chrysler, Plotnikov p. 12 — 241-3593 — 244-7235

Wesorta, Glazovskiy p. 7, kv. 6 — 203-5790 — 200-1248 — 413051

West International, Lavochkina ul. 19 — 451-5364 — 455-8470

	Phone	Fax	Telex
Westdeutsche Landesbank Europa AG,			
Krasnopresnenskaya nab. 12, Office 1207-1208	255-6464	253-9093	413098
Westdeutscher Rundfunk (ARD & ARD TV),			
Kutuzovskiy prosp. 7/4, kv. 121-124	243-4355	243-0795	413124
Westdeutscher Rundfunk (ARD),			
Kutuzovskiy prosp. 7/4, kv. 125	243-9744	243-6068	413551
Western Atlas International, Inc.,			
Leninskiy prosp. 2, 3rd floor, office 22	974-1277		414834
Western Union, (Sberbank) PO Box 9	119-8250	310-4709	
Bank Elita, ul. Meshchanskaya 20	971-6479		
Bank Orbita, Spasonalivkovskiy p.2. 7	223-8875		
Gloria Bank, Avtozavodskiy pr. 2. 2			
Inkombank, Sadovo-Triumfalnaya ul. 14/12			
Inkombank, Arkhangelskiy p. 12/8	209-1939		
Inkombank, ul. Nametkina 14, k. 1			
Westfalia Restaurant, Leninskiy prosp. 87	134-3026		
WestLB, see Westdeutsche Landesbank Girozentrale			
Westlink JV, Varshavskoye sh. 8	276-6507		
Westminster Motors, B. Cheremushkinskaya ul. 25/40	127-0832	127-0830	613022
Westrosso Insurance Co., Ltd.,			
Vozenko ul. 9/2, PO Box 226351	417-8149	417-8334	
White & Associates, Rokossovskovo bul. 7, k. 2, kv. 14	160-5539	230-2101	
White & Case, ul. Tverskaya 7, entrance 9	201-9292	201-9284	
Widik Auto Salon, Leningradskiy prospect 31	213-1156	213-8754	
Wild Orchid Lingerie, Petrovskiy bul. 9			
Willbros (overseas), Ltd.,			
Park Place, Leninskiy prosp. 18/1	956-5491	956-5492	
Willcox R.E.B., Dmitrovka M. ul. 31/22, office 8	299-2101	956-3271	
Willis Faber & Dumas Ltd, ul. Gilyarovskovo 65	281 1601	975-2012	
Willowcorp Russian Ltd., Zemlyanoy val 19	923-3436		
Wilma Sanatorium	496-9810		
Winebrant Life JV (US), Platovskaya ul. 4			
Winkler's, TsUM, 3rd fl.			
Wise Marketing and Management JV (UK),			
ul. Spartakovskaya 6a			
Wolff Aktiengesellschaft,			
see Otto Wolff Aktiengesellschaft			
Wolfgang Held, Petrovskiy Passazh, 1st fl.			
World Bank, Aerostar Hotel	155-5111		
World Bible Transl'n Center, Krylatskiye Kholmy 34	413-8294	413-8294	
World Mission Cultural Centre, ul. Krupskoy 12a	344-6759		
World Trade Consultants Corporation,			
Koroviy val 7, Office 64	238-9146	230-2035	413932
World Trade Telecom,			
Sovintsenter, Krasnopresnenskaya nab. 12	253-1308	253-8182	
World Transit	206-8781	206-9717	
World University Service, prosp. Vernadskovo 41	432-5782	434-8355	
World Vision, prosp. Vernadskovo 41a, room 812	432-2604	432-5744	
Worldwide Relocation Service,			
Novoyasenevskiy prosp. 5, kor. 8	425-8084	425-8084	
Worldwide Television News,			
Presnenskiy val 19, kv. 513	254-4758		412305
Wrigley's, Tryokhprudny p. 5, kv. 7	200-6525	956-3167	

	Phone	Fax	Telex
Writer's Union Restaurant, ul. Povarskaya 52	291-2169		
WTCC, see World Trade Consultants Corporation			
WTL international, Novy Arbat 36	290-7768	290-9303	

X

	Phone	Fax	Telex
Xerox Corporation, 4th Dobryninskiy p. 6/9, 1st floor	230-2744	230-2728	
Xerox Copy Center,			
Sovintsentr, Mezhdunarodnaya Hotel, 2nd fl.	205-6903		
Novinskiy bul. 15 Kutuzovskiy 22	205-7983	205-7708;	
Vorontsovskiy p. 5/7	271-2068		
Xinhau News Agency, ul. Druzhby 6	143-1951	938-2007	413983

Y

	Phone	Fax	Telex
Yagil International Corp., Serebryanicheskiy p. 2/5	227-1905	227-1905	
Yak Air Service JV, ul. Timiryazevskaya, 10/12			
Yakimanka cafe, B. Polyanka 2/10, Str. 1	238-8888		
Yakovlev & Co., GUM, 1st line, 2nd fl.			
Yakut, ul. Dolgorukovslaya 5	973-3452		
Yale Alumni Association	271-1622		
Yamaha Pianos, Petrovskiy Passazh, 2nd fl.			
Yamskoy Dvor, Leninskiy prosp. 30	135-8255		
Yantar Cinema, Otkrytoye sh. 4	168-6228		
Yanusles JV (FRG), ul. Volkhonka 5/6, str. 11		213-4747	
Yapi Ve Kredi Bankasi A.S.,			
Krasnopresnenskaya nab. 12. Office 1206a	253-1947	253-1647	413705
Yaroslavskaya Hotel, Yaroslavskaya ul. 8	283-1733		
Yaroslavskiy Train Station, Komsomolskaya pl. 5	266-0218		
Yauzkie Vorota cafe, Yauzkiy bul. 1/15	227-2405		
Yeiwa Trading Co., LTD, ul. Mytnaya 1, 2nd fl.	237-2040	230-2323	
Yemenia (Yemen Airlines)			
Sheremetevo 2 Airport, Office 646	578-2708		413973
Yenisey Cinema, 3rd Parkovaya ul. 53	164-4896		
Yerevan Cinema, Dmitrovskoye sh. 82	489-9464		
Yermolova Drama Theater, ul. Tverskaya 5			
Yermolova Museum, Tverskoy bul. 11	290-4901		
Yeruslan Coop, Sheremetevo 2 Airport	578-8879	578-6539	
Yokohama Trading Corp., Ltd., ul. Mytnaya 1, 2nd fl.	237-1628		
Young and Rubicam/Sovero JV (US),			
Mezhdunarodnaya Business Center, Ent. 3, #1404	253-1347	253-1348	412199
Young Fashion, Sadko Arcade (Expocenter)	253-9592	973-2185	
Young Millionaires Club,			
see Russian Club of Young Millionaires			
Yunona JV (Yugoslavia), Merzlyakovskiy p. 7/2	290-6223	230-2117	411160
Yunost Cinema, ul. Marshala Rybalko 1/4	194-0275		
Yunost Hotel, ul. Khamovnicheskiy val 34			
Yupiter, ul. Novy Arbat 25			
Yuridicheskaya Literatura, Nikitskaya M. ul. 14	202-8384		
Yustas JV, ul. Kasatkina 3a			

	Phone	Fax	Telex
Yuzhnaya Hotel, Leninskiy prosp. 87	134-3065		
Yuzhny Dvor, Butyrskiy val 7	250-2300	233-0405	
Yves Rocher, GUM, 2nd line, 1st fl.	926-3408		
ul. Tverskaya 4	923-5885		

Z

	Phone	Fax	Telex
ZA Art Action Agency JV, ul. Studencheskaya 22			
Za Rubezhom, ul. Pravdy 24	257-2387		
Zagorye Hotel, ul. Yagodnaya 15	329-3011		
Zagranreklama,			
see Interdepartmental Council for Foreign Advertising			
Zaidi i Poprobui cafe, prosp. Mira 124, k. 1	286-8165		
Zamoskvoreche Restaurant, ul. B. Polyanka 54	230-7333		
Zapchastexport, 2nd Skotoprogonnaya 35			
Zapsibinvest JV (FRG), Staraya Basmannaya ul. 4-405	925-0327		
Zarital JV (Italy), Kashirskoye sh. 65	398-8066		
Zarubezhgeologia, Kaloshin p. 10	241-1515		
Zarya Vostoka cafe, ul. 26 Bakinskikh Komissarov 4, k. 2	433-2201		
Zaryadye Cinema, Moskvoretskaya nab. 1	298-5687		
Zeiger International, ul. Ostozhenka 22	203-2548	203-1165	
Zeit (Die), ul. Sr. Pereyaslavskaya 14, kv. 19, 200-201	280-0385	288-9550	
Zeitung vum Letzbuerger Vollek,			
Leninskiy prosp. 68/100, kv. 33	930-1995		413303
Zenit Cinema, Taganskaya ul. 40/42	271-1440		
Zenit Interior JV Filial (Switz.), Gorodskaya ul. 2/7	954-0139	954-0148	
ZEOS International Ltd., prosp. Mira 186, str.2	286-2438	286-2438	
Zheldorbank, ul. Krasnoprudnaya 26/1	262-3666	262-3666	
Zhen Shen, Petrovskiy Passage	921-8460		
Zhilsotsbank of the USSR, see Mosbiznesbank			
Zhukovskiy Museum, ul. Radio 17	267-5054		
ZigZag Venture Group, Plotnikov p. 12	241-3593	244-7235	411636
Zika Chemie GmBH,			
Petrovskiye linii, 2/18, Budapest Hotel, room 401	921-4269	921-4269	
Zil and Stahl JV (FRG), ul. Avtozavodskaya 23		253-9800	411006
Zippo, ul. Energeticheskaya 5	362-8840	362-8840	
Znamenskiy Monastery Concert Hall, ul. Varvarka 8	298-3398		
Znaniye Publishers, Lubyanskiy pr. 4	928-1531		
Zolotaya Roza, Moskva Hotel	292-1194		
Zolotoy Kolos Hotel, Yaroslavskaya ul. 15, k. 3	286-2703		
Zolotoye Koltso (Belgrade II) Hotel,			
Smolenskaya ul. 15	248-6734		
Zoo, B. Gruzinskaya ul. 1	255-5375		
Zoo Beauty Salon, ul. Druzhinnikovskaya 30	252-2088		
Zoology Museum, Nikitskaya, B. ul. 6	203-8923		
Zormand Inc./Tazoma, p. Krasina 16	254-9537	254-7717	
Zvezda Cinema, Zemlyanoy val 18/22	297-6209		
Zvezdnaya Hotel, Zvyozdny bul. 42	215-4292		
Zvyozdny Cinema, prosp. Vernadskovo 14	133-9778		
Zweites Deutsches Fernsehen,			
ul. B. Dorogomilovskaya 14, kv. 46-47	243-4078	230-2054	413106
Zwemmer Bookstore, Kuznetskiy Most 18	928-2021		

RCMI, Inc.

Business Start-Up &
Market Entry in Russia

I. Strategy Planning and Market Entry

Business Plans

Project Analysis

Legal & Tax Updates

Competition Surveys

Market Analysis

II. Tax, Banking, Currency Conversion

Russian & International Taxation

Russian & International Accounting

Treaties & Tax Reduction

Local Banking Considerations

Currency Conversion

III. Company Registration and Visa Support

Joint Stock Companies

Limited Partnerships

Representative Offices

Non-Profit Organizations

Offshore Registration

Multi-Entry Visas

IV. Translation, Travel, Secretarial Services

Phone, Fax, Moscow Address

Translation Projects

Secretarial Services

Domestic Air & Rail Tickets

Logistics & Travel Coordination

Staffing Issues

IN THE U.S.:

19000 MacArthur Blvd., Suite 400
Irvine, CA 92715
(714) 476-7850
(714) 540-7108
Internet: <rcmi@igc.apc.org>

IN MOSCOW:

15 Ulitsa Chekhova
Moscow, Russia 103006
Tel +(7095) 209-98-14
Fax +(7095) 209-13-98
Glasnet: <rcmi@glas.apc.org>

Moscow Business
Yellow Pages

International Country and City Codes

To dial an international call from Russia, first dial 8, wait for a dial tone, then 10, then the country code, followed by the city code as listed below, then the local number.

Algeria	213	Germany	49	Kuwait	965	Singapore	65	
Argentina	54	Berlin	30	Latvia	371	Slovakia	42	
Buenos Aires	1	Bonn	228	Riga	2	South Africa	27	
Armenia	7	Dusseldorf	211	Liberia	231	Spain	34	
Australia	61	Frankfurt	69	Libya	218	Madrid	1	
Melbourne	3	Munich	89	Liechtenstein	4175	Sri Lanka	94	
Sydney	2	Greece	30	Lithuania	370	Suriname	597	
Austria	43	Athens	1	Vilnius	2	Sweden	46	
Vienna	1	Guatemala	502	Luxembourg	352	Stockholm	8	
Azerbaidzhan	7	Haiti	509	Malawi	265	Switzerland	41	
Bahrain	973	Honduras	504	Malaysia	60	Geneva	22	
Belarus	7	Hong Kong	852	Mexico	52	Zurich	1	
Belgium	32	Hong Kong	5	Mexico City	5	Tadzhikistan	7	
Brussels	2	Hungary	36	Moldova	373	Taiwan	886	
Bolivia	591	Budapest	1	Chisinau	2	Thailand	66	
Santa Cruz	33	Iceland	354	Monaco	3393	Bangkok	2	
Canada	1	India	91	Morocco	212	Tunisia	216	
Montreal	514	Bombay	22	Namibia	264	Turkey	90	
Ottawa	613	New Delhi	11	Nepal	977	Istanbul	1	
Toronto	416	Indonesia	62	Netherlands	31	Turkmenistan	7	
Vancouver	604	Jakarta	21	Amsterdam	20	Ukraine	7	
Cameroon	237	Iran	98	The Hague	70	United Arab		
Chile	56	Teheran	21	New Zealand	64	Emirates	971	
Santiago	2	Iraq	964	Nicaragua	505	UK	44	
China	86	Baghdad	1	Nigeria	234	Belfast	232	
Beijing	1	Ireland	353	Norway	47	Glasgow	41	
Columbia	57	Dublin	1	Oslo	2	London	71 (inner)	
Bogota	1	Israel	972	Oman	968		81 (outer)	
Costa Rica	506	Jerusalem	2	Pakistan	92	United States	1	
Croatia	385	Tel Aviv	3	Islamabad	51	Boston	617	
Cyprus	357	Italy	39	Panama	507	Chicago	312	
Czech Republic	42	Florence	55	Peru	51	Dallas	214	
Prague	2	Milan	2	Phillipines	63	Houston	713	
Denmark	45	Rome	6	Manila	2	Los Angeles	213	
Copenhagen	1 or 2	Venice	41	Poland	48	Montpelier	802	
Ecuador	593	Ivory Coast	225	Warsaw	22	New York	212	
Egypt	20	Japan	81	Portugal	351	San Francisco	415	
El Salvador	503	Tokyo	3	Lisbon	1	Seattle	206	
Estonia	372	Yokohama	45	Qatar	974	Washington	202	
Tallinn	2	Jordan	962	Romania	40	Uruguay	598	
Ethiopia	251	Amman	6	Bucharest	0	Uzbekistan	7	
Finland	358	Kazakhstan	7	Russia	7	Vatican City	396	
Helsinki	0	Kenya	254	Moscow	095	Venezuela	58	
France	33	Kirgizistan	7	St. Petersburg	812	Yemen Arab		
Paris	1	Korea, South	82	Saudi Arabia	966	Republic	967	
Georgia	7	Seoul	2	Senegal	221	Yugoslavia	381	
						Belgrade	11	

☑ See page 6 for Russian and CIS city codes.

Cross-reference Guide

The following is a list of cross-reference topics for use with the Moscow Business Yellow Pages. Bolded subheadings appear in the Yellow Pages.

Accounting
Advertising
Aerobics, see Gym
Airlines, Charter
Airlines, Commercial
Airports
Ambulance
American Express, see
    Credit Card Loss
Antiques
Apartments
Art galleries
Art museums
    see Museums
Associations
ATMs, see Cash advances
Autos, see Cars
Bakeries
Banks, Domestic
Banks, Foreign
Ballet
    see Theater/Ballet
Bars
Beauty salon
    see Hair cutting
Bodyguards, see Security
Boat Rides
Books
Bowling
Brunch
Business cards, see Printing
Business Centers
Business publications
    see Newspapers/
    Magazines
Cable Television
Calling home
    see International phone
Car phone
Cars, parts and supplies
Cars, rental
Cars, sales
Cars, service
Cash advances
Casinos/Gambling
Catering

Cellular phone
Changing money
    see Money changing
Chambers of Commerce
Charitable organizations,
    see Non-profits
Charters, see Airlines,
    Charters
Church
    see Religious services
Children, see Recreation,
    Schools, Clothing,
    children's, Toys
Circus
Clothing
Clothing, children's
Clubs
Coffee shops
Commercial department
Communication
    see International phone,
    Fax, Telegram/Telex,
    Telecom
Computer Sales
Computer Service
Computer, software
Concerts
Conference rooms, see
    Business Centers
Construction
Consulates
    see Embassies
Consulting firms

Contact lenses, see Optical
Copiers, Repair
Copiers, Sales
Copying
Cosmetics
Courier, Inter
Courier, City/Dom
Credit card loss
Customs
Decor
Delis
Dentists
Department stores
Desktop publishing
    see Printing
Dinner
    see Restaurants
Doctors
    see Medical care
Drug stores
Dry cleaning
Electronics
Electronic mail
Embassies
Engraving
Eye care, see Optical
Exercise
    see Swimming, Tennis,
    Gym, Horseback Riding,
    Gulf
Exchanges
Exhibitions
Express mail
Farmer's markets
    see Markets
Fax, see Business Centers
Film
Films
    see Movies
Fire
Flowers
Food

A

ACCOUNTING

Current Russian law requires regular auditing for all firms with foreign ownership. This has strained the already busy Western and joint venture accounting firms. Listed below are the major Western and Russian firms that can provide a full range of services.

Contact, Novaya Basmannaya ul. 37, ph. 261-0990

Coopers and Lybrand, ul. Shchepkina 6, ph. 288-9801

Deloitte & Touche, 2nd Samotyochny p. 1/23, ph. 281-5520

DRT Inaudit, 2nd Samotyochny p. 1/23, ph. 281-5520

Ernst & Young, Podsosenskiy p. 20/12, ph. 927-0569

Inaudit, ul. Konyushkovskaya 28, ph. 253-9505

KPMG Moscow, ul. Novaya Basmannaya 37, 3rd flr., ph. 261-7173

Master Ltd., ul. Marksa-Engelsa 15, kv. 5, ph. 202-3715

Price Waterhouse, B. Gruchcnovskiy p. 22/25, ph. 230-6185

ADVERTISING

See also Radio

The amazing increase in available media outlets in Russia has likewise increased options for advertising. Listed below are both Western and Russian firms that provide the full range of advertising services. To advertise in a specific newspaper, see the White Pages under the paper's name (some outlets are also listed below, under Advertising).

Akzent Media Russia, ul. Malomoskovskaya 21, ph. 286-2666 {billboards}

Arrange Media Service, ul. Lesnaya 27, ph. 251-5602

B&B&A, Frunzenskaya Nab. 30, pavilion 11, ph. 201-1929

BBDO Marketing, Staromonetny p. 31, ph. 231-3906

Begemot, M. Bronnaya 20a, ph. 202-1652

Bekar Advertising Agency, ph. 110-3993

Carat Russia, ul. Sheremetevskaya 2, ph. 971-0302

Cinema Service, Ltd., ul. Akademika Koroleva 8/1, ph. 216-8162

CIS Direct Mail, P.O. Box 85, ph. 229-7883 {direct mail services}

D'Arcy Masius Benton and Bowler, Tverskoy bul. 13, ph. 200-7286

Dentsu Inc., Radisson-Slavyanskaya Hotel, ph. 941-8112

Eurasia TV, ul. Lesnaya 63/43, ph. 250-1248

Friedman & Rose, 1st Baltiyskiy p. 6/21, k. 1, 3rd fl., ph. 151-8092

GGK Moscow, ph. 250-0196

Greatis, ul. Nagornaya 31, 4th Bld, ph. 127-5940

Hungexpo, Povarskaya ul. 21, ph. 291-1845

IMAX Show International JV (US), Tryokhgorny val 6, ph. 205-7279 {television ads}

Informlitsenzreklama JV (FRG), Leninskiy prosp. 146, office 1901, ph. 438-8100

Intercity Communications Agency (ICA), ul. Klary Tsetkin 11, Kor. 1, ph. 450-6788

Kamir Advertising Agency, ul. Goncharova 17a, ph. 219-0101

Key to Abbreviations

Abbrev.	Full word	English
bul./bulv.	bulvar	boulevard
kor.	korpus	building
kv.	kvartira	apartment
	most	bridge
nab.	naberezhnaya	embankment
p.	pereulok	lane
pl.	ploshchad	square
pod.	podyezd	entrance
prosp./pr.	prospekt	avenue
pro.	proyezd	passage
sh.	shosse	highway
str.	stroenie	building
	tupik	cul-de-sac
ul.	ulitsa	street
	val	rampart

Kosmos TV, ul. Akad. Koroleva 15, ph. 282-3360

Liniya-Poligraf Advertising Firm, ul. Sovkhoznaya 2, ph. 351-6173

LTW International, ul. B. Ordynka 14, ph. 233-1038

M BIS, ul. Goncharova 6, ph. 218-0860

Metapress Agency, 4th Tverskaya- ⇨ Yamskaya ul. 4, ph. 972-6453

Metroreklama JV (FRG), prosp. Mira 41, ph. 288-0309

MM & M, ul. Spartakovskaya 6A, ph. 267-4559

Moscow Times — Advertising, ph. 257-2574

News-Burda Advertising-Information Service JV, Pushkinskaya pl. 5, ph. 209-3674

Ogilvy & Mather, ul. Mytnaya 3, #3A, ph. 230-6606; prosp. Vernadskovo 33, ph. 131-5749

Premier SV, ul. Shchepkina 60/2, entr. A, ph. 281-4726

Premier SV-Print, Yeropkinskiy p. 16, ph. 201-3926

Red Square Productions, Kotelnicheskaya nab. 1/15, kv. 39, floor 8, ph. 227-4484

Russian Press Service Agency, Pitinkovskiy p. 1/2, ph. 209-7652

⇨ Russian Information Services, B. Kondratyevskiy p. 4, kor. 2, kv. 168, ph. 254-9275 {Where in Moscow, Where in St. Petersburg, Russia Survival Guide, Russian Travel Monthly}

Solidarnost Advertising, ph. 222-0961

Sovelan Aroma JV (US), Rublyovskoye sh. 26, k. 1, kv. 43, ph. 415-4039

Svetoreklama JV, ul. Polyarnaya 13V, ph. 473-9266

Tabani Corporation, Krasnopresnenskaya nab. 12, Office 1505, ph. 253-2462

Vigraf Studio, ul. Vavilova 24, ph. 238-4578

Vites, ul. Lesnaya 20/6, ph. 972-1755

Where in Moscow, (see Russian Information Services above).

Young and Rubicam/Sovero JV (US), Mezhdunarodnaya Business Center, Ent. 3, #1404, ph. 253-1347

AIRLINES, CHARTER

Aeroflot-Lufthansa and Partners JV, Sheremetevo 1 Airport, K-340, ph. 578-0540

Air Charter Service, ph. 939-0200

AJT Air International, ul. Varvarka 6, Hotel Rossiya, #503, ph. 298-1404

Akko-Universal, ul. Kosmonavta Volkova 6A, #1206, ph. 155-5644

Center-South, ul. Verkhnyaya Doroga 1, 16th fl., ph. 976-1112

⇨ EuroFlite Oy, via Helsinki office:

Ibusz (Hungarian Travel Company), Staropimenovskiy p. 5, ph. 299-7402

Korsar Airlines, pl. Suvorova 1, ph. 281-7452

Service 11 (Sluzhba 11) Air Charter Agency, ul. Profsoyuznaya 98 korp.1 kv.294, ph. 330-7508

Skytrump, Myusskaya pl. 6/5, 4th fl., ph. 250-5555

Transaero, Hotel Moskva, ph. 292-7513

TransSuper, ph. 177-1274

Vektor Joint Stock Co., Bolshevistskiy prosp., ph. 928-9953

AIRLINES, COMMERCIAL

See also Travel Agents

Most airlines have offices in Sheremetevo II airport and, if not listed here, can be contacted with the help of a hotel service bureau or, in any case, by calling one of these numbers. For addresses, fax or telex numbers, see the Telephone Directory **(numbers in bold are the airport phone numbers):**

For air tickets, contact a travel agent or:

Intourtrans, ul. Petrovka 15/13, ph. 927-1181

Ticket Express, Novokonyushenny p. 9/2, ph. 244-7260

World Transit, ph. 206-8781

Aeroflot, Leningradskiy pr., 37, ph. 155-6641, **578-9101**

Aeroflot Airport Information, Leningradskiy prosp. 37, ph. 155-0922
Departures, ph. **578-7816**
Arrivals, ph. **578-7518**

Air Algerie, Koroviy val 7, section 11, ph. 237-5257, **578-3386**

Air China, Kuznetskiy Most 1/8, Str. 5, ph. 292-3387, **578-2725**

Air France, Koroviy val 7, ph. 237-2325, **578-2757**

Air India, Koroviy val 7, k. 1, ph. 237-7494, **578-2747**

Air-BIJV, Sheremetevo 2 Airport, ph. **578-8268**

Alitalia, ul. Pushechnaya 7, ph. 923-9840, **578-2767**

All Nippon Airways, Hotel Mezhdunarodnaya II, #1405, ph. 253-1546, **578-5744**

Ariana Afghan Airlines, Koroviy val 7, fl. 2, kv. 8a, ph. 238-9779, **578-2719**

Austrian Airlines, Krasnopresnenskaya nab. 12, Office 1805, ph. 253-1670, **578-2734**

Balkan Air, Kuznetskiy Most 3, ph. 921-0267, **578-2712**

Bering Air, ph. 373-9664

British Airways, Krasnopresnenskaya nab. 12, Office 1905, ph. 253-2492, **578-2923**

Cascade Airlines, Trubnaya pl. 20/2, ph. 208-2090

Chosonminhang (N. Korean Airways), ul. Mosfilmovskaya 72, ph. 143-6307, **578-7580**

Continental Airlines, Kolokolnikov p. 11, ph. 925-1291

Croatia Airlines, Kutuzovskiy prosp. 13, #10-13, ph. 233-6797

CSA, Czechoslovak Airlines, 2nd Brestskaya 21/27, ph. 250-4571, **578-2704**

Cubana de Avacion, Koroviy val 7, sect. 5, ph. 238-0223, **578-2704**

Delta Airlines Inc., Krasnopresnenskaya nab. 12, Office 1102a, ph. 253-2658, **578-2738**

Deutsche BA, Sovintsentr, Mezhdunarodnaya Hotel I, #1905, ph. 253-2492

Egyptair, Sovintsentr, Mezhdunarodnaya Hotel, #831, ph. 253-2831

Ethiopian Airlines, Sheremetevo 2 Airport, office 641, ph. **578-2717**

Finnair, Kamergerskiy p. 6, ph. 292-8788, **578-2718**

Iberia Airlines, Sheremetevo 2, ph. **578-2791**

Iraqi Airways, ul. Pyatnitskaya 37, ph. 231-2974, **578-2707**

JAL, Japan Air Lines, Kuznetskiy Most 3, ph. 921-6448, **578-2942**

JAT Yugoslav Airlines, Kuznetskiy Most 3, ph. 921-2846, **578-2724**

KLM Royal Dutch Airlines, Krasnopresnenskaya nab. 12, Office 1307, ph. 253-2150, **578-2762**

Korean Air (South Korea), Hotel Cosmos, room 1629, ph. 217-1627, **578-2728**

LAL, Lithuanian Airlines, B. Rzhevskiy p. 7, ph. 203-6730

Libyan Arab Airlines, Koroviy val 7, ent. 2, ph. 237-2976, **578-2730**

LOT Polish Airlines, Koroviy val 7, Office 5, ph. 238-0003, **578-2706**

Lufthansa Airlines, Olympic Penta Hotel Olympiyskiy prosp. 18/1, ph. 975-2501, **578-3151**

Malev Hungarian Airlines, Kamergerskiy p. 6, ph. 292-0434, **578-2710**

MIAT Mongolian Airlines, Spasopeskovskiy p. 7/1, ph. 241-0754, **578-2759**

Romanian Air Transport, ul. Mosfilmovskaya 64, ph. 143-2640, **578-2716**

Royal Jordanian Air, Sheremetevo 2 Airport, ph. 578-2761, **578-2761**

Sabena Belgian World Airlines, Sheremetevo 2 Airport, ph. **578-2713**

Scandinavian Airlines, Kuznetskiy Most 3, ph. 925-4747, **578-2727**

Swissair, Krasnopresnenskaya nab. 12, Office 2005, ph. 253-8988, **578-2740**

Syrian Arab Airlines, Koroviy val 7, ph. 237-1727

TAAG, Angola Airlines, Koroviy val 7, #8, ph. 237-0010, **578-2773**

THY, Turkish Airlines, Kuznetskiy Most 1/8, ph. 292-5121, **578-2728**

Transaero Airlines, Okhotny Ryad 2 (Hotel 'Moscow'), ph. 292-7513

TWA, Radisson-Slavyanskaya Hotel, #5028, ph. 941-8146

Vietnam Airlines (Hang Khong Viet Nam), ul. Nikolskaya 17, #61, ph. 926-8378

Yemenia (Yemen Airlines), Sheremetevo 2 Airport, Office 646, ph. **578-2708**

AIRPORTS

Aerovokzal, Leningradskiy prosp. 37a, ph. 155-0922

Airline Ticket Booking, Leningradskiy prosp. 37, ph. 155-5003; **International**, ph. 156-8019

Bykovo Airport, ph. 155-0922

Domodedovo Airport, ph. 234-8656

Sheremetevo 2 Airport, ph. 578-5614

Vnukovo Airport, ph. 234-8656

AMBULANCE   DIAL 03

⇨ **American Medical Center**, Shmitovskiy proyezd 3, ph. 256-8212

ANTIQUES

Antikhvar, ul. 1st Tverskaya-Yamskaya 14, ph. 251-6548

Antikvariat, ul. B. Yakimanka 52, ph. 238-9545

Antique - Bukinist, Teatralny proyezd, 1, ph. 971-6181; ul. Arbat 36, ph. 241-3387

Antiques, ul. Arbat 9, ph. 291-7034

Bukinist, ul. Pushechnaya 4; ul. Maroseyka 8

Ikoni, ul. Arbat 34

Khrustal, ul. Tverskaya 15

Kommisioni, ul. Tverskaya-Yamskaya 16

Raritet, ul. Arbat 31, ph. 241-2381

Unisat, Nikopeskovskiy B. p. 5

APARTMENTS

There are hundreds of firms, varying in reputability, that will help you find an apartment. Below is a list of reliable Western and Russian agencies. The best of these provide both rental and renovation services.

A & A Relocations, Krapivinskiy p. 3, bldg. 2, ph. 299-2960

Art Salon, Ukrainskiy bul. 6-185, ph. 264-4109

BiSko JV (UK), ul. Bakhrushina 20, ph. 235-8254

Blackwood Apartment Rentals, Kotelnicheskaya nab. 1, ph. 387-7356

Clivedon Property Services, 1st Tverskaya-Yamskaya 13, #79, ph. 250-0152; Smolenskiy bul. 22/17, #2, ph. 134-0862

Dovesgate International/Russian Express, 2 Obydenskiy p. 14, ph. 202-5732

Ferguson Hollis, ul. Shchepkina 6, ph. 288-9801

First Russian Real Estate Corp., Shyolkovskoye Sh. 2, ph. 165-5511

Flat Finders, Kutuzovskiy prosp. 4/2, #328, ph. 413-9301

Global Properties, Tryokhprudny p. 11/13, 5th fl., #61, ph. 299-3759

Home Sweet Home, Kutuzovskiy prosp. 14, #155, ph. 255-4659

House Service Ltd., Nikopeskovskiy B. p. 7, ph. 241-7402

J.A.T. Ltd., Sushchyovskiy Val 5, ph. 973-0757

Moscow Enterprises Inc., ph. 291-3944

Nest International Ltd., ph. 921-5100

Orgkomitet Joint Stock Company, Nikitskaya B. ul. 12, ph. 202-1166

Oster and Company, Box 152, ph. 956-3300

Park Place Moscow, Leninskiy prosp. 113/1, ph. 956-5050

Quest Realty, Smolenskaya nab. 5/13, Suite 157, ph. 244-0527

Rodina, ph. 299-2096

Rosinka, Leningradskiy prosp. 39, ph. 213-6661

Russian Real Estate, ph. 244-2565

Technopark Business Center, VVTs, prosp. Mira 120, ph. 188-7776

ART GALLERIES

Aktsia Art Gallery, Krymskiy val 10/14, ph. 291-7509

Arlekin, Inc., pl. Zhurolova 1, ph. 928-6841

Art Moderne Gallery, ul. B. Ordynka 39, ph. 242-0175

Art Zone Gallery, Pullman Iris Hotel, ph. 488-8267

Contemporary Art Center, ul. B. Yakimanka 6, ph. 238-9666

Ensy Gallery, Mir Exhibition Hall, prosp. Mira 14, ph. 208-1403

Fedulov Gallery, ul. Pervaya Tverskaya Yamskaya 18, ph. 250-2774

First Gallery, The, Strastnoy bul. 7, ph. 299-0498

Gallery, ul. Malaya Gruzinskaya 28, ph. 253-7505

Gallery 1.0, ul. Bolshaya Yakomanks 2/6, ph. 238-6905

Georgian Cultural Center, ul. Arbat 42

Guelman Gallery, ul. B. Yakimanka 2/6, ph. 238-8492

Mars Gallery, M. Filevskaya ul. 32, ph. 146-2029

Nagornaya Gallery, ul. Remizova 10, ph. 123-6569

Neo-Shag Gallery, Petrovskiye liniye 1/20, ph. 200-0562

Peresvetov 4 Gallery, Peresvetov p. 4, ph. 275-2228

Rubens Gallery of Modern Art, Verkhnyaya Krasnoselskaya ul. 34, ph. 278-2584

Sadovniki Gallery, ul. Akad. Millionshchikova 35, ph. 112-1161

Savoy Art Gallery, Savoy Hotel, ph. 929-8660

Sevodnya Gallery, ul. Arbat 35, ph. 241-0209 {M-Su 12-18, exhibits change monthly}

Solyanka Art Gallery, ul. Solyanka 1/2, ph. 921-6332

Taganskaya 31/22 Gallery, Taganskaya ul. 31/22, ph. 278-5578

Theater Salon Gallery, Tverskoy bul. 11

Yakut, ul. Dolgorukovslaya 5, ph. 973-3452

ASSOCIATIONS

American Business Club, ph. 273-3101

American Women's Club, The, ph. 202-7175

British Women's Club, The, ph. 199-6907

Columbia Alumni Assn., ph. 252-2451

Foreign Correspondents' Association, International Press Center & Club, ph. 941-8746

Harvard Alumni Association, ph. 962-4464

International Women's Club, c/o US Embassy, ph. 253-2508

MIT Alumni Association, ph. 242-4701

Moscow Commercial Club, ul. B. Kommunisticheskaya 2A, ph. 274-0081

Moscow Rotary Club, ph. 284-7896

Press Club, Radisson-Slavyanskaya Hotel, ph. 941-8051

Princeton Alumni Assn., ph. 241-7086

UPenn Alumni Association, ph. 241-1337

Yale Alumni Association, ph. 271-1622

☑ *Where in Moscow* contains over 30,000 addresses, phone and fax numbers. The new Moscow City Map indexes over 1200 streets. Meanwhile, there are just 15 advertisements. That is all. Other guides make you tote around a ton of ads. The advertisements in *WIM* cover less than 3% of the total printed area of the book.

B

BAKERIES

Australian-Soviet Bakery, Pyatnitskaya ul. 29/8

Bakery, The, Olympic Penta Hotel, Olympiskiy prosp. 18/1, ph. 971-6101 {daily 8-20}

Baku-Livan Bakery, ul. Tverskaya 24, ph. 299-2322

Cheromushkinskiy Bread Kombinat, ph. 315-3810 {croissants, delivered, no min.}

Diana, ul. Mytnaya 74, ph. 230-3614

French Bread Bakery, Lazarevskiy pr. 4; ul. Generala Glagoleva 30, ph.

German Bakery, Pyatnitskaya ul. 29, ph.

Hol'N One Donuts, ph. 975-3392

Italian Bakery, ul. B. Polyanka 30, ph.

Lavash Bakery, B. Sadovaya 3, k. 6, ph. 251-7888

Montreal Bread Bakery, ul. Shipok, ph.

Praga Restaurant Bakery, Arbatskaya pl., ph. 290-6256 {one day advance notice}

Slastyona Bakery, Krasnokazarmennaya 3, ph. 261-8626

Swiss Bakery, Sadko Arcade (Expocenter), ph. 940-4068

Swiss Pastry Shop, Sadko Arcade (Expocenter), ph. 253-9592

BANKS, DOMESTIC

Russian banks continue to spring up faster than mushrooms after rain. Here is a list of the larger Russian banks.

Aeroflot Bank, Leningradskiy pr. 37a, ph. 292-0759

Agrica Commercial Bank, ul. Timiryazevskaya 26, ph. 210-1129

Agrokhimbank, Znamenskiy B. p. 2/16, ph. 202-3847

All Russian Exchange Bank, Yaroslavskoye sh. 13, ph. 188-8136

Atlant Commercial Bank, prosp. Mira 50, ph. 280-1302

Autobank, ul. Lesnaya 41, ph. 258-9412

Aviabank, Ulanskiy p. 16, ph. 207-5856

Avtobank, ul. Delegatskaya 11, ph. 973-3216

AvtoVAZ Bank, ul. Novy Arbat 36, ph. 926-7663

Central Bank of Russia, ul. Zhitnaya 12, ph. 237-5145; ul. Neglinnaya 12, ph. 928-9922

Centrocredit Commercial Bank, 2nd Kolobovskiy p. 9/2, ph. 299-6090

Cobra Bank, M. Gnezdnikovskiy p. 9 str. 4, ph. 229-0028

Commercial Bank of International Integration, Olympiyskiy prosp. 32, ph. 284-0630

Credit Bank Moscow, B. Ordynka 51, ph. 253-1430; Gospitalnaya ul. 16, ph. 263-2638

Credobank, Main office, Leontyevskiy p. 10, ph. 229-2252; Sadovnicheskaya ul. 15/2, ph. 220-3435

Delovaya Rossiya Bank, Strastnoy bul. 8, ph. 200-1465; Klenovy bul. 3, ph. 112-1310

Dialog Bank, Staropanskiy p. 4, ph. 921-9104; Radisson-Slavyanskaya Hotel, 1st fl., ph. 941-8434 {daily 8-20, lunch 13-14}

Elbim bank, 2nd Tverskaya-Yamskaya 15, ph. 251-0334; Krasnopresnenskaya nab. 12, pod. 3, #1707, ph. 253-2693; Krasnopresnenskaya nab. 12, room 1707, ph. 253-1200

Elektrobank, Voznesenskiy p. 20, str. 2, ph. 229-2279

Elektronika Research Institute, prosp. Vernadskovo 39, ph. 432-9223

Finistbank, Kutuzovskiy prosp. 26 str. 3, ph. 249-0256

Gazprombank, ul. Stroiteley 8, ph. 133-4610

Imperial Bank, Sadovnicheskaya ul. 63, str. 7, ph. 237-6601

Industry Service Bank, Miusskaya pl., 7, ph. 251-6004

Inkom Bank, Central Division, Sibirskiy proyezd 2, k. 2, ph. 270-9290; Arkhangelskiy p. 12/8, ph. 923-3709; ul. Nametkina 14, k. 1, ph. 332-0699

Innovation Land Bank, Nakhimovskiy prosp. 32, room 605, ph. 129-1211

International Bank of Economic Cooperation, ul. Mashi Poryvayevoy 11, ph. 975-3861

International Investment Bank, ul. Mashi Poryvayevoy 7, ph. 975-4008

International Moscow Bank, Kamergerskiy p. 6, ph. 292-9632

Izdatbank, ul. Petrovka 26, ph. 200-6869

Khimbank, ul. Myasnitskaya 20, ph. 928-9188

Komtorgbank, ul. Myasnitskaya 47, ph. 207-7096

Kontinent Bank, ul. Gostinichnaya 9, k. 4, ph. 482-1654

Konversbank, ul. B. Ordynka 24/26, ph. 239-2028

Koopbank Tsentrpotrebsoyuza, B. Cherkasskiy p. 15, ph. 923-2790

Lefortovskiy Commercial Bank, Lefortovskiy Val, 16a, ph. 362-4053

Menatep, Manezhnaya pl. 7, ph. 202-8556 Kolpachny p. 4, ph. 963-6013

Morbank, B. Koptevskiy pr. 6, ph. 151-5674

Mosbank, ul. Obrucheva 34/62, ph. 333-9070

Mosbusinessbank, Kuznetskiy Most 15, ph. 921-8582

Moscow Central Industrial Bank of Russia, ul. Zhitnaya 12, ph. 230-7962

Moscow Credit Bank, Orlikov per 7, ph. 204-0562

Moscow Industrial Bank, ph. 952-7408

Moscow International Bank, Dmitrovka B. ul. 5/6, ph. 292-8371

Mosstroybank, Dmitrovka M. ul. 21/18, ph. 209-4157

Mosstroyeconombank, ul. Vavilova 81, ph. 132-2897

Neftegazstroybank, ul. Zhitnaya 14, ph. 239-1159

Neftekhimbank, ul. Gilyarovskovo 31, ph. 284-8838

NGS Bank {answering machine}, ul. Zhitnaya 14, ph. 239-1508

North-Eastern Joint Stock Commercial Bank -Moscow Filial, prosp. Mira 9/18, str.1 , #18, ph. 207-7783

Optimum Commercial Bank, Nakhimovskiy prosp. 31, ph. 238-0089

Orbita Bank, 2nd Spasonalivkovskiy p. 5-7, ph. 238-8720

Promstroybank, Tverskoy bul. 13, ph. 200-7373

Resurs-Bank, 3rd Parkovaya ul. 24, ph. 306-7855

Rosbiznessbank, Tryokhprudny p. 9, ph. 299-5771

Rosinterbank, Orlikov p. 3, ph. 204-4350

Rospromstroybank, prosp. Mira 84, ph. 281-8936

Rosselkhozbank, ul. Neglinnaya 12, ph. 923-1032

Rosskommunbank, ul. Myasnitskaya 13, ph. 290-6036

Russian Bank for Foreign Trade, Kuznetskiy Most 16, ph. 921-3525

Russian Credit Association, Leningradskoye sh. 84, ph. 452-1143

Sbergatelny Bank, Head Office, ph. 928-2620 {see listings under this name in the White Pages for all major branches}

Stolichny Bank, GUM, 2nd line, 1st fl., ph. {M-Sa 8-19}; ul. Pyatnitskaya 72, ph. 233-5892

Technopolis Innovation Bank, Zelenograd k. 317a, ph. 534-1449

Tekhnobank, B. Gruzinskaya 56, ph. 254-4611

Telebank Mezhdunarodny Kommercheskiy Bank, ul. Znamenka 13, str. 3, ph. 203-5397

Tempbank, Krutitskiy val 26, ph. 276-4141

Tokobank, ul. Mashi Poryvayevoy 7, ph. 204-9100

Tovnarbank, Novopeschanaya ul. 20, ph. 943-4102

Transcapital Bank, ul. Vorontsovskaya 27/35, ph. 272-5450

Tsentrosoyuz Bank, B. Cherkasskiy p. 15, ph. 928-7683

Twenty-First Century Development Commercial Bank, Volokolamskoye shosse 88, stroyeniye 8, ph. 250-9641

Unikombank, Khrustalny p. 1, ph. 925-3462

VIZA Bank, Gogolevskiy bul. 3/2, ph. 291-9514

Vnesheconombank, ul. Plyushchikha 37, ph. 928-7116

Vostok Bank, ul. Yaroslavskaya 4, ph. 217-6165

Vozrozhdeniye Bank, Khrustalny per. 1, ph. 921-4415

Zheldorbank, ul. Krasnoprudnaya 26/1, ph. 262-3666

BANKS, FOREIGN

A recent law allows foreign banks to open full-service banks in Russia. Most of the offices listed below are just representations of Western banks, few have begun the process of actually opening banks on Russian soil.

Amro Bank, Krasnopresnenskaya nab. 12, Office 1209, ph. 253-1476

Banca Commerciale Italiana, Mamonovskiy p. 6, kv. 9, ph. 209-6518

Banca Nazionale Del Lavoro, Krasnopresnenskaya nab. 12, Office 1602, ph. 253-1802

Banco Central – Madrid, ul. Mytnaya 1, Office 4, ph. 230-0388

Banco di Napoli, Krasnopresnenskaya nab. 12, Office 1008, ph. 253-2590

Banco di Roma, Mamonovskiy p. 4, kv. 8, ph. 209-6625

Banco Do Estado De Sao Paulo, Serpukhovskaya Pl. 7, Office 220, ph. 238-9724

Banco Exterior de Espana, Krasnopresnenskaya nab. 12, Office 1408, ph. 253-2263

Banco Hispano Americano, Krasnopresnenskaya nab. 12, Office 1301, ph. 253-8176

Bank Austria, Dolgorukovskaya ul. 19, ph. 200-5221

Bank of America NT & SA, Krasnopresnenskaya nab. 12, Office 1605, ph. 253-7054

Bank of Scotland, Pokrovskiy bul. 4/17, kv. 34, ph. 207-5998

Bank-Melli-Iran, Smolenskiy bul. 22/14, kv. 3, ph. 248-2153

Banque Nationale de Paris, Pokrovskiy bul. 4/17, kv. 19, ph. 207-5888

Banque Paribas, Pokrovskiy bul. 4/17, kv, 31, ph. 297-5511

Barclays Bank PLC, Mamonovskiy p. 4, kv. 14, ph. 209-6452

Bayerische Vereinsbank, ul. Babayevskaya 1/8, kv. 23, ph. 269-2743

BFG Moskau, Kamergerskiy per 5/6, kv. 35, ph. 292-4839

Cariplo, Saimonovskiy p. 7, 3rd fl., ph. 202-3652

Chase Manhattan Bank N.A., Krasnopresnenskaya nab. 12, Office 1709, ph. 253-2865

Cho Hung Bank, Olympic Penta Hotel, Olympiyskiy prosp. 18/1, ph. 971-6101

CIC-Union Europeenne, Int'l ET CIE., Krasnopresnenskaya nab. 12, Office 609, ph. 253-1182

Citibank, M. Poryvaevoy ul. 7, #622, ph. 207-2679

Commerzbank Aktiengesellschaft, Mamonovskiy p. 4, kv. 9, ph. 209-6440

Credit Lyonnais, Pokrovskiy bul. 4/17, kv. 18, ph. 207-6489

Credit Lyonnais Russie (Moscow branch), ul. Ulianovskaya 15, 1st floor, ph. 221-7520

Credit Suisse, Palashevskiy B. p. 15/1, ph. 973-2413

Creditanstalt, Krasnopresnenskaya nab. 12, Office 1108, ph. 253-2752

Credito Italiano, Pokrovskiy bul. 4/17, kv. 40, ph. 207-0389

Den norske Bank, Dmitrovka B. ul. 5/6, kv. 34, ph. 292-0338

Deutsche Bank AG, ul. Ostozhenka 23, ph. 201-2988

Deutsche Genossenschaftsbank, Hotel Intourist, room 2009, ph. 203-1621

Donau-Bank AG, Wien, 1st Krasnogvardeyskiy proyezd, Exh. Complex, Pav. 2, ph. 256-7444

Dresdner Bank AG, Krasnopresnenskaya nab. 12, Office 1708, ph. 253-2681

Eurofinance Commercial Bank, Vspolny p. 5, str. 1, ph. 202-4902

Garanti Bank, Krasnopresnenskaya nab. 12, rm. 1425, ph. 253-1589

Generale Bank, Krasnopresnenskaya nab. 12, Office 1705-1706, ph. 253-7572

Gotabanken, Pokrovskiy bul. 4/17, kv. 4, ph. 207-3429

Guta Bank, ul. Dolgorukovskaya 5, ph. 251-0105

Hypo Bank, B. Gnezdnikovskiy p. 7, 4th fl., ph. 200-4627

Instituto Bancario San Paolo di Torino, ul. Mosfilmovskaya 54, ph. 143-6021

Inter-Alpha Group of Banks, The, ul. Skakovaya 3, 2nd fl., ph. 945-2479

International Monetary Fund (IMF), Novy Arbat 36, ph. 290-7133

Kansallis, Osaki, Pankki, Pokrovskiy bul. 4/17, kv. 4, ph. 207-3429

Lloyds Bank PLC, Krasnopresnenskaya nab. 12, Office 1808, ph. 253-8174

Midland Montagu, Krasnopresnenskaya nab. 12, Office 1305, ph. 253-2144

Monte Dei Paschi di Siena, Krasnopresnenskaya nab. 12, Office 1105-1106a, ph. 253-2677

Morgan Grenfell & Co. Ltd, B. Strochenovskiy p. 22/25, office 101, ph. 230-6154

National Westminster Bank PLC, Pokrovskiy bul. 4/17, kv. 33, ph. 207-5739

Nordbanken, Molochny p. 9/14, k. 3, ph. 201-3714

Okobank, Koroviy val 7, Office 13a, ph. 230-1387

Ost-West Handelsbank AG, Kamergerskiy p. 5/6, ph. 292-4839

Palms & Company Investment Bank, Zelenograd, building 342-22, ph. 214-6504

Postipankki, Molochny p. 9/14, str. 3, ph. 201-3714

Raiffeisen Zentralbank Austria, 1st Krasnogvardeiskiy per., pavilion 2, ph. 256-7444

Skandinaviska Enskilda Banken, Dmitrovka B. ul. 5/6, kv. 34, ph. 292-0338

Skopbank, Mamonovskiy p. 4, kv. 2, ph. 209-6836

State Bank of India, Pokrovskiy bul. 4/17, kv. 32, ph. 297-2190

Svenska Handelsbanken, Pokrovskiy bul. 4/17, kv. 35, ph. 207-6018

Swedbank, Mamonovskiy p. 4, kv. 2, ph. 209-6836

Unibank, Dmitrovka B. ul. 5/6, ph. 292-0338

Union Bank of Finland LTD, Dmitrovka B. ul. 5/6, kv. 34, ph. 292-0338

Union Bank of Switzerland, Pokrovskiy bul. 4/17, kv. 4, ph. 207-3429

Westdeutsche Landesbank Europa AG, Krasnopresnenskaya nab. 12, Office 1207-1208, ph. 255-6464

World Bank, Aerostar Hotel, ph. 155-5111

Yapi Ve Kredi Bankasi A.S., Krasnopresnenskaya nab. 12. Office 1206a, ph. 253-1947

BARS

Arbat Blues Club, Aksakov p. 11, kor. 2, ph. 291-1546

Arbat Irish House, Novy Arbat 13, ph. 291-7641 {daily 10-23, cc}

Armadillo Bar, Khrustalny p. 1, ph. 254-2832

⇨**Artists' Bar**, Hotel Metropol, Teatralny Proyezd 1/4, ph. 927-6159

Australian Down Under Club, Kropotkinskiy p. 13

Baltschug Bar, Hotel Baltschug, ul. Baltschuga 1, ph. 230-6500

Bar, The, Novotel Hotel, Sheremetevo-2, ph. 578-9407

Beer House, Sadko Arcade (Expocenter), ph. 940-4062

Bierstube, Pekin Hotel, 13th floor, ph. 209-4240

Borodino Bar, Aerostar Hotel, ph. 155-5030

British Club, Kutuzovskiy prosp. 7/4

Brown Bear Bar, Sadko Arcade, ph. 255-2742

Cafe Vienna, Sovintsentr, Mezhdunarodnaya Hotel I, Atrium, ph. 253-2491

Canadian Club, Starokonyushenny p. 23

Casino Portture, Hotel Mezhdunarodnaya, ph. 252-3440

⇨**Chalyapin Bar**, Hotel Metropol, ph. 927-6113

Champagne Bar, Hotel Baltschug, ph. 230-6500

Die Bierstube Restaurant, Olympic Penta Hotel, ph. 971-6101 {cc}

Galaxy Restaurant and Pub, Selsko-khozyaystvennaya pr. 2, ph. 181-2169

Hermitage, Savoy Hotel, ph. 929-8577

In Vino Restaurant, Ukraine Hotel, 3rd floor, ph. 243-2316 {cc}

Irish Bar, Sheremetevo 2 Airport, Duty Free Zone, ph. 578-6878

Italia Restaurant/Bar, ul. Arbat 49, ph. 241-4342 {cc}

Jacko's Piano Bar, Leningradskaya Hotel, ul. Kalanchovskaya 21/40, ph. 975-1967

Jever Pilsner, Detskiy Mir, 4th floor {daily 8:30-20}

Jever Stube, Hotel Izmailovo, k. D, ph. 166-3490

Jever-Bistro, Rossiya Hotel, East entrance, ph. 298-2923

Kosmos Cafe/ Bar, ul. Tverskaya 4, ph. 292-6544 {daily 11-19, 20-6}

Lis's, Olympic Stadium, Olympiskiy Pr., ph. 288-4027

Lobby Bar, Radisson-Slavyanskaya Hotel, ph. 941-8411

Lux Bar, Petrovskiy Passazh, 2nd fl. (See Passazh), {M-Sa 11-19:30, cc}

Medusa Bar, The, M.S. Alexander Blok (Inflotel), Krasnopresnenskaya Nab. 12, ph. 255-9284

Mozhayskiy Disco, Mozhayskoye sh. 163, ph. 447-3294

News Pub, ul. Petrovka 18, ph. 921-1585

Olympic Bar, Olympic Penta Hotel, ph. 971-6101

Palace Night Club, Izmailovskaya pl. 1, ph. 165-0283

Patio Bar, Intourist Hotel, ph. 203-4008

Peter's Place, Zemlyanoy val 72, ph. 298-3248

Piano Bar, Novotel Hotel, Sheremetyevo-II, ph. 578-9407 {live music}

Red Lion Pub, Mezhdunarodnaya Hotel I, ph. 253-2283 {daily 12-16, 17-23}

Remy Martin Piano Bar, Sadko Arcade (Expocenter), ph. 940-4065

Rosie O'Grady's, ul. Znamenka 9, ph. 203-9087 {Su-Th 12-24, F-Sa 12-1:30

Santa Lucia Bar, Hotel Intourist, 3rd floor, ph. 203-1632

Savoy Club, ul. Dovzhenko 1, Tumba Golf Club, ph. 147-7368 {closed Mon., bar open 9-21, rest. 17-23}

Shamrock Bar, At Latin Ish House, ul. Novy Arbat 19, ph. 291-7641

⇨**Teatro Mediterraneo**, Hotel Metropol, Teatralny proyezd 1/4, ph. 927-6739 {daily 11-14, cc}

TrenMos Bar, ul. Ostozhenka 1/9, ph. 202-5722; **TrenMos Bistro**, Ostozhenka ul. 1/9, ph. 202-5722 {daily 12-17, 19-23, cc}

BOAT RIDES

One of the most pleasant activities for a sunny, summer day is a cruise along the Moscow river. It offers great scenery for newcomers, and plenty of sunshine and water for experienced residents. There are stations all along the Moscow river (see the Moscow City Map in the back of the book for the one nearest you). There are also tour-boats with bars and restaurants that can be rented for special occasions.

Boat tours, from Ustinskiy Most (near Rossiya) to Krylatskoye; from Ustinskiy Most (near Rossiya Hotel) to Kolomenskoye, from South River boat station to

Serebriany Bor, ph. 118-7811 {daily from April to August}
Charter Boat Tours, from Northern river station to Ikshinskoye Reserv., ph. 459-7476 {runs May to August, with stops in Gorkiy, Bykhta Radosti, Solnechnay Polyana, Khvoiny Bor}
Intercar Moscow 189, B. Sadovaya 5/1, ph. 200-5200 {river cruise tickets}
Northern River Boat Station, Leningradskoye sh. 51, ph. 459-7476
River Boat Tickets, Leningradskiy prosp. 1, ph. 257-7109
Southern River Port, prosp. Andropova 11, k. 2, ph. 118-7811
Spartak Yacht Club, c/o Savoy Hotel, ph. 929-8569 {day cruises North of city}
Volga Yacht Charter, ul. Maksimova 6, kv. 121, ph. 254-7998

BOOKS

Quality art books, classics, and dictionaries are now available in many Russian book stores, but the best selection is still found in front of the big book stores like Progress and Dom Knigi, from 'private' vendors. Western literature is available in most hotels and stores, with the widest selection being found at the locations listed below. Good finds are also to be had at Bukinist and Antikvar shops, which are squirrelled away throughout the city. Die-hard book lovers will want to visit the book market held every weekend at Olympiyskiy Stadium.

Akademkniga, ul. Tverskaya 19
Antikvar, ul. 1st Tverskaya-Yamskaya 14, ph. 251-6548 {M-Su 10-19}
Antique - Bukinist, Teatralny proyezd, 1, ph. 971-6181; ul. Arbat 36, ph. 241-3387 {M-Sa 10-19, break 14-15}
Book Boutique, 1st Kadashevskiy p. 12, ph. 231-1020
Books and Prints, ul. Prechistenka 31, ph. 203-9262
Books, Moskniga, ul. Tverskaya 18, ph. 200-0146; Hotel Mezhdunarodnaya, ph. 253-2376
Bukinist, ul. Maroseyka 8, {M-Sa 10-19, break 14-15}
Dom Knigi, ul. Novy Arbat 26 {the largest indoor bookstore}

Dona, 2nd Tverskaya-Yamskaya 54, ph. 251-0245 {M-F 10-19, Sa 10-18, break 14-15}
Inostrannaya Kniga, Nikitskaya M. ul. 16, ph. 290-4082 {open 10-19}
K-Boutiques, Aerostar Hotel, ph. 155-5030 and Pullman Iris Hotel, ph. 488-8100 {Western paperbacks}
Krugozor, Pyatnitskaya ul. 25, ph. 231-2902
Moscow Book World, ul. Myasnitskaya 6, {M-Sa 10-19, break 14-15}
Mosgorspravka, ul. Tverskaya 7, ph. 292-5381 {reference books}
October 19 Literary Salon, 1st Kazachiy p. 8, ph. 238-6489 {Tu-Sa 11-19}
Poligrafresursy, ul. Petrovka 26, ph. 925-6112
Press and Book Shop, Leninskiy prosp. 113/1, ph. 206-9207
Souvenir, ul. Arbat 4, ph.
Zwemmer Bookstore, Kuznetskiy Most 18, ph. 928-2021 {English language foreign-published books; M-Sa 10-19, cc}

BOWLING

Kegelbahn in the basement of the Kosmos Hotel and the **Bowling Bar** at the Mezhdunarodnaya Hotel.

BRUNCH

Almost all the joint-venture hotels offer a Sunday brunch (see listing of Hotels, Foreign). The best bets are:

Cafe Taiga, Aerostar Hotel, ph. 155-5030 {cc}
Les Champs Elysees Restaurant, Pullman Iris Hotel, ph. 488-8000 {cc}
Metropol Restaurant, Hotel Metropol, ph. 927-6452 {Jazz Brunch, Su 10:30-14, cc}
Rosie O'Grady's, ul. Znamenka 9, ph. 203-9087 {Su-Th 12-24, F-Sa 12-1:30}
Skandia Restaurant, Radisson-Slavyanskaya Hotel, ph. 941-8020

BUSINESS CENTERS

Aerostar Business Center, Aerostar Hotel, Leningradskiy prosp. 37, kor. 9, ph. 155-5030
Americom Business Center, Radisson-Slavyanskaya Hotel, ph. 941-8427 {also rents offices for short-term use}

AMERIC⊛M™
BUSINESS CENTERS

Executive Office Suites

Elegantly furnished, fully staffed and serviced -
designed to take care of your every need.

Receptionist
Telephones
Telephone Message Service
Daily Mail Service
Courier Service
Interpretation Service
Translation Service

Photocopying Service
Executive Assistant
Conference Room
Word Processing
Fax Transmission
Transportation
Stationary & Supplies

Leasing Information: 941-8815 or 8892
Int. fax: (7502) 224-1107 Local fax 941-8376

Business Services

24-hours a day, equipped with the very best in
telecommunications and business support services.

PHOTOCOPYING

Copier Transparencies
Blueprint
Color Copies
Color Transparencies
Projector Color Copies

SPRINT MAIL SYSTEMS

Electronic Fax
Electronic Telex

EQUIPMENT RENTAL

Cellular Telephone
Portable TV/VCR
Computer Cassette Recorder

WORKSTATION RENTALS

IBM
Apple Macintosh
Laser Printing
Typewriter

PHONE

FAX

WORD PROCESSING

LAMINATING

BINDING

Business Center: 941-8427

Client Services

Making it easier to do business in Russia by providing you with a wide network of consulting services.
Whether it's organizing a conference or setting up
your offshore banking, we can help.

General Information: 941-8641
Meetings & Events: 941-8890

Artel, ul. Myasnitskaya 26, ph. 925-290; Novy Arbat 2, ph. 245-0026

Asteis JV (UK), Verkhniy Taganskiy tupik 2, ph. 272-1176

Big Business Center, Leninskiy prosp. 2, 9th floor, ph. 239-1021

Business Center of Pekin Hotel, Pekin Hotel, ul. B. Sadovaya 1/5, ph. 209-3323

Comstar Business Center, ul. Petrovka 10 (Passage), Room 301, ph. 924-0892

Hotel Mezhdunarodnaya Service Bureau, Hotel Mezhdunarodnaya, ph. 253-2762

International Press Center & Club, Radisson-Slavyanskaya Hotel, ph. 941-8621

⇨**Metropol Business Center**, Hotel Metropol, ph. 927-6090

Moscow Commercial Club, ul. B. Kommunisticheskaya 2A, ph. 274-0081

Penta Business Center, Olympic Penta Hotel, ph. 971-6101

Pullman Iris Business Center, Pullman Iris Hotel, ph. 488-8104

Red Square Business Center, GUM, 1st line, 2nd floor, ph. 921-0911 {open 24 hrs, cc}

Retour Business Center, Savyolevskiy p. 6, ph. 202-7610

Russian Business Center, Staromonetny p. 33 kv. 2, ph. 238-8389

Savoy Hotel Business Center, ul. Rozhdestvenka 3, ph. 928-3780

Sovincenter, Mezhdunarodnaya Hotel 1, Krasnopresnenskaya nab. 12, ph. 256-6303

Telekos JV (Holland), Dmitrovka M. ul. 5, ph. 209-7861

Telesource Business Center, Sheremetevo 2 Airport, ph. 578-4848

Tumba Golf Business Center, ul. Dovzhenko 1, ph. 147-5480

C

CABLE TELEVISION

Crosna Space Communications, Presnenskiy val 27, ph. 253-8603

Kosmos TV, ul. Akad. Koroleva 15, ph. 282-3360

Skiy Line Ltd., ul. Geroyev Panfilovtzev 22, korp.1, kv. 290, ph. 496-6013

Teleset Service, ph. 166-9763

Unitel Co., Ltd., ul. Mariny Raskovy 12, ph. 943-1506

CAR PHONE

AMT JV (Finland), Khoroshevskoye sh. 42a, ph. 941-3092

Moscow Cellular Communications, Vorontsovskaya ul. 18/20, ph. 271-3749

Radio Communications International Corp. (RCI), VVTs, Transport Pavilion, prosp. Mira, ph. 181-6552

CARS, PARTS & SUPPLIES

See also Hardware, Security

Asto, ul. Gorbunova 14, ph. 447-3804 {Ford, Toyota}

Autoshop Toyota, prosp. Marshala Zhukova 49/1, ph. 199-5977

Avtodom, ul. Zorge 17, ph. 943-1001 {BMW dealer, Michelin}

BC Business Car, Ovchinnikovskaya nab. 18/1, ph. 233-1796

Bosch Auto Parts Store, Petrovskiy Passazh, 1st fl., {M-Sa 9-20, cc}

Diplomat Auto Service, ul. Kievskaya 8, ph. 249-9197 {American and German models}

Do It Yourself, Sadko Arcade (Expocenter), ph. 253-9588

Express Motors, ul. Alabyana 12, ph. 198-0034 {American cars}

F & C Trade Corporation, ul. Oktyabrskaya 7, ph. 556-6877

General Motors Moscow, Krasnopresnenskaya nab. 12, office 1004B, ph. 253-2577

Incomtrade, ul. Kulakova 22, ph. 944-9793 {new and used}

Inmart, ul. Rabochaya 63, #1026, ph. 270-3054

Moscow X-Service, ul. Mytnaya 18, entrance 2, ph. 238-6634

Mosrentservice JV (FRG), ul. Krasnobogatyrskaya 79, ph. 963-9145

MTDS, ul. Gorbunova 14, ph. 448-9531 {Volvo}

Nefto Agip JV (Italy), B. Cherkasskiy p. 7, k. D, ph. 930-7973; Leningradskoye sh. 63, ph. 457-2013 {cc}

Robert Bosch GMBH, ul. Mytnaya 4, ph. 230-6082

Rosartson, 2nd Baumanskaya 9/23, k. 18, ph. 265-7094 {Volkswagen, Audi, Porsche}

Service-Resource, ul. Aviamotornaya, 44, ph. 273-1733 {Volvo}

Sovautocapital, ul. Birysinka, 6, ph. 462-5120

Sovinteravtoservice, Institutskiy p. 2/1, ph. 299-7773

⇨**Stockmann Home Electronics and Car Supplies Store**, ul. Lyusinovskaya 70/1, ph. 954-8234

UVL Plus, ul. Svobody 79, ph. 496-5163 {Monarch, Goodyear tires}

CARS, RENTAL

See also Limos

A number of car rental opportunities are available. As in the West, your best bet is to call around and compare prices and models, and bargain. For fax and/or telex numbers of the companies below, see the Telephone Directory **(phone numbers in bold type are Sheremetevo desk phone numbers).**

Auto-sun, Sheremetevo 2 Airport, ph. **280-3600**

AVIS Car Rental, Sheremetevo 2 Airport, ph. **578-5646**

BC Business Car, Ovchinnikovskaya nab. 18/1, ph. 233-1796

Budget Rent-a-Car, ul. Novoryazanskaya 28, ph. 262-2876

Europcar, *Pullman Iris Hotel*, ph. 488-8000; *Olympic Penta Hotel*, ph. 971-6101 {daily 8:30-20:20}; *Hotel Novotel*, K 339, ph. 578-9407 {daily 8:30-20:30}; Krasnaya Presnya ul. 23B, ph. 255-9190 {daily 8:30-20:30}; *Hotel Mezhdunarodnaya* l, ph. 253-1369 {daily 8:30-20:30}; Novaya pl. 14, ph. 923-9749 {M-F 9:30-18:30}, **578-3878** {daily 10-22}

Fobit Car Rental, 1st Dorozhny proyezd 3a, ph. 315-0134

Galaktika Agency, ul. Metallurgov 23/13 kv. 56, ph. 304-1968 {Zil Limo, 3 days notice, 9-23}

Hertz Car Rental, Leninskiy prosp. 152, ph. 434-5332 , **578-7532**

InNis JV (Japan), ul. B. Ordynka 32, ph. 238-3077; Mozhayskoye sh. 165, ph. 599-9222

Intourist Car Rental, Hotel Kosmos, ph. 215-6191

Intourservice Car Rental, ul. Varvarka 6 Hotel 'Rossiya', ph. 298-5853

Iris Car Rental, Pullman Iris Hotel, ph. 488-8106

Mosrent Car Rental, Zemledelcheskiy per 14/17, str. 2, ph. 248-3607

Mosrentservice, Sheremetevo 2 Airport, ph. **963-9173**; ul. Krasnobogatyrskaya 79, ph. 963-9145

MTDS, ul. Gorbunova 14, ph. 448-9531; Leninskiy prosp. 152, ph. 434-5332 {Volvo}

Olga Co., Ltd., Hotel Metropol, Teatralny proyezd 1/4, ph. 927-6139

Rozec Car Rental, ul. Kulakova 20, ph. 233-2202

⇨**Service Globus (US)**, B. Kommunistiches-kaya 1/5, ph. 298-6146, **578-7534**

Vesta Car Rental, Leningradskaya Hotel, room 61, ph. 248-2657

CARS, SALES

Car sales is one of the fastest growing businesses in Russia. This is directed not such much to the Western community, as it is to the nouveau-riche Russian business class. You can now purchase virtually any make or model of car in Moscow. Call around to get complete information and verify taxation expenses.

ABC Opel, ul. Sergeya Eyzenshteyna 1, ph. 181-0407 {Opels}

Alankom, ul. Letchika Babushkina 26, ph. 186-5301

Alfa Technology, Dmitrovka B. ul. 4-2-10, ph. 923-4476

Aoyama Motors Ltd., ul. Tverskaya 29/3, ph. 209-6490; Zemlyanoy val 41/2, ph. 297-4128 {Honda}

Auto Clemert, ul. Vorontsovo pole 3, ph. 297-2271 {Volvo, Orel, Chevrolet}

Auto Sun JV (Japan), Grokholskiy p. 29, ph. 280-3600 {Nissan cars and minibuses, road construction equipment}

Avtodom, ul. Zorge 17, ph. 943-1001 {BMW dealer, Michelin}

Avtoimport, ul. Marksa-Engelsa 8, ph. 202-6221

BC Business Car, Ovchinnikovskaya nab. 18/1, ph. 233-1796; Showroom, prosp. Marshala Zhukova 49/1, ph. 199-5977 {Toyota}

California Trading Company, Litovskiy bul. 5/10-32, ph. 427-0140

Daimler-Benz Akziengesellschaft, Park Place, Leninskiy prosp. 113/1, ph. 956-5055

Diplomat Auto Service, ul. Kievskaya 8, ph. 249-9197 {American and German models}

Express Motors, ul. Alabyana 12, ph. 198-0034 {American cars}

F & C Trade Corporation, ul. Oktyabrskaya 7, ph. 281-2964 {Ford, all models}

Ferado Trade Co., ul. Ryabinovaya 39/2, ph. 242-0765

Fisherman's Harbor, Krasnobogatyrskaya 79, ph. 963-8780

Ford Motor Company, ul. Gorbunova 14, ph. 447-3804, ul. Marx-Engelsa 8, ph. 203-9237

Forto, ul. Mytnaya 11, ph. 236-4467

Forward International, Teatralny proyezd 5, ph. 926-2765 {10-19 Mon-Sat}

Gebr. Helbig MOS-Auto GmbH, Krasnaya Presnaya, Krasnogvardeyskiy 1 pr. 12, ph. 255-2551 {VW, Audi}

General Motors Moscow, Krasnopresnenskaya nab. 12, office 1004B, ph. 253-2577

Genser, VVTs, bldg. 1, prosp. Mira 120, ph. 187-2781 {new and used}

Gewika Autoservice GMBH, ul. Kotlyakovskaya 3a, ph. 113-7803 {BMW}

Hantarex S.U., ul. Obrucheva 36, ph. 334-2974 {Fiat, Alfa Romeo}

Hyundai Motors, Krasnopresnenskaya nab. 12, #1809A, ph. 253-1683

Incar, ul. Marksa-Engelsa 8, ph. 202-4917 {Ford}

Incomtrade, ul. Kulakova 22, ph. 944-9793 {new and used}

Independence, Selskokhozyastvenny pr. 2. 6, ph. 181-5149 {Renault, Volvo}

Interavtocom JV (Italy), Volgogradskiy prosp. 42, ph. 179-5367

Intrada, ul. M. Pirogovskaya 1a, ph. 256-4570; Showroom, Okhotny ryad 2, first floor, ph. 925-9336

Island Jeep Eagle/Chrysler Corp., ph. 147-8610

Jacob Hohermuth AG, B. Starodanilovskiy p. 5, Danilovskiy Complex, #33, ph. 954-0624 {Landrovers, Masaratti}

Kairin Co. Ltd., ul. 2nd Baumanskaya 9/23 - 18, ph. 261-6336 {Audi, Porsche, VW}

Kanematsu Corporation, Krasnopresnenskaya nab. 12, 1508, ph. 253-2488 {Honda}

KPA, ph. 123-5364

Kristal Motors, TsUM, ul. Petrovka 2, 1st fl., ph. 292-2347; ul. Tverskaya 29/3, ph. 209-6596 {Chrysler, Jeep, Dodge}

Lada Export, Otkrytoye sh. 48a, ph. 168-2828

Land Rover, B. Starodanilovskiy p. 5, ph. 954-0624

Locarus, prosp. Vernadskovo 7, ph. 430-5219 {Peugot}

LogoVaz, ul. Volgina 6A, ph. 330-3231 {Mercedes-Benz}

LogoVaz JV (Switzerland), ul. Prechistenka 17/8, str. 2, ph. 203-1724 {Volvo}

Mercedes-Benz AG, prosp. Vernadskovo 9/10, kv. 602, ph. 131-3448

Mosrentservice JV (FRG), ul. Krasnobogatyrskaya 79, ph. 963-9145

MTDS, ul. Gorbunova 14, ph. 448-9531 {Volvo}

Olivier S.A., Mamonovskiy p. 6, kv. 5, ph. 209-6705 {Citroen}

Optintorg, ul. Krzhizhanovskovo 16, k. 1, ph. 127-7011 {Citroen}

Park Avenue, Volgogradskiy prosp. 18, ph. 276-1074 {General Motors}

Peugeot Moscow, Leninskiy prosp. 2, 9th floor, ph. 231-1442

Resource, ul. Vorontsovo pole 3, ph. 297-2271 {Volvo}

Rimag Co., ul. Varvarka 15, ph. 206-3474

Rimpex, Dmitrovka M. ul. 16, ph. 299-4012

Rolls-Royce of Moscow, ul. Mytnaya 11, ph. 237-7069

Rosavtoservis, Volgogradskiy prosp. 139, ph. 172-8781 {Renault}

Rubicon International Ltd., ul. Letchika Babushkina 26, ph. 186-5301 {Chrysler, Ford, Volvo}

Rubicon International Ltd. — Showroom, prosp. Andropova 22/30, ph. 186-5301

Saab, Swedish Embassy, ph. 147-9009

Satra Automotive, Tryokhprudny p. 11/13, ph. 299-9169 {Land Rover}

Savva Car Land, ul. Energeticheskaya 6, ph. 362-7264

SDS, ph. 258-0149

Servoimport, ul. Profsoyuznaya 88/20, ph. 335-4987

Sovautocapital, bul. Generala Karbusheva 8, str.1, ph. 212-8581

Stolitsa International Trade House, B. Filevskaya ul. 35, ph. 181-1500

Summit Motors Moscow, Ltd., Mezhdunarodnaya Hotel I, #1202-1205, ph. 253-2280 {Toyota}

Trinity Motors, ul. Tverskaya 18, ph. 230-2535 {General Motors}

US Impex Inc., Dmitrovskoye Sh. 98, ph. 488-3102 {Ford}

Viko, Sherbakovskaya 9, ph. 369-1757

Volvo Auto Oy Ab, ph. 336-6565

Wesak Chrysler, Plotnikov p. 12, ph. 241-3593

Westminster Motors, B. Cheremushkinskaya ul. 25/40, ph. 127-0832 {new and used}

Widik Auto Salon, Leningradskiy prospect 31, ph. 213-1156

CARS, SERVICE

ABC Opel, ul. Sergeya Eyzenshteyna 1, ph. 181-0407 {Opels}

Autodesignservice JV (Japan), Trubnikovskiy pr. 1, ph. 290-2322

Autohaus 'Helbig', Dobrolyubova ul. 2A, ph. 218-1613 {VW, Audi}

CASOV, Hotel Mezhdunarodnaya 2, ph. 253-1830

Emergency Towing Service, Varshavskoye sh. 91, ph. 380-2101; Ryazanskiy p. 13, ph. 267-0113 {24 hour towing}

Forto, ul. Mytnaya 11, ph. 236-4467

Gewika Autoservice GMBH, ul. Kotlyakovskaya 3a, ph. 113-7803 {BMW}

Inmart, ul. Rabochaya 63, #1026, ph. 270-3054

Kairin Co. Ltd., ul. 2nd Baumanskaya 9/23 - 18, ph. 261-6336 {Audi, Porsche, VW}

Land Rover Service, ul. Dubininskaya 55, ph. 235-6580

Moscow X-Service, ul. Mytnaya 18, entrance 2, ph. 238-6634

Nefto Agip JV (Italy), B. Cherkasskiy p. 7, k. D, ph. 930-7973

Olivier S.A., Mamonovskiy p. 6, kv. 5, ph. 209-6705 {Citroen}

Raduga Car Service, 1st Dorozhny proyezd 3a, ph. 315-3736

Rolls-Royce of Moscow, ul. Mytnaya 11, ph. 237-7069

Saab Service, Volgogradskiy prosp. 177, ph. 379-6245

Service Station No. 7, 2nd Selskokhozyaystvenny pr. 6, ph. 181-1374

Sims & Klein, ul. Tverskaya 36, ph. 251-8950

Sovinteravtoservice, Institutskiy p. 2/1, ph. 299-7773

Spetzavtosentr, Kiyevskaya ul. 8, ph. 240-2092

US Impex Inc., Dmitrovskoye Sh. 98, ph. 488-3102 {Ford}

CASH ADVANCES

The locations below provide cash advance services off AMEX, VISA, MC or Eurocards. You can also have money wired to you instantly via Western Union.

AMEX

American Express, ul. Sadovaya-Kudrinskaya 21a, ph. 956-9000

Dialog Bank, Radisson-Slavyanskaya Hotel, ph. 941-8434 {daily 8-20, lunch 13-14}

VISA/MC/Eurocard

Belgrade Hotel, Smolenskaya pl. 4, ph. 248-1268, 10am-7pm

Elbim Bank, Mezhdunarodnaya Hotel, ph. 205-6560

Inkombank, Telegrafny per. 12/8, ph. 923-3810, 9am-4pm

Manezh Exhibition Hall, Manezhnaya Pl. 1, ph. 202-4836, 202-8556, 9:30 am-7 pm;

Mezhdunarodnaya hotel (24 hours), Krasnopresnenskaya nab. 12 , ph. 252-6481

NGSBank, Zhitnaya ul. 14, ph. 238-7210, 10 am-3 pm

Olympic-Penta Hotel, Olimpiysky prosp. 18/1, ph. 235-9003 (ext. 26-60), 9am-9pm

Pekin Hotel, ul. B. Sadovaya 5, ph. 209-2317 (Roskredit)

Pullman-Iris Hotel, Korovinskoye shosse 10, ph. 488-8102

WESTERN UNION

Call 119-8250 to get a current listing of banks where a WU wire can be picked up or sent from. At press time, the following banks were among those on the list:

Bank Orbita, Spasonalivkovskiy p. 27, ph. 223-8875

Bank Elita, ul. Meshchanskaya 20, ph. 971-6479

Inkombank, Sadovo-Triumfalnaya ul. 14/12; Arkhangelskiy p. 12/8, ph. 209-1939; ul. Nametkina 14, k. 1

Number to call in the US: 1-800-325-6000

CASINOS/GAMBLING

Alexander's, Kolonny Zal, Entrance 6, ph. Dmitrovka B. ul. 1 292-7123

Bingo Club Gabriela, ul. Pravdy 1, ph. 214-0787 {open 24 hours}

Bombay Restaurant, Rublyovskoye sh. 91, ph. 141-5504

Casino Aleksander Blok, Krasnopresnenskaya nab. 12, docking, ph. 255-9284 {daily 20-3}

Casino Arbat, Novy Arbat 29, ph. 291-1172

Casino Bombay, Rublyovskoye Sh. 91, ph. 141-5504

Casino Club Fortuna, Hotel Mezhdunarodnaya, 2nd fl., ph. 253-2236

Casino Club N, Leninskiy prosp. 88, ph. 131-1603

Casino Gabriela, Hotel Intourist, Tverskaya ul. 3/5, ph. 203-9608

Casino Moscow, Leningradskaya Hotel, ul. Kalanchovskaya 21/40, ph. 975-1967

Casino Okhotny Ryad, Hotel Moskva, ph. {open 14-5}

Casino Portture, Hotel Mezhdunarodnaya, ph. 252-3440 {bar open 16-4, casino 8-4}

Casino Ralina, ul. B. Yushunskaya 1a, Hotel Sevastopol, ph. 318-6474

Casino Riga, Volgogradskoye sh. 54, ph. 179-2350

Casino Savoy Club, Hotel Savoy, 2nd fl., ph. 929-8500

Casino Tars, Hotel Ukraina, ph. 243-3004

Casino U Arkadia, Spartakovskaya pl. 1/2, ph. 261-8040

Casino Valery, pl. Indira Gandi 1, ph. 939-9611

Cherry Casino, Metelitsa Entertainment Complex, ul. Novy Arbat 21, ph. 291-1170 {jacket required, daily 13-8}

Club Golden Ostap, Shmitovskiy proyezd 3, ph. 259-4795

⇨**Club Royale**, Begovaya ul. 22, ph. 945-1410 {daily 8-4}

Elite, ul. Krzhizhanovskovo 24/35, korp. 3, ph. 124-5941

Kings Casino, Izmailovo Hotel, Beta Bldg, ph. 166-6735 {open 24 hours}

Metelitsa Moscow, Novy Arbat 21, ph. 291-1130 {open 13-8}

Okhotny Ryad, Moskva Hotel, 2 Okhotny Ryad, ph. 924-6500 {open daily}

Oriental Excelsior Club, ul. Novy Arbat 21, ph. 291-1172

Queens, ul. Nizhegorodskaya 8, ph. 272-6680

Russian Club, Voznesenskiy p. 7, ph. 291-6965 {daily 12-9}

CATERING

Big Village Leisure Company, Ltd., The, ul. Tverskaya 15/2, #208, ph. 244-9432

Hopf Catering, Krasnogvardeyskiy proyezd 1, ph. 259-5384

Jack's Sandwiches, ph. 281-3536 {M-F 9-18, free deliv.}

Just Subs, Kutuzovskiy prosp. 22, ph. 243-0109 {M-S 8-21}

Kan, ul. Solyanskaya 8A, ph. 300-8721

Kombi's Deli, prosp. Mira 46/48, ph. 280-6402 {daily 11-22}

McDonald's Delivery, ul. B. Bronnaya 29, ph. 200-1655

Moscow Catering Company, B. Kalitnikovskaya 36, ph. 270-5197

Moveable Feasts, ph. 309-0449

Panda Catering, ph. 298-6565

Pekin in Moscow JV, ul. B. Sadovaya 1/7, ph. 209-1387

Pizza Hut Restaurant, ul. Tverskaya 12, ph. 229-2013 {daily 11-23, cc}

Potel et Chabot Restaurant, B. Kommunisticheskaya 2A, ph. 271-0707 {cc, banquets at Kremlin and prestig. lodges}

Pullman Catering Service, Korovinskoye Shosse 10, ph. 488-8279

SHRM International, Korovinskoye Sh. 10, Pullman Office Complex, Entr 2, ph. 906-0991

CELLULAR PHONE

AMT JV (Finland), Khoroshevskoye sh. 42a, ph. 941-3092

Moscow Cellular Communications, Vorontsovskaya ul. 18/20, ph. 271-3749

Moscow Rent-a-Phone, Novotel Hotel, #718, ph. 578-7252

Plexsys International, ul. Tverskaya 16/2, #508, ph. 292-2092

Radio Communications International Corp. (RCI), VVTs, Transport Pavilion, prosp. Mira, ph. 181-6552

CHAMBERS OF COMMERCE

British-Russia Chamber of Commerce, Krasnopresnenskaya nab. 12, Office 1904, ph. 253-2554

Canada-Russia Business Council, Novy Arbat 21, suite 712, ph. 291-3292

Canadian Business Council, Tabaskiy p.8, ph. 157-7619

Finnish-Russian Chamber of Commerce, Pokrovskiy bul. 4/17, kv. 2, ph. 925 9001

Franco-Russian Chamber of Commerce, Pokrovskiy bul. 4/17, kv. 3, ph. 297-9092

Hungarian Chamber of Commerce, Krasnopresnenskaya nab. 12, Mezhdunarodnaya 2, kv. 91, ph. 253-2921

Italian-Russian Chamber of Commerce, Denezhny p. 7, ph. 241-6517

Japan-Russian Trade Association, ul. Mytnaya 1, floor 2, ph. 237-2465

Mission of the Israeli Federation of Chambers of Commerce, Krasnopresnenskaya nab.12, Office 809, ph. 253-2809

Moscow Chamber of Commerce, M. Dmitrovka ul. 13, ph. 299-7612

Russian Chamber of Commerce, ul. Ilyinka 6, ph. 924-5645

CIRCUS

Circus (New) on Lenin Hills, prosp. Vernadskovo 7, ph. 930-2815; **(Old)**, Tsvetnoy bul. 13, ph. 200-0668 {Wkdys (ex Tu) at 7pm, Sa at 15 and 19}

Circus-Europe JV (France), 3rd Frunzenskaya ul. 10, kv. 88, ph. 424-8004

CLOTHING

There are hundreds of hard currency shops that sell clothing around Moscow. Many of them are simply hard-currency versions of the old Russian "kommissioni", and the quality is not very high. Check out the the following locations if you're looking for better-quality work or casual wear.

ABR Consortium, 1st Kolobovskiy Pereulok 27/3, ph. 921-2952

Agimpex, Detskiy Mir, 4th floor, ph. {daily 8:30-20}

AISI International JV (Italy), Dmitrovka M. ul. 8, ph. 209-7553

Alain Manoukian Shop, ul. Druzhinnikovskaya 11, ph. 255-9140 {daily 12-20}

Alma, ul. Kluchevaya 8, ph. 342-8848

Alternative JV & IPLV, Orlyonok Hotel, {daily 10-20}

American Store, ul. Profsoyuznaya 84/32, ph. 333-2313

American Wholesale Center: Pervomaiskiy Center, 9th Parkovaya ul. 62, ph. 468-4119

Ana-1, ul. Lublinskaya 117/4, ph. 351-4028 {daily 10-20}

Apollo Store, ul. Arbat 32, ph. 241-6060

Arrow, GUM, 1st line, 1st fl., ph. 926-3474

Atelier Modnie Golovnie Ubori, Nikitskaya B. ul. 16, ph. 229-0663 {hats}

Baginskiy Fashion, Sovintsentr, Mezhdunarodnaya Hotel I, 1st fl., ph. 253-2697 {M-Sa 10-21, Su 11-19, lunch 15-16}

Benetton, Hotel Moskva, ul. Okhotny Ryad 2, ph. 924-2734; ul. Arbat 13, ph.

Beriozka, ul. Fersmana 5, ph. 124-5024

Bonita, Leninskiy prosp. 91, ph. 132-5474

Botany 500, GUM, 1st line, 2nd fl., ph. 926-3215 {M-Sa 9-20, cc}

Bradley's of London, ul. Stary Arbat 4, ph. 291-7067

Burda Moden Showroom, ul. Generala Belova 18, ph. 399-1460 {M-F 10-18}

Centaur Shop, Smolenskaya pl. 8, Hotel Belgrade 2, ph. 248-2828

Cezar's, Radisson-Slavyanskaya Hotel, ph. 941-8398 {daily 10-21, cc}

Charles Jourdan, Sadko Arcade (Expocenter), ph. 253-9592 {daily 9-21}

Danata, Radisson-Slavyanskaya Hotel, ph. 941-8028 {M-Sa 11-23 Su 15-23, cc}

Di Style, Petrovskiy Passazh, ul. Petrovka 10, 2nd fl., ph. 292-4056

Dom Modi, prosp. Mira 55, {puts out racks of nice clothing designed and made there}

Donna, Sadko Arcade (Expocenter), ph. 253-9588

Elsa Moda Italia, ul. 60 Let Oktyabr 2, ph. 135-4085

Escada, GUM, 1st line, 2nd fl., ph. 926-3231 {M-Sa 8-20, cc}

Etienne Aigner, Petrovskiy Passazh, 1st fl. (See Passazh), {M-Sa 9-20, cc}

Eve Fashion, Petrovskiy Passazh, 2nd fl., {M-Sa 9-20, cc, lingerie}

Franco-Serra Italia, ul. Tverskaya 1, {M-Sa 11-14, 15-20}

Free Way, ul. Baumanskaya 32/6, ph. 265-2963

Galeries Lafayette, GUM, 1st line, 1st fl., ph. 926-3457 {M-Sa 9-19:30, cc}

Golden Lady, Detskiy Mir, 4th floor, {daily 8:30-20}

Gumir, GUM, 1st floor, ph. 926-3250 {M-Sa 8-20, cc}

Hom Clothing Store, Petrovskiy Passazh, 1st fl., {M-Sa 9-20, cc}

InterArt Bazar, Serpukhovskiy val 24, kor.2, ph. 952-3008

Ital-moda, Leninskiy prosp. 41/1

Jindo Rus, Hotel Kosmos, prosp. Mira 150, ph. 217-0025; Hotel Intourist, ph. 203-9742

Kalinka Tekseks, ul. Profsoyuznaya 15, ph. 129-7711

Karstadt, GUM, 1st line, 1st fl., ph. 926-3229 {M-Sa 9-20, cc}

Kutuzovskiy 9, Kutuzovskiy prosp. 9, ph. 243-7501 {M-Sa 10-20, Su 10-18, cc}

Kuznetskiy Most Clothing Store, Kuznetskiy Most 10, ph. 921-6971 {M-F 10-19, Sa 10-17, break 14-15, cc}

La Pantera, prosp. 60-Letiya Oktyabrya 12, ph. 126-8510

La Victoria Clothing Store, Petrovskiy Passazh, 2nd fl., {M-Sa 9-20, cc}

Le Monti, TsUM, 4th fl., ph. 292-4057 {M-Sa 8-20, cc}; VVTs, prosp. Mira 120, ph. 188-6474 {daily 11-19, cc}

Levi Strauss Store, Stoleshnikov p. 9, {M-Sa 10-20, cc}

Little Rome, Kutuzovskiy prosp. 18, ph. 243-0080

Love Fashions, ul. B. Yakimanka 26, ph. 237-4114

LUX, ul. Pelshe 4, ph. 437-6438

M & S Clothing Store (Oltes), ul. Pushechnaya 4, ph. 921-4907; ul. B. Gruzinskaya 39, ph. 253-8298; 1st Tverskaya-Yamskaya ul. 11, ph. 250-5032 {daily 9-21, cc}

M-1, Leninskiy prosp. 24/4, ph. 203-5103 {daily 9-21}

Magazin del Mondo, Ukraine Hotel, 8th floor, ph. 243-4682

Maksimilian, GUM, 2nd line, 2nd fl., ph. 926-3304

Male Fashion (Muzhskaya Moda), 1st Tverskaya-Yamskaya 26, ph. 251-1294 {M-Sa 9-20, cc}

Merkury, ph. 207-3139

Michael Paris, ul. Druzhinikovskaya 11A, ph. 255-9140

Modus Vivendi, Sovintsentr, Mezhdunarodnaya Hotel I, 1st fl., {M-Sa 10-20, Su 10-18}

Montana, Novy Arbat 21, ph. 203-5103 {daily 8-19:30, cc}

Nofkoh, ul. B. Krasnoselskaya 15A, ph. 264-8318

Noris International Trading, Leningradskiy prosp. 33a, ph. 945-8504 {M-Sa 10-20, Su 10-18}

Olympic Supermarket, Krasnaya Presnya 23, ph. 252-6591

Oscar Jacobson, ul. Nikolskaya 5/1, ph. 921-8333 {M-Sa 10-20 cc}

Patrick's, Petrovskiy Passazh, 1st fl., {M-Sa 9-20, cc}

Peppino Conte, Krasnopresnenskaya nab. 1/2, ph. 205-3115

Queen of Saba, ul. Tverskaya 9, ph. 229-2068 {M-Sa 10-19, cc}

Real American Clothing Store, Leninskiy prosp. 36, ph. 137-6960

REP, TsUM, 2nd fl., ph. 292-4484 {M-Sa 8-20, cc}

Rosfratex, Milyutinskiy p. 13/4, ph. 921-2557

RusLan Shop, Smolenskaya-Sennaya pl. 27/29, ph. 244-0568 {M-Sa 9-20}

Sadko, ul. B. Dorogomilovskaya 16, ph. 243-7501; Kutuzovskiy prosp. 9, ph. 243-3730

Sadko Arcade, Krasnogvardeyskiy pr. 1, Expocenter, ph. 259-5656

Salentini, ul. Tverskaya 37, ph. 973-3846; Dokuchayev p. 13, ph. 207-5607

Samos JV (Poland), Komsomolskiy prosp. 7, ph. 202-5955

San Francisco in Moscow, Komsomolskiy prosp. 15, ph. 246-2142

Seawise, Karmanny p. 9, ph. 241-8770

Shtayelman, ul. B. Polyanka 30, ph. 238-4166 {M-Sa 9-14, 15-20}

Sima Clothing Store, Petrovskiy Passazh, 2nd fl., {M-Sa 9-20, cc}

Sizai, GUM, 2nd line, 1st fl., ph. 926-3412 {M-Sa 8-20, cc}

Slava Zaitsev, prosp. Mira 21, ph. 971-0547

Steilmann, GUM, 1st line, 2nd fl.

⇨ Stockmann Fashion and Business Store, Leninskiy prosp. 73/8, ph. 134-0386 {daily 10-20}

Temkas Clothing Store, Petrovskiy Passazh, 2nd fl., {M-Sa 9-20, cc, outerwear}

Tip Top Mode, ul. Krasnaya Presnya 44, ph. 255-1498

Top Sport, Sadko Arcade (Expocenter), ph. 253-9589

Trussardi, Radisson-Slavyanskaya Hotel, ph. 941-8397 {M-Sa 11-22 Su 14-20, cc}

U2 Family Superstore, ul. Bakuninskaya 32, ph. 265-2963 {M-Sa 10-19}

Valentin Yudashkin Salon, Petrovskiy Passazh

Vera Moda, Dmitrovka M. ul. 8, ph. 299-7448 {daily 10-19, lunch 14-15}

Via Montenapoleone, Kutuzovskiy prosp. 22, ph. 243-1250

Vossen Clothing Store, Petrovskiy Passazh, 2nd fl., {M-Sa 9-20, cc, cotton robes and towels}

Waltham Shopping Center, ul. Tverskaya 9, ph. 229-2869 {daily 10-19, cc}

Wild Orchid Lingerie, Petrovskiy bul. 9, {M-F 10-21, Sat 10-20, Sun 12-18}

Winkler's, TsUM, 3rd fl., {M-Sa 8-19, cc}

Wolfgang Held, Petrovskiy Passazh, 1st fl., {M-Sa 9-20, cc}

Young Fashion, Sadko Arcade (Expocenter), ph. 253-9592 {daily 9-21}

CLOTHING, CHILDRENS'

Ana-1, ul. Lublinskaya 117/4, ph. 351-4028 {daily 10-20}

Benetton, GUM, 2nd line, 1st fl., ph. 926-3420; ul. Arbat 13 {M-Sa 8-20, cc}

Beriozka, Luzhnetskiy pr. 12, ph. 246-2742 {M-Sa 10-19}

Boys and Girls, Sadko Arcade (Expocenter), ph. 253-9588

Detskiy Mir (Children's World), Teatralny proyezd 5, ph. 927-2007

Grant Clothing Store, Petrovskiy Passazh, 2nd fl. {M-Sa 9-20, cc}

Karstadt-Kids, GUM, 1st line, 2nd fl., ph. 956-3556

Mia Shoe, Tikhvinskiy p. 1/50

Rosso di Libiege, Petrovskiy Passazh, 2nd fl. {daily 9-20}

Stockmann Fashion and Business Store, Leninskiy prosp. 73/8, ph. 134-0386 {daily 10-20}

CLUBS

See also Bars

For the more-adventurous, Russian clubs are frequently a special cross-breed of disco, bar, and floor show. Security is not tight at most of them, so be careful with your belongings.

Arkadia Jazz Club, Teatralny pr. 3, ph. 926-9008

Banzai, ul. Novopeshchannaya 12, ph. 157-7552

Bunker Club, ul. Trifonovskaya 56, ph. 278-7043 {open Wed, Fri & Sat to midnight}

Cenerentola, Novosushchevskaya ul. 26, ph. 972-1450

Cherry Casino, Metelitsa Entertainment Complex, ul. Novy Arbat 21, ph. 291-1170 {jackets required, daily 13-8}

Concord Night Club, ul. Lavochkina 32, ph. 454-6155

FAB Club, Proyezd Zhukova 4, ph. 195-1031 {open 19-23}

Hermitage, Karetny ryad 3, Hermitage Theater, ph. 299-9774 {open Tue, Thu, Fri, Sat 21-4}

Jump, Luzhniki Sports Complex, Universalny Sportivny Zal, ph. 247-0343 {Tue-Sun 23-5:30}

Karo, Pushkinskaya pl. 2, ph. 229-0003

Lis's, Olympic Stadium, Olympiskiy Pr., ph. 288-4027

M & S, ul. Ostozhenka 42, ph. 291-3232 {open 20-5}

Manhattan Express, Hotel Rossiya, ph. 298-5355

Moscow Hill Night Club, Trubnaya pl. 4, ph. 208-4637

Night Flight, ul. Tverskaya 17, ph. 229-4165

O-II Club, Sadovaya-Kudrinskaya 19 {open Thu-Sun 23-5}

Peter's Place, Zemlyanoy val 72, ph. 298-3248

Red Zone, Leningradskiy prosp. 39, TsSKA Ice Palace, ph. 212-1676 {open 23-6, closed Mon}

Russkaya Troyka, ul. Kosygina 15, Hotel Orlyonok, ph. 939-8683 {open 23:30-5:30}

Sexton FOZD, 1st Baltiyskiy p. 6/21, corp. 2, ph. 237-5477 {closed 10-12}

Sovincenter Business Club, Mezhdunarodnaya Hotel I, 1st fl., ph. 253-1792 {daily 13-5}

COFFEE SHOPS

Meeting for coffee in Moscow can be a real challenge if you don't know where to turn. Below are a few sure-fire places to get a cup of coffee or tea during the day:

Cafe Berlin, Hotel Baltschug, ph. 230-6500 {cc}

⇨ **Cafe Confectionery,** Hotel Metropol, Teatralny pr. 1/4, ph. 927-6122

Cafe Mozart, Palace Hotel, ul. Tverskaya 19, ph. 956-3152

Cafe Vienna, Mezhdunarodnaya Hotel I, Atrium, ph. 253-2491 {daily 8-12:30}

Carpigiana, Hotel Mezhdunarodnaya {Italian gelatto}

Coffee House (Pizza Pazza), Sadko Arcade (Expocenter), ph. 940-4071

Garden Bar, Hotel Intourist Lobby

Le Cafe Francais, Pullman Iris Hotel, ph. 488-8000 {cc}

Union Supermarket Cafe JV (Germany), Bernikov p. 2/6, ph. 227-2805 {daily 10-22}

COMMERCIAL DEP'T

See also Chambers of Commerce

Check with your embassy as to whether it has a commercial department to help you. The American, British, Canadian, Italian, German, and Finnish embassies (among others) all have Commercial counselors. (see "Embassy of..." in Telephone Directory for address, phone, fax and telex numbers).

COMPUTER SALES

Computers (and peripherals and supplies) are widely available. Be sure you know what you are buying. Warranties do not usually apply here. There are, however, a number of Western firms that offer full system installation and maintenance programs (with guarantees).

Many of the firms listed below also sell and support software.

Absolut, ul. Pokrovka 12, ph. 227-3985

AF Computers, Sudostroitelnaya ul. 15, ph. 112-6204

American Technology, Raushskaya nab. 4/5, ph. 239-3046

Apple Computer (RUI a.r.), Petrovskiy p. 8, ph. 229-1136; Kazenny M. p. 12/1, apt. 20, ph. 207-4570

Aquarius Systems Integral, Dmitrovka B. ul. 32, ph. 200-0459

Avstrosoft JV, ul. Garibaldi 21b, ph. 128-8072

Awer, ul. Olkhovskaya 16/6, ph. 265-0535

Belaya Rus, ul. Krasnoprudnaya 26/28, #3, ph. 264-2572

CAT Software Ltd., ph. 209-7256

Cherus, Profsoyuznaya ul. 130, k. 3, kv. 217, ph. 338-1225

Commodity-Credit Partnership, ph. 271-0730

Comptrade Marketing PTE, VVTs, bldg. 8, prosp. Mira 120, ph. 181-0495

Computer Aided Technology JV, Krutitskiy val 3, k. 2, ph. 276-4714

Computer Automated Systems JV, Studencheskaya ul. 39, k. 2, ph. 200-4671

Computer Center Moscow, Pervy Krasnoselskiy p. 7/9, kor. 4, ph. 264-7669; ul. B. Yakimanka 31, ph. 238-1223

Computer Support Services Moscow (CSS), Bryanskaya ul. 9, ph. 240-0544

Computer Systems and Technology JV (US), ul. Pokrovka 10, ph. 924-5969

Computerland, Leninskiy prospect 146, Dom Turista, ph. 434-9758; Dmitrovka M. ul. 5, ph. 200-4171; Kutuzovskiy prosp. 8, ph. 243-7882

Computerland Training System Dev., ul. Ostrovityanova 1, ph. 434-2192

Control Data Corp., Krasnopresnenskaya nab. 12, Office 1704A, ph. 253-8379

Dialog JV (US), ul. Spartakovskaya 13, ph. 932-4762

Eksimer, Leninskiy prosp. 76a, ph. 930-7193

Elex Vest, M. Sukharevskiy p. 9A, ph. 208-4190

Excimer Computers, ul. Ivana Babushkina 24A, ph. 125-7001

Fort Info International Trading, ul. Baumanskaya 56/17, ph. 261-5164

Future Technology, ul. Festivalnaya 22, ph. 453-4204

Global USA, ul. Usacheva 35, ph. 245-5657 {M-Su 10-20, cc}

Hadler International Ltd., ul. Donskaya 6, ph. 236-2310

Hard Soft, ul. Butyrskiy Val 24, ph. 258-8256

Hewlett Packard, VVTs, bldg. 2, prosp. Mira 120, ph. 181-8002

Hewlett Packard Co., ul. Pokrovskiy bul. 4/17, office 12, ph. 923-5001

IBM Russia, ul. Bakrushina 18, ph. 235-6602

Image, ul. Petrovka 26/104, ph. 925-6021 {Apple}

Intelligent Technologies, Baltiyskaya ul. 14, ph. 155-4450

Intergraph Graphic Systems, ul. Bakhrushina 20, Room 401, ph. 235-4652

InterMicro, ul. Nizhnyaya Krasnoselskaya 39, ph. 267-3210 {Apple}

International Computers Ltd. (ICL), ul. Vavilova 83, kv. 5, ph. 134-9549

Istok-K Computer Network, ph. 245-5165

IVK SYSTEMS, ul. Dubininskaya 96, ph. 955-6519

Konica Complex (Fort), ul. Malaya Pereyaslavskaya 7/12, ph. 284-4396

Korona, ul. Geroyev Panfilovtsev 20, ph. 496-6375

Lotus Development Russia, 2nd Frunzenskaya ul. 8, ph. 242-8929

Mac Shop, ul. Pokrovka 43, ph. 297-4987 {Apple}

MagSoft, Michurinskiy pr. 3, ph. 430-0001

MicroAge Computers, Balaklavskiy prosp. 3, ph. 316-2111

Mikrodin, ul. Novozavodskaya 18, ph. 145-8966

Mosad, ul. Oktyabrskaya 58, ph. 219-3128

Nilstar Co. Ltd., 1st proyezd Marinoy Roschi 11, #606, ph. 515-1577

Olan, ph. 425-9322

Ortex, Litovskiy bul. 3a, ph. 427-1101

P.R. Lotus Trading GmbH, 2nd Brestskaya ul. 5, Room 1, ph. 973-0602

PC Center Techno, ul. Pervomaiskaya 126, ph. 461-8775

Pirit, Kolomenskiy pr. 1A, ph. 112-7210

Quest Automation PLC, Koroviy val 7, Office 4, ph. 236-2135

R-Style, Simferopolskiy pr. 5, ph. 316-9646

Silicon Technology Corporation, prosp. Vernadskovo 82, ph. 433-2575

Silid, Rusakovskaya nab.1, ph. 268-3318

Steepler Ltd., ul. Prechistenka 7, ph. 246-8192

Systems & Strategy, ul. Novoslobodskaya 36/1, ph. 973-1325 {Apple}

Talus Corporation, ph. 255-9698

Technotex USA Inc., Park Place, Leninskiy prosp. 113/1, #E307, ph. 956-5124

Trident International Ltd., Raushskaya Nab. 4/5, ph. 239-3046

Union of Info. and Mgmt. Centers, Kozhevnicheskaya ul. 3, ph. 253-1053

Vektor SP Brokerage Firm, ul. Safonovskaya 17/43, ph. 415-7734

Wang Computer Systems, VVTs, bldg. 1, unit 17, prosp. Mira 120, ph. 263-9906

Wang/Management Data, Rubtsovskaya nab. 3, ph. 265-3708

West International, Lavochkina ul. 19, ph. 451-5364

COMPUTER SERVICE

Most of the companies in the previous listing can arrange computer repairs, as can:

AISI JV, P.O. Box 332, ph. 925-7158

C&P&S Technical Center, Chelonikhinskaya nab. 18, ph. 259-8818

Computerland, Verkhnyaya Radishevskaya ul. 14/2, ph. 298-1102

Salma Service Center, Zelyony pr. 2/19, ph. 306-0283

Znamenskiy Monastery Concert Hall, ul. Varvarka 8, ph. 298-3398

COMPUTERS, SOFTWARE

Borland, Okruzhnoy pr. 19, ph. 366-4298
Informatika NPC JV, ul. Skhodnenskaya 6, ph. 497-6378
Microsoft, Leningradskiy prosp. 80, ph. 158-1112
Summit Systems, Vorotnykovskiy p. 7/2, 10, ph. 299-1162

CONCERTS

Concert Hall in the Church of Pokrova v Filyakh, Novozavodskaya 6, ph. 148-4552
Dom Khudozhnikov (House of Artists), Krymskiy val 10, ph. 238-9634
Dom Uchonikh (House of Scientists), ul. Prechistenka 16, ph. 201-4555
Estrada Theater, Bersenevskaya nab. 20/2, ph. 230-0444
Glinka Concert Hall, ul. Fadeyeva 4, ph. 251-1066
Gnesin Institute Opera Studio, Povarskaya ul. 30/36, ph. 290-6737
House of Trade Unions (Kolonny Zal), Dmitrovka B. ul. 1, ph. 292-0178
Izmailovo Concert Hall, Izmaylovskoye sh. 71, ph. 166-7844
Luch Concert Hall, Varshavskoye sh. 71, ph. 110-3758
Moscow Conservatory, Nikitskaya B. ul. 13, ph. 229-7412
Oktyabr Concert Hall, Kalininskiy prosp. 42, ph. 291-2263
Olympic Village Concert Hall, Michurinskiy prosp. 1, ph. 437-5650
Rossiya Concert Hall, Moskvoretskaya nab. 1, ph. 298-1124
Russian Academy of Music, Rzhevskiy M. p. 1, ph. 290-6737
Russian Library Concert Hall, ul. Vozdvizhenka 3, ph.
Tchaikovskiy Concert Hall, Triumfalnaya pl. 4/31, ph. 299-3487
Tsentralny Dom Sovetskoy Armii, Suvorovskaya pl. 2, ph. 281-5550
Tsentralny Dom Turista Concert Hall, Leninskiy prosp. 146, ph. 434-9492

CONSTRUCTION

Academinvest JV (Austria), ul. Gubkina 14, kv. 11, ph. 129-0443
AEC, ul. Skakovaya 3, ph. 945-2477
All American Renovation, Tverskoy bul. 152, ph. 229-7097
Bechtel International Inc., Povarskaya ul. 21, ph. 230-2006
Budimpex, Milyutinskiy p. 9, ph. 208-0636
Caterpillar Overseas S.A., Pokrovskiy bul. 4/17, kv. 13, ph. 207-1007
Domus Construction, ul. Rossalimo 4, ph. 246-9258
Form & Technik, Hotel Mezhdunarodnaya 2, #506, ph. 253-2506
Greentec (MGU), Nikitskaya B. ul. 31, ph. 291-0510
JSR Holdings Company Ltd., B. Strochenovskiy p. 22/25, ph. 236-1237
McHugh International, M. Bronnaya ul. 19A, ph. 203-5679; B. Pirogovskaya ul. 9a, str. 2, ph. 246-7700
Moscow-Carroll JV (UK), Presnenskiy val 1/5, ph. 238-0635
Perestroika JV (Finland), ul. Kosmonavtov 2/4
Vneshstroyimport, Tverskoy bulv. 6, ph. 220-3204

CONSULTING FIRMS

See Legal Advice
See Accounting, Advertising
Listed below are only better known firms:

AEC, ul. Skakovaya 3, ph. 945-2477
AG Plan, Mezhdunarodnaya Assotsiatsiya 'Moskva', prosp. Mira 176, ph. 286-6316
Akva, ul. Fonvizina 5a, ph. 210-6546
Americom Business Center, Radisson-Slavyanskaya Hotel, ph. 941-8427
ASET Consultants, Inc., Zagorodnoye sh. 9, ph. 958-6273
Bain and Company, Inc., ul. Shcherbakovskaya 40-42, ph. 369-5948
Business Consulting Agency, Leninskiy prosp. 36, ph. 248-3360

Cannon Associates, Bogoslovskiy p. 7, kv. 40, ph. 956-3050

Clivedon Property Services, Smolenskiy bul. 22/17, #2, ph. 134-0862

ConsultAmerica, ul. Krasnokholmskaya 1/15, office 73, ph. 271-2580

Contact, Novaya Basmannaya ul. 37, ph. 261-0990

Coopers and Lybrand, ul. Shchepkina 6, ph. 288-9801

Dateline International, Inc, 3rd Golutvinskiy p. 2, ph. 233-3972

DRI, PO Box 15, ph. 396-0853

Dun & Bradstreet Russia, Bumazhny proyezd 14, ph. 250-2025

East Consult, Ltd., ul. Rozhdestvenka 12, ph. 924-1233

Ernst & Young, Podsosenskiy p. 20/12, ph. 927-0569

Esa Seppanen Consulting Ltd., Dmitrovka B. ul. 21/7, #6, ph. 200-3388

Eurasia Global, ul. Baumanskaya 43/1, 5th floor, room 505, ph. 261-1392

Gadfly, Ltd., The, Novoshukinskaya 3-21, ph. 193-5096

Galla, B. Kozikhinskiy p. 7, #2, ph. 202-3002

Global Edge-Moscow, Gorokhovskiy p. 18, str 2, ph. 267-1850

ICF/ EKO, Novoalekseevska 20A, ph. 283-3015

Informcom, Merzlyakovskiy p. 8, ph. 925-6644

Intercinema Agency, ul. Druzhinnikovskaya 15, ph. 255-9052

International Business Service (IBS), 1st Tverskoy-Yamskoy p. 18/3, #326, ph. 956-1525

Joint Stock Service Company, B. Gnezdnikovskiy p. 10, Suite 108, ph. 229-2618

Link JV (Switz.), ul. Shcherbakovskaya 40/42, ph. 369-2643

Manakey Global, Inc., Parusny proyezd 32/9, ph. 193-1804

MCBE Company, Ltd, B. Gnezdnikovskiy p. 10, ph. 229-5810

McHugh International, M. Bronnaya ul. 19A, ph. 203-5679; B. Pirogovskaya ul. 9a, str. 2, ph. 246-7700

Moscow Finance Group, ul. Kedrova 15, ph. 129-6700

National Market Research Institute, ul. Pudovkina 4, ph. 143-8664

Newstar, ul. Tverskaya 6, Suite 65, ph. 292-5057

Novosti-Inform, Zubovskiy bul. 4, rm 5010, ph. 201-7193

PBN Company, Radisson-Slavyanskaya Hotel, Room 3025, ph. 941-8433

Pencil Group, Pokrovskiy bul. 4/17, kv. 25, ph. 230-2955

Preng & Associates, ul. Lyusinovskaya 72, kv. 50, ph. 952-7421

Progressor, Nakhimovskiy prosp. 27, ph. 316-6901

Quinta, B. Cherkasskiy p. 4, str. 1, ph. 923-1403

⇨RCMI, Inc. (Research Consultation Management Intl.), Dmitrovka M. ul. 15, ph. 209-9814

Rotterdam Consult, Novy Arbat 16, #10, ph. 291-0677

Roy International Consultancy, Smolenskiy bul. 4, #11, ph. 246-4439

Rus Implant, 1st Tverskoy-Yamskoy p. 18/3, ph. 251-5369

⇨Russian Information Services, B. Kondratyevskiy p. 4, kor. 2, kv. 168, ph. 254-9275

⇨Scott-European Co., Krasnopresnenskaya nab. 12, Office 501, ph. 253-1094

Taroco Enterprises, Inc., prosp. Mira POB 29, Moscow office VVC, ph. 974 6033

Team Training Russia, ul. B. Spasskaya 10, #183, ph. 280-0018

White & Associates, Rokossovskovo bul. 7, k. 2, kv. 14, ph. 160-5539

ZigZag Venture Group, Plotnikov p. 12, ph. 241-3593

COPIERS, REPAIR

See also Repair Services

Atlas, Zemlyanoy val 14/16, ph. 297-4937 {Rank Xerox dealer}

Copia Moscow, Pechatnikov p. 26, ph. 208-4007

H.G.S. JV (Austria), ul. Gilyarovskovo 10, ph. 281-7445

MB, ul. Pokrovka 12, ph. 924-5133

Oko JV (England), Vorontsovskiy pereulok 5/7, ph. 272-0882 {authorized agent for Rank Xerox}

Xerox Copy Centre, Vorontsovskiy p. 5/7, ph. 271-2068

COPIERS, SALES

See also Electronics

Buying a copier, as with all office equipment, has become much easier. If you choose a ruble, or Russian option, be sure you check out the merchandise and guarantee. For sure-fire copier purchases try:

Atlas, Zemlyanoy val 14/16, ph. 297-4937 {Rank Xerox dealer}

Copia Moscow, Pechatnikov p. 26, ph. 208-4007

Koloss, ul. Shvernika 14/1, ph. 126-0208

Konica Complex (Fort), ul. Malaya Pereyaslavskaya 7/12, ph. 284-4396

Konica Copiers, ph. 277-3819

MB, ul. Pokrovka 12, ph. 924-5133

Pan Fun Copiers, ul. Levchenko 1, ph. 943-4101

Rank Xerox Limited, ul. B.Yushunskaya 1a, corp.2, 15-th floor, ph. 237-6842

Xerox Copy Centre, Vorontsovskiy p. 5/7, ph. 271-2068

COPYING

See also Business Centers

Copy centers have sprung up all over Moscow and, odds are, you will be able to find one in your neighborhood (or hotel; see Business Centers). It's a good idea to carry a few sheets of stationary or letterhead with you, if you need a quick, but quality copy. For full-service copying, try:

Copia Moscow, Pechatnikov p. 26, ph. 208-4007

Copy Shop, Petrovskiy Passazh, 1st fl., ph. 923-6055 {M-Sa 9-20}

Copyrus, ul. Vavilova 11/19, ph. 235-1475

Dona, 2nd Tverskaya-Yamskaya 54, ph. 251-0245 {M-F 10-19, Sa 10-18, brk 14-15, cc}

Informpravo JV, Neglinnaya ul. 29/14, bldg. 3, ph. 200-2775 {paper}

MB, ul. Pokrovka 12, ph. 924-5133

Reprocenter (Rank Xerox), Ukraine Hotel, ph. 243-3007

Reprocenter (Rank Xerox), Kutuzovskiy prosp. 22, ph. 243-1290

Sovaminco Quick Printing, Aviamotornaya 2, korp. 18, ph. 362-9081

Team Design, Americom Business Center, ph. 941-8389

Tektron, ul. 2nd Vladimirskaya 31A, ph. 176-8911

Xerox Copy Center, Sovintsentr, Mezhdunarodnaya Hotel, 2nd fl., ph. 205-6903 {M-F 9-18}; Novinskiy bul. 15, ph. Kutuzovskiy 22, 205-7983

COSMETICS

Avon, Lavrushinskiy p. 15, 2nd fl., ph. 230-6532

Avon Cosmetics Store, Petrovskiy Passage, 1st fl. (see Passazh), {cc}

Christian Dior, ul. Tverskaya 4, ph. 292-0722; GUM, 1st line, ph. 926-3430 {M-Sa 10-20 cc}; Mezhdunarodnaya Hotel 1, ph. 253-9297

Drug Store, Sadko Arcade (Expocenter), ph. 253-9592

Dzintars, Pushkinskaya pl. 12

Estee Lauder, Passazh, ph. 923-6057; GUM, 1st line, 1st fl., ph. 921-7064 {M-Sa 9-20, cc}; Plotnikov 12, ph. 244-7235

Gabi's Drugstore, Hotel Mezhdunarodnaya 2, ph. 253-7692

Julius Meinl Supermarket, Leninskiy prosp. 146, ph. 438-3444 {M-Sa 10-20, Su 10-18}

L'Oreal, Petrovskiy Passazh, 1st fl., {M-Sa 9-20}; GUM, 2nd line, 1st fl. (see GUM), {M-Sa 8-20}

Lakme, GUM, 2nd line, 1st fl., ph. 926-3370 {M-Sa 8-20, cc}

Mary Kay Cosmetics, 3rd Samotechny p. 3, Floor 1, ph. 974-1000

Nina Ricci, ul. Tverskaya 9, ph. 229-2967

Olympic Boutique, Olympic Penta Hotel, Olympiyskiy prosp. 18/1, ph. 971-6101

Red Line, Petrovskiy Passazh, 1st fl., {M-Sa 9-20, cc}

Sadko, Kutuzovskiy prosp. 9, ph. 243-3730

Sana Medical Center JV (France), ul. Nizhnyaya Pervomayskaya 65, ph. 464-1254 {Tu-Su}

Siren, Novy Arbat 44, ph. 291-1225

Yves Rocher, ul. Tverskaya 4, ph. 923-5885 {hair cutting: daily 10-12}; GUM, 2nd line, 1st fl., ph. 926-3408 {M-Sa 8-20, cc}

Zolotaya Roza, Moskva Hotel, ph. 292-1194

COURIER, INT'L

See also Express Mail

All Express Services (AES), Shmitovskiy pr. 33, ph. 256-4502

BMT Courier Service, Hotel Mezhdunarodnaya 2, #940, ph. 271-2609 {weekly document courier via London}

⇨ **DHL Worldwide Express Mail**, I Chernyshevskovo p. 3, ph. 956-1000 {see white pages for listing of express centers}

⇨ **Post International, Inc.**, Pushkin Square, Novoe Vremya building, ph. 209-3118 {Subscriber-based twice-weekly courier service, M-Fr 8-20}

⇨ **PX Post**, ul. Kusinena 9, kv. 26, ph. 956-2230 {document and letter courier/mail service}

COURIER, CITY/DOMESTIC

Moscow Messengers, ul. B. Polyanka 28/295, ph. 238-5308

City Express 2B, ph. 946-1368

⇨ **DHL Worldwide Express Mail**, I Chernyshevskovo p. 3, ph. 956-1000

Express Mail Service (USA), Varshavskoye sh. 37, ph. 114-4613

Falcon Express, ul. Shukhova 17/3, ph. 954-0233

Inservice Courier, ul. Mayakovskaya 17/7, ph. 203-9945

Krasnaya Gorka, ul. Podelskikh 6, bldg. 2, room 106, ph. 381-2746

Pony Express, Komsomolskiy prosp. 42, #206, ph. 245-9447 {M-F 9-18}

Prompt International, ul. Mayakovskaya 17/7, ph. 203-9945

CREDIT CARD LOSS

If your credit card is lost or stolen, here are the offices in Moscow to report the situation to:

American Express, ul. Sadovo-Kudrinskaya 21a, ph. 956-9000

Diners' Club, ph. 284-4873

Eurocard/Mastercard, ph. 284-4794

Visa, ph. 284-4802

CUSTOMS

See also Shipping

There are a large number of customs clearing agents. Some are listed below. For an up-to-date list, call InformVes at the number below. As well, most Western transport agencies with services to and from Moscow can provide such services.

Customs clearing agents:

Aeroservice JV, Sheremetevo 2 Airport, ph. 578-9030

All Express Services (AES), Shmitovskiy pr. 33, ph. 256-4502

Cargo International Services, Ltd., Radisson-Slavyanskaya Hotel, 6th floor, ph. 941-8880

Marine Transport & Trade Co., Plotnikov p. 12, ph. 241-3593

Sofi Courier Services JV (Finland), ul. Myasnitskaya 22, room 404, ph. 209-6207

Yeruslan Coop, Sheremetevo 2 Airport, ph. 578-8879

Customs points:

Dmitrovskiy, ph. 587-3391

Fryazinskiy, ph. 734-59

Klinskiy/Zelenogradskiy, ph. 535-1793

Kolomenskiy, ph. 344-25

Moscow Central Customs (Rostrans), 4th ul. Marinoy Roshchy 12, ph. 971-1178

Oktabrskaya Tovarnaya Stantsiya, Komsomolskaya pl., ph. 975-4460

Pavlovo-Posadskiy, ph. 44-751

Pochtoviy (postal), Varshavskoye Shosse 37A, ph. 114-4581

Podolskiy, ph. 30-375

Ramenskiy/ 'Kuntsevo', ph. 417-1324

Sergievo-Posadskiy, ph. 447-51

Serpukhovskiy, ph. 07-980

Sheremetevo 2 Airport, ph. 578-2120

Stupinskiy, ph. 546-8681

Tschelkovskiy, ph. 435-82

Voskresenskiy, ph. 2-26-03

Other important numbers/addresses:

InformVES, Ovchinnikovskaya nab. 18/1, ph. 220-1606

Ministry of Foreign Economic Relations, Smolskaya-Sennaya 32-34, 6th podyezd, ph. 244-1320

D

DECOR

See also Renovation
There are several stores with everything you need to decorate your apartment or office.

Amigo JV (Spain), Komsomolskiy prosp. 19, ph. 248-2225 {wallpaper}
Curtains Company, The, Kutuzovskiy prosp. 74, kv. 27, ph. 243-6102 {by appointment}
Decor Espana, Varshavskoye sh. 46, ph. 111-5201
Essor Carpets, Leninskiy prosp. 85, ph. 134-0531
European Paints and Wallpaper Shop, Ul. Vavilova 55, ph. 125-3479
Klemm, Petrovskiy Passazh, 2nd fl., ph. 921-3915 {M-Sa 9-20, cc}
Radial, B. Gruzinskaya ul. 20, ph. 254-1344 {window blinds}
Renlund M, Stolyarny p. 3, ph. 253-4173
Ruscan JV (Canada), Smolenskaya-Sennaya pl. 27/29, ph. 244-0568 {carpets}
Scandecor, Detskiy Mir, 4th floor, {daily 8:30-20}
⇨**Stockmann Home Electronics and Car Supplies Store**, ul. Lyusinovskaya 70/1, ph. 954-8234
TOO Dekorativny Kamen, Trifonovskaya ul. 61, str. 1, ph. 281-1857

DELIS

Bistro, Leninskiy prosp. 37, {M-Sa 10-20} H20(14)
Kombi's Deli, ul. Tverskaya-Yamskaya 2, ph. 251-2578 H13(18); prosp. Mira 46/48, ph. 280-6402 {daily 11-22} K12(7)

DENTISTS

Adventist Health Center, 60-Letiya Oktyabrya prosp. 21a, ph. 126-7906 {physiotherapy, M-Th 9-17:30, F 9-13}
Dental Clinic, The, Pullman Iris Hotel, ph. 488-8279 {open 10-17}
Dental-Beker JV (FRG), Kuznetskiy Most 9/10, ph. 923-5322 {M-F 8:30-20}

Ildent, 10 Letiya Oktyabrya ul. 2, ph. 245-4078
Intermed, ul. Durova 26, floor 4, kor. 1 & 6, ph. 971-2836 {acupuncture, contactless massage, remedial gymnastics}
Intermedservice JV (Switzerland), Hotel Intourist, rooms 2030-2031, ph. 203-8631
Medstar, Lomonosovskiy prosp. 43, 2nd fl., ph. 143-6076 {M-F 9-20}
Mosta Clinic, Bolshoy Cherkasskiy Per.15, 2nd floor, ph. 927-0765 {M-F 10-17}
Swiss-Medical Interline, Hotel Intourist, room 2030, ph. 203-8631 {daily M-F 9-20}

DEPARTMENT STORES

Detskiy Mir (Children's World), Teatralny proyezd 5, ph. 927-2007
GUM, Krasnaya pl. 3 (Red Square), ph. 921-5763 {M-Sa 8-20}
Petrovskiy Passage, ul. Petrovka 10, ph. 923-6055 {all stores accept checks from Business Rossiya bank}
Sadko Arcade, Krasnogvardeyskiy proyezd 1, Expocenter, ph. 259-5656
St. George Street, Radisson-Slavyanskaya Hotel, Berezhovskaya nab. 2
Symetrie Champagne Showroom, Leninskiy prosp. 85, ph. 134-0531 {french goods}
Taki-Moscow, ul. Mnevniki 10, ph. 191-1377 {M-Sa 10-14, 15-19}
TsUM (Central Department Store), ul. Petrovka 2, ph. 292-7600 {M-Sa 8-20}
Univermag, ul. Krasnoprudnaya 12
VVTs - All-Russian Exhibition Center (former VDNKh), prosp. Mira 120, ph. 181-9332 {100's of shops, get guide from info for listing}

DRUG STORES

See also Medical Care
⇨**American Drug Store**, Shmitovskiy pr. 3, ph. 259-7181 {M-F 8:30-18, Sat 10-14, cc}
Apteka, Beskudnikovskiy bul. 59A, ph. 905-4227 {M-F 11-16:30, cc}; Detskiy Mir, 4th floor, {daily 8:30-20}
Diplomatic Polyclinic Drugstore, 4th Dobryninskiy p. 4, ph. 237-5335
Drug Store, Sadko Arcade (Expocenter), ph. 253-9592

Eczacibasi Drug Store, Arkhangelskiy p. 5, str. 4, ph. 923-3615; ul. Maroseyka 2/15, ph. 928-9189 {M-Sa 9-19}

European Medical Center, Gruzinskiy p. 3, ph. 253-0703 {M-F 9:30-18:30}

Farmakon Drugstore, ul. Tverskaya 4, ph. 292-0843

International Pharmacie in UPDK, Gruzinskiy p. 3, kor. 2, ph. 254-4946

Interoko Drug Store, Petrovskiy Passazh, 2nd fl., ph. 292-3451 {M-Sa 9-20, cc}

Medicine Man, The, ul. Chernyakhovskovo 4, ph. 155-7080

Mikrokhirurgiya Glaza, Beskudnikovskiy bul. 59a, ph. 484-8120

Pfizer International (USA), VVTs, bldg. 5, prosp. Mira 120, ph. 181-7510

Pharmacy Rossiskaya, ul. Novy Arbat 31, ph. 205-2135 {M-F 8-20, Sat 10-18}

Primula Pharmacy, Ukrainskiy bul. 5, ph. 243-5119

Rimos Pharma, Kashirskoye sh. 24, ph. 324-9624

Sana Medical Center JV (France), ul. Nizhnyaya Pervomayskaya 65, ph. 464-1254 {Tu-Su}

Stariy Arbat, ul. Arbat 25, ph. 291-7101 {M-Sa 10-20, cc}

Unipharm JV (UK), Skatertny p. 13, ph. 202-5071

VITA, ul. Poklonnaya 6, ph. 249-7818

Vitas Corp., ul. Rossolimo 4, ph. 246-9366 {medicine, chemicals}

DRY CLEANING

California Cleaners, ph. 497-0005 {free pickup and delivery on $10 min. order}

Eurosam Express Drycleaning, ul. Krasnopresnenskaya 11/3, ph. 259-4157

Express Dry Cleaners, ul. Polbina 6, ph. 259-4157

Hotel Mezhdunarodnaya Dry Cleaning, Hotel Mezhdunarodnaya, ph. 253-2776

Khimvak, ul. Ryabinovaya 8, #209, ph. 362-1740

Mayers International (Hong Kong), Frunzenskaya nab. 30, pavil. 15, level 3, ph. 242-8946 {M-Sa 10-18}

MBTS Dry Cleaning, ul. Volgina 6, ph. 335-6192 {M-F 9:30-19}

Moscow Laundry Service, ph. 480-9452 {laundry pick-up and drop-off}

Savoy Hotel Dry Cleaning, ul. Rozhdestvenka 3, ph. 929-8693

Service A.N. Dry Cleaning, ph. 248-1573

ELECTRONIC MAIL

Prices and services are fast becoming very competitive in this, the easiest, cheapest and most reliable way to establish East-West (or East-East) communications. See Chapter 7 of our Russia Survival Guide for more details and for Western addresses of email service providers. Below are the Moscow addresses of major email services.

Glasnet, ul. Yaroslavskaya 8/3, #216, ph. 207-0704

Infocom JV (Finland), Teterenskiy p. 10, ph. 915-5093

Relcom, ph. 198-3796

⇨**Sovam Teleport**, Bryusov p. 2a, ph. 229-3466

Sprint, ul. Tverskaya 7, entrance 7, ph. 201-6890

ELECTRONICS

Home appliances and audio-video equipment is very widely available. There are a lot of clones and counterfeits on the ruble market. Let the buyer beware.

AMO Ltd., Kashirskoye sh. 57, k. 2, ph. 344-6604; ul. Avtozavodskaya 5, 'Ogonyek', ph. 275-4314

Ana-1, ul. Lublinskaya 117/4, ph. 351-4028 {daily 10-20}

Arbat Irish House, Novy Arbat 13, ph. 291-7641 {daily 10-23, cc}

Bang and Olufsen, Kutuzovskiy prosp. 8, ph. 243-0229

Beriozka, Krasnokholmskaya nab. 5/9, ph. 272-0474

Blaupunkt, ul. Mytnaya 3, #4, ph. 230-6080

Dartland International, Vtoroy Minaevskiy pr. 2, Bldg. 2, k. 7 {daily 9-19}; ul. Nikolskaya 5/1, 2nd fl., ph. 923-4745 {daily 9-19}; Park Place, Leninskiy prosp. 113, Bldg. E,

#320, ph. 956-5790 {daily 9-19, wholesale and contracts}

DL Lota, ul. Solyanka 9 str.1, ph. 924-5010 {daily 10-20:30, cc}

Do It Yourself, Sadko Arcade (Expocenter), ph. 253-9588

Dorin Electronics, Khimkiy, Spartakovskaya ⇨ 12, ph. 571-8108

Elektronika, Leninskiy prosp. 99, ph. 134-9009

ERLAN, Leninskiy prosp. 57, ph. 135-8245

Fairn & Swanson Ltd., Sovintsentr, Mezhdunarodnaya Hotel I, 1st fl., ph. 253-9408 {M-Sa 10-20, Su 10-19}; **office**, Olympiyskiy prosp. 18, ph. 288-1512

Firta Partia, prosp. 60-letiya Oktyabrya, 9, ph. 135-6072

Frost, ul. Kuntsevskaya 4/1, ph. 417-9400

Glarus, TsUM, 4th fl., ph. 292-4786 {M-Sa 8-20}

Goldstar Co., Ltd., Khlebny p. 19, 4th fl., ph. 291-7430

Grundig, ul. Obratsova 17, ph. 956-3409

Infatel JV (Japan), ul. Tverskaya 7, ph. 201-9174

JVC, GUM, 1st line, 1st fl., ph. 923-8200 {M-Sa 9-19, cc}; Leninskiy prosp. 60, ph. 137-2025

Kami Corp., Bolshaya Kommunisticheskaya ul. 11, ph. 272-4963

Konica (Tokyo Boeki), ul. Leninskaya Sloboda 9, ph. 275-1674

M & S Electronics Store (Oltes), Strastnoy bul. 7, ph. 229-7641 {daily 9-21, cc}

Maar, ul. Rusakovskaya 23A, ph. 264-9977

Mikrodin, ul. Novozavodskaya 18, ph. 145-8966

Montana, B. Cherkasskiy p. 15, ph. 923-8271 {M-Sa 10-18}

Moscow Duty Free, Sheremetevo 2 Airport, ph. 578-9089

Moskva Electronics Store, Kutuzovskiy prosp. 31

Neglinka, Kuznetskiy Most 9/10, ph. 924-0660 {M-Sa 10-19, break 13-14, cc}

Olbi Diplomat, Petrovskiy Passazh, 2nd fl., {M-Sa 9-20, cc}

Olbi Store, ul. D. Ulyanova 3, ph. 135-6567

Optintorg Electronics, ul. Krzhizhanovskovo 16, k. 1, ph. 124-8056

Orbita-Service, Krivorozhskaya ul. 33, ph. 113-4490

P.R. Lotus Trading GmbH, 2nd Brestskaya ul. 5, Room 1, ph. 973-0602

Panasonic, ul. B. Polyanka 30, ph. 238-4122 {M-Sa 9-14, 15-20}; Petrovskiy Passazh, 2nd fl., ph. 923-7080 {M-Sa 9-20, cc}; ph. 253-1939; VVTs, prosp. Mira 120, ph. 181-9263

Pioneer Electronics Store, Petrovskiy Passazh, 2nd fl. (see Passazh), {M-Sa 9-20, cc}

Radiotovary, prosp. Mira 27, ph. 280-3047 {closed Su}

Robert Bosch GMBH, ul. Mytnaya 4, ph. 230-6082

Roditi, GUM, 3rd line, 1st fl., ph. 921-1529 {M-Sa 8-20, cc}

San Francisco in Moscow, Komsomolskiy prosp. 15, ph. 246-2142

Shablen-Shop, Frunzenskaya nab. 30, pav. 12, ph. 242-8953

Sharp, GUM, 3rd line, 1st fl., ph. 926-3455

Siemens, 1st Donskoy pr. 2, ph. 237-6624

Sony, Petrovskiy Passazh, 2nd fl. (see Passazh), {M-Sa 9-20, cc}

Sony Europa Gmbh, B. Tishinskiy p. 38, ph. 205-3234

Stockmann Home Electronics and Car Supplies Store, ul. Lyusinovskaya 70/1, ph. 954-8234

Sunbreeze Electronics, Petrovskiy Passazh, {M-Sa 9-20}

Tamada Duty Free Shop, Hotel Moskva, ph. 292-2874

Technotex USA Inc., Park Place, Leninskiy prosp. 113/1, #E307, ph. 956-5124

Teleset Service, ph. 166-9763

Tomo JV (Canada), ul. Karetny ryad 5/10, str. 6, ph. 429-1377

Toshiba Shop, ul. Kosmonautov 4, ph. 283-5613

Waltham Shopping Center, ul. Tverskaya 9, ph. 229-2869 {daily 10-19, cc}

EMBASSIES

See the Telephone Directory under "Embassy of..." for a complete listing.

ENGRAVING

Engraving Shop, TsUM, 1st fl.

Engraving Shop, ul. Petrovka 8, ph. 928-2954 {M-Sa 11-19, lunch 14-15}

EXCHANGES

Thousands of exchanges have sprung up in the past year. These are just some of the major ones.

Alisa Construction Exchange, Leninskiy prosp. 45, ph. 137-6819

All Russian Commodity Exchange, B. Matrosskiy p. 1/1, ph. 217-6027

AVEX Commodities Exchange, ph. 921-1430

Chemical Goods Exchange, ph. 281-9258

Computer Exchange SM, ph. 236-9613

Fininvest, Nikitskiy bul. 8, ph. 203-2355

Inter-Republican Universal Trade Exchange, ph. 208-6681

International Compensations Exchange, ul. Sretenka 19, ph. 207-1622

International Exch. of Information and Telecom, Leningradskiy prosp. 80/2, ph. 158-7492

International Exchange of Intellectual Property, Staraya pl. 10/4

International Exchange of Secondary Resources, B. Matrosskiy p. 1/1, ph. 269-0211

Moscow Central Stock Exchange, Romanov p. 5, kv. 37, ph. 229-7635

Moscow Commodity Exchange, VVTs, bldg. 4, prosp. Mira 120, ph. 187-8614; **Energy Dept.,** VVTs, bldg. 4, prosp. Mira 120, ph. 187-8505

Moscow Interbanking Currency Exchange (MICE), Zubovskiy bul. 4, #6026, ph. 201-2817

Moscow International Agricultural Exchange, ul. Koroleva 15, ph. 283-3693

Moscow International Stock Exchange, ul. Neglinnaya 23, ph. 238-3632

Moscow Non-Ferrous Metals Exchange, ul. Gorbunova 20, ph. 449-7783

Moscow Oil Exchange, ph. 233-8981

Moscow Trade House, Dmitrovka M. ul. 2, ph. 299-1333

Russian Commodity and Raw Materials Exchange, Novaya pl. 3/4, ph. 262-8080

Russian Fish Exchange, VVTs, prosp. Mira 120, ph. 181-0918

Russian Forestry Exchange (Roslesbirzha), B. Kisselny p. 13/15, ph. 923-3350

Russian Fur and Leather Commodity Exchange, Kolpachny p. 14, ph. 227-1013

Russian Investment and Joint Stock Company, Novaya pl. 3/4, entr. 6, ph. 936-0766

Tyumen Commodity and Stock Exchange, ph. 245-6265

Umitec Exchange, ul. Profsoyuznaya 113, k. 3, ph.

EXHIBITIONS

Construction Exhibition, Frunzenskaya nab. 30, ph. 242-8968

Expocenter, Sokolnicheskiy val. 1a, ph. 268-1340

Service Exhibit, ul. Pokrovka 43, str. 1, ph. 925-7129

Sokolniki Exhibition Complex, Sokolniki Park, ph. 268-7151

EXPRESS MAIL

See also Courier

Several options are now available. The types and prices of services vary and not all will pick up and deliver.

Airborne Express, Spasoplinishchevskiy B. p. 9/1, ph. 262-9515

⇨**DHL Express Centers,** Olympic Penta Hotel, 4th fl. Olympiyskiy prosp. 18/1, ph. 971-610; Krasnopresnenskaya nab. 12 Entrance 4 Room 902A, ph. 253-1194; Radisson-Slavyanskaya Hotel, IPC & C, ph. 941-8621; **Drop off box** at Metropol Hotel

⇨**DHL Worldwide Express Mail** (Head Office), 1 Chernyshevskovo p. 3, ph. 956-1000

EMS Garantpost, Varshavskoye sh. 37, ph. 117-8560

Federal Express, Krasnopresnenskaya nab. 12, fl. 1, ent. 3, ph. 253-1641

TNT Express Worldwide, 3rd Baltiyskiy p. 3, ph. 156-5771

UPS Express Mail JV (Finland), B. Ochakovskaya ul. 15a, ph. 430-6373

F

FILM

See Photo

Western Kodak and Fuji film can be purchased at all hotels and in many stores. It is also available at the new, and numerous photo-development shops. When buying film, always check the expiration date. Also, avoid purchasing ORWO NC-21 or DC-4 film, which can only be developed in Russia. For video film, see Video. For film developing, see Photo.

Fuji Center, Mezhdunarodnaya Hotel I, Krasnopresnenskaya nab. 12, ph. 253-2914 {M-F 9-18}

Fuji Film Center, Novy Arbat 25, ph. 203-7307 {M-Sa 10-21}

Kodak Express, Detskiy Mir, 4th floor {daily 8:30-20}; Leningradskiy prosp. 74, ph. 151-0826 {M-Sa 10-19}; ul. Tverskaya 25, ph. 299-5483 {daily 10-19}

Kodak Film Developing, Hotel Mezhdunarodnaya, ph. 253-1643

Kodak Film Shop, Petrovskiy Passage, ul. Petrovka 4, ph. 928-5468 {M-F 9-20, I hour photo}

Office Club, ul. Ogrucheva 34/63, ph. 336-0550 {M-Sa 9-21, Su 9-18}

Polaroid Shop, Leninskiy prosp. 70/11, ph. 930-9627

Polaroid Studio Express, GUM, 3rd line; Leninskiy prosp. 150; Leningradskiy prosp. 33; Dobrininskaya pl. 36/71; Komsomolskiy prosp. 7; Leningradskiy prosp. 71; ul. Novy Arbat 30/9; Vetoshny p. 5/4; Dmitrovka B. ul. 14; 70 Leninskiy prosp.; Teatralny pr., Detskiy Mir; Pyatnitskaya ul. 28; Ukrainskiy bul. 7; Serpukhovskiy val 14

Yupiter, ul. Novy Arbat 25

FIRE   DIAL 01

FLOWERS

Bouquets can be bought year-round at most major metro stations, usually in underpasses. Prices vary greatly from season to season. For the cheapest bouquets, look for vendors who seem to be selling from their own garden. The best flowers are consistently available at:

Flower markets

Byelorusskiy, next to this train station Pushkin Square underpass.

Tsentralny Market, Tsvetnoy bul. 15, open 7-18

Florist shops

Elite Flora, B. Gruzinskaya 32, ph. 254-3992 {phone orders, delivery}

Flower Shop, ul. Tverskaya 16, ph. 229-0468 {M-Sa 10-19}; Leningradskiy prosp. 74, ph. 151-2283 {M-Sa 10-19}; Novy Arbat 23, ph. 203-0321

Flowers, Novy Arbat 15, ph. 203-0204 {M-Sa 10-20, break 14-15}

Flowers, prosp. Mira 74, ph. 281-6281

GUM Flower Market, GUM, 1st fl., 2nd row, ph. 926-3346 {delivers}

Nataly Flora Service, ul. Krasina 7, ph. 255-9480 {made to order}

Petrovskiy Passage Flower Shop, ul. Petrovka 10. 1st fl., ph. 923-6005 {M-Sa 9-20}

Polskaya Gvozdika, Leninskiy prosp. 79, ph. 134-5416

Priroda, Kutuzovskiy prosp. 5/3, ph. 243-5528

Sakura, ul. Tverskaya 15, ph. 229-3709 {dried, bonsai trees}

Swiss Flora, Leninskiy prosp. 43, ph. 237-3942 {daily 10-19}

FOOD

See also Shopping, Markets, Food Delivery

The past year has brought a full blossoming of grocery stores stocking Western products. These are the biggest and best:

Alberto Beski - Products of Italy, GUM, 3rd line, 1st fl., ph. 926-3246 {M-Sa 8-20, cc}

Arbat Irish House, Novy Arbat 13, ph. 291-7641 {daily 10-23, cc}

Australian Pie Co., Ltd., Varshavskoye sh. 46, ph. 111-0522

Avantat, Dmitrovka B. ul. 2, ph. 292-1175

Capricorne International, Simferopolskiy Blvd. 7A, #15/16, ph. 113-2933

Cheromushkinskiy Bread Kombinat, ph. 315-3810 {croissants, delivered, no minimum}

Chico, Detskiy Mir, 4th floor {baby food}

Colognia Supermarket, ul. B. Sadovaya 5/1, ph. 209-6591

Danone, ul. Tverskaya 4, ph. 292-0512 {cc}

Diplomat Food Store, ul. B. Gruzinskaya 63, ph. 251-2589 {daily 10-19, cc}

Exposhop Supermarket, Krasnopresnenskaya nab. 14, ph. 259-4017 {M-Sat 10-20, Sun 10-18}

Food Line Supermarket, Krasnaya Presnya ul. 23, ph. 252-6591 {M-Sa 10-20}

Food Orders Store, Biryulevskaya ul. 37, ph. 326-4477

Foodland, Sadko Arcade (Expocenter), ph. 256-2213 {open 7 days}

Franco-Serra Italia, ul. Tverskaya 1 {M-Sa 11-14, 15-20}

Garden Ring Supermarket, B. Sadovaya 1, ph. 209-1572 {daily 9-21, cc}; Leninskiy prosp. 146, Dom Turistov, ph. 956-5458; ul. Serafimovicha 2, ph. 230-0718

Giminey Foodstore, ul. B. Yakimanka 22, ph. 238-6262

Intercar Minishop (and offices), ul. Pilyugina 14, k. 3, ph. 936-2469 {M-F 10-20, Sa-Su 11-19}

Julius Meinl Supermarket, Leninskiy prosp. 146, ph. 438-3444 {M-Sa 10-20, Su 10-18}

Lux Supermarket, Olympic Village, Michurinskiy prosp. 4, ph. 932-1000 {M-Sa 11-20, Su 10-18}

M. Leader, Leningradskiy prosp. 39, ph. 157-8345 {daily 10-21, cc}

Mega-Inter, B. Dorogomilovskaya ul. 8, ph. 240-0331 {daily 9-21}

Montana, B. Cherkasskiy p. 15, ph. 923-8271 {M-Sa 10-18}

Montana Coffee Traders, ul. Marksistskaya 1/1, ph. 271-9280 {imported coffee}

Morozko, ul. Lva Tolstovo 2, ph. 246-0504

Morozko, ul. Kedrova 7a

Olwis, Leninskiy prosp. 60/2, ph. 137-4660 {M-Sa 10-20, Su 11-21}

Olympic Supermarket, Krasnaya Presnya 23, ph. 252-6591

Riglich Dina Market, Velozavodskaya ul. 3/2, ph. 275-6986 {M-F 9-20, S-Sun. 9-19, cc}

Rus-H Supermarket, Novy Arbat 26 (Dom Knigi)

Sadko, ul. B. Dorogomilovskaya 16, ph. 243-7501

SCM Center (Julius Meinl), Varshavskoye sh. 46, ph. 111-2200 {M-Sa 10-20, Su 10-18}

SIAG Food Store, ul. Tverskaya 22, ph. 299-1223 {daily 9-23, cc}

Sinti, Leninskiy prosp. 30, ph. 952-1343

Sovincenter Supermarket, Mezhdunarodnaya Hotel I, 1st fl., ph. 253-1389 {daily 9:30-20}

⇨Stockmann Grocery Store, Zatsepskiy val 4/8, ph. 233-2602 {daily 10-20, cc}

Sweet Way, ul. Tverskaya 12 {candy, M-F 9-20, break 14-15}

Swiss Butchery, Sadko Arcade (Expocenter), ph. 940-4068

Taganka II Supermarket, ul. Marksistskaya 1/1, ph. 272-2417 {daily 11-20}

Tamada Duty Free Shop, Hotel Moskva, ph. 292-2874

Tea, Coffee and Other Colonial Wares, Khudozhestvenny pr. 2, ph. {M-Sat 10-19}

Union JV (Germany), Bernikov p. 2/6, ph. 227-2805 {daily 10-22, cc}

Virginia-American Food Store, M. Bronnaya ul. 27/14, ph. 290-3531 {daily 8-20}

FOOD DELIVERY

See also Pizza

The following options exist for delivery of fast food (some coop restaurants will also deliver).

Hol'N One Donuts, ph. 975-3392

Jack's Sandwiches, ph. 281-3536 {M-F 9-18, free deliv.}

Just Subs, Kutuzovskiy prosp. 22, ph. 243-0109 {M-S 8-21}

McDonald's Delivery, ul. B. Bronnaya 29, ph. 200-1655

Montana Coffee Traders, ul. Marksistskaya 1/1, ph. 271-9280 {imported coffee}

Panda Restaurant, Tverskoy bul. 3/5, ph. 298-6505 {daily 12-14, 16-23, cc}

Pettina Hamburgers, ul. Kosmonavtov 2/4, ph. 286-5217 {cc}

Pizza Hut Restaurant, Kutuzovskiy prosp. 17, ph. 243-1727 {daily 11-22, cc}; ul. Tverskaya 12, ph. 229-2013 {daily 11-23, cc}

FOOD, WHOLESALE

Exposhop Cash & Carry, Krasnopresnenskaya nab. 14, ph. 256-5571 {M-Sat 10-20, Sun 10-18}

K & S Fruits and Vegetables, Leninskiy prosp. 42, ph. 938-7986

MAXA Cash and Carry, Silikatny pr. 13, ph. 583-6502 {M-Sa 9-17:30}

Moscow Cash and Carry Mozhaisk, ul. 20-ovo Yanvarya 20, Mozhaisk, ph. 238-24104

Sadko Distribution, Krasnogvardeyskiy proyezd, 1, ph. 255-2650

SCM Center (Julius Meinl), Varshavskoye sh. 46, ph. 111-2200 {M-Sa 10-20, Su 10-18}

Scorpio Cash & Carry, Zaporozhskaya ul. 1, ph. 449-7791; Berezhkovskaya nab. 8, ph. 240-2264 {cc}; Dubininskaya ul. 10, ph. 481-2400

Scorpio Trade Center, Kutuzovskiy prosp. 17, ph. 207-9815 {cc}

FURNITURE

See Office Supplies, Decor, Hardware

For home furniture, try:

A & A Relocations, Krapivinskiy p. 3, bldg. 2, ph. 299-2960

Business Furniture International (BFI), ul. D. Ulyanova 4/1, ph. 135-2105

C.C.I. Capital Contracts International Ltd., ul. Spartakovskaya 6A, ph. 267-3783

Essor Carpets, Leninskiy prosp. 85, ph. 134-0531

First Trading Consortium Limited, Gogolevskiy Bul. 31, ph. 291-1663

Holding Center, Shyolkovskoye sh. 7, ph. 241-5014

Intermebel JV, ul. Litvina-Sedova 9/26, ph. 259-6933

Interoko JV (FRG), Frunzenskaya nab. 30, ph. 242-8941

Inzhener Ltd., prosp. Mira 20, kor. 2, ph. 288-7177

Linea-M, B. Starodanilovskiy p. 6, ph. 235-0402

Queen-Mosmebel JV (Egypt), ul. Garibaldi 26, ph. 128-7835

Ramsey Furniture, Uldatsova ul. 85, ph. 931-9207

REM, Yaroslavskoye sh. 13

Ryugen, ul. Malygina 9a, ph. 474-4433

San Giacomo Furniture, Shyolkovskoye sh. 7, ph. 167-2527

Supply Side, ph. 238-5308

Swedish Furniture, Leninskiy prosp. 64, ph. 137-0291

Taki-Moscow, ul. Mnevniki 10, ph. 191-1377 {M-Sa 10-14, 15-19}

VIT Worldwide, Povarskaya ul. 21, 2nd fl., #14, ph. 291-1844

FURS

Fur hats can be easily purchased on the street near major tourist sights. You can also try some of the markets, the Arbat and Izmailovskiy Park on the weekends. Many of the major Russian department stores also now have furs available.

Claude Litz, GUM, 1st line, 2nd fl., ph. 925-1227 {M-Sa 8-20, cc}

Jindo Rus, Hotel Intourist, ph. 203-9742; Hotel Kosmos, prosp. Mira 150, ph. 217-0025

Rosenberg & Lenhart, GUM, 1st line, 1st fl.

Sovmekhastoria, ul. Dorogomilovskaya 14, ph. 243-7672

Tsoukas Bros., Kutuzovskiy prosp. 18, ph. 243-3089

Yakovlev & Co., GUM, 1st line, 2nd fl.

GAS STATIONS

See also Cars, Service and Cars, Parts & Supplies

Below is a list of Moscow city gas stations, by region (see also the stations shown on map):

Center

ul. Trifonovskaya, 36/38 • Frunzenskaya nab. • Luzhnetskaya nab.

North

ul. Pryanishnikova, 10 • Sheremetevskaya ul. 85a • Signalny prospect • Dmitrovskoye shosse, 104 • ul. Rimskovo-Korskakova • ul. Abramtsevskaya 26.

Northwest
ul. Begovaya, 3a • Leningradskiy prospekt, 43 • ul. Marshala Biryuzova, 2 • Staropetrovskiy per., 4 • 1st Krasnogorskiy prospekt • ul. Festivalnaya • Belomorskaya ul. 2 • Svetlogorskiy prospekt, 12 • Nemanskiy prospekt, str. 14 • **Nefto Agip**, Leningradskoye sh. 63, ph. 457-2013 {cc}

Northeast
ul. Dokukina, 4 • Izmailovskiy prospekt, Gorodok Baumana • Ostashkovskoe shosse, at Outer Ring Road • Rusakovskiy nab. • Yaroslavskoe shosse, 107 • 10th ul. Krasnoy Sosny

South
Varshavskoe shosse, 21 km • ul. Kakhovka, 28 • Varshavskoe shosse, 26 & 77 • 7th Kozhukhovskaya ul., 7 • Proletarskiy prospekt, 60a • ul. Y. V. Andropova, 6 • Vostryakovskiy prospekt, Outer Ring Road

Southwest
ul. Lobachevskovo, 92a • Leninskiy prospekt, kvartal 42 • Leninskiy prospekt, at Outer Ring Road

Southeast
ul. Lublinskaya • Volgogradskiy prospekt, 166 & 135 • Shipilovskaya ul., 31a

East
ul. Semyonovskiy val, 4 • Poluyarovskaya nab. • ul. Stalevarov, 12a • Shchelkovskoe shosse, at Outer Ring Road • Sokolnicheskiy val

West
Khoroshovskoe shosse, 37/39 • Nizhnegorodskaya ul. 25 • Belobezhskaya ul. • Minskaya ul. • Kastanaevskaya ul. • 2nd Kuskovskaya ul., 16 • Vereyskaya ul. • ul. Gorbunova • ul. Konobalova, 9/2

If you have questions about the assortment of gasoline available at a certain station or about the location of a certain station, you can call 473-0345 or 473-0346 for such information. You can get oil and grease for Russian cars at

stores located at: Dmitrovskoe shosse, 65b • Leningradskoe shosse, 21a • Volokolamskoe shosse, 83 • ul. Vilisa Latsisa, 16 • Taganskaya ploshchad • Krasnobogatyrskaya ul. • Rusakovskaya nab.

GIFTS

Almaz Independent Group, Kutuzovskiy prosp. 35, ph. 249-5049

Beriozka, Rossiya Hotel, ph. 298-3620

Gzhel Store, Radisson-Slavyanskaya Hotel, ph. 941-8928

Gzhel Store, Mezhdunarodnaya Hotel I, 1st fl., ph. 253-2359 {daily 9-22}

Gzhel Store, GUM, 2nd line, 1st fl., {M-Sa 8-20}

K-Boutiques, Pullman Iris Hotel, ph. 488-8100

K-Boutiques, Aerostar Hotel, ph. 155-5030

Rus, Mezhdunarodnaya Hotel I, 1st fl., ph. 253-1785 {daily 9-20}

Russian Enamel Miniatures, ph. 336-3444

Russian Style Souvenirs, Petrovskiy Passazh, 1st fl., {M-Sa 9-20}

Souvenir Trading JV (US), ul. Miklukho-Maklaya 37, ph. 335-1444

Souvenirs, GUM, 2nd line, 1st fl., {M-Sa 8-20}

GOLF

Moscow Country Club, Krasnogorskiy District, Makhabino, ph. 561-2977

Tumba Golf Course (Finland), ul. Dovzhenko 1, ph. 147-8330

GOVERNMENT

Some government offices are listed here. For Russian ministries, see the Telephone Directory under "Ministry of...," for state committees and other bodies, see "Russia, Government of," for city regional government, see "Prefecture of."

CIS
Committee for Cooperation of CIS States, ph. 925-9051

Russia
Agency for International Cooperation and Development, ul. Vozdvizhenka 18, ph. 290-0903

Government of the Russian Federation (Admin. Info.), Staraya pl. 4, ph. 925-3581

Kremlin Palace of Congresses, Kremlin, ph. 926-7901

Presidium of the Russian Supreme Soviet, Krasnopresnenskaya nab. 2, ph. 205-6847

State Duma – International Department, ph. 290-7391

Moscow

Moscow City Council
Executive Committee, ul. Tverskaya 13, ph. 229-5431
Interagency Commission, ph. 202-2782
Planning Committee, Leontyevskiy p. 24, ph. 925-3123
Orgkomitet, Nikitskaya B. ul. 12, ph. 203-2655

GYM

See also Swimming, Tennis
⇨**Metropol Hotel Health Club**, Hotel Metropol, ph. 927-6148 {$5/hr. gym, $17/hr. pool, $30/hr. massage}

Mezhdunarodnaya Health Club, Hotel Mezhdunarodnaya, Ent. 1, ph. {$9/swim}

Olympic Health Club, Olympic Penta Hotel, Olympiyskiy prosp. 18/1, ph. 971-6101

Olympic Penta Hotel, Olympiyskiy prosp. 18/1, ph. 971-6101

Slavyanskaya Health Club, Radisson-Slavyanskaya Hotel, ph. 941-8027

H

HAIR CUTTING

Africana Beauty Center, The, ul. Zelenodolskaya 41, ph. 172-7671

Charodeika, Novy Arbat 17, ph. 290-5339

City Looks Hair Salon, ul. Pokrovka 2/1 str. 1, ph. 928-7084

Entourage Beauty Salon, Radisson-Slavyanskaya Hotel, main lobby, ph. 941-8157 {M-F 10-19, Sa 10-15}

Ginseng salon, ul. Pokrovka 32, ph. 227-1641

Kudesnitsa, Nikitskaya B. ul. 37, ph. 291-2111

⇨**Metropol Salon**, Hotel Metropol, ph. 927-6024 {for men and women}

Mezhdunarodnaya Hotel salon, ph. 953-2378

Pullman Hairdressers, Pullman Iris Hotel, ph. 488-8101

Wella, ul. Mayakovskovo 12, ph. 290-5137

Yves Rocher, ul. Tverskaya 4, ph. 923-5885 {hair cutting: daily 10-12}

Zhen Shen, Petrovskiy Passage, ph. 921-6460 {for men and women}

Zoo Beauty Salon, ul. Druzhinnikovskaya 30, ph. 252-2088 {for men and women}

HARDWARE

Intermarket, Degtyarny p. 5, ph. 299-7968 {M-Sa 10-19}

Perestelf Hardware Store, Kosmodemyankich Zoi i Alexandra 17/2, ph. 450-0896

Renlund Biurobin, Prechistenskiy p. 37-39, ph. 237-7612

Scanflot-Scanior Design, ul. Biryuzovaya 19, ph. 194-8811

Star Progress, Frunzenskaya nab. 30, pav. 15, ph. 201-0692

⇨**Stockmann Home Electronics and Car Supplies Store**, ul. Lyusinovskaya 70/1, ph. 954-8234

HORSEBACK RIDING

Bitsa Horseback Riding Complex, Balaklavskiy prosp. 35, ph. 318-6820

Equestrian Center, Balaklavskiy prosp. 33, ph. 318-0581

Hippodrome, ul. Begovaya 22, ph. 945-4516

Moscow Tourist Club, Sadovaya-Kudrinskaya 4, ph. 203-1094

Yamskoy Dvor, Leninskiy prosp. 30, ph. 135-8255

Can't find it?

Check the Cross-reference Guide on the first pages of the Yellow Pages section for a complete listing of subject headings.

HOSTELS

Travellers Guest House, ul. B. Pere-yaslavskaya 50, 10th fl., ph. 971-4059 {Email: tgh@glas.apc.org} **K11(7)**

HOTELS

All major (and most minor) hotels are listed below. Following the address and phone of each is (in bold type) a map reference to the hotel's location (i.e. F15(10)) is map page 10). For fax and telex numbers, see the Telephone Directory.

Aerostar Hotel, Leningradskiy prosp. 37, k. 9, ph. 155-5030 **E11(5)**

Akademicheskaya Hotel I, Leninskiy prosp. 1, ph. 238-0902 **I26(14)**

Altay Hotel, Botanicheskaya ul. 41, ph. 482-5703 **H4(3)**

Arbat Hotel, Plotnikov p. 12, ph. 244-7635 **H16(22)**

Arena Hotel, ul. 10-letiya Oktyabrya 11, ph. 245-2802 **F18(10)**

Baltschug Kempinski Hotel, ul. Baltschuga 1, ph. 230-6500 **J15(19)**

Baykal Hotel, Selskokhozyaystvennaya ul. 15/1, ph. 189-7515 **K6(7)**

Belgrade I Hotel, Smolenskaya Ploshchad 5 (see also Zolotoye Koltso), ph. 248-1643 **G16(21)**

Booking for Voskresensskoe Hotel /Sa-voy/, Rozhdestvenka 3, ph. 929-8569

Budapest Hotel, Petrovskiye linii 2/18, ph. 921-1060 **J14(19)**

Cosmos Hotel, prosp. Mira 150, ph. 217-8680 **L7(7)**

Danilov Hotel, Danilovskiy Monastery, B. Stary Danilov per., ph. 954-0503 **I20(14)**

Druzhba Hotel, prosp. Vernadskovo 53, ph. 432-9629 **B24(13)**

Hotel Mezhdunarodnaya I, Krasnopres-nenskaya nab. 12, ph. 253-2382 **F15(17)**

Hotel Mezhdunarodnaya II, Krasnopres-nenskaya nab. 12, ph. 253-2760 **F15(17)**

Infa-Otel JV (Finland), ul. Rozhdestvenka 3, ph. 928-9169 **J14(19)**

Inflotel, Krasnopresnenskaya nab. 12, dock-ing, ph. 255-9278 **F15(17)**

Intourist Hotel, ul. Tverskaya 3/5, ph. 203-4008 **I14(19)**

Izmailovo Tourist Complex, Izmaylovskoye sh. 69A, ph. 166-0109 **R11(8)**

Kievskaya Hotel, Kiyevskaya ul. 2, ph. 240-1444 **F16(21)**

Kuzminki Hotel, Volzhskiy bul. 114a, k. 9, ph. 179-0879 **R20(16)**

Leningradskaya Hotel, ul. Kalanchevskaya 21/40, ph. 975-3032 **L13(20)**

Lesniye Dali Hotel, Rublyovskoye sh., 29th km, ph. 592-3628

Lokomotiv Hotel, ul. B. Cherkizovskaya 125a, ph. 161-8133 **R9(8)**

Marco Polo Presnaya Hotel, Spirido-nevskiy Pereulok 9, ph. 202-0381 **H14(18)**

Mayak Hotel, ul. B. Filevskaya 25, ph. 142-2384 **A16(9)**

⇨ **Metropol Hotel**, Teatralny proyezd 1/4, ph. 927-6000 **J14(19)**

Minsk Hotel, ul. Tverskaya 22, ph. 299-1300 **I13(19)**

Mir Hotel, B. Devyatinskiy p. 9, ph. 290-9519 **G15(17)**

Molodyozhnaya Hotel, Dmitrovskoye sh. 27, ph. 210-9311 **G7(6)**

Moskva Hotel, Okhotny Ryad 7, ph. 292-1100 **J14(19)**

Mozhayskaya Hotel, Mozhayskoye sh. 165, ph. 447-3434

National Hotel, Okhotny ryad 14/1, ph. 203-6539 **J14(19)**

Neptune Hotel, ul. Ibragimova 30, ph. 369-6383 **Q11(8)**

Novotel Hotel, Sheremetevo 2 Airport, ph. 578-9401

Olympic Penta Hotel, Olympiyskiy prosp. 18/1, ph. 971-6101 **J11(7)**

Orlyonok Hotel, ul. Kosygina 15, ph. 939-8853 **F20(14)**

Ostankino Hotel, ul. Botanicheskaya 29, ph. 219-2880 **H6(6)**

Palace Hotel, ul. Tverskaya Yamskaya 19, ph. 956-3152 **H13(18)**

Peking Hotel, ul. B. Sadovaya 1/5, ph. 209-3400 **H13(18)**

President Hotel, ul. B. Yakimanka 24, ph. 238-7303 **I17(23)**

Pullman Iris Hotel, Korovinskoye Shosse 10, ph. 488-8000 **E2(4)**

Radisson Slavyanskaya Hotel, Berezhkovskaya nab. 2, ph. 941-8020 **G16(21)**

Rossiya Hotel, ul. Varvarka 6, ph. 298-5400 J15(19)

Rossiyanka Hotel, ul. Donskaya 1, ph. 238-0508 I18(23)

Royal Zenith Hotel, Tamanskaya ul. 49 B, ph. 199-8001

RusOtel JV (US), Varshavskoye sh., 21st km, ph. 382-0586 J25(15)

Salyut Hotel, Leninskiy prosp. 158, ph. 438-6565 A26(13)

Savoy Hotel, ul. Rozhdestvenka 3, ph. 929-8500 J14(19)

Sayani Hotel, Yaroslavskoye sh. 116, k. 2, ph. 183-1456 N4(2)

Sevastopol Hotel, ul. Yushunskaya 1a, ph. 318-2263 H26(14)

Severnaya Hotel, ul. Sushchyovskiy val 50, ph. 289-6413 J11(7)

Sheremetevo Hotel, Sheremetevo 2 Airport, ph. 578-7663

Sovetskaya Hotel JV (France), Leningradskiy prosp. 32/2, ph. 250-7255 G11(6)

Soyuz Hotel, ul. Levoberezhnaya 12, ph. 457-9004 A1(4)

Soyuz II Hotel, 1st Krasnogvardeyskiy pr. 25b, ph. 259-3004 E15(9)

Sport Hotel, Leninskiy prosp. 90/2, ph. 131-1191 C24(13)

Spros Hotel JV (Switz.), Leninskiy prosp. 95/15, ph. 133-4393 D24(13)

Sputnik Hotel, Leninskiy prosp. 38, ph. 938-7096 G20(14)

Tourist Hotel, ul. Selskokhozyaystvennaya 17/2, ph. 187-6018 K6(7)

Travellers Guest House, ul. B. Pereyaslavskaya 50, 10th fl., ph. 971-4059 {Email tgh@glas.apc.org} K11(7)

Tsaritsino Hotel, Shipilovskiy prosp. 47/1, ph. 343-4343

Tsentralnaya Hotel, ul. Tverskaya 10, ph. 229-8589 I14(19)

Tsentralny Dom Turista (Central House of Tourism), Leninskiy prosp. 146, ph. 434-2782 B25(13)

Ukraina Hotel, Kutuzovskiy prosp. 2/1, ph. 243-2895 F15(17)

Universitetskaya Hotel, Michurinskiy prosp. 8/29, ph. 939-9731 C20(13)

Ural Hotel, ul. Pokrovka 40, ph. 297-4258 L14(20)

Varshava I Hotel, Leninskiy prosp. 2, ph. 238-1970 I18(23)

Varshava II Hotel, Kotelnicheskaya nab. 1/15, ph. 227-4078 K16(24)

Villa Peredelkino Hotel, 1st Chobatovskaya Alleya 2a, ph. 435-8184

Volga Hotel, Dokuchayev p. 10, ph. 280-7729 K13(20)

Volga II Hotel, ul. B. Spasskaya 4, ph. 280-1364 K13(20)

Voskhod Hotel, Altufyevskoye sh. 2, ph. 401-9822 H4(3)

Yaroslavskaya Hotel, Yaroslavskaya ul. 8, ph. 283-1733 L8(7)

Yunost Hotel, ul. Khamovnicheskiy val 34, F18(21)

Yuzhnaya Hotel, Leninskiy prosp. 87, ph. 134-3065 D23(13)

Zagorye Hotel, ul. Yagodnaya 15, ph. 329-3011

Zolotoy Kolos Hotel, Yaroslavskaya ul. 15, k. 3, ph. 286-2703 L7(7)

Zolotoye Koltso (Belgrade II) Hotel, Smolenskaya ul. 15, ph. 248-6734 G16(21)

Zvezdnaya Hotel, Zvyozdny bul. 42, ph. 215-4292 J8(7)

HOUSEWARES

AMO Ltd., ul. Avtozavodskaya 5, 'Ogonyek', ph. 275-4314; Kashirskoye sh. 57, k. 2, ph. 344-6604

Decor Espana, Varshavskoye sh. 46, ph. 111-5201

Eden International, ul. Novy Arbat 21, 8th fl., ph. 291-4392

ERLAN, Leninskiy prosp. 57, ph. 135-8245

Fairn & Swanson Ltd., Sovintsentr, Mezhdunarodnaya Hotel I, 1st fl., ph. 253-9408 {M-Sa 10-20, Su 10-19}

JVC, GUM, 1st line, 1st fl., ph. 923-8200 {M-Sa 9-19, cc}

Moulinex, Koroviy val 7, #74, ph. 238-3479

Peter's Shop, Zemlyanoy val 72, ph. 298-3248

Renlund M, Stolyarny p. 3, ph. 253-4173

Siemens, 1st Donskoy pr. 2, ph. 237-6624

⇨ Stockmann Home Electronics and Car Supplies Store, ul. Lyusinovskaya 70/1, ph. 954-8234

Tefal, GUM, 1st line, 1st fl., ph. 926-3463

U2 Family Superstore, ul. Bakuninskaya 32, ph. 265-2963 {M-Sa 10-19}

Wedgewood, Sadko Arcade (Expocenter), ph. 253-9588 {daily 10-22}

I

ICE CREAM

Baskin Robbins, ul. Arbat 20, ph. 291-7114; ul. Graivoronovskaya 19; ul. Udaltsova 19A; Lesnaya alleya 1111, Zelenograd, ph. 530-9091; ul. Tverskaya 27/5, ph. 299-5829; ul. Varvarka 6, Hotel Rossiya, ph. 298-3594

Caffe Gelateria, prosp. Mira 58, ph. 280-9679 {cc}

Carpigiana, Hotel Mezhdunarodnaya

Pinguin Ice Cream, Nikolskaya ul. 4/5, ph. 927-1726 {M-Sa 8-20, Su 8-19}; Leninskiy prosp. 37, ph. 954-6466 {M-Sa 10-20, Su 10-19}

INFORMATION

Directory Assistance: 09

Several companies also provide a wide range ⇨ *of business information services. The range of services is very diverse and requires inquiry:*

AIT Information Systems, Lusinovskaya 72, ph. 236-3717

Americom Business Center, Radisson-Slavyanskaya Hotel, ph. 941-8427

ASU-Impuls, ul. Nelidovskaya 18, kv. 38, ph. 497-2047

Commersant, Kiosk, ph. 202-9951

Commersant Information Center, ul. Vrubelya 4, ph. 943-9710

Dialog Data Bank, ph. 932-5610

Fakt, Khoroshevskoye sh. 41, ph. 299-0004

Foliant, ph. 202-9505 {pay via phone bill}

Forepost Information Service, ul. Skhodnenskaya 26, ph. 555-5510

Formula Information Technologies Center, Kiselny N. p. 5, ph. 925-6897

Garant, ul. Krzhizanovskaya 14/1, ph. 129-0154

Glavk Ltd., ph. 120-9568

Gosstatistika Information Center, ul. Myasnitskaya 39, ph. 207-4681

Information Moscow, Leninskiy prosp. 45, ent 15, kv 426, ph. 135-1164 {M-F 10-18}

Information on City Phone Numbers, ph. 927-0009 {paid service}

Informbank Agency, ul. Timura Frunze 8/5, ph. 245-0213

Interlink JV (FRG), ul. Narodnovo Opolcheniya 34, ph. 946-8711

Intourist Information, ph. 203-6962

Klever Corporation, P.O. Box 745, ph. 297-5628

Legal information by phone, ph. 946-2550

Maria Information, Butyrskiy Val 24, ph. 251-7766

Marketing Information Center JV (Finland), Kolpachny p. 7, ph. 924-7941

Moscow Business Telephone Guide, Khoroshevskoye shosse 4, ph. 316-6130

Moscow Center for Scientific-Technical Information, Lubyanskiy pr. 5, ph. 928-6605

Moscow Central Address Information Bureau, Krasnoproletarskaya 10, ph. 258-2820

Noviye Razrabotki i Technologiy, Leninskiye Gory, ph. 939-2494

Russian Information Services, B. Kondratyevskiy p. 4, kor. 2, kv. 168, ph. 254-9275

Russian-American Press and Information Center, Khlebny p. 2/3, West Wing, ph. 203-5724

Russica Information Inc., Vinnitskaya ul. 4, ph. 932-4760

Sotrudnichestvo, ul. Rozhdestvenka 8, stroenie 2, ph. 923-6405

Vneshterminalkomplex, ul. Zenlyachkiy 3. str. 2

Weather forecast by phone, ph. 975-9222

INSURANCE

American International Group (AIG), Radisson-Slavyanskaya Hotel, ph. 941-8879

Asko Insurance Company, Universitetskiy pr. 21, ph. 143-4692

Ingosstrakh Insurance Company, ul. Pyatnitskaya 12, ph. 231-1677

Insurance Company IMKO, ul. Yartsevskaya 30, kom. 1105-1106, ph. 141-3396

Rosgosstrakh, Neglinnaya ul. 23, ph. 200-2995; Nastasinskiy per. 3, k. 2, ph. 299-8945

Russian-European Insurance Co. (RESO), PO Box 33, ph. 238-0467

Westrosso Insurance Co., Ltd., Vozenko ul. 9/2, PO Box 226351, ph. 417-8149

INTERNATIONAL PHONE

See Business Centers, Telecom
See Car phone
International phones (in booths) payable by credit card or pre-pay card are available in most major tourist hotels. Always be sure of the costs before you dial; these booths are very expensive! International calls can now be dialed directly from apartments as well.

Long distance call
  booking: 8-194 or 8-196
  booking from a hotel: 333-4101

Also try calling from the Central Telegraph Office (the crowd is large, except early in the a.m.), at ul. Tverskaya. 7.
Certain business centers and hotel service desks also have direct international lines which can be used for fax or phone calls.
Here are the numbers for international calling card access from Moscow:

AT&T USA Direct, ph. 155-5042
MCI Call USA (Helsinki), ph. 8-10-358-9800-102-80
Sprint Express , ph. 155-6133

J

JAZZ

Call ahead to verify the program.
All-Star Jazz Club, ul. Generala Yermolova 6
Arbat Blues Club, Aksakov p. 11, kor. 2, ph. 291-1546
Arkadia Jazz Club, Teatralny Pr. 3, ph. 926-9008
⇨ **Club Royale**, Begovaya ul. 22, ph. 945-1410 {daily 8-4}
Francaise (La), Pullman Iris Hotel, ph. 488-8000
⇨ **Jazz Brunch**, Hotel Metropol, ph. 927-6452
Jazz Club, Kuznetskiy Most, ph. 921-9744

Rock and Jazz Laboratory, Staropanskiy p. 1/5, ph. 923-1604
Savoy Restaurant, Savoy Hotel, ph. 928-0450 {Sunday jazz brunch 11:30-15}

L

LANGUAGE COURSES

See also Translation
The opportunities are virutally endless; call around, bargain for the best rate. Listed below are just a few of the potential options, those which have been most widely advertised and/or around the longest.
Many institutes and technical colleges also have courses which are very good.

Aescom, ul. Parshina 23, Ap. 89, ph. 197-6760
Berlitz, Sovintsentr, Mezhdunarodnaya Hotel I, ph. 253-8223
Center for Intensive Language Training, ph. 291-3727
Goethe Institute Moscow, Leninskiy prosp. 95a, ph. 936-2457
Marchi-Intensiv, ul. Rozhdestvenka 11, ph. 928-1269
Patriarchi Dom, B. Kozikhinskiy p. 17, #20, ph. 299-5971
Study Company, ph. 237-4572

LEGAL ADVICE

Adams and Reese, Dmitrovka B. ul. 4/2, #1b, ph. 925-8430
Baker & McKenzie, B. Strochenovskiy 22/25, ph. 230-6036
Bureau Francis Lefebvre, Nikitskaya B. ul. 22, kv. 18, ph. 202-1170
Chadbourne, Parke, Hedman & Union of Advocates, Maxim Gorkiy nab. 38, ph. 231-1064
Clifford Chance, Palashevskiy B. p. 15a, ph. 973-2415
Coudert Brothers, Staraya Basmannaya ul. 14, ph. 262-2744

> **To add or correct information appearing in this guide, call (in Moscow) 254-9275.**

Duval Khinchuk Ljanders, ul. B. Ordynka 61, str. 2, ph. 238-1744

Firestone, Duncan & Associates, ul. B. Polyanka 28/1, 4th fl., Ste 295, ph. 237-5657

Gibson, Dunn & Crutcher, Kazenny M. p. 10, kv 6, ph. 297-3784

Inform-Pravo JV, ul. Druzhby 10/32, ph. 143-6771

Inyurcolleguia, ul. Tverskaya 5, ph. 203-6864

Lamport Co. Ltd., ul. Prechistenka 40, ph. 246-6845

Latham & Watkins, Park Place, Leninskiy prosp. 113/1, #C200, ph. 956-5555

Leboeuf, Lamb, Leiby & MacRae, Novy Arbat 36, City Administration Bldg., 14th fl., ph. 290-9000

Lord, Day & Lord Barrett Smith, Ltd., ul. Vavilova 72/13, kv. 33, ph. 134-8293

Macleod Dixon, 7th M. Levshinkiy 3, ph. 201-4073

Mannheimer Swartling, Pokrovskiy bul. 4/17, apt. 35, ph. 207-6008

Milbank, Tweed, Hadley & McCloy, ul. Pokrovka 28, ph. 975-2524

Moscow Legal Advice Center, M. Poluyaroslavskiy per 3/5, ph. 227-1248

Moscow Legal Collegium, Dmitrovka B. ul. 9, str. 6, ph. 229-9033

Pepper, Hamilton & Scheetz, Grokholskiy p. 19/27, ph. 280-5279

Public Notary, Bobrov p. 6, ph. 923-6281

Russin & Vecchi, Danilov Hotel Complex, 5 Bol. Starodanilovskiy per., ph. 954-0652

Salans, Hertzfeld & Heilbronn, Gazetny p. 17/9, ph. 940-2944

Sarpinservis, ul. Nikolskaya 5/1, ph. 923-1739

Shaines & McEachern, Michurinskiy prosp. 14A, ph. 437-6667

Skadden, Arps, Slate, Meagher & Flom, Pleteshkovskiy p. 1, ph. 940-2304

Steptoe and Johnson, 7th M. Levshinsky, #3, ph. 201-4073

Vinson & Elkins, Povarskaya ul. 21, ph. 291-3156

White & Case, ul. Tverskaya 7, entrance 9, ph. 201-9292

For arbitration boards, see Government in the White Pages

LEISURE

See also Parks, Concerts, Horseback Riding, Sports

Dyen i Noch Restaurant, Kolomenskiy pr. 12, ph. 112-5092 {cc, dinner cabaret}

Moscow Parachute Club, ph. 111-3315

Obninsk, Vodolei International, ph. 357-7758

Villa Peredelkino Restaurant, 1st Chobatovskaya Alleya, Solntsevskiy District, ph. 435-1478

Wilma Sanatorium, ph. 496-9810

LIBRARIES

Russian State Library, ul. Vozdvizhenka 3, ph. 202-5790

This is the largest library in the world. You'll need a passport to get in. No roaming the stacks here, but you can request a book from the counter and they will bring it to you. Hours are 9 a.m. to 10 p.m. daily, except Sundays in summer and the last Monday of every month, when it is closed. Also try:

American Cultural Center Library, Nikoloyamskaya ul. 1, 2nd floor, Foreign Lit. Libra, ph. 297-6985 {open M-F 10-20:45, S 11-17:45}

British Council Resource Center, Nikoloyamskaya ul. 1, 2nd fl., Foreign Lit. Library, ph. 297-7733 {open M-F 10-20, S 11-18}

Central Polytechnic Library, Polytechnicheskiy pr. 2, ph. 928-6465

Foreign Literature Library, Nikoloyamskaya ul. 1, ph. 227-8810

French Cultural Center, Nikoloyamskaya ul. 1, 2nd fl., Foreign Lit. Library {open M-F 13-17}

Library of the Inst. for Scienific Info. on Social Sciences RAS, Nakhimovskiy prosp. 28/21/21, ph. 128-8881

LIMOS

Express Motors, ul. Alabyana 12, ph. 198-0034 {American cars}

Jetta, ph. 307-8351 {Lincoln, Ford, Cadillac}

Olga Co., Ltd., Hotel Metropol, Teatralny proyezd 1/4, ph. 927-6139

Savva Car Land, ul. Energeticheskaya 6, ph. 362-7264
Sunrise Limousines, ul. Zolotaya 11, ph. 366-4656

LIQUOR

See also Food, Shopping
Most all food stores stock liquor, wine and beer, as do hotels. Street corner kiosks carry a wide variety of liqueurs and beers, but try to make sure you are getting what you pay for, there have been cases of food and alcohol poisoning from liquor purchased at such kiosks.

Diplomat Food Store, ul. B. Gruzinskaya 63, ph. 251-2589 {daily 10-19, cc}
Galerie Du Vin, Kutuzovskiy prosp. 1/7, ph. 243-0365 {M-F 14-19:30, Sa 10-19:30}
Moscow Duty Free, Sheremetevo 2 Airport, ph. 578-9089
Office Club, ul. Obrucheva 34/63, ph. 336-0550 {M-Sa 9-21, Su 9-18}
⇨**Stockmann Grocery Store**, Zatsepskiy val 4/8, ph. 233-2602 {daily 10-20, cc}
Symetrie Champagne Showroom, Leninskiy prosp. 85, ph. 134-0531 {french goods}

LOST PROPERTY

In the metro, ph. 222-2085
In a taxi/public transport, ph. 923-8753

LUGGAGE

Etienne Aigner, Petrovskiy Passazh, 1st fl. (See Passazh), {M-Sa 9-20, cc}
Samsonite, GUM, 1st line, 2nd fl., ph. 926-3466 {M-Sa 8-20, cc}
Samsonite, Petrovskiy Passazh, 2nd fl., ph. {M-Sa 9-20, cc}
U2 Family Superstore, ul. Bakuninskaya 32, ph. 265-2963 {M-Sa 10-19}

Where in St. Petersburg, this book's parallel guide to Russia's imperial capital, is the only guide you'll need to the "Venice of the North." Call Russian Information Services at: (in the US) 802-223-4955, (in Moscow) 095-254-9275, (in St. Petersburg) 812-292-7420.

M

MAIL ORDER

Ostermann, ul. Sadovaya-Samotechnaya 5, kv. 21, ph. 292-5110
Peter Justensen, 4th ul. Marinoy Roshchi 12, ph. 971-1178
Quelle Catalogue Sales, ul. B. Molchanovka 34, str. 2, ph. 291-4735

MAPS

See also Books
For the most detailed Moscow city map available (identical to that in the back of this book, only full-sheet – laminated version also available, contact Russian Information Services at 254-9275; in the US call 802-223-4955. For other, Russian-made maps, try:

Atlas, Kuznetskiy most 9
Knigi, Kuznetskiy most 20
Dom Knigi, Novy Arbat
Mosgorspravka, ul. Tverskaya 5

MARKETS

The best farmers' markets are:

Cheremushkinskiy, Lomonosovskiy pr. 1
Tsentralny, Tsvetnoy bulv. 15
Rizhskiy, prosp. Mira 94-6
Dorogomilovskiy, ul. Mozhaiskiy val 10
Yaroslavskiy, prosp. Mira 122
Danilovskiy, ul. Mytnaya 74

MASSAGE

See also Gym
The Moscow Times classifieds are overflowing with ads for massage providers. If a massage is what you are really after, that avenue is not recommended. This is:

Ginseng salon, ul. Pokrovka 32, ph. 227-1641
Intermed, ul. Durova 26, floor 4, kor. 1 & 6, ph. 971-2836 {acupuncture, contactless massage, remedial gymnastics}
Massage Russkaya Amerika, Luzhnetskaya nab. 10, ph. 201-1680

MEDICAL CARE

See also Drug Stores, Dentists
The health care alternatives have dramatically improved over the last few years and several options now exist where none were present previously.

Adventist Health Center, 60-Letiya Oktyabrya prosp. 21a, ph. 126-7906 {physiotherapy, M-Th 9-17:30, F 9-13}

Aesop Center, PO Box 27, ph. 141-8315 {information center}

⇒**American Medical Center**, Shmitovskiy proyezd 3, ph. 256-8212

Athens Medical Center, Michurinskiy prosp. 6, ph. 143-2387

Avicenna JV, 2nd Romyatnicheskiy p. 11/16, ph. 229-5593

Barocenter (Center of Social Reabilitation), ul. Bolshaya Kosinskaya 139, ph. 700-0445 {daily 9-16, cc}

Biocard Health Center JV (Belgium), 3rd Cherepkovskiy ul. 15a, ph. 149-0533

Botkin Clinic, 2nd Botkinskiy proyezd 5, k. 5, ph. 945-0033

Delta Consulting Medical, Berezhkovskaya nab. 12, pod. 15, ph. 245-9999

Diplomatic Polyclinic, 4th Dobryninskiy p. 4, ph. 237-8338

Euromedical Emergency Service, ph. 432-1616

Europ Assistance, Berezhkovskaya nab. 12, pod. 15, ph. 240-9999

European Medical Center, Gruzinskiy p. 3, ph. 253-0703 {M-F 9:30-18:30}

Intermed, ul. Durova 26, floor 4, kor. 1 & 6, ph. 971-2836 {acupuncture, contactless massage, remedial gymnastics}

Intermedservice JV (Switzerland), Hotel Intourist, rooms 2030-2031, ph. 203-8631

MediClub, Profsoyuznaya ul. 65, Ste. 380, ph. 956-5081 {24 hour availability for members}

Medservice, Trifonovskaya ul. 61, kv. 65, ph. 288-5875

Mikrokhirurgiya Glaza, Beskudnikovskiy bul. 59a, ph. 484-8120

Moscow Medical Center, ul. Mosfilmovskaya 31a, ph. 432-1616

Moscow Medical International Centre JV (FRG), ul. Vorontsovo pole 14, ph. 297-1848

Recovery Treatment Center (AA), ul. D. Ulyanova 37/3, ph. 129-4366

Sana Medical Center JV (France), ul. Nizhnyaya Pervomayskaya 65, ph. 464-1254 {Tu-Su}

Tourist's Clinic, Gruzinskiy proyezd 2, ph. 254-4396

For an **Ambulance, dial 03**

To trace persons known to be in a hospital, call 928-9572; 208-9157
Information on hospitals: 208-7584

MONEY CHANGING

See Banks, Domestic
See American Express, Cash Advances
More liberal Russian hard-currency regulations, combined with mass-printing of large denomination bills has eased many of the former difficulties of changing money.

Money exchange points have popped up on practically every street corner, and almost every bank has an Обмен валюты–'Obmen valyuty' (Bureau de change). Bank rates are usually pegged to the MICE (Moscow Interbank Currency Exchange) rate, which is based on twice-weekly currency auctions. In theory, a commercial bank's buy and sell rates are not to differ by more than 10%, but this is rarely adhered to. There is also a change bureau in the Central Telegraph office (ul. Tverskaya 7).

MOVIES

See also Video Rental
The theaters listed frequently run quality films, many of them in English or with sub-titles. There are also billboards with theater listings at strategic points throughout the city. You can also call theaters directly to find out their programs – you will find the address and phone of most theaters in the Telephone Directory

Illuzion Cinema, Kotelnicheskaya nab. 1/15, ph. 227-4339 {occasional foreign films

French Embassy, {French films, Monday & Wednesday at 7 pm, call 236-0003 or 236-1223 to find out how to attend}

Mir Cinema, tsvetnoy bul. 11, ph. 200-1695
Tsentralny Detskiy Kinoteatr, ul. Bakhrushina 25, ph. 233-4206 {foreign films in foreign languages once per month}

MOVING

A & A Relocations, Krapivinskiy p. 3, bldg. 2, ph. 299-2960

All Express Services (AES), Shmitovskiy pr. 33, ph. 256-4502

Allied Pickfords, ul. B. Dorogomilovskaya 16, #12, ph. 243-7609

Dragun GmbH, Rublyovskoye sh. 36, k. 2, kv. 212, ph. 415-4296

Heinrich Klingenberg International Moving, pr. Vernadskovo 103, k. 1, kv. 49, ph. 434-2414

Huolintakeskus OY, Staraya Basmanaya 18, office 37-38, ph. 261-9440

Interdean AG, Rublyovskoye sh. 36, k. 2, kv. 212, ph. 415-4296

John Nurminen Oy, ul. B. Ochakovskaya 15a, ph. 430-7861

Klingenberg, prosp. Vernadskovo 103, kor 1, kv. 48, ph. 434-2414

Logimix, Leningradskiy prosp. 37, k. 5, ph. 155-5880

S.C. Inc. Freight Forwarders, ph. 229-1379

Worldwide Relocation Service, Novoyasenevskiy prosp. 5, kor. 8, ph. 425-8084

MUSEUMS

See the Telephone Directory under the museum you wish to visit for address and telephone number. For guided tours of selected museums, call Intourist Moscow at 928-4515 or 927-1372.

All-Russia Decorative and Folk Art Museum, ul. Delegatskaya 3, ph. 921-0139 {closed Fri.}

Andrei Rublyov Museum (Museum of Early Russian Art), Adronyevskaya pl. 10 (Andronnikov Monastery), ph. 278-1489 {closed Wed.}

Architecture Museum (Shchusev Museum), Don Monastery, Donskaya pl. 1, ph. 232-0221; ul. Vozdvizhenka 5, ph. 291-2109

Armed Forces Museum, ul. Sovetskoy Armii 2, ph. 281-1880

Armoury Palace, Kremlin, ph. 221-4720

Aviation and Space Travel Museum (Frunze Central Museum), Krasnoarmeyskaya ul. 4

Bakhrushin Theater Museum, ul. Bakhrushina 31/12, ph. 235-3820

Biology Museum (Timiryazev Museum of Biology), M. Gruzinskaya ul. 15, ph. 252-0749

Borodino Panorama, Kutuzovskiy prosp. 38, ph. 148-1967

Central Exhibition Hall (Manezh), Manezhnaya pl. 1, ph. 202-9304

Central Lenin Museum, pl. Revolyutsii 2, ph. 295-4808 {Tue-Sun 10:30-18}

Central Revolution Museum, ul. Tverskaya 21, ph. 299-5217 {closed Mon.}

Chekhov Museum, ul. Sadovaya-Kudrinskaya 6, ph. 291-6154 {closed Mon.}

Church of the Trinity in Nikitniki, Nikitnikov p. 3, ph. 298-5018

Darwin Museum, M. Pirogovskaya ul. 1, ph. 246-6470

Dostoyevskiy House Museum, ul. Dostoyevskovo 2, ph. 281-1085

Durov Corner, ul. Durova 4, ph. 281-2914

Exhibition Hall of Moscow Artists' Trade Union, ul. M. Gruzinskaya 28, ph. 253-7355

Exhibition Hall of the Academy of Arts, ul. Prechistenka 21, ph. 201-3704

Exhibition Hall of the Union of Artists, ul. Tverskaya 25/9, ph. 299-2289; ul. Vavilova 65, ph. 125-6809; ul. 1st Tverskaya-Yamskaya 46b, ph. 250-1412; ul. Kuznetskiy Most 20, ph. 928-1844

Gorkiy House Museum, Nikitskaya M. ul. 6/2, ph. 290-0535 {closed Mon., Tues.}

Gorkiy Museum of Literature, Povarskaya ul. 25a, ph. 290-5130

Historical Museum, Krasnaya pl. 1/2, ph. 928-8452

History of Moscow Museum, Novaya pl. 12, ph. 924-8490 {closed Mon.}

Horse-breeding Museum, Timiryazevskaya ul. 44, ph. 216-1003

Intergorizont, Stoleshnikov p. 11, ph. 928-4515

Kolomenskoye Museum, prosp. Andropova 39, ph. 115-2713 {closed Mon., Tues.}

Korolyov House Museum, 6th Ostankinskiy p. 2/28, ph. 283-8197

Krasnaya Presnya Museum, Bolshevitskaya ul. 4, ph. 252-3035

Kuskovo (Ceramics Museum), ul. Yunosti 2, ph. 370-0160

Kutuzov Hut, Kutuzovskiy prosp. 38, ph. 148-1967

Lenin Funeral Train, Paveletskaya pl. 1, ph. 235-2898

Lenin Museum in Gorkiy (Gorkiy Leninskiye), ph. 136-2334

Literary Museum, ul. Petrovka 28, ph. 221-3857

Lunacharskiy House Museum, Denezhny p. 9/5, ph. 241-0877

Mayakovskiy House Museum, Lubyanskiy pr. 3/6, ph. 921-6607 {closed Wed.}

Memorial Cosmonaut Museum, Alleya Kosmonavtov (VVTs), ph. 283-1837

Mineralogy Museum (Fersman Museum of Mineralogy), Leninskiy prosp. 18, k. 2, ph. 232-0067

Moscow Artists' House Hall, Kuznetskiy Most 11, ph. 925-4264

Moscow Theater of the Arts Museum, Kamergerskiy p. 3a, ph. 229-0080

Museum of Applied Folk Art, Delegatskaya ul. 5, ph. 221-0139

Museum of Folk Art, Leontyevskiy p. 7, ph. 291-8718

Museum of Oriental Art, Nikitskiy bul. 12a, ph. 291-9614

Museum of the Defense of Moscow, Michurinskiy prosp. 3, ph. 437-3616

Museum of the Ministry of the Interior, Seleznevskaya ul. 11, ph. 258-0659

Music Museum (Glinka Museum of Music Culture), ul. Fadeyeva 4, ph. 972-3237

Nemirovich-Danchenko House Museum, Glinishchevskiy p. 5/7, ph. 209-5391

Oriental Art Museum, Nikitskiy bul. 12a, ph. 202-4555

Ostankino Museum (Museum of Serf Art), 1st Ostankinskaya ul. 5, ph. 283-4575

Ostrovskiy Museum (N.A. Ostrovskiy), ul. Tverskaya 14, ph. 209-1222

Palace of the 16-17th Centuries in Zaryadye, ul. Varvarka 10, ph. 298-3235

Paleontology Museum, Leninskiy prosp. 16, ph. 234-2985

Planetarium, ul. Sadovaya-Kudrinskaya 5, ph. 254-1838

Polytechnical Museum, Novaya pl. 3/4, ph. 923-0756 {closed Mon.}

Pushkin Museum, ul. Prechistenka 12/2, ph. 202-3293

Pushkin Museum of Fine Art, Volkhonka ul. 12, ph. 203-7998 {closed Mon.}

Rerikh Museum, ul. Marksa-Engelsa 5, ph. 203-6419 {open Wed & Sat 11-18}

Scriabin Museum, Nikopeskovskiy B. p. 11, ph. 241-0303

Shalyapin House Museum, Novinskiy Bul. 25, ph. 444-0306 {closed Mon.}

Soil Science and Agronomy Museum, Timiryazevskaya ul. 55, ph. 216-1619

St. Basil's Cathedral, Red Square, ph. 928-3304

Stanislavskiy House Museum, Leontyevskiy p. 6, ph. 229-2855

Sytin Museum, Tverskaya 12, kv. 274, ph. 229-0755

Tolstoy House, ul. Lva Tolstovo 21, ph. 246-6112

Tolstoy Museum, ul. Prechistenka 11, ph. 202-2190

Tretyakov Gallery (New), Krymskiy val 10, ph. 230-1116 {closed Mon.}

Tretyakov Gallery (Old), Lavrushinskiy p. 10, ph. 230-1116 {closed Mon.}

Tropinin Museum, Shchetininskiy p. 10, ph. 231-1799

Underground Press Museum, Lesnaya ul. 55, ph. 251-2593

Vasnetsov House (A.M. Vasnetsov) Museum, Vasnetsova p. 13, ph. 208-9045 {closed Thurs.}

Vernadskiy Museum, ul. A.N. Kosygina 47a, ph. 137-0011

Yermolova Museum, Tverskoy bul. 11, ph. 290-4901

Zhukovskiy Museum, ul. Radio 17, ph. 267-5054

Zoo, B. Gruzinskaya ul. 1, ph. 255-5375

Zoology Museum, Nikitskaya B. ul. 6, ph. 203-8923

MUSIC STORES

See Books, Electronics
You can purchase records and good quality CDs (made in Moscow on German and Dutch equipment) at the stores below. You can also

buy them at many stores selling Western non-food items. Beware those being sold in street kiosks, as they are often of substandard quality.

DL Lota, ul. Solyanka 9 str.1, ph. 924-5010 {daily 10-20:30, cc}

Melodia, Novy Arbat 22, ph. 291-1421

Noty, ul. Neglinnaya 14, ph. 248-0153 {Tu-Sa 10-19, break 14-15, cc}

Slami,Sadovaya-Triumfalnaya 14/12,ph. 209-2195 {M-Sa 10-19, cc}

Yamaha Pianos, Petrovskiy Passazh, 2nd fl., ph. {M-Sa 9-20, cc}

NEWS

See also Cable Television

Most joint-venture hotels are equipped with cable television with CNN to help you keep up with the world. The CBS Evening News in English is also shown every morning on the Super Channel 2x2 (Channel 3) at 7:30. 2x2 (Channel 3) also has regular broadcasts of BBC and ITN newscasts, dubbed into Russian.

A "decimetrovy" antenna bought at an electrical supply store should allow you to receive CNN in your apartment. Your television must have UHF reception and CNN is at 20-25 on the dial.

NEWSPAPERS/MAGAZINES

There are a number of publications available in English which you can obtain in Moscow and/or subscribe to there. Most important Russian language periodical publications are listed under their title in the White Pages phone directory.

Commersant {weekly English language version of the most popular business daily in Russia}

Delovie Lyudi, ph. 333-3340 {monthly magazine, printed in Russian and English}

Financial and Business News, ul. Bozhenko 14/4, ph. 945-5375

Interfax, 1st Tverskaya-Yamskaya 2, ph. 250-9840

LA Times NewsFax, a same-day digest of the *LA Times*, can be purchased at Alpha-Graphics, ul. 1st Tverskaya-Yamskaya 22.

Literary Gazette, Kostyanskiy p. 13, ph. 208-8594

Moscow Guardian, ul. Vrubelya 4, ph. 943-9738 {English language weekly}

Moscow News, ul. Tverskaya 16/2, ph. 200-2010

Moscow Times, ul. Pravdy, ent. 2, ph. 257-3201 {English language daily for foreign community; 5 times/wk, free at drop points in Moscow; subscription delivery available}

Moscow Tribune, Leninskiy prosp. 45/426-429, ph. 135-1114 {ditto previous note, but twice weekly, free around the city}

Postfactum, Khoroshevskoye sh. 41, ph. 195-1820.

⇨**Russian Travel Monthly**, B. Kondratyevskiy p., 4, ph. 254-9275 {published in the US by publishers of this guide, available worldwide by airmail}

Sovaminco JV, Nikitskaya B. ul. 11/4 str. 2, ph. 229-3307{delivery of Western periodicals, such as *Economist, IHT, Le Monde* and *USA Today.*

NON-PROFITS

There are numerous charitable, non profit and non-governmental organizations now operating in Moscow and providing various types of aid or technical assistance. Some of the major ones are listed below. See the White Pages for other listings.

Aesop Center, PO Box 27, ph. 141-8315 {information center}

Amnesty International, ph. 291-2904

CARE Deutschland, ul. Petrovka 22, ph. 227-1312

CARE USA, prosp. Vernadskovo 41, #801, ph. 431-2660

Citizen Democracy Corps, ul. Spiridonovka 22/2, kv. 36, ph. 290-6948

Committee on UNESCO Affairs, ul. Vozdvizhenka 9, ph. 290-0853

Cultural Initiative Foundation, B. Kozlov per., ph. 928-4632

Doctors Without Borders, Dokuchayev p. 10, kv. 841-843, ph. 207-4593

Gaia International Women's Center, Khlebny p. 2/3, ph. 135-3207

German Red Cross, ph. 126-0021
Greenpeace, ul. Dolgorukovskaya 21, ph. 258-3950
International Center for Children's Health, ph. 236-2594
International Committee of the Red Cross, Smolenskaya nab. 5/13, kv.125, ph. 241-5160
International Science Foundation (Soros), ph. 939-1092
IREX - International Research and Exchange Board, Khlebny p. 8, 4th fl., ph. 290-6233
Jamestown Foundation, ph. 208-9512
MacArthur Foundation, ph. 290-5088
Moscow House of Charity, ph. 925-3042
Moscow Kennan Project, Vspolny p. 16, kv. 38, ph. 299-6875
MSF (Belgium), ph. 207-4618
Open World Association, ul. Petrovka 19, bldg. 6, #3, ph. 923-9504
Peace Fund, ul. Prechistenka 10, ph. 202-4347
Project HOPE, Smidskiy proyezd 29, Detskaya Bolnitsa #9, ph. 259-7990
Red Cross and Red Crescent, Cheremushinskiy pr. 5, 2nd fl., ph. 230-6620
Russian Commission for Humanitarian Assistance, ul. Vozdvizhenka 18, ph. 290-0903
Salvation Army, Slavyanskaya pl. 4, str. 1, ph. 213-8392
UN Information Center, Glazovskiy p. 4/16, ph. 241-2894
UNESCO Assistance (Moscow Club), ul. Miklukho-Maklaya 22, ph. 330-6546
United Way International, ul. Yaroslavskaya 8, k. 3, ph. 243-9726
VOCA, Boyarskiy p. 3, ph. 207-2000
World University Service, prosp. Vernadskovo 41, ph. 432-5782
World Vision, prosp. Vernadskovo 41a, room 812, ph. 432-2604

O

OFFICE SPACE

See also Real Estate

⇨ Aengevelt Immobilien KG, ul. Burdenko 14a, ph. 248-1855
⇨ American Trade Center, Radisson-Slavyanskaya Hotel, ph. 941-8815
⇨ Americom Business Center, Radisson-Slavyanskaya Hotel, ph. 941-8427
Barrington Development, Nikoloyamskaya ul. 13, ph. 297-3454
C.C.I. Capital Contracts International Ltd., ul. Spartakovskaya 6A, ph. 267-3783
Ferguson Hollis, ul. Shchepkina 6, ph. 288-9801
First Russian Real Estate Corp., Shyolkovskoye sh. 2, ph. 165-5511
Jacob Hohermuth AG, B. Starodanilovskiy p. 5, Danilovskiy Complex, #33, ph. 954-0624 {Landrovers, Masaratti}
Jones Development Group, ul. Tverskaya 6, #97, ph. 229-7201
McDonald's Office Center, Nikopeskovskiy B. p. 15, str. 2, ph. 241-4146
Moscow Enterprises Inc., ph. 291-3944
Mosenka JV, Tsvetnoy bul. 25/3, ph. 291-3952
Negrelli, Nikoloyamskaya ul. 15, ph. 111-5407
Oster and Company, Box 152, ph. 956-3300
Park Place Moscow, Leninskiy prosp. 113/1, ph. 956-5050
Rodina, ph. 299-2096
Russian Real Estate, ph. 244-2565
Taroco Enterprises, Inc., prosp. Mira POB 29, Moscow office VVC, ph. 974-6023
Technopark Business Center, VVTs, prosp. Mira 120, ph. 188-7776

OFFICE SUPPLIES

See also Furniture, Copiers, Telecom

3M (Minnesota Mining & Manufacturing), Samarskiy p. 3, ph. 288-9701
Anson Trade Ltd., Staraya Basmanaya 18/1, ph. 267-4130

Apiko Ltd., ul. Sretenka 36, ph. 975-4342

Colve Austria, ul. Delegatskaya 16/1, ent. 0, ph. 281-8447

Colve Austria, Leninskiy prosp. 49, ph. 135-8210

Complete Ltd., Krzhizhanovskovo ul. 24/35, kor. 4, ph. 125-7041

Complex Systems Co., Ltd., ul. Kerchenskaya 1, kor. 3, ph. 121-3102

Dona, 2nd Tverskaya-Yamskaya 54, ph. 251-0245 {M-F 10-19, Sa 10-18, break 14-15, cc}

Druzhba Trading House, Voznesenskiy p. 1, ph. 229-6603 {M-Sa 10-20, cc}

ERLAN, ul. Ozernaya 46, ph. 437-3701

Euronetics, ul. Dubininskaya 65, ph. 235-2251 {wholesale}

Excimer, Leninskiy prosp. 76, ph. 939-0692

Fairn & Swanson, Ltd., Olympiyskiy prosp. 18, ph. 288-1512

Fias, Leninskiy prosp. 72/12A, ph. 131-9968

Global USA, ul. Usacheva 35, ph. 245-5657 {M-Su 10-20, cc}

Informpravo JV, Neglinnaya ul. 29/14, bldg. 3, ph. 200-2775 {paper}

Interartbazaar JV (British/Russian), Serpukhovskiy val 24, kor. 2, ph. 952-3008

Inzhener Ltd., prosp. Mira 20, kor. 2, ph. 288-7177

Khrustal, ul. Tverskaya 15

Moscow Messengers, ul. B. Polyanka 28/295, ph. 238-5308 {they deliver}

Office Club, ul. Ogrucheva 34/63, ph. 336-0550 {M-Sa 9-21, Su 9-18}

Office Equipment, Petrovskiy Passazh (see Passazh), {M-Sa 9-20}

Olivetti Synthesis, ph. 197-5283 {cc}

Olmi Center, Olympiyskiy prosp. 18, ent. 5, ph. 288-2488

Parker, Petrovskiy Passazh, 2nd fl. (see Passazh), {M-Sa 9-20, cc}

Planshop, Krasnopresnenskaya nab. 12, ph. 253-2773

Statfall, TsUM, 3rd fl., ph. 954-0493 {M-Sa 8-20, cc}

⇨ Stockmann Fashion and Business Store, Leninskiy prosp. 73/8, ph. 134-0386 {daily 10-20}

Supply Side, ph. 238-5308

Technotex USA Inc., Park Place, Leninskiy prosp. 113/1, #E307, ph. 956-5124

OPTICAL

See also Drug Stores

For contact lens solutions or items related to eye care, try:

Mikrokhirurgiya Glaza, Beskudnikovskiy bul. 59a, ph. 484-8120

Optic Moscow, ul. Arbat 30, bldg 2, ph. 241-1577 {open 10-19}

Optika, Kuznetskiy most 4, ph. 292-0573 {open 9-19}

Optika Moscow Center JV (Finland), Frunzenskaya nab. 54, ph. 242-3650

Sana Medical Center JV (France), ul. Nizhnyaya Pervomayskaya 65, ph. 464-1254 {Tu-Su}

Task Optic, Goncharnaya ul. 12, ph. 921-0518 {binoculars and lenses}

P

PAGING SYSTEMS

AFCO-Pager, prosp. Mira 51, ph. 290-2704

AMT JV (Finland), Khoroshevskoye sh. 42a, ph. 941-3092

Moscom Paging, ph. 199-0300 {Motorola}

Moscow Cellular Communications, Vorontsovskaya ul. 18/20, ph. 271-3749

Radio Communications International Corp. (RCI), VVTs, Transport Pavilion, prosp. Mira, ph. 181-6552

Vessolink Paging Systems, Skakovaya ul. 32, ph. 945-2843

PARKS

See also Leisure

If you're going to be staying in Moscow over a weekend, a park in Moscow is a nice place to spend a Sunday afternoon. Best among these are Izmailovskiy park, Sokolniki park, the Academy of Sciences Botanical Gardens, and, of course, Gorkiy Park. Kolomenskoe and Novodevichy are must see's. Also recommended is the view from Sparrow (formerly Lenin) Hills at the University. Most parks are open 10-22.

Botanical Gardens, Botanicheskaya 4, metro VDNKh

Gorkiy Park, Krimskiy val 9, metro Park Kultury

Izmailovskiy Park, Narodny prosp. 17, metro Izmailovskiy Park

Kolomenskoye, Proletarskiy pr., ph. 115-2309

Novodevichy Convent, Novodevichy prosp. 1, ph. 245-3268

Sokolniki Park, Sokolnicheskiy val, metro Sokolniki

PASSPORT PHOTOS

See also Photo

If you are not in a rush, most Photografia salons in the city offer one day service for passport photos, but black and white only. For instant color photos, try:

AlphaGraphics, ul. 1st Tverskaya-Yamskaya 22, ph. 251-1215

PERSONNEL

Ancor Agency, ph. 261-9262

Ernst & Young, Podsosenskiy p. 20/12, ph. 297-3121

Eurospan Human Resources, ul. Baumanskaya 43/1, 5th fl., suite 106, ph. 261-5228

Hill International, Sovintsentr, Mezhdunarodnaya Hotel I, #1329, ph. 253-1329

Interdialekt, Glazovskiy p. 1, 2nd flr., ph. 241-6307

International Business Service (IBS), 1st Tverskoy-Yamskoy p. 18/3, #326, ph. 956-1525

Olex Agency, Pokrovskiy bul. 14/5, ph. 137-6469

Personnel Agency International, Shchipovskiy p. 1. 20, ph. 237-3643

Preng & Associates, ul. Lyusinovskaya 72, kv. 50, ph. 952-7421

Professional Recruiting Group, ul. Petrovka 24, ph. 200-7521

⇨**Service Globus (US)**, B. Kommunisticheskaya 1/5, ph. 298-6146

Slava Ltd., ul. Usacheva 62, ph. 245-5128

Triza Agency, Sokolnicheskaya Pl. 7, ph. 268-8701

PHOTO

There are lots of options for photo developing in Moscow. Kodak equipment and paper are widely used, and you can even have photos developed in one or two hours. Listed below are the more central locations:

Fuji Centers, Mezhdunarodnaya Hotel I, Krasnopresnenskaya nab. 12, ph. 253-2914 {M-F 9-18}; Stoleshnikov p. 5/20, ph. 229-0100 {M-F 10-19, Sa 10-17, break 14-15, cc}; Novy Arbat 25, ph. 203-7307 {M-Sa 10-21}

Kodak Express, Detskiy Mir, 4th floor {daily 8:30-20}; Leningradskiy prosp. 74, ph. 151-0826 {M-Sa 10-19}; ul. Tverskaya 25, ph. 299-5483 {daily 10-19}; Hotel Mezhdunarodnaya, ph. 253-1643

Kodak Film Shops, Komsomolskiy prosp. 25, ph. 245-1594; Petrovskiy Passage, ul. Petrovka 4, ph. 928-5468 {M-F 9-20, one hour photo}; Americom Business Center, ph. 941-8941 {one hour photo}

Lokus, TsUM, ph. 941-3523 {M-Sa 8-20}

Office Club, ul. Obrucheva 34/63, ph. 336-0550 {M-Sa 9-21, Su 9-18}

Polaroid Shop, Leninskiy prosp. 70/11, ph. 930-9627

Polaroid Studio Express {throughout the city: see the listings under this heading in the White Pages}

PIZZA

Patio Pizza, Volkhonka ul. 13A, ph. 201-5000 {daily 12-24, cc}

Pizza Hut Restaurant, Kutuzovskiy prosp. 17, ph. 243-1727 {daily 11-22, cc}; ul. Tverskaya 12, ph. 229-2013 {daily 11-23, cc}

Pizza Hut Take-out, Kutuzovskiy prosp. 17, ph. 243-1727 {cc}

Pizza JV (Canada), ul. Marksistskaya 1/1, ph. 272-3828

Pizza Pazza, Sadko Arcade (Expocenter), ph. 940-4071

РАДИО 7 RADIO
73.4 FM 104.7 FM

ENGLISH PROGRAMMING IN THE MORNING

6 A.M. - 10 A.M.
- 104.7 -

Moscow's First Dual FM Radio Station
English News on the half hour
24 hours a day.

Анжлийские новости в середине каждого
часа кружлосуточно.
Русские новости в начале каждого часа.

*The Best Buy in Moscow for your
Advertising Dollars.*

*Featuring Adult Contemporary
and Oldies Rock*

TEL.: (095) 946-6864 FAX 946-6456

POLICE   DIAL 02

See also Legal Advice

Most hotels have a militia department attached or assigned to them. The need to call upon the police is becoming more and more frequent among both full-time residents and visitors. Be sure you know your rights as a foreign resident or visitor to Russia (see our Russia Survival Guide).

POSTAL

The Russian mail system is legendary for its ineffectiveness. More frequently than not, letters and packages simply do not reach you or your friends at home. There are reliable mail and courier services (see Courier), that have weekly international deliveries.

To post a letter or package, or to get current postal rates (which are being hiked monthly), go to or call:

Central Post Office, ul. Myasnitskaya 26/2, ph. 928-6311

Central Telegraph, ul. Tverskaya 7, ph. 924-9004

International Post Office, Varshavskoye sh. 37, ph. 114-4584

⇨**PX Post**, ul. Kuusinena 9-26, ph. 956-2230 {Express international mail to/from Russia}

PRINTING

See also Copying

AlphaGraphics, ul. 1 Tverskaya-Yamskaya 22, ph. 251-1215

Anson Trade Ltd., Staraya Basmanaya 18/1, ph. 267-4130

Domino Print Shop, B. Vatin p. 4, ph. 227-3125

GlavUPDK Printing, Kursovoy p. 1/1, ph. 203-2294

Grafica M, ul. B. Kommunisticheskaya 23, ph. 272-0069

Informpravo JV, Neglinnaya ul. 29/14, bldg. 3, ph. 200-2775 {paper}

NPO Polygrafmash-YAM International Trading Ltd., ul. Profsoyuznaya 57, rm. 601, ph. 332-6420

Offset Print Moscow, Krasnogvardeyskiy 1. pr., pavilion #2, ph. 259-7367

Offset Printshop, Nagornaya ul. 20, k. 7, ph. 123-4477

Painoanson Printing Services, Staraya Basmannaya 18/1, #17, ph. 267-4130

Poligran, Pakgauznoye sh. 1, ph. 153-1021

Premier SV-Print, Yeropkinskiy p. 16, ph. 201-3926

Print Shop, Petrovskiy Passazh, 1st fl. (see Passazh), {M-Sa 9-20, cc}

Sovaminco Quick Printing, Aviamotornaya 2, korp. 18, ph. 362-9081

Trinity Graphics, ul. Serpukhovskaya 72, kv. 2, ph. 952-6484

R

RACING (HORSE RACING)

Hippodome, ul. Begovaya 22. Races are held Sunday at 13:00 and Wednesdays and Saturdays at 18:00.

RADIO

A number of frequencies have been opened up by the authorities for commercial use. There are now a number of good radio stations that broadcast in English and Russian.

Delovaya Volna (Business Wave) Radio Company, ph. 217-9162

Open Radio, Pyatnitskaya ul. 25, ph. 233-7640 {pop, rock, BBC, VOA, 102.3 FM, 918 KHz}

Prestige Radio, Radisson-Slavyanskaya Hotel, #6034-5, ph. 941-8811 {jazz Mon-Fri 23 hrs, break 4-5, Sat-Sun 24 hrs., 104.7 FM}

⇨**Radio 7**, ul. D' Bednovo 24, ph. 946-6864 {English news on half hour, 73.4 & 104.7 FM}

Radio Evropa Plus, ul. Akad. Koroleva 19, ph. 215-9938 {pop, dance, news on the half-hour, weather, traffic, 69.9 FM, 1116 AM}

Radio Maximum, ph. 200-1088 {rock, pop, Moscow in the Morning (English) 7-10, Top 40 sound 103.7 FM}

Radio Rocks, ph. 116-4374 {rock, 103FM}

SNC Radio Station (Stas Namin Center), Krymskiy val 9, ph. 191-1026

MOSCOW'S *ONLY* CHOICE FOR INTERNATIONAL MAIL

REAL ESTATE

⇨ **Aengevelt Immobilien KG**, ul. Burdenko 14a, ph. 248-1855

Aikon JV (UK), Uglovoy p. 27, ph. 972-3135

BANSO Real Estate Agency, ul. Novozavodskaya 21, ph. 148-0806

Barrington Development, Nikolo-yamskaya ul. 13, ph. 297-3454

Brok Invest Service, Nikitskaya B. ul. 60/3, ph. 291-4017

Catherine Mamet Real Estate Agency, Tverskoy bul. 25, ph. 291-1941

Clivedon Property Services, Smolenskiy bul. 22/17,#2, ph. 134-0862; 1st Tverskaya-Yamskaya 13, #79, ph. 250-0152

Dovesgate International/Russian Express, 2nd Obydenskiy p. 14, ph. 202-5732

Esa Seppanen Consulting Ltd., Dmitrovka B. ul. 21/7, #6, ph. 200-3388

First Russian Real Estate Corp., Shyolkovskoye sh. 2, ph. 165-5511

Global Properties, Tryokhprudny p. 11/13, 5th fl., #61, ph. 299-3759

Hines Interests, Park Place, Leninskiy prosp. 113/1, #E100, ph. 956-5051

Home Sweet Home, Kutuzovskiy prosp. 14, #155, ph. 255-4659

House Service Ltd., Nikopeskovskiy B. p. 7, ph. 241-7402

InterOccidental, Izmailovskoye sh. 44, ph. 367-9645

J.A.T. Ltd., Sushchyovskiy val 5, ph. 973-0757

Jones Development Group, ul. Tverskaya 6, #97, ph. 229-7201

Menatep Real Estate, pl. Suvorova 1, pod. 3, ph. 971-7958

Mosc-American Real Estate, Nizhegorodskaya ul. 3/23, ph. 278-4947

Moscow Country Club, Krasnogorskiy District, Makhabino, ph. 561-2977

Moscow Finance Group, ul. Kedrova 15, ph. 129-6700

Negrelli, Nikoloyamskaya ul. 15, ph. 111-5407

Oster and Company, Box 152, ph. 956-3300

Park Place Moscow, Leninskiy prosp. 113/1, ph. 956-5050

Quest Realty, Smolenskaya nab. 5/13, Suite 157, ph. 244-0527

Samuel M. Spiro & Associates, ph. 272-4101

Tierney & Associates, Kuznetskiy Most 19, ph. 928-5793

Tumanskiy Real Estate Co., Staropanskiy p. 4, ph. 921-8412

Yagil International Corp., Serebryani-cheskiy p. 2/5, ph. 227-1905

RECREATION, CHILDREN

Cat Theater, Kutuzovskiy prosp. 25, ph. 249-2907

Children's Music Theater, prosp. Vernadskovo 5, ph. 930-7021

Kosmonaut Museum, prosp. Mira, Space Monument, {Tu-Su 10-19, closed last Friday of every month}

Moscow Puppet Theater, Spartakovskaya ul. 26, ph. 261-2197

Moscow Youth Theater, Sadovskiy p. 10, ph. 299-5360

RECREATION, SPORTS

See also Leisure, Tennis

Brezhnev's hunting dacha, ph. 203-4820

Chaika Sports Complex, Turchaninov p. 1/3, ph. 246-1344

Dinamo Sports Palace, ul. Lavochkina 32, ph. 453-6501

Dinamo Stadium Gym, Leningradskiy prosp. 36, ph. 212-7092

Druzhba, Luzhnetskaya nab. 10, ph. 201-1655

Hash House Harriers, ph. 280-5493

Krylatskoye Olympic Sports Center, Krylatskaya ul. 10, ph. 140-7369

Lenin Stadium, Luzhniki, ph. 246-5515

Moscow International Peace Marathon JV (US), Milyutinskiy p. 18, ph. 924-0824

Olympic Sports Complex, Olympiyskiy prosp. 16, ph. 288-3777

Sokolniki Sports Palace, Sokolnicheskiy val 1b, ph. 268-6958

Sports Palace, Luzhniki, ph. 201-0955

Tais Sport JV, Luzhnetskaya nab. 10, ph. 201-1129

RELIGIOUS SERVICES

To get times of services call the numbers listed below:

Antiakhilskoye Podvorje, Arkhangelskiy p. 15a, ph. 923-4605

Baptist Services, M. Tryokhsvyatitelskiy p. 3, ph. 297-5167

Bulgarian Orthodox Services, Uspenskaya Church, Goncharnaya ul. 29, ph. 271-0124

Christian Scientist Church, ph. 928-7370

Church of Jesus Christ of Latter Day Saints, ph. 240-6332

Church of Saint George, ul. Varvarka 12, ph. 298-3872

French Church of St. Louis (Catholic), ul. M. Lubyanka 12, ph. 925-2034

German Evangelical Church Services, German Embassy Mosfilmovskaya ul. 56, ph. 238-1324

International Baptist Fellowship, Druzhinnikovskaya ul. 15, 5th fl., #6, ph. 150-3293

International Christian Assembly, Lenin Children's Library, Kaluzhskaya pl., ph. 138-8293

Jewish Services, Maria Roshcha Synagogue, 2nd Veshlavtzev per. 5a

Jewish Synagogue (choral), ul. Akhipova 10, ph. 923-9697

Jewish Youth Cultural Center Tkhiya, ul. B. Tulskaya 44, ph. 234-5297

Moscow Christian Center, October Theater, ul. Novy Arbat, ph. 344-9067

Moscow Patriarchate, Chistoprudny p. 5, ph. 201-3416

Moscow Protestant Chaplaincy, ul. Olaf Palme 5, kor. 2, ph. 143-3562

Old Believers, Rogozhskiy p. 29

Roman Catholic Services, Kutuzovskiy prosp. 7/4, k. 5, kv. 42, ph. 243-9621

Russian Orthodox, Yelokhovskiy Cathedral, ul. Spartakovskaya 15, ph. 261-6913

Russian Orthodox Patriarchate (Information Center), ul. Pogodinskaya 20, ph. 245-2013

Seventh Day Adventist Services, ph. 297-5167

Seventh Day Adventists, M. Tryokhsvyatitelskiy p. 3, ph. 297-0568

St. Andrew's Church, Voznesenskiy p. 9, ph. 143-3562

St. George's Church, ul. Varvarka 12, ph. 928-3872

World Mission Cultural Centre, ul. Krupskoy 12a, ph. 344-6759 {non-denominational, English}

RENOVATION (REMONT)

A & A Relocations, Krapivinskiy p. 3, bldg. 2, ph. 299-2960

All American Renovation, Tverskoy bul. 152, ph. 229-7097

Business Furniture International (BFI), ul. D. Ulyanova 4/1, ph. 135-2105

Clivedon Property Services, Smolenskiy bul. 22/17, #2, ph. 134-0862

Clivedon Property Services, 1st Tverskaya-Yamskaya 13, #79, ph. 250-0152

Danish Remont Trading, ul. Strominka 20, ph. 268-2889

Di Pace SRL, ul. Fedotovoy 6, kv. 5, ph. 241-1743

Dovesgate International/Russian Express, 2nd Obydenskiy p. 14, ph. 202-5732

Global Properties, Tryokhprudny p. 11/13, 5th fl., #61, ph. 299-3759

Home Sweet Home, Kutuzovskiy prosp. 14, #155, ph. 255-4659

Manyam & Associates, Inc., Parusny proyezd 32/9, ph. 193-1804

Moscow Enterprises Inc., ph. 291-3944

Phoenix Engineering, B. Kozikhinskiy p. 22, str. 1, fl. 5, ph. 299-4345

Renlund M, Stolyarny p. 3, ph. 253-4173

Russian Real Estate, ph. 244-2565

REPAIR SERVICES

A1 Trade International Systems Ltd., ul. Myasnitskaya 15/17, ph. 923-1353 {copy machines, office equipment}

Dorin Electronics, Khimkiy, Spartakovskaya 12, ph. 571-8108

Eureka JV, ul. Narodnovo Opolcheniya 38 k. 2, ph. 943-0893

GlavUPDK, ul. Prechistenka 20, ph. 201-2326; **Appliance Repair**, ph. 202-2865; **Home Service**, ph. 201-2706; **Office Equipt. Repair**, ph. 143-1502; **Phone Repair**, ph. 202-2706

Interstroy Service Division, ph. 972-0232
Siemens Service Hotline, ul. Dubininskaya
98, ph. 236-4644
Toshiba Service Center, Maloafanasyevskiy
p. 7, ph. 291-9210

RESTAURANTS

The Russian government's imposition of a "ruble-only" policy for cash settlements means that all meals in all restaurants may be paid for with rubles. In reality, many restaurants still post prices in dollars or deutschemarks. The client may then choose to pay in rubles, at a "house rate" of exchange, or with a credit card. Usually the latter is a better deal. Restaurants below which are known to accept credit cards are so indicated {cc}. Information in bold (i.e., F14(17) – section F14, page 17) is the map coordinates for the restaurant.

AMERICAN
Exchange, The, Radisson-Slavyanskaya Hotel, ph. 941-8333 **G16(21)**
Manhattan Express, Hotel Rossiya, ph. 298-5355 **J15(19)**
Steak House, Sadko Arcade (Expocenter), ph. 256-2206 {daily 11:30-23:30, cc} **E15(9)**
TrenMos Bistro, Ostozhenka ul. 1/9, ph. 202-5722 {daily 12-17, 19-23, cc} **I16(23)**
TrenMos Restaurant, Komsomolskiy prosp. 21, ph. 245-1216 {daily 12-17, 19-23, cc} **H18(22)**

ARABIAN
1001 Nights, Leninskiy prosp. 146, ph. 434-9739

ARMENIAN
Ayastan Restaurant, Flotskaya 3, summer on board 'Sviatoy Giorgiy', ph. 456-9503 **A4(4)**
Moosh cafe, ul. Oktyabrskaya 2/4, ph. 284-3670 {cc} **J11(7)**
Sayat-Nova cafe, ul. Yasnogorskaya 17, k. 1, ph. 426-9011 {cc}
Tsakhkadzor cafe, ul. Lesnaya 15, ph. 251-0257 {cc} **H12(6)**
Viktoria (Hard Rock Cafe) cafe, Zelyony Theater, Krymskiy val 9, ph. 237-0709 **K17(24)**

AZERI
Baku Restaurant, ul. Tverskaya 24, ph. 299-8506 {cc} **I13(19)**
Farkhad cafe, B. Marfinskaya 4, ph. 218-4136 {cc} **H6(6)**
Karabakh Restaurant, ul. Lipetskaya 52, ph. 329-7100 {cc}
Nargiz cafe, Lebedyanskaya 22, k. 4, ph. 329-7187

CAUCASIAN
Abkhaskiy Dvor Restaurant, Nakhimovskiy prosp. 35, ph. 124-9833 **F23(14)**
Araks cafe, Sirenevy bul. 11, korp. 2, ph. 164-3630
Bistro-Nedelya cafe, Oktyabrskaya ul. 18, ph. 288-9398 **J11(7)**
Dukhan Shavo Restaurant, Karamyshevskaya nab. 58, ph. 197-1975 {cc}
Golden Horseshoe Club, Leningradskiy prosp. 32, ph. 214-8070 **G11(6)**
Na Sretenke, Turgenevskaya pl. 2/4, ph. 928-7444 **K14(20)**

CHINESE
Chopsticks, Tumba Golf Course, ul. Dovzhenko 1, ph. 147-7368 {cc} **C18(9)**
Golden Dragon na Ordynke Restaurant, ul. B. Ordynka 59, ph. 231-9251 {daily 12-17, 18-5, cc} **J17(23)**
Golden Dragon Restaurant, ul. Plyushchikha 64, ph. 248-3602 {cc} **E15(9)**
Golden Lotus Restaurant, Expocenter, 1st Krasnogvardeyskiy proyezd 12, ph. 255-2510 {daily 12-14, 16-23, cc} **E15(9)**
Mei-hua Restaurant, ul. Rusakovskaya 2/1, str. 1, ph. 264-9574 {daily 12-23, cc} **M12(7)**
Orient, Nikoloshchepovskiy p. 1/9, ph. 241-1078 **H15(18)**
Panda Restaurant, Tverskoy bul. 3/5, ph. 298-6505 {daily 12-14, 16-23, cc} **I14(19)**
Peking Restaurant, Hotel Pekin, ul. B. Sadovaya 1/7, ph. 209-1815 {daily 12-16, 18-23, cc} **H13(18)**

DANISH
Glazur cafe, Smolenskiy bul. 12, ph. 248-4438 {daily 12-14, 16-2, cc} **H16(22)**

DELIS
Bistro, Leninskiy prosp. 37, {M-Sa 10-20} **H20(14)**

Kombi's Deli, ul. Tverskaya-Yamskaya 2, ph. 251-2578 H13(18)

Kombi's Deli, prosp. Mira 46/48, ph. 280-6402 {daily 11-22} K12(7)

EUROPEAN

Amadeus Cafe, Radisson-Slavyanskaya Hotel, ph. 941-8333 G16(21)

Ambassador, ul. Prechistenka 29, ph. 201-4014 {daily 12-24} H16(22)

Anchor Restaurant, Palace Hotel, ul. Tverskaya-Yamskaya 19, ph. 956-3152 {lunch 12-17, dinner 19-24} H13(18)

Anna Mons Restaurant, ul. Krasnokazarmennaya 3, ph. 261-8626 {cc} N14(11)

Annushka Tea Tram, ph. 236-8272

Arkadia Restaurant, Teatralny proyezd 3, str. 4, ph. 926-9545 {cc} J15(19)

Atrium Cafe, Leninskiy prosp. 44, ph. 137-3008 {daily 12-23, cc} F20(14)

Bely Lebed cafe, Sivtsev Vrazhek 3/18, ph. 203-1283 H15(18)

⇨ **Boyarskiy Zal Restaurant**, Hotel Metropol, 4th floor, Teatralny proyezd 1/4, ph. 927-6089 {cc} J14(19)

Brasserie Restaurant, Olympic Penta Hotel, Olympiyskiy prosp. 18/1, ph. 971-6101 {cc, reservations recommended} J11(7)

Budapest Restaurant, Hotel Budapest, Petrovskiy linii 2/18, ph. 924-4283 {daily 8-10, 12-23} J14(19)

Cafe Berlin, Hotel Baltschug, ph. 230-6500 {cc} J15(19)

Cafe Taiga, Aerostar Hotel, ph. 155-5030 {cc} E10(5)

Cafe Viru, ul. Ostozhenka 50, ph. 246-6107 I16(23)

Club na Taganka, ul. Verkhnyaya Radishchevskaya 19, ph. 272-7320 L16(24)

Continental Restaurant, Sovintsentr, Hotel Mezhdunarodnaya I, ph. 253-1934 {daily 12-16,18-22} F15(17)

DAB Beer Bar, Belgrade Hotel, ul. Smolenskaya 8, ph. 248-2684 {cc} G16(21)

Danilovskiy Monastery Restaurant, Danilovskiy val 22, ph. 954-0566 {cc} J20(15)

Dom na Tverskoy cafe, ul. Gotvalda 12, ph. 251-8419 H12(6)

Druzhba Restaurant, prosp. Vernadskovo 53, ph. 432-9939 {cc} F15(17)

Dubrava Restaurant, Hotel Kosmos, ph. 217-0495 L7(7)

Dyen i Noch Restaurant, Kolomenskiy proyezd 12, ph. 112-5092 {cc, dinner cabaret} K25(15)

⇨ **Evropeyskiy Restaurant**, Hotel Metropol, Teatralny proyezd 1/4, ph. 927-6039 {daily 11:30-23:30 cc} J14(19)

Galaxy Restaurant and Pub, Selskokhozyaystvennaya pr. 2, ph. 181-2169 L6(7)

Golden Ostap Restaurant, Shmitovskiy proyezd 3, ph. 259-4795 {cc} F14(17)

In Vino Restaurant, Ukraine Hotel, 3rd floor, ph. 243-2316 {cc} F15(17)

Karina Restaurant, Solyanskiy proyezd 1/3, ph. 924-0369 K15(20)

Kropotkinskaya 36 cafe, ul. Prechistenka 36, ph. 201-7500 {daily 12-17, 18-23, cc} H16(22)

Lomonosov Restaurant, Palace Hotel, ul. Tverskaya-Yamskaya 19, ph. 256-3152 {daily 7-10:30, 12-15, 19-23} H13(18)

Luchnik, ul. Maroseyka 6/8, ph. 928-0056 K14(20)

Margarita cafe, M. Bronnaya 28, ph. 299-6534 {cc} H14(18)

Merkator, Moscow Commercial Club, B. Kommunisticheskaya 2A, ph. 274-0081 L16(24)

Moskovskiye Zori cafe, M. Kozikhinskiy p. 11, ph. 299-5725 {cc} H14(18)

Moskva Restaurant, Okhotny ryad 7 (Hotel Moskva), ph. 292-6227 J14(19)

Nevka, Volokolamskoye sh. 15, ph. 943-4152 A8(5)

Night Flight, ul. Tverskaya 17, ph. 229-4165 I14(19)

Olimp Restaurant, Luzhnetskaya nab., ph. 201-0148 F19(10)

Po Dvorye Restaurant, ul. Maroseyka 9, ph. 923-8949 {cc} K14(20)

Prague Restaurant, ul. Arbat 2, ph. 290-6171 I15(19)

Restaurant Baltschug, Hotel Baltschug, ph. 230-6500 J15(19)

Rus Restaurant, Krasnozvozdnaya 13, Saltykova Settlement, ph. 524-4202 {cc}

Rusalochka (Little Mermaid) Restaurant, Smolenskiy bul. 12, ph. 248-4438 {cc} H16(22)

Ruslan cafe, Vorontsovskaya 32/36, ph. 272-0632 {cc} L17(24)

Russian Hall Restaurant, ul. Tverskaya 3, ph. 203-0150 J14(19)

Ryleeva 9 cafe, Gagarinskiy p. 9/5, ph. 291-6063 {cc} H16(22)

Savoy Club, ul. Dovzhenko 1, Tumba Golf Club, ph. 147-7368 {closed Mon., bar open 9-21, rest. 17-23} C18(9)

Savoy Restaurant, Savoy Hotel, ul. Rozhdestvenka 3, ph. 929-8600 {cc} J14(19)

Serebryany Vek, Teatralny proyezd 3, ph. 926-1352 J14(19)

Sirena Bolshaya Spasskaya cafe, ul. B. Spasskaya (across from Hotel Volga), {cc} K13(20)

Skazka II Restaurant, Yaroslavskoye sh., 43rd km, ph. 584-3436

Sorok Cheterie (44) cafe, Leningradskoye sh. 44, ph. 159-9951 {cc} B7(5)

Soyuz Restaurant, Gospitalny val 22, ph. 360-7432 P13(12)

Stoleshniki cafe, Stoleshnikov p. 6, ph. 229-2050 I14(19)

Strastnoy 7, Strastnoy bul. 7, ph. 299-0498 {daily 12-23} I13(19)

Supriz cafe, Medynskaya 5, k. 1, ph. 384-4400

Talisman cafe, ul. Shchepkina 1, ph. 208-9055 J13(19)

Terrace Bar, Aerostar Hotel, ph. 155-5030 {cc} E11(5)

Theater cafe, ul. Tverskaya 5, I13(19)

Tsentralny Restaurant, ul. Tverskaya 10, ph. 229-0241 I14(19)

U Bankira Restaurant, Chasovaya 24/1, ph. 151-8681 D9(5)

U Kamina cafe, ul. Pokrovka 32, ph. 297-0840 K14(20)

U Margarity cafe, Gagarinskiy p. 9, ph. 291-6063 {cc} H16(22)

Uzbekistan Restaurant, ul. Neglinnaya 29, ph. 924-6053 {cc} J13(19)

Vareniki cafe, Rzhevskiy M. p. & Skatertny p., {cc} H14(18)

Vienna cafe, Olympic Penta Hotel, Olympiyskiy prosp. 18/1, ph. 971-6101 {cc} **J11(7)**

Vienna Restaurant, Palace Hotel, ul. Tverskaya-Yamskaya 19, ph. 956-3152 {daily 17-23} H13(18)

Viktoria Restaurant, prosp. Mira 78, ph. 971-0721 {cc} K11(7)

Vladimir Restaurant, 5th Kotelnicheskiy p. 1, ph. 272-4566 L16(24)

Vltava cafe, Vasilyevskaya ul. 15/24, ph. 251-6898 H13(18)

Votchina cafe, ul. Ostozhenka 18, ph. 203-7173 I16(23)

Writer's Union Restaurant, ul. Povarskaya 52, ph. 291-2169 {cc} H14(18)

Yakimanka cafe, B. Polyanka 2/10, Str. 1, ph. 238-8888 {cc} J16(23)

Yauzkie Vorota cafe, Yauzkiy bulv. 1/15, ph. 227-2405 {cc} L15(20)

Zaldi I Poprobui cafe, prosp. Mira 124, k. 1, ph. 286-8165 K8(7)

FAST FOOD

Burger Queen, Nikitskiy bul. 25, ph. 291-3262 I14(19)

Chicken Grill, Sadko Arcade (Expocenter), ph. 255-2638 {eat-in or take-out} E15(9)

McDonald's, ul. B. Bronnaya 29, ph. 200-1655 I14(19); Gazetny p. 15, ph. 956-9818 {daily 10-22} I14(19); ul. Arbat 50/52, ph. 241-3681 {daily 10-22} H15(18)

Pettina Hamburgers, ul. Kosmonavtov 2/4, ph. 286-5217 {cc} L7(7)

Rostik's, GUM, 3rd line, 2nd fl., ph. 921-1529 {fried chicken} J15(19)

FISH

Anchor Restaurant, Palace Hotel, ul. Tverskaya-Yamskaya 19, ph. 956-3152 {lunch 12-17, dinner 19-24} H13(18)

⇨ **Lobster Grill,** Hotel Metropol, Teatralny proyezd 1/4, ph. 927-6739 J14(19)

⇨**Teatro Mediterraneo**, Hotel Metropol, Teatralny proyezd 1/4, ph. 927-6739 {daily 11-14, cc} J14(19)

FRENCH
Le Cafe Francais, Pullman Iris Hotel, ph. 488-8000 {cc} E2(4)

Les Champs Elysees Restaurant, Pullman Iris Hotel, ph. 488-8000 {cc} E2(4)

Potel et Chabot Restaurant, B. Kommunisticheskaya 2A, ph. 271-0707 {cc, banquets at Kremlin and prestig. lodges} L16(24)

Sovincenter Business Club, Mezhdunarodnaya Hotel I, 1st fl., ph. 253-1792 {daily 13-5} F14(17)

GEORGIAN
Aragvi Restaurant, ul. Tverskaya 6, ph. 229-3762 {cc} I14(19)

Arena cafe, ul. 10-letiya Oktyabrya 11, ph. 245-2972 F18(21)

Cafe Mziuri, ul. Arbat 42, ph. 241-0313 H15(18)

Guria cafe, Komsomolskiy prosp. 7/3, ph. 246-0378 {cc} H17(22)

Iberia Restaurant, ul. Rozhdestvenka 5, str. 2, ph. 928-2672 {daily 12-17, 19-24, cc} J14(19)

Kolkhida cafe, ul. Sadovaya-Samotechnaya 6, stroen. 2, ph. 299-6757 J13(19)

U Pirosmani cafe, Novodevichy proyezd 4, ph. 247-1926 {cc} F17(21)

GERMAN
Beer House, Sadko Arcade (Expocenter), ph. 940-4062 F15(17)

Die Bierstube Restaurant, Olympic Penta Hotel, Olympiyskiy prosp. 18/1, ph. 971-6101 {cc} J11(7)

Westfalia Restaurant, Leninskiy prosp. 87, ph. 134-3026 D23(13)

GREEK
Greek Restaurant, Inflotel, Krasnopresnenskaya N12, ph. 255-9284 {cc} E15(9)

INDIAN
Bombay Restaurant, Rublyovskoye sh. 91, ph. 141-5504 C18(9)

Delhi Restaurant, ul. Krasnopresnenskaya 23b, ph. 255-0492 {cc} G14(17)

Moscow Bombay, Glinishchevskiy p. 3, ph. 292-9731 {cc} I14(19)

ITALIAN
Arlecchino Restaurant JV (Italy), ul. Druzhinnikovskaya 15, ph. 205-7088 {cc, Night Club: 255-9759} G14(17)

Bistro Restaurant, Hotel Baltschug, ph. 230-6500 {cc} J15(19)

Italia Restaurant/Bar, ul. Arbat 49, ph. 241-4342 {cc} H15(18)

La Cipolla D'oro, ul. Gilyarovskovo 39, ph. 281-9498 K11(7)

Lasagne cafe, Pyatnitskaya ul. 40, ph. 231-1085 {cc} J17(23)

Le Stelle Del Pescatore, ul. Pushechnaya 7/5, ph. 924-2058 J14(19)

Pasta House, Sadko Arcade (Expocenter), ph. 255-2638 E15(9)

Patio Pizza, Volkhonka ul. 13A, ph. 201-5000 {daily 12-24, cc} I16(23)

Pescatore Restaurant, prosp. Mira 36, ph. 280-2406 {cc} L7(7)

Ristorante Belfiore, Petrovskiy Passazh, ul. Petrovka 10, ph. 924-6469 {cc, daily 12-20} J13(19)

⇨**Teatro Mediterraneo**, Hotel Metropol, Teatralny proyezd 1/4, ph. 927-6739 {daily 11-14, cc} J14(19)

Tino Fontana Restaurant, Hotel Mezhdunarodnaya, 3rd floor, ph. 253-2241 {cc} F15(17)

Trattoria Restaurant, Sadko Arcade (Expocenter), ph. 940-4066 {cc} E15(9)

Villa Peredelkino Restaurant, 1st Chobatovskaya Alleya, Solntsevskiy District, ph. 435-1478

Vstrecha cafe, ul. Gilyarovskovo 3, ph. 208-4597 {cc} K11(7)

JAPANESE
Sakura Restaurant, Hotel Mezhdunarodnaya, ph. 253-2894 {cc} F15(17)

Sapporo Restaurant, prosp. Mira 12, ph. 207-8253 K12(7)

Tokyo Restaurant, Hotel Rossiya, Varvarka ul. 6, West block, 1st fl., ph. 298-5707 {cc, reservations suggested} J15(19)

JEWISH

U Yuzefa, ul. Dubininskaya 11/17, ph. 238-4646 K18(24)

KOREAN

Korea House, Volgogradskiy prosp. 26, ph. 270-1300 P19(12)

Seoul Plaza, Serpukhovskiy val 14, ph. 952-8254 J20(15)

Zarya Vostoka cafe, ul. 26 Bakinskikh Komissarov 4, k. 2, ph. 433-2201 {cc} A25(13)

LEBANESE

Baku-Livan-Nasr Restaurant, ul. Tverskaya 24, ph. 299-8506 {cc} I13(19)

PHILIPINE

Manila Restaurant, The, ul. Vavilova 81, ph. 132-0055 {cc} E23(13)

PIZZA

Patio Pizza, Volkhonka ul. 13A, ph. 201-5000 {daily 12-24, cc} I16(23)

Pizza Hut Restaurant, Kutuzovskiy prosp. 17, ph. 243-1727 {daily 11-22, cc} F15(17); ul. Tverskaya 12, ph. 229-2013 {daily 11-23, cc} I14(19)

Pizza Hut Take-out, Kutuzovskiy prosp. 17, ph. 243-1727 {cc} F15(17)

Pizza Pazza, Sadko Arcade (Expocenter), ph. 940-4071 F15(17)

RUSSIAN

Aist, M. Bronnaya 1/8, ph. 291-6692 H14(18)

Aromat Restaurant, ul. Rogova, 12, kor. 2, ph. 947-0024 {daily 18-5, cc}

⇨**Boyarskiy**, Hotel Metropol, ph. 927-6000

Gourmet Restaurant, Hotel Baltschug, ph. 230-6500 {cc} J15(19)

Havana Restaurant, Leninskiy prosp. 88, ph. 131-0091 {daily 12-23} D23(13)

Imperial Restaurant, Gagarinskiy p. 9/5, ph. 291-6063 H16(22)

Kashtan Restaurant, Taganskaya ul. 40/42, ph. 272-6242 M16(11)

Le Romanoff, Hotel Baltschug, ph. 230-6500 J15(19)

Lesnaya Skazka, ul. Vvedenskovo 11a, ph. 334-7334

Nemetskaya Sloboda Restaurant, ul. Baumanskaya 23, ph. 267-4476 {daily 12-23 break 17-18, cc} N13(11)

Ordynka Restaurant, ul. B. Ordynka 71/36, ph. 237-9905 J17(23)

Paradise Restaurant and Bar, Hotel Moskva, Okhotny Ryad 2, ph. 292-2073 {cc} J18(23)

Pokrovka Restaurant, ul. Maroseyka 4, ph. 923-0282 {cc} K14(20)

Razgulyai Restaurant, ul. Spartakovskaya 11, ph. 267-7613 {cc} M13(11)

Robin Hood Restaurant, ul. B. Gruzinskaya 42, ph. 254-0738 H13(18)

Rossiya Restaurant, Hotel Rossiya, ph. 298-4133 {cc} J15(19)

Russian Club, Voznesenskiy p. 7, ph. 291-6965 {daily 12-9} I14(19)

Russkaya Izba, Ilyinskoye Village, ph. 561-4244

Russkiy Traktir Restaurant, ul. Arbat 44, ph. 241-9853 H15(18)

Sedmoye Nebo, Ostankino Tower, ul. Akademika Korolyova 15, ph. 282-2293 {midway up the the Ostankino TV tower} J7(7)

Skazka, Tovarishcheskiy p. 1, ph. 271-0998 {cc} L16(24)

Slavyanskiy Bazaar, ul. Nikolskaya 13, ph. 921-1872 J14(19)

Stanislavskovo 2, Leontyevskiy p. 2, ph. 291-8689 I14(19)

Taganka Bar, ul. Verkhnyaya Radishchevskaya 15, ph. 272-4351 {cc} L16(24)

U Babushki, ul. B. Ordynka 42, ph. 239-1484 J17(23)

U Nikitskikh Vorot, Nikitskaya B. ul. 23, ph. 290-4883 I14(19)

Viktoria (Hard Rock Cafe) cafe, Zelyony Theater, Krymskiy val 9, ph. 237-0709 K17(24)

Vyecherni Siluett, Taganskaya pl. 88, ph. 272-2280 L16(24)

Zamoskvoreche Restaurant, ul. B. Polyanka 54, ph. 230-7333 J17(23)

SCANDINAVIAN

Skandia Restaurant, Radisson-Slavyanskaya Hotel, ph. 941-8020 G16(21)

SPANISH

Don Quixote Restaurant, Pokrovskiy bul. 4/17, ph. 297-4757 **L15(20)**

El Rincon Espanol Restaurant, Hotel Moskva, Okhotny Ryad, 7, ph. 292-2893 {cc} **J14(19)**

SWISS

Le Chalet Restaurant, Korobeynikov per., 1/2, ph. 202-2611 {cc} **H16(22)**

Swiss House Restaurant, Sadko Arcade (Expocenter), ph. 940-4069 {cc} **E15(9)**

TATAR

Serebryany Slonyonok cafe, Bolotni-kovskaya 52, ph. 121-2011 **H25(14)**

VIETNAMESE

Hanoi Restaurant, prosp. 60-letiya Oktyabrya 20/21, ph. 125-6001 **G21(14)**

Khram Luny Restaurant, Koslovskiy B. p. 1, ph. 291-0401 **I15(19)**

Kuilong cafe, Litovskiy bul. 7, ph. 425-1001

Phen Khuan Restaurant, ul. Sretenka 23/25, ph. 208-0654 **K13(20)**

RUBBER STAMPS

Shops in the city make stamps to order. Here are two, in case you can't find one nearby.

Eurostyle, Pokrovskiy bul. 3, #1204, ph. 206-7313, 227-5621

Print and Stamp Shop, ul. Festivalnaya 13

Trinity Graphics, ul. Serpukhovskaya 72, kv. 2, ph. 952-6484

S

SAUNAS

See also Massage, Swimming
Most of the newer hotels have saunas and swimming pools. For public baths, try:

Krasnopresnenskiy baths, Stolyarny p. 7

Lianozovo Club Courts, Lianozovskiy Park, ul. Uglicheskaya 13/2, ph. 909-3011

Sandunovskaya Sauna, Sandunovskiy p. 1a, ph. 925-4631

SCHOOLS

Anglo-American School, Leninskiy prosp. 78, ph. 131-8700; B. Devyatinskiy p. 8, ph. 255-0326

Arab School, ul. Ulofa Palme 5, ph. 147-4083

Finnish School, Kropotkinskiy p. 15/17, ph. 246-4027

French School, Spasonalivkovskiy p. 12/16, ph. 237-4636

Hungarian School, ul. Olaf Palme 5, k. 2, ph. 143-6057

Indian School, Dorogomilovskaya 32, ph. 240-6437

Indonesian School, Novokuznetskaya 12, ph. 231-9549

Italian School, ul. Lobachevskovo 38, ph. 431-4966

Japanese School, Leninskiy prosp. 78, ph. 131-8733

Pakistani School, ul. Sadovaya-Kudrinskaya 17, ph. 254-7201

Playschool, ul. Tverskaya 28, ph. 214-9406

Playschool Moscow, Leninskiy prosp. 83 kv. 5, ph. 131-2471

Polish School, ul. Mosfilmovskaya 60, ph. 147-1354

Swedish School, Leninskiy prosp. 78, ph. 131-8766

US Embassy Day Care and Pre-School, US Embassy, ph. 252-2451

SEAMSTRESS/TAILOR

ALS JV, B. Strochenovskiy p. 13, ph. 236-1041

Andy's Fashion, prosp. Vernadskovo 9, ph. 131-0420 {daily 9-17}

Atelier, Mozhayskiy val 4; ul. B. Yakimanka 19; Leninskiy prosp. 21; Lomonosovskiy pr. 23

Mayers International (Hong Kong), Frunzenskaya nab. 30, pavil. 15, level 3, ph. 242-8946 {M-Sa 10-18}

Mr. Tillani's Hong Kong Fashions, ul. Oktyabrskaya 105, kor. 2 (Hotel Good Luck), ph. 289-4575

Slava Zaitsev, prosp. Mira 21, ph. 971-0547

UPDK Atelier, ul. B. Pereyaslavskaya 7, ph. 280-2763 {M & Th 9-19, Tu & F 9-16:30}

SECURITY

Alarm Center, Lomonovskiy prosp. 27, ph. 939-0098

Aleks Detective Agency, ph. 255-2901 {bodyguards}

Benxon Worldwide, ph. 205-1416 {car security}

Betatron, Inc., Park Place, Leninskiy prosp. 113, #713, ph. 956-5055

CEZAM, Zvonarskiy p. 7 str.1, ph. 255-6148 {steel doors}

Dorin Electronics, Khimkiy, Spartakovskaya 12, ph. 571-8108

Honeywell Inc., Tryokhprudny p. 11/13, 3rd fl., ph. 299-6543

Intermarket, Degtyarny p. 5, ph. 299-7968 {M-Sa 10-19}; Patriarshiy B. p. 12, ph. 291-7655 {daily 10-20, home and auto security hardware}

Iskra, ph. 312-1205 {steel doors and window bars}

Megasoft, ph. 576-2400

Oy Esmi, ph. 238-5520

Security Formula, Kolpachny p. 7, ph. 925-6380

Star Progress, Frunzenskaya nab. 30, pav. 15, ph. 201-0692

Trust, ph. 249-5252 {steel doors and window bars}

Wackenhut, Sadovaya-Kudrinskaya ul. 21A, ph. 254-0202 {security personnel}

Willowcorp Russian Ltd., Zemlyanoy val 19, ph. 923-3436

SHIPPING AGENTS

See also Moving, Customs

Aerofreight, P.O. Box 47, ph. 954-8879

Aeroservice JV, Sheremetevo 2 Airport, ph. 578-9030

Air-Troyka, Kuznetskiy Most 6/3, ph. 927-8303

Akko-Universal, ul. Kosmonavta Volkova 6A, #1206, ph. 155-5644

Amoco Eurasia Petroleum Co., Moscow Region, Krasnogorsk, Gorki-6, #3, ph. 418-4359

Anglo-Soviet Shipping Co. Ltd., Pokrovskiy bul. 4/17, kv. 25, ph. 230-2955

Autoserve JV, ul. B. Molchanovka 36, ph. 291-9631

Baltes Moebelspedition, Vekovaya ul. 5, kv. 14, ph. 274-0746

Cargo International Services, Ltd., Radisson-Slavyanskaya Hotel, 6th floor, ph. 941-8880

⇨**Corporate Forwarding**, ul. Festivalnaya 28, ph. 454-1345

Dileon, Rublyovskoye sh. 36, k. 2, ph. 415-4904

Dragun GmbH, Rublyovskoye sh. 36, k. 2, kv. 212, ph. 415-4296

Etex Ligne Reguliere, Pokrovskiy bul. 4/17, kv. 1, ph. 297-4835

Finnair Cargo, Sheremetevo 2 Airport, ph. 578-2718

Froesch K.G., Kutuzovskiy prosp. 7/4 kv. 115, ph. 243-1930

Huolintakeskus OY, Staraya Basmanaya 18, office 37-38, ph. 261-9440

International Shipping Lines, Novy Arbat 21, ph. 291-9331

Interoceanic Shipping and Oil Inc., Protopovskiy p. 16, kv. 37, ph. 280-6692

John Nurminen Oy, ul. B. Ochakovskaya 15a, ph. 430-7861

KLM Cargo, Sheremetevo 2 Cargo Terminal, ph. 578-4541

Logimix, Leningradskiy prosp. 37, k. 5, ph. 155-5880

Lufthansa Airlines Cargo, Sheremetevo 2 Cargo Terminal, ph. 578-6758

Marine Liner Services, ul. Petrovka 20/1, ph. 925-9433

Marine Transport & Trade Co., Plotnikov p. 12, ph. 241-3593

Moscow Diplomatic Transport Service JV (Sweden), ph. 434-0160

MosTransEurope, Butyrskiy val 22, kom. 48/49, ph. 973-0076

Panalpina, Gogolevskiy bul. 17, Ste. 205, ph. 202-1713

Port Service Ltd., ul. Michurinskaya 31/1, ph. 973-1346

S.C. Inc. Freight Forwarders, ph. 229-1379

Scan-Cargo, Head Office, Institutskiy p. 2/1, ph. 200-1522

SeaLand Service, Inc., ul. Petrovka 20/1, ph. 200-3588

Sofi Courier Services JV (Finland), ul. Myasnitskaya 22, room 404, ph. 209-6207

Sovfrakht, ul. Rozhdestvenka 1/4, ph. 926-1032
Sovmortrans, ul. Petrovka 20/1, ph. 925-0803
Sovtransavto, Institutskiy p. 2/1 (Butovo), ph. 971-3663; Oktybraskaya ul. 2/4, ph. 292-8965
Sovtransavto-Expeditsia, ul. B. Ochakovskaya 15a, ph. 548-7675
Sovtranzit, Smolenskaya 34, ph. 244-3951
Soyuzvneshtrans, Gogolevskiy bul. 17, ph. 203-1179
Spetzagrotrans JV, Volzhskiy bul. 3, ph. 179-9901
Stroykomplektexport, Ovchinnikovskaya nab. 18/1, ph. 233-9512
Tekhnopromexport, Ovchinnikovskaya nab. 18/1, ph. 220-1523
Trade and Management, ul. Udaltsova 89/3, #765, ph. 931-4419
TransCargo, Putevoy proyezd 3, ph. 901-1700
Vektor Joint Stock Co., Bolshevistskiy prosp., ph. 928-9953
Vneshstroyimport, Tverskoy bulv. 6, ph. 220-3204

SHOES

Alternative JV & IPLV, Orlyonok Hotel, {daily 10-20}
Baginskiy Fashion, Sovintsentr, Mezhdunarodnaya Hotel I, 1st fl., ph. 253-2697 {M-Sa 10-21, Su 11-19, lunch 15-16}
Bradley's of London, ul. Stary Arbat 4, ph. 291-7067
Di Style, Petrovskiy Passazh, ul. Petrovka 10, 2nd fl., ph. 292-4056
Emanuelle, Hotel Moskva, Teatralnaya pl., ph. 924-3776 {M-Sa 11-19, break 14-15, cc}
Magazin del Mondo, Ukraine Hotel, 8th floor, ph. 243-4682
Mia Shoe, Tikhvinskiy p. 1/50
Red Line, Petrovskiy Passazh, 1st fl. {M-Sa 9-20, cc}
Salamander, GUM, 1st line, 2nd fl.

SHOPPING

See Food, Souvenirs, Electronics, Books

Shopping hours throughout Moscow can vary greatly. Beware the afternoon break, which usually falls between 13-14:00 for food stores, and 14-15:00 for all others. The major department stores like GUM and TsUM work without a lunch break, as do the many Western-owned stores. Most all shops are open six days a week and some stores, particularly food stores and bread stores, are open on Sundays.

Typical hours for food stores are 9-20:00, while for central department stores it is 8-21:00. Expect to encounter the infamous "sanitary day", "closed for technical reasons" or "closed for inventory". These days occur at random and mean the store is closed for the entire day. They are more likely to happen at the start of the month.

SOUVENIRS

See Gifts

The Arbat every day, and the Vernisage at Izmailovskiiy Park on Saturdays and Sundays, are the best known spots for souvenir shopping, and have the widest selection in one location. However, state stores (newly-or soon-to-be-privatized) have a much better selection than previously, and prices are usually more reasonable. See the listings under Gifts for the better private and state shops.

SPORTING GOODS

Adidas-Moscow Ltd., Leningradskiy prosp. 39A, ph. 213-6525
Diadora Sporting Goods, Petrovskiy Passazh, 2nd fl., ph. {M-Sa 9-20, cc}
Karstadt Sports, GUM, 1st line, 1st fl., ph. 926-3326 {M-Sat 8-20}
Lianozovo Club Courts, Lianozovskiy Park, ul. Uglicheskaya 13/2, ph. 909-3011 {4 outdoor courts, private/group lessons, racquet sales, sauna & massage}
Okhotnik, ul. Tverskaya 10, ph.
Olimp, ul. Krasnaya Presnya 23, ph.
Puma, Sadovaya-Spasskaya 19, ph. 975-1992
Reebok Russia, pl. Suvorova 1, ent. 2, off 464, ph. 281-7969
Tennis Shop, ul. Profsoyuza 18, ph.
Top Sport, Sadko Arcade, ph. 253-9588

SWIMMING

In all instances, bathing caps are recommended.

Outdoor pool
Moscow Outdoor Swimming Pool, Prechistenskaya nab. 38, ph. 202-4725

Indoor pools
Cosmos Hotel Indoor Pool, ph. 217-1183
Dinamo Swimming Pool, Leningradskiy prosp. 36, ph. 212-8483
Hotel Mezhdunarodnaya Indoor Pool, Hotel Mezhdunarodnaya, ph. 255-6691
Lenin Stadium Swimming Pool, Luzhniki, ph. 201-0764
Olympic Complex Swimming Pool, Olympiyskiy prosp. 16, ph. 288-1333
Palace of Water Sports, ul. Mironovskaya 27, ph. 369-7444
Radisson Slavyanskaya Swimming Pool, Radisson Slavyansksya Hotel, ph. 941-8027
Swimming Pool of TsSKA, Leningradskiy prosp. 39, ph. 213-2583

T

TAXIS

See Car Rental

Price hikes due to the increase in gas prices have, in general, made taxis more available. Prices are usually agreed upon with the driver beforehand. There are very few taxis that work by the meter anymore. Many private cars also try to make some money on the side by giving rides ('gypsy cabs').

With recent increases in crime, it is best to avoid gypsy cabs if you are not a Russian speaker or do not know your way around the city fairly well. NEVER get into a taxi or gypsy cab with more than the driver in it.

Taxi prices are climbing too fast to be worth quoting.

Express Taxi, ph. 254-6590
Krasnaya Gorka, ul. Podelskikh 6, bldg. 2, room 106, ph. 381-2746

Ochakovo Taxi Service, ul. B. Ochakovskaya 47a, ph. 437-1564
Pride Taxi Service, ph. 451-0858
Taxi Reservations, 24 hours a day, ph. 927-0000 {one hour's notice req'd}; 9am - 6pm (Medvedkovo), ph. 477-7068; 9am - 6pm, ph. 227-0000 {for advanced booking, one to seven days}
Vesta Taxi Service, ph. 447-5481

Private taxi agencies (see also the listings under Car Rental, most hire cars with drivers):

TELECOM

See Electronic Mail, International Phone
The companies listed below offer services related to obtaining telecommunications equipment and services for firms setting up offices and/or communications capabilities.

3M (Minnesota Mining & Manufacturing), Samarskiy p. 3, ph. 288-9701
Aerocom Corp., Leninskiy prosp. 32A, ph. 938-1811
AISI JV, P.O. Box 332, ph. 925-7158
Alcatel BSR, Pokrovskiy bul. 4/17, #21, ph. 207-9998
Alcatel Trade International, Spasonalivkovskiy per. 24, ph. 230-0334
AMT JV (Finland), Khoroshevskoye sh. 42a, ph. 941-3092
Andrew Corp., ul. Volkhonka 3/4, 2nd fl., ph. 203-0280
Artel, ul. Myasnitskaya 26, ph. 925-2901; **Business Center**, Novy Arbat 2, ph. 245-0026
Belcom, ul. Usacheva 35, ph. 245-5766
Bell Atlantic, Degtyarny p. 2, ph. 209-6256
Combellga, Kutuzovskiy prosp. 9, kor. 2, #64, ph. 244-9158; Mytnaya 3, ent. 2, 14 fl., ph. 239-1149
Crosna Space Communications, Presnenskiy val 27, ph. 253-8603
Direct Net Telecommunications, Novy Arbat 36, Room 2834, ph. 290-9541 {direct Phone and Fax from the U.S.}
Hughes Network Systems/General Motors Corp., Krasnopresnenskaya nab. 12, Office 10041, ph. 253-2577
Infatel JV (Japan), ul. Tverskaya 7, ph. 201-9174

Infocom JV (Finland), Teterenskiy p. 10, ph. 915-5093

Inkom JV, Zubovskiy bulv. 3, ph. 299-4937

International Network Connections, ul. Profsoyuznaya 61, office 326, ph. 334-8249

Istok-K Computer Network, ph. 245-5165

Morsvyazsputnik, Novoslobodskaya 14/19, ph. 258-7045

Moscow Cellular Communications, Vorontsovskaya ul. 18/20, ph. 271-3749

Moscow City Telephone Network, Degtyarny p. 6, ph. 299-2885

Moscow Rent-a-Phone, Novotel Hotel, #718, ph. 578-7252

Multivision, Inc., ul. Bolshaya Yakimanka 24, ph. 230-7813

Novosibirsk-Seattle International, ph. 939-3741 {CB and two-way radios}

Phoenix International, Suvorovskaya pl. 2, ph. 974-1031

Promed JV, Promyshlenniy pr., garazhn. kooperativ 'Volga3', ph. 148-5557 {cb radios}

Pulse Soft, ul. Burdenko 12, ph. 245-0406

Radio Communications & Computers, PO Box 666, ph. 220-2818

Segol, Ltd., Leningradskoye sh. #116, ph. 262-1452

Sovam Teleport, Bryusov p. 2a, ph. 229-3466

Sovintel JV (US), Dubovaya Roscha 25, ph. 215-6097

Sprint International Communications Corp., ul. Tverskaya 7, entrance 7, ph. 201-6890

STET, Palashevskiy B. p. 11/1, 3rd floor, ph. 973-2478

Teleset Service, ph. 166-9763

U.S. West International, Inc., Krasnopresenskaya nab. 12, Office 809, ph. 253-2058

World Trade Telecom, Sovintsenter, Krasnopresnenskaya nab. 12, ph. 253-1308

TELEGRAM/TELEX

Central Telegraph Office, ul. Tverskaya 7

Communications House, Novy Arbat 22

Both are open 24 hours (hotels also have telex and telegram services)

Dictate a telegram by phone (in Russian) by calling 927-2002

TENNIS

Chaika Tennis Courts, Korobeynikov p. 1/2, ph. 202-0474 {cc, 4 indoor courts, private lessons, open daily 7-22}

Druzhba Tennis Courts, Luzhnetskaya nab. 10, ph. 201-1780 {in Luzhniki Park, indoor/outdoor courts, private/group lessons, open 7-16}

Lianozovo Club Courts, Lianozovskiy Park, ul. Uglicheskaya 13/2, ph. 909-3011 {4 outdoor courts, private/group lessons, racquet sales, sauna & massage}

Luzhniki Tennis Courts, Luzhnetskaya nab. 10, ph. 201-1655

Petrovskiy Park Tennis Club 36, Leningradskiy prosp. 36, ph. 212-8351

THEATER/BALLET

Hotel service desks (often a separate theater desk exists) are the best place to turn to for tickets. For places like the Bolshoy, you can often hang around outside the theater the day of the performance and buy tickets from scalpers, for varying prices and seat locations. Russian speakers should also try the Teatralniye kassi (on the streets are at a specific theater) since the dramatic increase in ruble ticket prices for Russians has also made tickets more widely available. Also try:

IPS Theater Box Office, Hotel Metropol, Teatralny proyezd 1/4, ph. 927-6728 {M-F 10-18, Sa-Su 10-15}

Animal Theater, ul. Durova 4, ph. 281-2914

Bat Cabaret Theater, B. Gnezdnikovskiy p. 3, ph. 229-8661

Bolshoy Theater, Teatralnaya pl. 1, ph. 292-9986

Cat Theater, Kutuzovskiy prosp. 25, ph. 249-2907

Central Children's Theater, Teatralnaya pl. 2/7, ph. 292-0069

Central Puppet Theater, ul. Sadovaya-Samotechnaya 3, ph. 299-3310

Chamber Music Theater, Leningradskiy prosp. 71, ph. 198-7204

Chelovek Studio Theater, Skatertny p. 23a, ph. 291-1656

Conservatory, Nikitskaya B. ul. 13, ph. 229-8183

Drama Theater on Malaya Bronnaya, M. Bronnaya 4, ph. 290-4093

Ermitage Theater, Karetny ryad 3, ph. 209-6742

Fifth Floor Studio (Na Pyatom Etazhe), Kostomarovskiy p. 3, ph. 297-6564

Glinka Museum Hall, ul. Fadeyeva 4, ph. 972-3237

Gogol Theater, ul. Kazakova 8a, ph. 261-5528

Gypsy Theater 'Romen', Leningradskiy prosp. 32/2, ph. 250-7353

Jewish Drama Studio Theater, Varshavskoye sh. 71, ph. 110-3758

Jewish Music Theater, Taganskaya pl. 12, ph. 272-4924

Kamernaya Tsena Theater, Zemlyanoy val 64, ph. 297-3718

Lenkom Theater, Dmitrovka M. ul. 6, ph. 299-0708

Lyetuchaya Mysh Cabaret, B. Gnezdnikovskiy p. 3, ph. 930-7021

Maly Theater, Teatralnaya pl. 1/6, ph. 924-4083; **filial,** ul. B. Ordynka 69, ph. 237-6420

Mayakovskiy Theater, Nikitskaya B. ul. 19, ph. 925-3070; **filial,** Pushkareva p. 21, ph. 208-3312

Moscow Ballet Theater, ul. Skakovaya 3, ph. 251-3221

Moscow Detective Theater, ul. B. Lubyanka 13, ph. 222-5213

Moscow Puppet Theater, Spartakovskaya ul. 26, ph. 261-2197

Moscow Theater of the Arts
New, Tverskoy bul. 22, ph. 203-8744
Old, Kamergerskiy p. 3, ph. 229-0443
Filial, Petrovskiy p. 3, ph. 229-9631

Moscow University Students Theater, Nikitskaya B. ul. 1, ph. 203-6876

Moscow Youth Theater, Sadovskiy p. 10, ph. 299-5360

Mossoviet Theater, B. Sadovaya 16, ph. 299-2035; Sivtsev Vrazhek 44, ph. 241-0225; **Small stage,** Khamovnicheskiy val 2, ph. 242-1707

Musical Comedy Theater (Operetta Theater), Dmitrovka B. ul. 6, ph. 292-0405

New Drama Theater, ul. Prokhodchikov 2, ph. 182-0347

O. Tabakov's Studio Theater, ul. Chaplygina 1a, ph. 928-9685

Oblastnoy Teatr Yunovo Zritelya, Prokhladnaya ul. 28, ph. 321-6277

Onegin Hall, Konstantine Stanislavskiy Museum, Leontyevskiy p. 6, ph. 299-2855

Pantomime Theater (Mimiki i Zhesta), Izmaylovskiy bul. 39/41, ph. 163-8130

Pushkin Drama Theater, Tverskoy bul. 23, ph. 203-4221

RosInterTeatr JV (USA), Strastnoy bul. 10, ph. 924-5496

Russian Academic Youth Theater, Teatralnaya pl. 2, ph. 292-6572

Russian Army Theater, Suvorovskaya pl. 2, ph. 281-5120

Satire Theater, B. Sadovaya 18, ph. 299-9042

Satirikon Theater, Sheremetevskaya ul. 8, ph. 289-7844

Shadow Theater, Izmaylovskiy bul. 60/10, ph. 465-6592

Shkola Dramaticheskovo Isskustva, Povarskaya ul. 20, ph. 290-5888

Sovremennik Theater, Chistoprudny bul. 19a, ph. 921-1790

Sphera Theater, Karetny ryad 3, ph. 299-9645

Stanislavskiy & Nemirovich-Danchenko Musical Theater, Dmitrovka B. ul. 17, ph. 229-8388

Stanislavskiy Drama Theater, ul. Tverskaya 23, ph. 299-7224

Studio Theater on Yugo Zapade, prosp. Vernadskovo 125, ph. 434-7483

Taganka Drama and Comedy Theater, Zemlyanoy val 76, ph. 272-6300

Teatr Kinoaktyora (Filmactor Theater), Povarskaya ul. 33, ph. 290-5524

U Nikitskikh Vorot Studio Theater, Nikitskaya B. ul. 23/9, ph. 291-8419; **Lebed Hall,** Leningradskoye sh. 35, ph. 159-7844

Union of Theater Workers, ul. Tverskaya 12, str. 7, kv. 228, ph. 209-2436

V. Spesivtsev's Experimental Studio Theater, ul. Rustaveli 19, ph. 218-2332

Vakhtangov Theater, ul. Arbat 26, ph. 241-0728

Yermolova Drama Theater, ul. Tverskaya 5

TIME   DIAL 100

*Seasonal time changes are as follows: clocks are set one hour ahead the last weekend of March and back one hour the last weekend in September. Check time differences across Russia on the map on pages 2 and 3 of our **Russia Survival Guide**.*

TOYS

Barbie, Detskiy Mir, Teatralny proyezd 5, {daily 8:40-20}

Lego, GUM, 2nd line, 1st fl., ph. 926-3264 {M-Sa 10-20, cc}, TsUM, 3rd fl., ph. 923-7704 {M-Sa 8-20, cc}

San Francisco in Moscow, Komsomolskiy prosp. 15, ph. 246-2142

Statfall, TsUM, 3rd fl., ph. 954-0493 {M-Sa 8-20, cc}

U2 Family Superstore, ul. Bakuninskaya 32, ph. 265-2963 {M-Sa 10-19}

TRAIN INFORMATION

Train Information Service (24 hrs), Komsomolskaya pl. 5, ph. 266-9000

Train Ticket Delivery Service, ph. 262-8684

TRAIN STATIONS

Byelorusskiy Train Station, Tverskaya zastava 7, ph. 973-8464 {Belarus}

Kazanskiy Train Station, Komsomolskaya pl. 2, ph. 266-2843 {to Tartarstan}

Kievskiy Train Station, pl. Kiyevskovo ⇨ Vokzala, ph. 262-6230 {Ukraine}

Kurskiy Train Station, pl. Kurskovo Vokzala, ph.

Leningrad Train Station, Komsomolskaya pl. 3, ph. 262-4281 {St. Petersburg, Estonia, Lithuania}

Paveletskiy Train Station, Paveletskaya pl. 1, ph. 235-0522 {Southbound, Westbound}

Rizhskiy Train Station, Rizhskiy pl., ph. 266-9535 {Baltics}

Savyolovskiy Train Station, pl. Savyolovskovo Vokzala, ph. 285-9000 {Northbound}

Yaroslavskiy Train Station, Komsomolskaya pl. 5, ph. 266-0218 {central Russia}

TRANSLATION

Services of this nature are widely available and have a very wide quality range. For best results, make sure the service can draw on native speakers of the language you are having something translated into. The better written and oral translation services available are listed below.

AT&T offers a unique over-the-phone translation service. You call them up, any time day or night in the US at (800) 628-8486, and for $3.50 per minute, plus long distance charges, you can have a translated telephone conversation. From outside the US, call (800) 843-8420.

Aescom, Ul. Parshina 23, Ap. 89, ph. 197-6760

ASET Consultants, Inc., Zagorodnoye sh. 9, ph. 958-6273

Atlas Language Service, Vorontsovskiy p. 2, office 206, ph. 272-6257

Fonetiks, Semyonovskaya nab. 2/1, ph. 360-0874

Interdialekt, Glazovskiy p. 1, 2nd flr., ph. 241-6307

Interperevod, Sadovaya-Kudrinskaya 11, ph. 252-7388

Intourguideservice, Milyutinskiy p. 13/1, ph. 923-8575

Intrakon, Kiselny N. p. 5, ph. 200-6921

Machmir Perevod, 2nd Frunzenskaya 8, ph. 242-5441

⇨**NewEurope International**, ul. Smolenskaya 10, ent. 4, kv. 125, ph. 241-3463

Polyglot, ul. Rybalko 13, ph. 194-7781

RR Translations, B. Kondratyevskiy p. 4, kv. 168, ph. 254-9275

Russian-Italian Foundation, Michurinskiy prosp. 1, ph. 146-7001

RussLan JV (US), ul. Miklukho-Maklaya 21, blok 9, ph. 299-1549

⇨**Service Globus (US)**, B. Kommunisticheskaya 1/5, ph. 298-6146

Statistica, Inc., ul. Skakovaya 9, 4th fl, kv. 22, ph. 945-3412

World Bible Translation Center, Krylatskiye Kholmy 34, ph. 413-8294

TRAVEL AGENCIES

Most Western travel agencies in Moscow exist to serve their clients when they are in Moscow. But they can often help you solve travel-related problems while in the Commonwealth or help you arrange travel to other parts of the Commonwealth. The major agencies with offices in Moscow are listed below, along with better Russian firms.

AEC, ul. Skakovaya 3, ph. 945-2477

American Express, ul. Sadovo-Kudrinskaya 21a, ph. 956-9000

Amitra Inc., ul. Nezhdannaya 15, 4th fl., kom. 70, ph. 925-1991

Area Travel Agency Ltd., ul. Rozhdestvenka 3, ph. 929-8665

Autoserve JV, ul. B. Molchanovka 36, ph. 291-9631

Barry Martin Travel, ul. Vorontsovskaya 26, ph. 271-9232

Bear Travels, prosp. Andropova 35, k. 2, apt. 172, ph. 114-4223

Business Tour, Hotel Mezhdunarodnaya 2, office 701, ph. 253-2940

Cedok (Czech Travel Bureau), Tverskaya-Yamskaya ul.4. 33/39, ph. 258-8932

Europaeishes Reiseburo GmbH, ul. B. Spasskaya 12, ph. 280-6438

Express-Boyd, ph. 203-2675

Gadfly, Ltd., The, Novoshukinskaya 3-21, ph. 193-5096

GlavUPDK Travel and Tickets, ph. 202-2725

Griphon Travel, Hotel Ukraine, rm. 743, ph. 243-2595

Ibusz (Hungarian Travel Company), Staropimenovskiy p. 5, ph. 299-7402

Inatours, ph. 253-1529

Inntel, ul. Nemchinova 12, ph. 211-0983

Interbusinesstour, Molodyozhnaya Hotel, #1520, ph. 210-9438

Interguide Tour Agency, proyezd Yakushina 3, #52, ph. 903-5303

Interperevod, Sadovaya-Kudrinskaya 11, ph. 252-7388

Intourservice, Nikitskiy p. 4a, ph. 203-9898; **Central Excursion Bureau**, ul. Tverskaya 1, ph. 292-5133

Intourtrans, ul. Petrovka 15/13, ph. 927-1181

Intravel, ul. Vavilova 55, ph. 124-5888

IT Club, ul. Novaya Basmannaya 4/6/342, ph. 262-1027

Kaleva Travel Agency Ltd., Intourist Hotel, Room 801, ph. 203-6108

MCBE Company, Ltd, B. Gnezdnikovskiy p. 10, ph. 229-5810

McCall Tours, ph. 201-5895

Messe-Reisen Falk, Vsevologskiy p.3, stroyeniye 1, ph. 201-2149

MGPO Tourist, Izmailovskoye sh. 71, k. V, 4th flr., ph. 166-2036

Palmira Travel Ltd., ul. Vavilova 48, entr. 5-a, ph. 135-1200

Panaramatour Travel Services, Leningradskiy prosp. 10, ph. 257-0533; ul. Levoberezhnaya 32, ph. 458-5786

Pilgrim Tours, 1st Kirpichny p. 16, ph. 369-0389

Podmoskovye Travel Association, Kalanchevskaya ul. 4/2, ph. 975-9545

REI Adventures, 1st Kerpichny p. 17a, ph. 365-4563

Representation of Tourist's Committee of Bulgaria, Kuznetskiy Most 1/8, ph. 292-7042

Rinata Travel, ul. Zamarenova 5, ph. 252-3814

Savoy Travel Club, Rozhdestvenka 3, Savoy Business Center, ph. 929-8559 {daily 9-21}

⇨ **Service Globus**, B. Kommunisticheskaya 1/5, ph. 298-6146, Sheremetevo 2 Airport, ph. 578-7534

Skurimpeks, ul. 1st Tverskaya-Yamskaya 28, kv. 88, ph. 250-1780

Sovit-tours JV (Italy), ul. Angarskaya 15a, ph. 290-3270

Sputnik Tourist Agency, M. Ivanovskiy p. 6, str. 2, ph. 925-9278

Super Nova, ul. Petrovka 2, ph. 292-9979 {also ticket sales}

SVO Travel, Ltd., ul. Novy Arbat 15, 18th fl., #1820, ph. 202-2293

Thomson Holidays, ph. 203-4025

Travellers Guest House, ul. B. Pereyaslavskaya 50, 10th fl., ph. 971-4059

TrekKingtour JV (FRG), ul. M. Yakimanka 2/1, ph. 230-7426

Unisel Network (US), Leninskiy prosp. 85, ph. 134-0521

VAO 'Intourist' (Adventure Tours), ul. Mokhovaya 13, ph. 292-2791

World Transit, ph. 206-8781

V

VETERINARIAN

Every region has a regional veterinary clinic. If you don't know where yours is, ask at a pet store listed under pets above.

Vet pharmacy, ul. Kirova 34, ph. 923-6659

VIDEO RENTAL

American Video Store, B. Gnezdnikovskiy p. 10, kv. 834, ph. 229-7459 {also delivers}

Barus Video JV (Holland), Skatertny p. 20, ph. 290-4258

Cinema Service, Ltd., ul. Akademika Koroleva 8/1, ph. 216-8162

Entertainment World, GUM Department Store, 3rd line, ph. 926-3454

Garden Ring Supermarket, B. Sadovaya 1, ph. 209-1572 {daily 9-21, cc}

VideoForce, Mezhdunarodnaya Hotel, 1st floor, ul. Korovy Val 7, ph. 253-7708; Koroviy val 7, ent. 1, ph. 238-3136 {open daily 11-20, Sun 11-18}

Videoline JV (Switz.), 2nd Frunzenskaya ul. 10, k. 1, ph. 242-0110

VISA OFFICE

UVIR, ul. Pokrovka 42, ph. 207-0113 (private visa); 207-0239 (business visa), open Mo, Tu, Th 10-18, lunch 13-15; open Fr 10-13, 15-17

W

WAREHOUSES

Autoserve JV, ul. B. Molchanovka 36, ph. 291-9631

Dileon, Rublyovskoye sh. 36, k. 2, ph. 415-4904

Euronet, 2nd Skotoprogonnaya ul. 35, ph. 278-0029

Items Warehouse and Storage, B. Cherkasskiy p. 4, ph. 924-6495

Jones Development Group, ul. Tverskaya 6, #97, ph. 229-7201

Karavan, ul. Zoologicheskaya 1, ph. 285-8584

Marine Transport & Trade Co., Plotnikov p. 12, ph. 241-3593

Pony Express, Komsomolskiy prosp. 42, #206, ph. 245-9447 {M-F 9-18}

TransCargo, Putevoy proyezd 3, ph. 901-1700

WATER

Clear Water, ph. 247-1945 {bottled water systems}

Z

ZOO

Moscow Zoo, ul. Bolshaya Gruzinskaya 1, open 9-17 in winter, 9-20 in summer

---

Unequaled Access

Where in Moscow reaches over ten thousand active users inside Russia and out. It is the only guide of its type with national bookstore distribution in North America and Europe. It has earned a reputation as an objective, detailed, qualitative and easy-to-use guide. And it is used year-round as a reference tool and guide. A very limited number of advertising spaces are available in this guide (limited so as to maximize each ad's value). To find out how your company can become a part of *Where in Moscow*, contact Russian Information Services at 89 Main St., Suite 2, Montpelier, VT 05602, ph. 802-223-4955, fax 802-223-6105. In Moscow, call our office at 095-254-9275.

Moscow City
Street Map

MOSCOW

Scale 1:35,000

✦	Cafe	⚓	Boat Stop
♈	Restaurant	🎬	Cinema
Ⓜ	Metro Station	⊞	Embassy
⊡	Ring Line Metro Station	⛽	Gas Station
		⬛	Market
		♨	Theater
	Park or Cemetery	✚	Christian Church
		✚	Russian Orthodox
	Railroad & Station	✡	Synagogue
		☪	Mosque

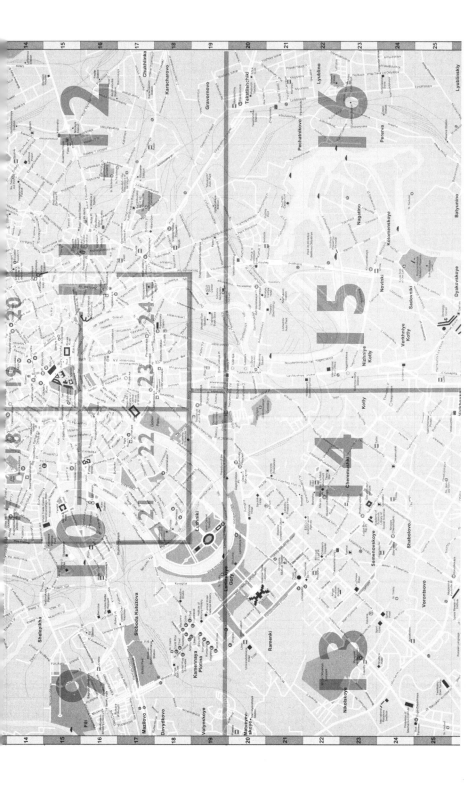

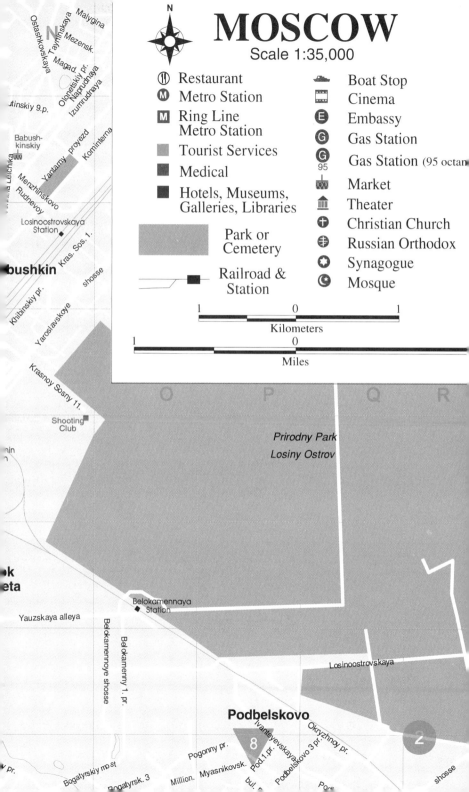

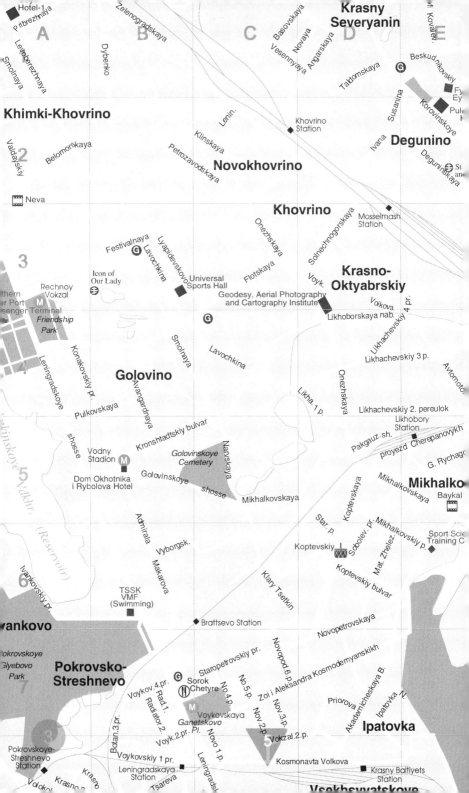

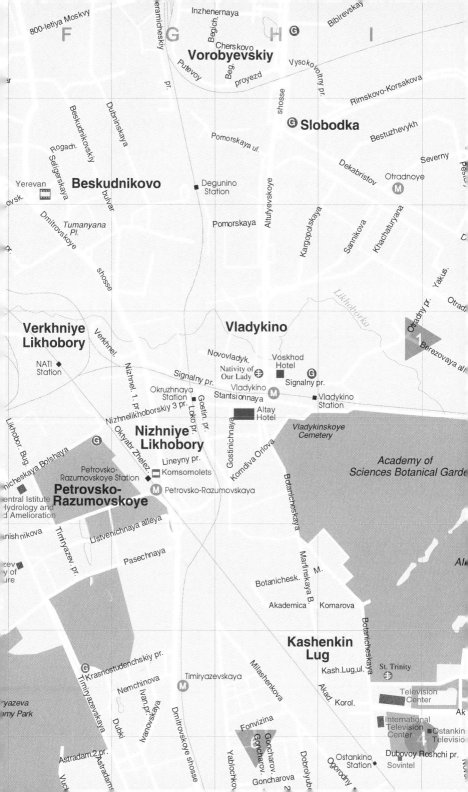

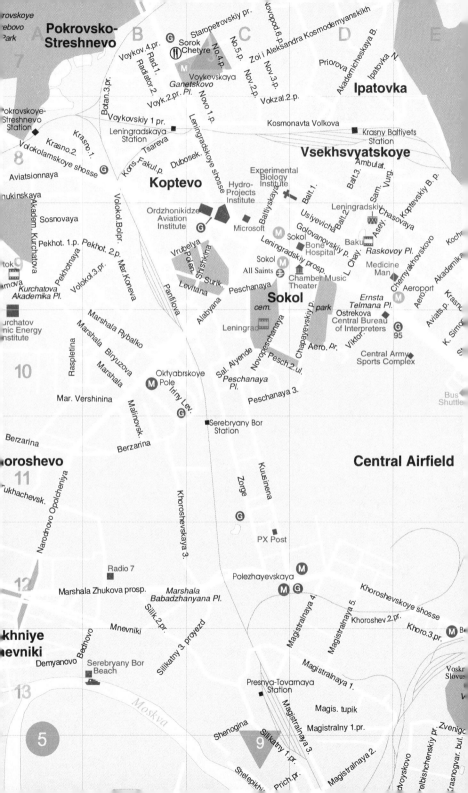

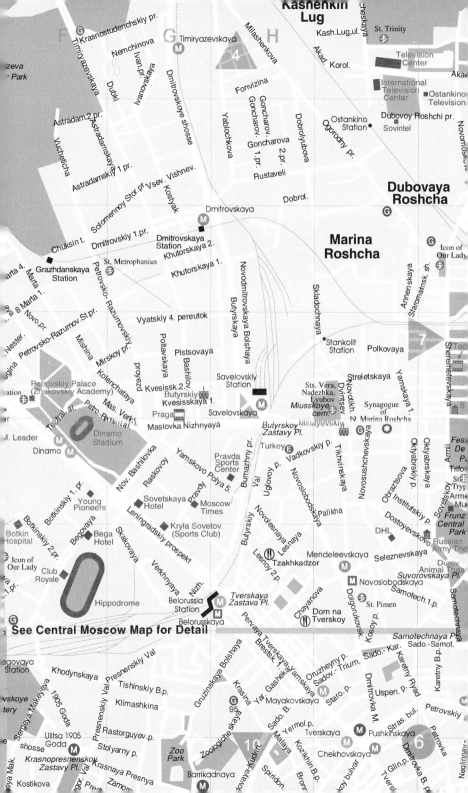

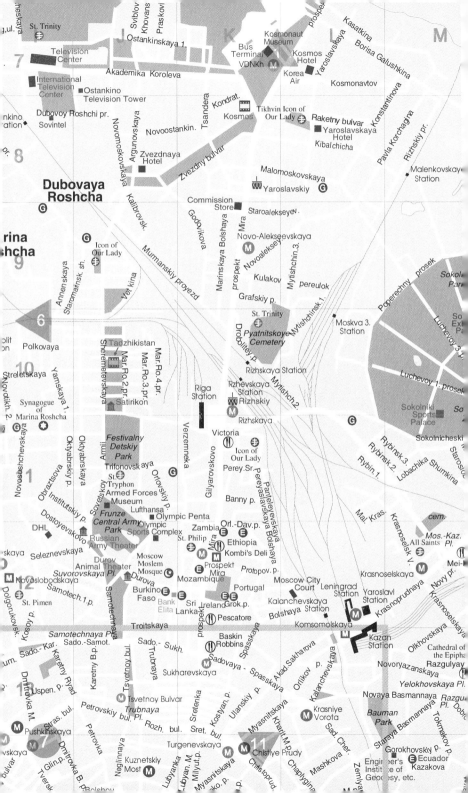

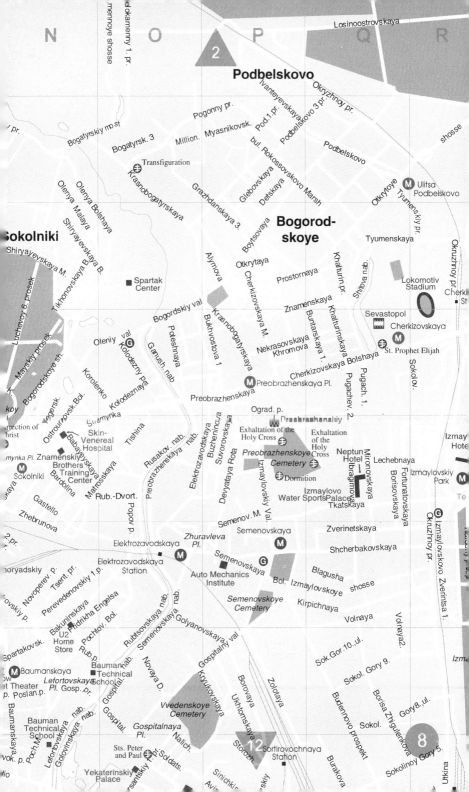

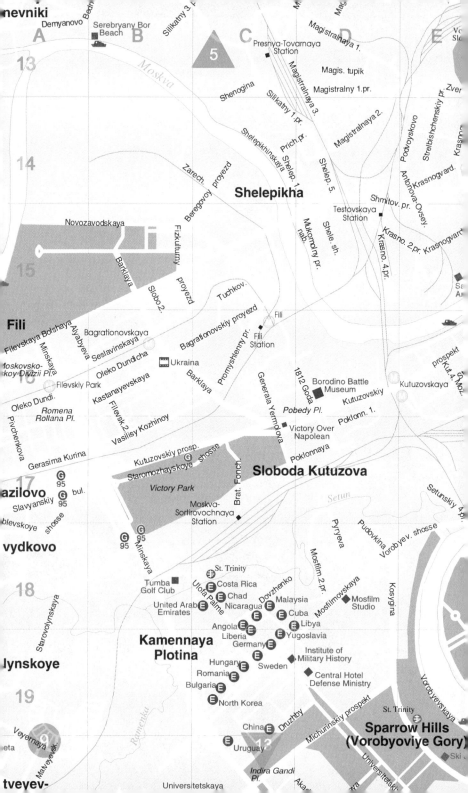

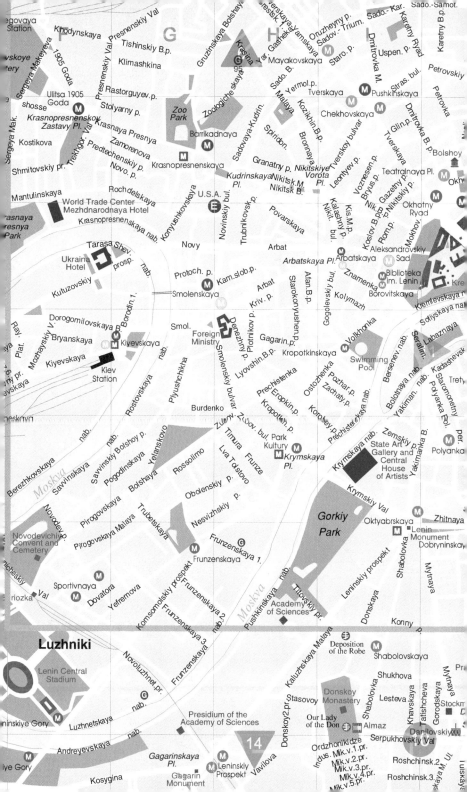

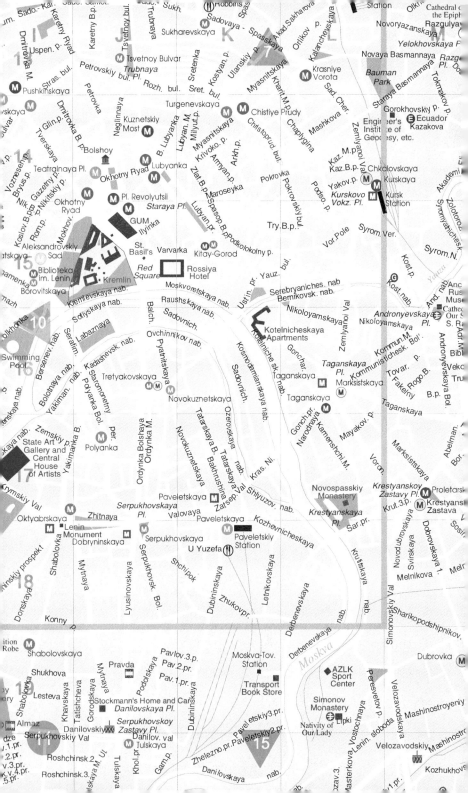

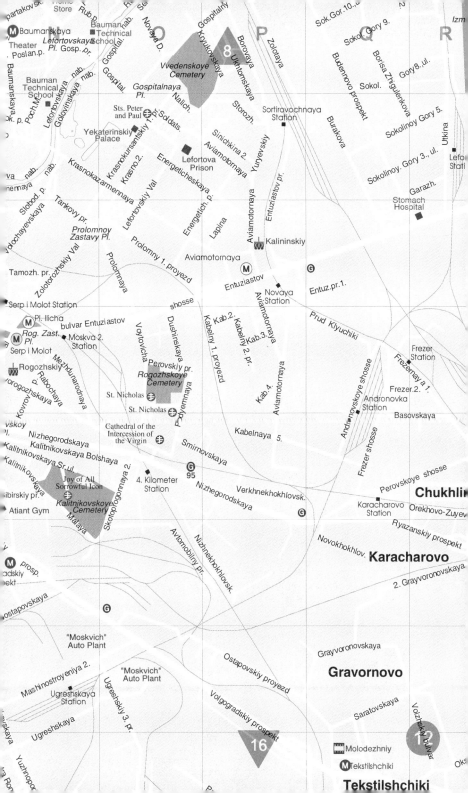

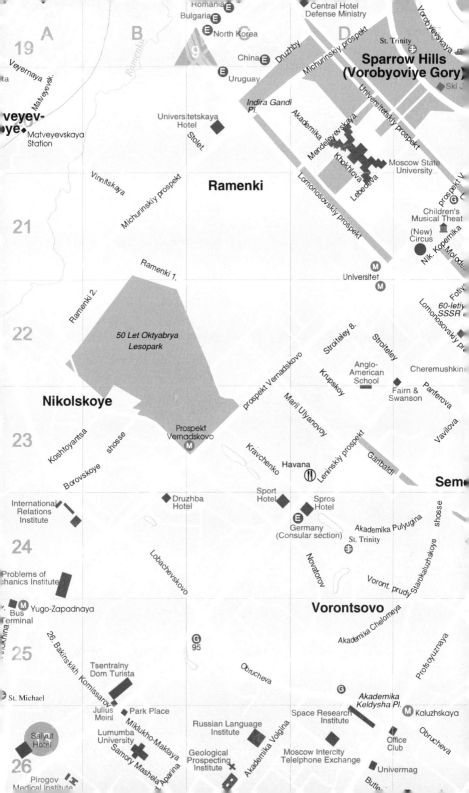

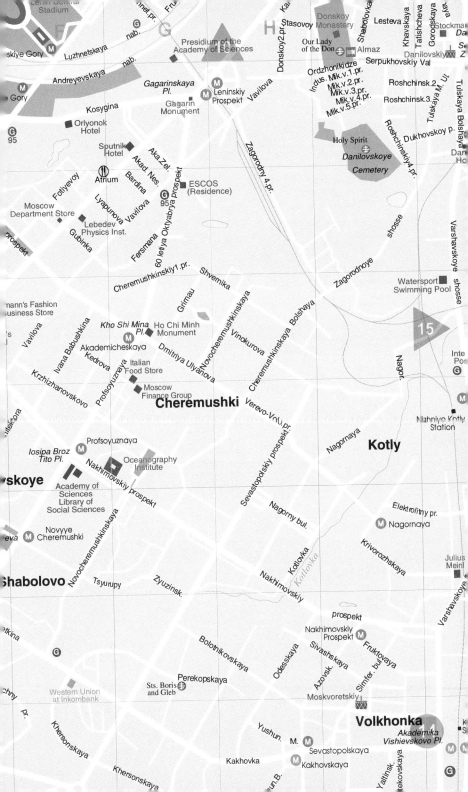

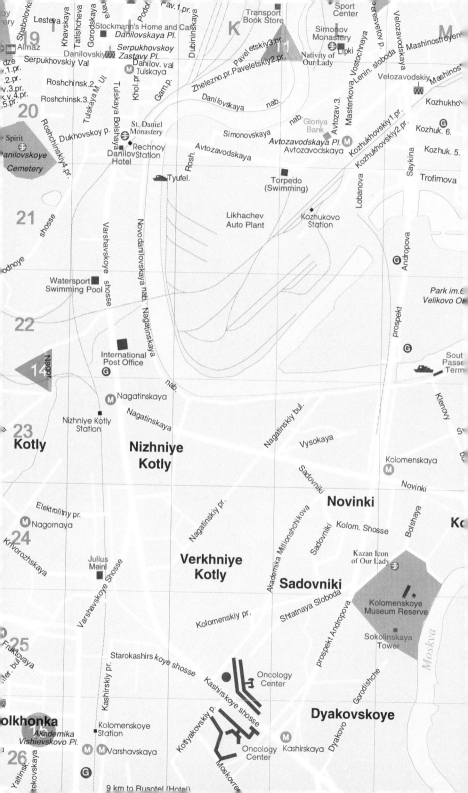

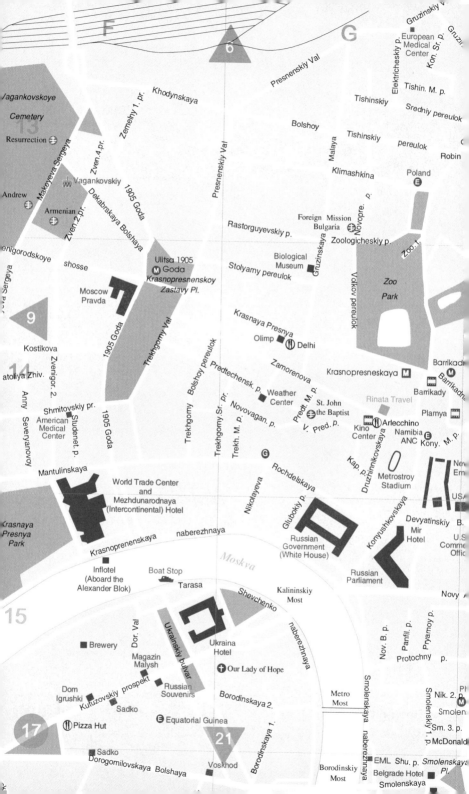

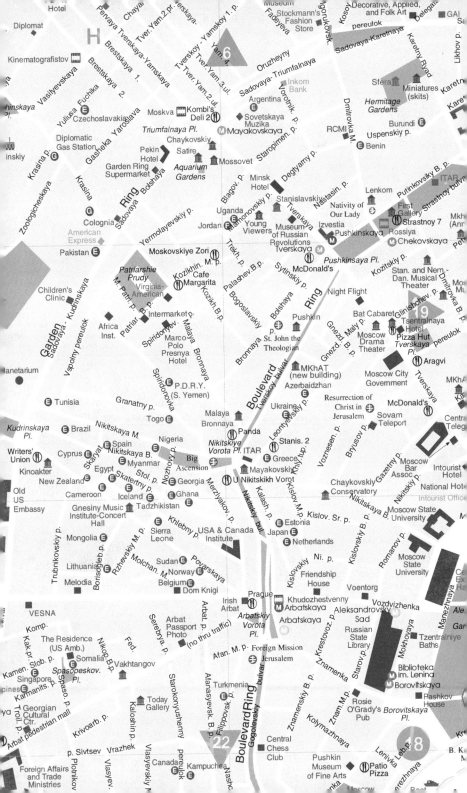

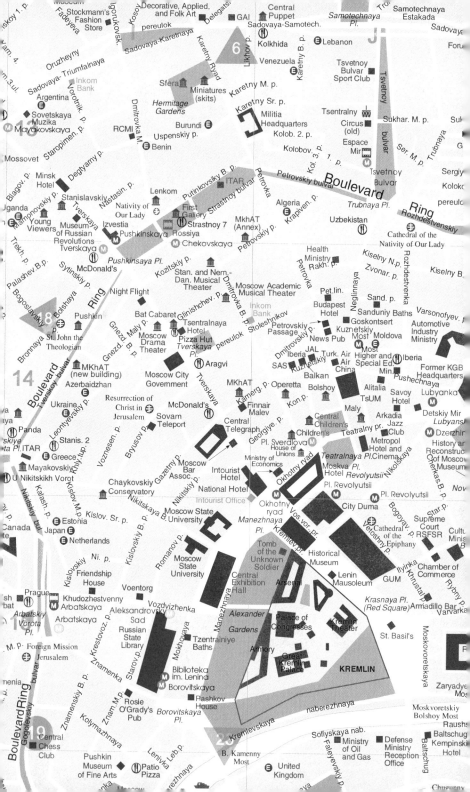

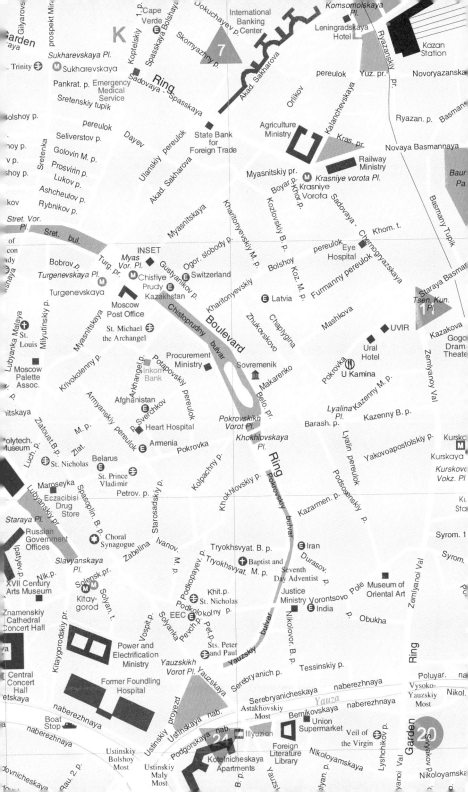

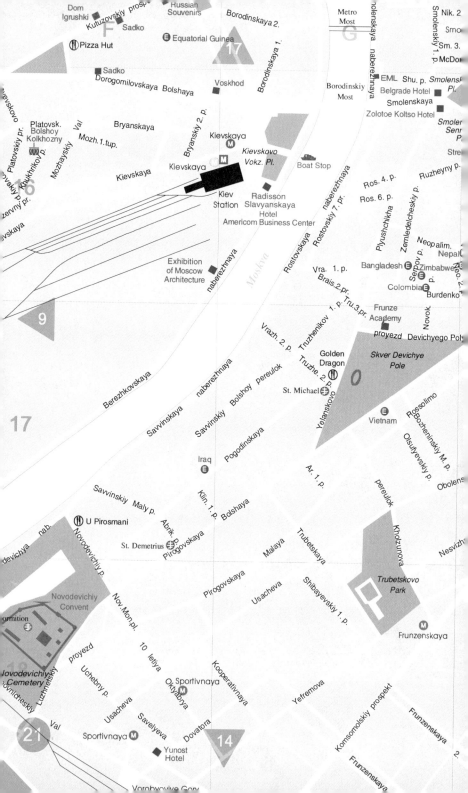

Dom Igrushki
Kutuzovskiy prospekt
Sadko
Pizza Hut
Sadko
Dorogomilovskaya Bolshaya
Russian Souvenirs
Borodinskaya 2.
Equatorial Guinea
17
Voskhod
Borodinskaya 1.
Metro Most
G
Smolenskaya naberezhnaya
Borodinskiy Most
Nik. 2
Smolenskiy 1. p.
Sm. 3. p.
Smo
McDo
EML
Shu. p.
Smolensk
Belgrade Hotel
Pl.
Smolenskaya
Zolotoe Koltso Hotel
Smoler
Senr
P.
Stre

Platovsk. Bolshoy Kolkhozny
Platovskiy pr.
Khutrikov p.
Mozhayskiy
Val
Mozh.1.tup.
Bryanskaya
Bryansky 2. p.
Kievskaya
Kievskaya
Kievskaya
M
M
Kievskovo Vokz. Pl.
Boat Stop

16
zervny pr.
vskaya

Kiev Station
Klev
Radisson Slavyanskaya Hotel
Americom Business Center

Rostovskaya
Rostovskiy 7. pr.
Ros. 4. p.
Ros. 6. p.
Plyushchikha
Zemledelcheskiy p.
Ruzheyny p.
Neopalim.
Nepal
Bangladesh E
Serpov p.
Zimbabwe
Zio.
Colombia E
Burdenko
Vra. 1. p.
Brais.2.pr.

9

Exhibition of Moscow Architecture
naberezhnaya
Muskva

Frunze Academy
proyezd Devichyego Pol
Golden Dragon
St. Michael
Skver Devichye Pole
Novok.
0
Vrazh. 2. p.
Truzhenikov 1. p. Tru.3.pr.
Truzhe. 2. p.
Yelanskovo
Vietnam
Rossolimo
Bozheninskiy M. p.

Berezhkovskaya
Savvinskaya naberezhnaya
Savvinskiy Bolshoy pereulok
Pogodinskaya
Olsufyevskiy p.
Obolens

17
Iraq
E
Ar. 1. p.
pereulok
Khodzunova
Nesvizh

Savvinskiy Maly p.
Abrik.
Klin. 1. p.
Bolshaya
U Pirosmani
Novodevichiy p.
St. Demetrius
Pirogovskaya
Malaya
Trubetskaya
Pirogovskaya
Usacheva
Shibayevskiy 1. p.
Trubetskovo Park

devichya nab.
Novodevichiy Convent
Nov.Mon.pl.
ormition

18
Novodevichiy Cemetery
proyezd
Uchebny p.
Usacheva
10 letiya
Sportivnaya
Oktyabrya
Kooperativnaya
Dovatora
Yefremova
Komsomolskiy prospekt
Frunzenskaya

M
Frunzenskaya

21
Val
Sportivnaya
M
Savelyeva
14
Yunost Hotel
Frunzenskaya
Frunzenskaya 2.

Vorobyovye Gory

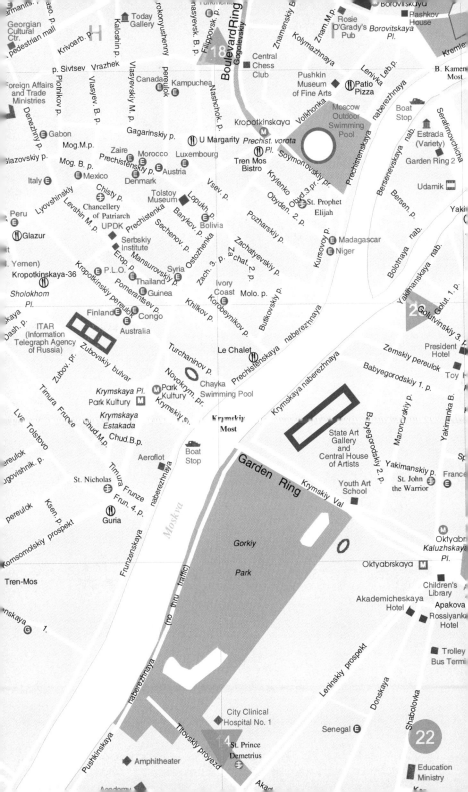

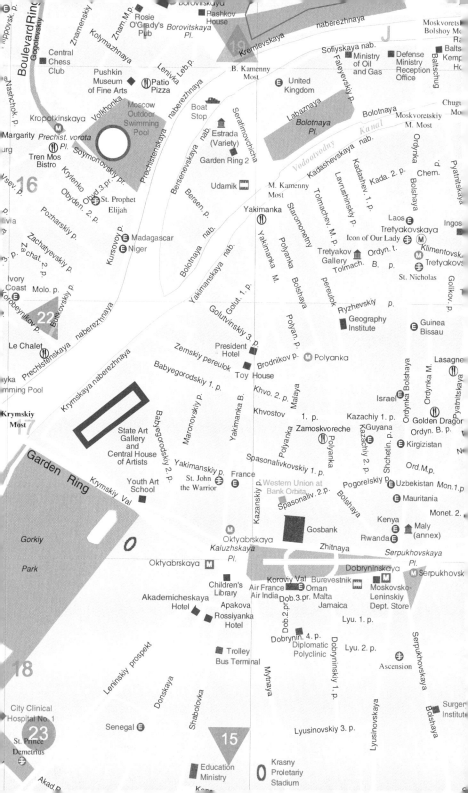

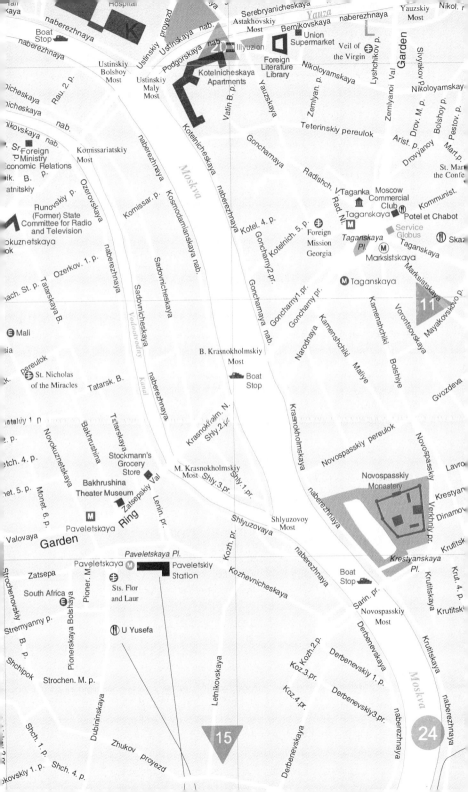

Moscow City Street Map Index

ABBREVIATIONS AND GLOSSARY

B. Bolshoy, -aya, -oye: big, great
bul. bulvar: boulevard
estakada: overpass
M. Maly, -aya, -oye: small, little
most: bridge
nab. naberezhnaya: embankment
Nizhniy, -yaya, -oye: lower
Novy, -aya, -oye: new
p. pereulok: side street
pl. ploshchad: square
pr. proyezd: passage
prosek: lane
prosp. prospekt: avenue
sh. shosse: highway
Sr. Sredniy, -yaya, -oye: middle
St. Stary, -aya, -oye: old
tupik: blind alley
ul. ulitsa: street, avenue
V. Verkhniy, -yaya, -oye: upper
val: rampart, embankment

This map utilizes the most current "official" names of streets, squares and metro stations, as designated by the Moscow City government and in force in early 1994. This index lists both the previous and current street names, with appropriate cross-referencing. The maps label all features with *current names only*. In fact, many street names may have been officially changed, while the newly designated name is not yet in common use.

The index includes the Russian generic terms (abbreviated, see table at left) for all the streets listed. Please note that the generic "ulitsa" (street) has been omitted from the street names on the map.

FINDING STREETS

This index lists streets alphabetically by the "main word" in the street's name, rather than by the way in which the street name is commonly written (i.e. in the Yellow and White Pages) or spoken. Thus, "ulitsa Arkhipova" or "prospekt Mira" would be found in the index under "Arkhipova, ul." or "Mira, prosp.," respectively. Under this convenient system, the reader need not know whether the road in question is a prospekt, alleya, shosse or ulitsa to find it in the index or on the map.

STREETS

Street	Coord.	Pg.
10 letiya Oktyabrya ul.	F18	21
1812 Goda, ul.	D16	9
1905 Goda ul.	F13	17
25th Oktyabrya, ul., see Nikolskaya ul.	J14	19
26 Bakinskikh Komissarov ul.	B25	13
60-letiya Oktyabrya prosp.	G21	14
8 Marta 1., ul.	F9	6
8 Marta 4., ul.	F9	6
800-letiya Moskvy, ul.	E1	4
Abelmanovskaya ul.	M17	11
Abrikosovskiy p.	F17	21
Adama Mitskevicha, ul., see Patriarshiy B. p.	H14	18
Admirala Makarova ul.	B5	4
Adronyevskaya M. ul.	M16	11
Aeroporta, pr.	D10	5
Aeroportovskaya ul.	E9	5
Afanasyevskiy B. p.	H15	18
Afanasyevskiy M. p.	I15	19
Akademicheskaya B. ul.	F5	3
Akademika Anokhina, ul.	A25	13
Akademika Aparina, ul.	B26	13
Akademika Chepomeya, ul.	D25	13
Akademika Ilyushina, ul.	E9	5
Akademika Khokhlova ul.	D20	13
Akademika Komarova, ul.	I6	6
Akademika Koroleva, ul.	K7	7
Akademika Kurchatova, ul.	A9	5
Akademika Millionshchikova, ul.	L24	15
Akademika Nesmeyanova, ul.	G21	14
Akademika Petrovskovo, ul.	I18	23
Akademika Pulyugina, ul.	D24	13
Akademika Tupoleva nab.	N14	11
Akademika Volgina ul.	C26	13
Akademika Zelinskovo ul.	G20	14
Aksakova, p., see Filippovskiy p.	I15	19
Alabyana, ul.	C9	5
Alekseya Tolstovo ul., see Spiridonovka, ul.	H14	18
Altufyevskoye sh.	H3	3
Alyabyeva, ul.	A16	9
Alymova, ul.	P9	8
Ambulatornaya ul.	D8	5
Amundsena, ul.	M4	2
Anatoliya Zhivova, ul.	F14	17
Andreyevskaya nab.	F20	14
Andronyevskaya B. ul.	M16	11

Street	Coord.	Pg.
Andronyevskaya nab.	M15	11
Andropova, prosp.	M21	15
Angarskaya ul.	D1	4
Annenskaya ul.	I9	6
Anny Severyanovoy ul.	F14	17
Antonova-Ovseyenko, ul.	E14	9
Apakova, ul.	I18	23
Arbat pedestrian mall	H15	18
Arbatskiy p.	H15	18
Argunovskaya ul.	J8	7
Arkadiya Gaydara, p., see Kazenny B. p.	L14	20
Arkhangelskiy p.	K14	20
Arkhipova, ul., see Spasoplinishchevskiy B. p.	K14	20
Arkhitektora Vlasova ul.	F23	14
Arkhivny 1. p.	G17	21
Armavirskaya ul.	R24	16
Armyanskiy p.	K14	20
Artekovskaya ul.	I26	14
Artyukhinoy ul.	Q21	16
Aseyeva, ul.	D9	5
Ashcheulov p.	K13	20
Astakhovskiy p., see Pevcheskiy p.	K15	20
Astradamskaya ul.	G8	6
Astradamskiy 1. pr.	G8	6
Astradamskiy 2. pr.	F8	6
Avangardnaya ul.	B4	4
Aviamotornaya ul.	P15	12
Aviatsionnaya ul.	A8	5
Aviatsionniy p.	E10	5
Avtomobilny pr.	P18	12
Avtomotornaya ul.	E4	4
Avtozavodskaya ul.	K20	15
Avtozavodskiy 3. pr.	L20	15
Azovskaya ul.	I25	14
Babayeyskaya ul.	N11	7
Babushkina Letchika ul.	N2	2
Babyegorodskiy 1. p.	I17	23
Babyegorodskiy 2. p.	I17	23
Bagrationovskiy pr.	C16	9
Bakhrushina, ul.	K17	24
Bakuninskaya ul.	N12	7
Balchug, ul.	J15	19
Baltiyskaya 1. ul.	D8	5
Baltiyskaya 2. ul.	D9	5
Baltiyskaya 3. ul.	D8	5
Baltiyskaya ul.	C8	5
Banny p.	K11	7
Barashevskiy p.	L14	20

Street	Coord.	Pg.	Street	Coord.	Pg.
Cherkizovskaya M. ul.	P9	8	Dobryninskaya ul.,		
Chernyakhovskovo ul.	E9	5	see Koroviy val, ul.	J18	23
Chernyshevskovo, ul.,			Dobryninskiy 1- 4. p.	J18	23
see Pokrovka, ul.	L14	20	Dokhturovskiy p.	F16	21
Cherskovo, pr.	H1	3	Dokuchayev p.	K13	20
Chicherina, ul.	L3	2	Dokukina, ul.	L5	2
Chistoprudny bul.	K14	20	Dolgorukovskaya ul.	I12	6
Chistova, ul.	R21	16	Donskaya ul.	I18	23
Chisty p.	H16	22	Donskoy 2. pr.	H19	10
Chkalova ul.,			Dorogomilovskaya B. ul.	F16	21
see Zemlyanoy val, ul.	L14	20	Dorogomilovskiy val	F15	17
Chudov B. p.	H17	22	Doronina ul.	M3	2
Chudov M. p.	H17	22	Dostoyevskovo, ul.	I11	6
Chukotskiy pr.	L3	2	Dovatora, ul.	F18	21
Chuksin tupik	F9	6	Dovzhenko ul.	C18	9
Danilovskaya nab.	K20	15	Droboliteyny p.	K10	7
Danilovskiy val	J20	15	Drovyanoy B. p.	L16	24
Dashkov p.	H17	22	Drovyanoy M. p.	L16	24
Dayev, p.	K13	20	Druzhby, ul.	D19	9
Degtyarny p.	I13	19	Druzhinnikovskaya ul.	G14	17
Deguninskaya ul.	E2	4	Dubininskaya ul.	K18	24
Dekabristov ul.	J3	2	Dubki, ul.	G7	6
Dekabrskaya B. ul.	F13	17	Dubninskaya ul.	G2	3
Delegatskaya ul.	I13	19	Dubovoy Roshchi, pr.	I8	6
Demidovskiy B. p.	M14	11	Dubrovskaya 1. ul.	M18	11
Demyana Bednovo, ul.	B12	5	Dudosekovskaya ul.	B8	5
Denezhny p.	H16	22	Dukhovskoy p.	J20	15
Derbenevskaya nab.	L18	24	Dunayevskovo, ul.	E16	9
Derbenevskaya ul.	L18	24	Durasovskiy p.	L15	20
Derbenevskiy 1. p.	L18	24	Durova, ul.	J12	7
Derbenevskiy 3. pr.	L18	24	Dushinskaya ul.	O16	12
Desyat-letiya Oktyabrya ul.,			Dvintsev, ul.	I10	6
see 10 letiya Oktyabrya ul.	F18	21	Dyakovo Gorodishche, ul.	L26	15
Detskaya ul.	P8	8	Dybenko, ul.	B1	4
Devichyevo Polya, pr.	G17	21	Dzerzhinskovo, ul.,		
Devyataya Rota, ul.	P11	8	see Lubyanka, B., ul.	K14	20
Devyatinskiy B. p.	G15	17	Elektricheskiy p.	G13	17
Dezhneva pr.	L2	2	Elektrolitny pr.	J24	15
Dezhneva ul.	L2	2	Elektrozavodskaya ul.	P11	8
Dimitrova, ul.,			Elizavetinskiy p.	M14	11
see Yakimanka B., ul.	I17	23	Energeticheskaya ul.	P14	12
Dinamovskaya ul.	L17	24	Entuziastov, bul.	O16	12
Dmitriya Ulyanova, ul.	G22	14	Entuziastov, pr.	P14	12
Dmitriyevskovo, ul.,			Entuziastov pr. 1., ul.	Q15	12
see Zachatyevskiy p.	I16	23	Entuziastov, sh.	P15	12
Dmitrovka B. ul.	I14	19	Eropkinskiy p.	H16	22
Dmitrovka M. ul.	I13	19	Fadeyeva, ul.	I13	19
Dmitrovskiy 1. pr.	G9	6	Fakelny B. p.	M16	11
Dmitrovskiy p.	J14	19	Fakultetskiy p.	B8	5
Dmitrovskoye sh.	G7	6	Faleyevskiy p.	J15	19
Dobrolyubova, p.	H8	6	Fedotovoy ul.	H15	18
Dobrolyubova, ul.	H8	6	Fersmana ul.	G21	14
Dobroslobodskaya ul.	M13	11	Festivalnaya ul.	B3	4

Street	Coord.	Pg.	Street	Coord.	Pg.
Filevskaya 2. ul.	B16	9	Golutvinskiy 1. p.	I16	23
Filevskaya B. ul.	A16	9	Golutvinskiy 3. p.	I17	23
Filippovskiy p.	I15	19	Golyanovskaya ul.	P13	12
Fizkulturny pr.	B15	9	Goncharnaya nab.	L16	24
Flotskaya ul.	C3	4	Goncharnaya ul.	L16	24
Fonvizina, ul.	H7	6	Goncharny 1- 2. pr.	L16	24
Fortunatovskaya ul.	Q11	8	Goncharny pr.	L16	24
Fotiyevoy ul.	F21	14	Goncharova, ul.	H8	6
Frezer sh.	Q17	12	Goncharovskiy 1- 2. pr.	H8	6
Frezernaya 1- 2. ul.	R16	12	Gorkovo ul. (between Manezh-		
Fridrikha Engelsa, ul.	N13	11	naya Pl. and Mayakovskaya		
Fruktovaya ul.	I25	14	Pl.), see Tverskaya ul.	I13	19
Frunze, ul., see Znamenka, ul.	I15	19	Gorkovo ul. (between Maya-		
Frunzenskaya 1- 2. ul.	H18	22	kovskaya Pl. and Tverskaya		
Frunzenskaya 3. ul.	G18	21	zastava) see,		
Frunzenskaya nab.	H17	22	Tverskaya-Yamskaya 1 ul.	H13	18
Frunzenskiy 4. p.	H17	22	Gorodskaya, ul.	J19	11
Furkasovskiy p.	K14	20	Gorokhovskiy p.	M14	11
Furmanny p.	L14	20	Gospitalnaya nab.	O13	12
Furmanova, ul.,			Gospitalnaya ul.	O13	12
see Nashchokinskiy p.	I16	23	Gospitalny pr.	N13	11
Gagarinskiy p.	H16	22	Gospitalny val	P13	12
Gamsonovskiy p.	J20	15	Gostinichnaya ul.	H5	3
Ganushkina, nab.	O10	8	Gostinichny pr.	G4	3
Garazhnaya ul.	R14	12	Gotvalda ul.,		
Garibaldi, ul.	D23	13	see Chayanova ul.	H13	18
Gasheka Yaroslava, ul.	H13	18	Grafskiy p.	K9	7
Gastello, ul.	N11	7	Granatny per.	H14	18
Gazetny p.	I14	19	Granovskovo, ul.,		
Generala Karbysheva, bul.	A12	5	see Romanov p.	I15	19
Generala Rychagova ul.	E5	4	Grayvoronovskaya 2. pr.	R18	12
Generala Yermolova, ul.	C16	9	Grayvoronovskaya ul.	Q19	12
Georgiu Dezha, ul.,			Grazhdanskaya 3. ul.	P8	8
see Peschanaya 2. ul.	C10	5	Griboyedova, ul.,		
Georgiyevskiy p.	J14	19	see Kharitonyevskiy M. p.	L13	20
Gerasima Kurina ul.	A17	9	Grimau, ul.	G22	14
Gertsena ul.,			Gritsevetskaya, ul.,		
see Nikitskaya B. ul.	I15	19	see Znamenskiy B. p.	I15	19
Gilyarovskovo, ul.	K11	7	Grokholskiy p.	K12	7
Glazovskiy p.	H16	22	Gruzinskaya B. ul.	H13	18
Glebovskaya ul.	P8	8	Gruzinskaya M. ul.	G13	17
Glinishchevskiy p.	I14	19	Gruzinskiy p.	H13	18
Glubokiy p.	G15	17	Gruzinskiy val, ul.	G13	17
Gnezdnikovskiy B. p.	I14	19	Gubinka, ul.	F21	14
Gnezdnikovskiy M. p.	I14	19	Guryanova, ul.	P22	16
Godovikova ul.	K9	7	Gustyanikov p.	K14	20
Gogolevskiy bul.	I15	19	Gvozdeva, ul.	L17	24
Golikovskiy p.	J16	23	Ibragimova, ul.	Q11	8
Golovanovskiy p.	D9	5	Igarskiy pr.	L3	2
Golovin B. p.	K13	20	Ilmenskiy pr.	E3	4
Golovin M. p.	K13	20	Ilovayskaya ul.	P26	16
Golovinskaya nab.	N13	11	Ilyinka, ul.	J15	19
Golovinskoye sh.	C5	4	Industrialny p.	I20	14

Street	Coord.	Pg.	Street	Coord.	Pg.
Krasnogorskaya 2. ul.	A8	5	Kutuzovskiy 4. pr.	E16	9
Krasnogvardeyskaya ul.	E14	9	Kutuzovskiy prosp.	B17	9
Krasnogvardeyskiy 1- 2. pr.	E15	9	Kuusinena, ul.	C11	5
Krasnogvardeyskiy 4. pr.	D15	9	Kuybysheva, ul.,		
Krasnogvardeyskiy bul.	E14	9	see Ilyinka, ul.	J15	19
Krasnokazarmennaya nab.	N14	11	Kuybyshevskiy pr.,		
Krasnokazarmennaya ul.	O14	12	see Bogoyavlenskiy p.	J15	19
Krasnokholmskaya N. ul.	K17	24	Kuznetskiy Most, ul.	J14	19
Krasnokholmskaya nab.	L17	24	Kvesisskaya 1- 2. ul.	G10	6
Krasnokursantskiy 1-2. pr.	O14	12	Labaznaya ul.	J16	23
Krasnopresnenskaya nab.	G15	17	Lapina, ul.	P15	12
Krasnoprudnaya ul.	M12	7	Lavochkina ul.	C4	4
Krasnoselskaya N. ul.	M12	7	Lavrov p.	L17	24
Krasnoselskaya V. ul.	M11	7	Lavrushinskiy p.	J16	23
Krasnostudencheskiy pr.	G7	6	Lazorevy pr.	K4	2
Krasnovorotskiy pr.	L13	20	Lazovskiy p.	E10	5
Krasnoy Sosny 1. ul.	N3	2	Lebedeva, ul.	D21	13
Krasnoy Sosny 11. ul.	N4	2	Lebezhiy p.	I15	19
Kravchenko, ul.	C23	13	Lechebnaya ul.	R11	8
Kremlevskaya nab.	J15	19	Lefortovskaya nab.	N13	11
Kremlevskiy pr.	J15	19	Lefortovskiy p.	N13	11
Krestovozdvizhenskiy p.	I15	19	Lefortovskiy val, ul.	O14	12
Krestyanskiy tupik	L17	24	Leningradskaya ul.	C2	4
Krivoarbatskiy p.	H15	18	Leningradskiy prosp.	G11	6
Krivokolenny p.	K14	20	Leningradskoye sh.	C8	5
Krivorozhskaya ul.	I24	14	Leninskaya sloboda, ul.	L20	15
Kronshtadtskiy bul.	C5	4	Leninskiy pr.	K17	24
Kropotkinskaya nab.,			Leninskiy prosp.	I18	23
see Prechistenskaya nab.	I16	23	Lenivka, ul.	I16	23
Kropotkinskaya ul.,			Lenskaya ul.	M2	2
see Prechistenka, ul.	H16	22	Leonova, ul.	K5	2
Kropotkinskiy p.	H16	22	Leontyevskiy p.	I14	19
Krupskoy ul.	D22	13	Lepidevskovo, ul.	B3	4
Krutitskaya nab.	L18	24	Lesnaya ul.	H12	6
Krutitskaya, ul.	L18	24	Lesnoryadskaya ul.	M12	7
Krutitskiy 1. p.	L18	24	Lesnoryadskiy 1-2. pr.	N12	7
Krutitskiy 3. p.	L17	24	Lesnoy 2. p.	H12	6
Krutitskiy 4. p.	L18	24	Lesteva, ul.	I19	10
Krylenko ul.,			Letchika Babushkina ul.	N2	2
see Obydenskiy 1. p.	I16	23	Letnikovskaya ul.	K18	24
Krymskaya nab.	I17	23	Letnyaya ul.	R22	16
Krymskiy pr.	H17	22	Levitana, ul.	C9	5
Krymskiy val, ul.	I17	23	Levoberezhnaya ul.	A1	4
Kryukovskaya p.	P13	12	Levshinskiy M. p.	H16	22
Krzhizhanovskovo ul.	F22	14	Likhachevskiy 1. p.	D4	4
Kseninskiy p.	H17	22	Likhachevskiy 2- 3. p.	E4	4
Kubanskaya ul.	R23	16	Likhachevskiy 4 pr.	E3	4
Kudrinskiy p.	H14	18	Likhoborskaya nab.	D4	4
Kukhmisterova ul.	P22	16	Likhoborskiye Bugry ul.	F5	3
Kulakov p.	L9	7	Likhov p.	I13	19
Kursovoy p.	I16	23	Lineyny pr.	G5	3
Kuryanovskaya 1-4. ul.	O26	16	Listvenichnaya alleya	G5	3
Kuryanovskiy 2. pr.	O26	16	Lizy Chaykinoy, ul.	D9	5

Street	Coord.	Pg.	Street	Coord.	Pg.
Lobachevskovo, ul.	B24	13	Maratovskiy M. p.,		
Lobachika, ul.	M11	7	see Ordynskiy M. p.	J17	23
Lobanova, ul.	L21	15	Marfinskaya B. ul.	H6	6
Lokomotivny pr.	G4	3	Marii Ulyanovoy, ul.	D23	13
Lomonosovskiy prosp.	E22	13	Marinoy Roshchi 2-4. pr.	J10	7
Lopukhinskiy p.	H16	22	Marinskaya B. ul.	K9	7
Losinoostrovskaya ul.	Q7	8	Mariupolskaya ul.	Q24	16
Lubyanka B., ul.	K14	20	Markhlevskovo, ul.,		
Lubyanka M., ul.	K14	20	see Milyutinskiy p.	K14	20
Lubyanskiy pr.	K14	20	Marksa i Engelsa, ul.,		
Luchevoy 1. prosek	M10	7	(Volkhonka to Znamenka)		
Luchevoy 3. prosek	M10	7	see Znamenskiy M. p.	I15	19
Luchevoy 6. prosek	N9	7	Marksa i Engelsa, ul.,		
Luchnikov p.	K14	20	(Znamenka to Vozhdvizhenka)		
Lukov p.	K13	20	see Starovagankovskiy p.	I15	19
Lunacharskovo, ul.,			Marksa, prosp.		
see Glazovskiy p.	H16	22	(Teatralnaya pl. to Lubyan-		
Luzhnetskaya nab.	G19	10	skaya pl.), see Teatralny pr.	J14	19
Luzhnetskiy pr.	F18	21	Marksa, prosp. (Teatralnaya pl.		
Lva Tolstovo, ul.	H17	22	to Pushkinsakaya), see		
Lyalin p.	L14	20	Okhotny Ryad	I14	19
Lyapunova ul.	G21	14	Marksa, prosp. (Znamenka to		
Lyovshinskiy B. p.	H16	22	Gertsena), see Mokhovaya ul.	I15	19
Lyshchikov p.	L15	20	Marksistskaya ul.	L16	24
Lyublinskaya ul.	Q25	16	Maronovskiy p.	I17	23
Lyusinovskaya ul.	J18	23	Maroseika, ul.	K14	20
Lyusinovskiy 1-3. p.	J18	23	Marshala Biryuzova, ul.	B10	5
Magadanskaya, ul.	N1	2	Marshala Grechko ul.,		
Magistralnaya 1. ul.	D13	9	see Kutuzovskiy pr.	B17	9
Magistralnaya 2. ul.	D14	9	Marshala Koneva ul.	B9	5
Magistralnaya 3. ul.	D13	9	Marshala Malinovskovo, ul.	B10	5
Magistralnaya 4. ul.	D12	5	Marshala Rokossovskovo, bul.	Q8	8
Magistralnaya 5. ul.	D13	9	Marshala Rybalko, ul.	B10	5
Magistralny 1. pr.	D13	9	Marshala Shaposhnikova ul.,		
Magistralny tupik	D13	9	see Kolymazhnaya ul.	I15	19
Makarenko, ul.	L14	20	Marshala Tukhachevskovo, ul.	A11	5
Maksima Gorkova, p.,			Marshala Vershinina ul.	B10	5
see Khitrovskiy p.	K15	20	Marshala Zhukova, prosp.	B12	5
Maksima Gorkovo, nab.,			Marta ul.	F9	6
see Kosmodamianskaya nab.	K16	24	Martynovskiy p.	L16	24
Maksimova, ul.	A9	5	Mashinostroyeniya 1., ul.	M19	11
Malakhitovaya ul.	M6	7	Mashinostroyeniya 2., ul.	N19	11
Malaya Bronnaya ul.	H14	18	Mashkova, ul.	L14	20
Malaya Krasnoselskaya ul.	L11	7	Maslovka Nizhnyaya, ul.	H11	6
Malenkovskaya ul.	M11	7	Maslovka Verkhnyaya, ul.	G10	6
Malygina, ul.	N1	2	Masterkova ul.	L20	15
Malysheva ul.	R21	16	Matrosa Zhelezneka, ul.	D6	5
Mamonovskiy p.	I13	19	Matrosskaya Tishina ul.	O11	8
Manezhnaya ul.	I15	19	Matveyevskaya ul.	A20	13
Mansurovskiy p.	H16	22	Mayakovskovo p.	L17	24
Mantulinskaya ul.	F14	17	Mayskiy prosek	N10	7
Maratovskiy B. p.,			Mechnikova, p.,		
see Ordynskiy B. p.	J17	23	see Kazenny M. p.	L14	20

Street	Coord.	Pg.	Street	Coord.	Pg.
Ostankinskaya 1. ul.	J7	7	Perekopskaya ul.	G25	14
Ostapovskiy pr.	P19	12	Pererva, ul.	P26	16
Ostashkovskaya ul.	N1	2	Peresvetov p.	L19	11
Ostozhenka, ul.	H16	22	Pereva ul.	P26	16
Ostrekova, ul.	D10	5	Perevedenovskiy 1. p.	N12	7
Ostroumovskaya B. ul.	N10	7	Pereyaslavskaya B. ul.	K11	7
Ostrovskovo A.N., ul.,			Pereyaslavskaya Sr. ul.	K11	7
see Ordynka M. ul.	J17	23	Perovskiy pr.	O16	12
Ostrovskovo N.A., p.,			Perovskoye sh.	R17	12
see Prechistenskiy p.	H16	22	Pervaya Tverskaya-		
Ostuzheva ul.,			Yamskaya ul.	H13	18
see Kozikhinskiy B. p.	H14	18	Peschanaya 2- 3. ul.	C10	5
Otkrytaya ul.	P9	8	Peschanaya ul.	C9	5
Otkrytoye sh.	R8	8	Pestelya, ul.	J2	2
Otradnaya ul.	J3	2	Pestovskiy p.	L16	24
Otradny pr.	I4	3	Petra Romanova ul.	N20	15
Ovchinnikovskaya nab.	K16	24	Petropavlovskiy p.	K15	20
Ovchinnikovskiy B. p.	K16	24	Petroverigskiy p.	K14	20
Ovchinnikovskiy Sr. p.	K16	24	Petrovka, ul.	J13	19
Ozerkovskaya nab.	K16	24	Petrovskiy bul.	J13	19
Ozerkovskiy 1. p.	K16	24	Petrovskiy p.	J13	19
Pakgauznoye sh.	D5	4	Petrovskiye linii, ul.	J14	19
Paliashvili, ul.,			Petrovsko-Razumovskaya		
(Povarskaya to Stolovy p.)			alleya	F10	6
see Rzhevskiy M. p.	H14	18	Petrovsko-Razumovskiy pr.	G10	6
(Stolovy p. to Nikitskaya B. ul.)			Petrovsko-Razumovskiy		
see Nozhovy p.	H14	18	Stary pr.	F10	6
Palikha, ul.	I11	6	Petrozavodskaya ul.	C2	4
Palshevskiy B. p.	I14	19	Pevcheskiy p	K16	20
Panferova ul.	E23	13	Pilota Nesterova, ul.	E10	5
Panfilova, ul.	B9	5	Pionerskaya B. ul.	K18	24
Panfilovskiy p.	G15	17	Pionerskaya M. ul.	K18	24
Pankratyevskiy p.	K13	20	Pionerskiy M. p.,		
Panteleyevskaya ul.	K11	7	see Patriarskiy M. p.	H14	18
Pasechnaya ul.	G6	6	Pirogovskaya B. ul.	G17	21
Patriarshiy B. p.	H14	18	Pirogovskaya M. ul.	G17	21
Patriarskiy M. p.	H14	18	Pisemskovo, ul.,		
Paveletskiy 2. pr.	K20	15	see Borisoglebskiy p.	H15	18
Paveletskiy 3. pr.	K19	11	Pistsovaya ul.	G10	6
Pavla Andreyeva, ul.	J18	23	Pivchenkova, ul.	A17	9
Pavla Korchagina, ul.	M8	7	Planetnaya ul.	E9	5
Pavlika Morozova p.,			Platovskaya ul.	F16	21
see Novovagankovskiy p.	G14	17	Platovskiy pr.	F16	21
Pavlovskiy 1. pr.	J19	11	Pleteshkovskiy p.	M13	11
Pavlovskiy 2. pr.	J19	11	Plotnikov p.	H16	22
Pavlovskiy 3. p.	K19	11	Plyushchikha, ul.	G16	21
Pechatnikov, p.	K13	20	Pnevaya ul.	E9	5
Pechorskaya ul.	M3	2	Pochtovaya B. ul.	O12	8
Pekhotnaya 1. ul.	A9	5	Pochtovaya M. ul.	N13	11
Pekhotnaya 2. ul.	B9	5	Podbelskovo 1. pr.	P8	8
Pekhotnaya ul.	A9	5	Podbelskovo 3. pr.	Q8	8
Pekhotny 1. p.	A9	5	Podbelskovo ul.,		
Pelovskaya ul.	E3	4	see Ivanteyevskaya, ul.	Q8	8

Street	Coord.	Pg.	Street	Coord.	Pg.
Podgorskaya nab.	K15	20	Privolnaya ul.	Q22	16
Podkolokolny p.	K15	20	Profsoyuznaya ul.	G22	14
Podkopayevskiy p.	K15	20	Prolomnaya ul.	O15	12
Podolskaya ul.	J19	11	Prolomny 1. pr.	O15	12
Podsosenskiy p.	L14	20	Promyshlenny pr.	C16	9
Podvoyskovo, ul.	E14	9	Prostornaya ul.	Q9	8
Podyemnaya ul.	O16	12	Prosvirin p.	K13	20
Pogodinskaya ul.	G17	21	Protochny p.	G15	17
Pogonny pr.	P8	8	Protopopovskiy p.	K12	7
Poklonnaya 1. ul.	D16	9	Proyektiruemy pr.	P20	16
Poklonnaya ul.	D17	9	Prud Klyuchiki ul.	Q16	12
Pokrovka, ul.	K14	20	Pryamoy p.	G15	17
Pokrovskiy bul.	L14	20	Pryanishnikova, ul.	F6	6
Pokryshkina, ul.	A25	13	Pudovkina, ul.	D18	9
Polbina ul.	Q23	16	Pugachevskaya 1-2. ul.	Q10	8
Polenova, ul.	C9	5	Pugovishnikov p.	H17	22
Polikarpova, ul.	E12	5	Pulkovskaya ul.	B4	4
Polkovaya ul.	I10	6	Pushechnaya ul.	J14	19
Poltavskaya ul.	G10	6	Pushkarev p.	K13	20
Poluyaroslavskaya nab.	L15	20	Pushkinskaya nab.	H18	22
Poluyaroslavskiy M. p.	L15	20	Pushkinskaya ul.,		
Polyanka B., ul.	J16	23	see Dmitrovka B. ul.	I14	19
Polyanka M., ul.	J17	23	Putevoy pr.	H1	3
Polyanskiy p.	J17	23	Putinkovskiy B. p.	I13	19
Polyarnaya ul.	K1	2	Putyayevskiy pr.	M8	7
Pomerantsev p.	H16	22	Pyatnitskaya ul.	J16	23
Pomorskaya ul.	H2	3	Pyryeva, ul.	D18	9
Poperechny prosek	M9	7	Rabochaya ul.	N16	11
Popov p.	O11	8	Radiatorskaya 1. ul.	B7	5
Poselka Tekstilshchiki 1., ul.	Q21	16	Radio, ul.	N14	11
Poselka Tekstilshchiki 7., ul.	R21	16	Radiomorskaya 2. ul.	B8	5
Poselka Tekstilshchiki 8., ul.	R21	16	Radishchevskaya N. ul.	L16	24
Poselka Tekstilshchiki 10., ul.	R20	16	Radishchevskaya V. ul.	L16	24
Poselka Tekstilshchiki 11., ul.	Q20	16	Raduzhnaya ul.	M3	2
Poslannikov p.	N13	11	Raketny bul.	L8	7
Posledniy p.	K13	20	Rakhmanovskiy p.	J14	19
Potapovskiy p.	K14	20	Ramenki 1., ul.	B21	13
Poteshnaya ul.	O10	8	Ramenki 2. ul.	B22	13
Povarskaya ul.	H15	18	Raskovoy, ul.	G11	6
Pozharskiy p.	I16	23	Raspletina, ul.	A10	5
Praskovina ul.	J7	7	Rastorguyevskiy p.	G13	17
Pravdy, ul.	G11	6	Raushskaya nab.	K15	20
Prechistenka, ul.	H16	22	Raushskiy 2. p.	K16	24
Prechistenskaya nab.	I16	23	Rayevskovo, ul.	F16	21
Prechistenskiy p.	H16	22	Razina, ul., see Varvarka, ul.	J15	19
Predtechenskiy B., p.	G14	17	Rechnikov ul.	N23	15
Predtechenskiy M. p.	G14	17	Rezervny pr.	F16	21
Preobrazhenskaya nab.	O11	8	Rimskovo-Korsakova, ul.	I1	3
Preobrazhenskaya ul.	P10	8	Rizhskiy pr.	M8	7
Presnenskiy val	G13	17	Rochdelskaya ul.	G14	17
Pribrezhnaya ul.	A1	4	Rogachevskiy p.	F2	3
Prichalny pr.	C14	9	Rogoshskiy B. p.	M16	11
Priorova, ul.	D7	5	Rogozhskiy val, ul.	N16	11

Street	Coord.	Pg.	Street	Coord.	Pg.
Starokonyushenny p.	H15	18	Taganrogskaya ul.	R23	16
Starokoptevskiy p.	D5	4	Taganskaya ul.	L16	24
Staromarinskoye sh.	J9	7	Talalikhina, ul.	N17	11
Staromonetny p.	J16	23	Taldomskaya ul.	D1	4
Staromozhayskoye sh.	C17	9	Tamozhenny pr.	N15	11
Staropanskiy p.	J15	19	Taneyevykh, ul.,		
Staropetrovskiy pr.	C7	5	see Vlasyevskiy M. p.	H16	22
Staropimenovskiy p.	I13	19	Tankovy pr.	N15	11
Starosadskiy p.	K14	20	Tarasa Shevchenko nab.	G15	17
Staroslobodskaya ul.	M11	7	Tatarskaya B. ul.	K17	24
Starovagankovskiy	I15	19	Tatarskaya ul.	K17	24
Starovolynskaya ul.	A18	9	Tatishcheva, ul.	J19	11
Starozykovskiy pr.	E9	5	Tatyanoy Makorovoy, ul.,		
Stasovoy, ul.	H19	10	see Bolotnaya ul.	J16	23
Stavropolskaya ul.	Q23	16	Tayninskaya ul.	N1	2
Stepana Supruna, ul.	E10	5	Teatralnaya alleya	F10	6
Stoleshnikov, p.	J14	19	Teatralny pr.	J14	19
Stoletova, ul.	C20	13	Telegrafny p.,		
Stolovy p.	H14	18	see Arkhangelskiy p.	K14	20
Stolyarny p.	G14	17	Tessinskiy p.	L15	20
Stopani, p.,			Teterinskiy p.	L16	24
see Ogorodnoy slobody, p.	K14	20	Tikhonovskaya B. ul.	N9	7
Storozhevaya ul.	P14	12	Tikhvinskaya ul.	I11	6
Strastnoy bul.	I13	19	Timiryazevskaya ul.	F7	6
Strelbishchenskiy pr.	E14	9	Timiryazevskiy pr.	F6	6
Streletskaya ul.	I10	6	Timura Frunze, ul.	H17	22
Stremyanny p.	K18	24	Tishinskiy B. p.	G13	17
Strochenovskiy B. p.	K18	24	Tishinskiy M. p.	G13	17
Strochenovskiy M. p.	K18	24	Tishinskiy Sr. p.	G13	17
Stroiteley 8. ul.	D22	13	Titovskiy pr.	H18	22
Stroiteley ul.	D22	13	Tkatskaya ul.	Q11	8
Stromynka, ul.	O11	8	Tokmakov p.	M13	11
Stroykovskaya ul.	M17	11	Tolmachevskiy B. p.	J16	23
Studencheskaya ul.	E16	9	Tolmachevskiy M. p.	J16	23
Studenetskiy p.	F14	17	Tolmachevskiy Stary p.	K16	24
Sudakova, ul.	R24	16	Tovarishcheskiy p.	M16	11
Sudostroitelnaya ul.	N23	15	Trekhgorny B. p.	F14	17
Sukharevskiy B. p.	K13	20	Trekhgorny M. p.	G14	17
Sukharevskiy M. p.	J13	19	Trekhgorny Sr. pr.	G14	17
Sukhonskaya ul.	L2	2	Trekhgorny val, ul.	F14	17
Surikova, ul.	C9	5	Trekhprudny p.	I14	19
Suvorovskaya ul.	P11	8	Trekhsvyatitelskiy B. p.	L15	20
Suvorovskiy bul.,			Trekhsvyatitelskiy M. p.	L15	20
see Nikitskiy bul.	I14	19	Trifonovskaya ul.	J11	7
Sverchkov, p.	K14	20	Trofimova, ul.	M21	15
Sviblovskaya B. ul.	J6	7	Troilinskiy p.	H15	18
Svirskaya ul.	M18	11	Troitskaya ul.	J12	7
Syromyatnicheskaya N. ul.	M15	11	Troitskaya ul.	J13	19
Syromyatnicheskaya nab.	M15	11	Trubetskaya ul.	G17	21
Syromyatnicheskaya V. ul.	L15	20	Trubnaya ul.	J13	19
Syromyatnicheskiy 1. p.	L15	20	Trubnikovskiy p.	H15	18
Syromyatnicheskiy pr.	M15	11	Truda, ul.	M16	11
Sytinskiy p.	I14	19	Truzhenikov 1. p.	G17	21

Street	Coord.	Pg.	Street	Coord.	Pg.
Vospitatelny p.	K15	20	Yeniseyskaya ul.	M2	2
Vostochnaya ul.	L19	11	Yermolayevskiy p.	H13	18
Voyevodina, p.,			Yermolovoy, ul.,		
see Kamennoy slobody, p.	H15	18	see Karetny B. p.	J13	19
Voykova ul.	D3	4	Yeyskaya ul.	R23	16
Voykovskiy 1. pr.	B8	5	Yuliusa Fuchika, ul.	H13	18
Voykovskiy 4. pr.	B7	5	Yunykh Lenintsev, ul.	R21	16
Voytovicha, ul.	O16	12	Yurlovskiy pr.	K2	2
Vozdvizhenka, ul.	I15	19	Yuryevskiy ul.	P14	12
Voznesenskiy p.	I14	19	Yushunskaya M. ul.	H26	14
Vrazhskiy 1. p.	G16	21	Yuzhinskiy p.,		
Vrazhskiy 2. p.	G17	21	see Palashevskiy B. p.	I14	19
Vrubelya, ul.	C9	5	Yuzhnoportovaya ul.	N20	15
Vsevoloda Vishnevskovo, ul.	G8	6	Yuzhnoportovy 2. pr.	N21	15
Vsevolozhskiy p.	I16	23	Yuzhnoportovy pr.	O21	16
Vspolny p.	H14	18	Yuzhny p.	L13	20
Vucheticha ul.	F8	6	Zabelina, ul.	K15	20
Vuzovskiy B. p.,			Zachatyevskiy 2. p.	I16	23
see Tryokhsvyatitelskiy B. p.	L15	20	Zachatyevskiy 3. p.	H16	22
Vuzovskiy M. p.,			Zachatyevskiy p.	I16	23
see Tryokhsvyatitelskiy M. p.	L15	20	Zagarodnoye sh.	I21	14
Vyatskiy 4. p.	G10	6	Zagorodny 4. pr.	H21	14
Vyborgskaya ul.	B6	5	Zamorenova ul.	G14	17
Vysokaya ul.	L23	15	Zapovednaya ul.	K2	2
Vysokovoltny pr.	H1	3	Zarechnaya ul.	C14	9
Yablochkova, ul.	H8	6	Zatonnaya ul.	N23	15
Yakimanka B., ul.	I17	23	Zatsepa ul.	K18	24
Yakimanka M., ul.	J16	23	Zatsepskiy val, ul.	K17	24
Yakimanskaya nab.	I16	23	Zelenogradskaya ul.	B1	4
Yakimanskiy p.	I17	23	Zemelny 1. pr.	F13	17
Yakornaya ul.	N23	15	Zemledelcheskiy p.	G16	21
Yakovoapostolskiy p.	L14	20	Zemlyachki, ul.,		
Yakushkina, ul.	J3	2	see Tatarskaya B., ul.	K16	24
Yaltinskaya ul.	I26	14	Zemlyanoy val, ul.	L14	20
Yamskaya 1. ul.	I10	6	Zemskiy p.	I17	23
Yamskovo Polya 5., ul.	H11	6	Zhdanova, ul.,		
Yantarny pr.	N2	2	see Rozhdestvenka ul.	J14	19
Yanysheva ul.,			Zheleznodorozhnaya ul.	M4	2
see Krestovozdvizhenskiy p.	I15	19	Zheleznodorozhny pr.	K20	15
Yaroslavskaya ul.	L7	7	Zherbunova, ul.	N11	7
Yaroslavskoye sh.	N4	2	Zhitnaya ul.	J17	23
Yasny pr.	K1	2	Zholtovskovo, ul.,		
Yauzskaya alleya	N6	7	see Yermolayevskiy p.	H13	18
Yauzskaya ul.	K15	20	Zhukov pr.	K18	24
Yauzskiy bul.	L15	20	Zhukovskovo, ul.	L14	20
Yazykovskiy p.	H17	22	Zhuzha, ul.	M24	15
Yefremova, ul.	G18	21	Zlatoustinskiy B. p.	K14	20
Yegerskaya ul.	N10	7	Zlatoustinskiy M. p.	K14	20
Yegorevskaya ul.	Q23	16	Znamenka, ul.	I15	19
Yegorevskiy pr.	Q24	16	Znamenskaya ul.	Q9	8
Yelanskovo, ul.	G17	21	Znamenskiy B. p.	I15	19
Yelizarovoy, ul.,			Znamenskiy M. p.	I15	19
see Yakovoapostolskiy p.	L14	20			

BRIDGES

LOCALITIES

Locality	Coord.	Pg.	Metro	Coord.	Pg.
Sokolniki	N9	7	Kropotkinskaya	I16	23
Sviblovo	K4	2	Kurskaya	L14	20
Tekstilshchiki	R20	16	Kutuzovskaya	D16	9
Vekhniye Mnevniki	A13	9	Kuznetsky most	I14	19
Verkhniye Kotly	K24	15	Leninskiye gory	F20	14
Verkhniye Likhobory	F4	3	Leninsky pr.	H20	14
Vladykino	H4	3	Lubyanka	L14	20
Volkhonka	I26	14	Marksistskaya	L16	24
Volynskoye	A19	9	Mayakovskaya	I13	19
Vorobyevskiy	G1	3	Mendeleevskaya	I12	6
Vorobyevskiye Gory	E19	9	Nagatinskaya	I23	14
Vorontsovo	D25	13	Nagornaya	I24	14
Vsekhsvyatskoye	D8	5	Nakhimovsky pr.	I25	14
			Noviye Cheremushki	F24	14

METRO STATIONS

Metro	Coord.	Pg.
Aeroport	E9	5
Akademicheskaya	G22	14
Aleksandrovsky sad	I15	19
Arbatskaya	I15	19
Aviamotornaya	P15	12
Avtozavodskaya	L20	15
Babushkinskaya	M2	2
Bagrationovskaya	B16	9
Barrikadnaya	G14	17
Baumanskaya	N13	11
Begovaya	E13	9
Biblioteka imeni Lenina	I16	23
Borovitskaya	I15	19
Botanicheskiy sad	K5	2
Byelorusskaya	H12	6
Chekhovskaya	I14	19
Cherkizovskaya	Q10	8
Christiye Prudy	K14	20
Dinamo	F11	6
Dmitrovskaya	G9	6
Dobryninskaya	J18	23
Elektrozavodskaya	O12	8
Filevskiy park	A16	9
Fili	C16	9
Frunzenskaya	G18	21
Izmailovskiy park	R11	8
Kakhovskaya	H26	14
Kaluzhskaya	E26	13
Kashirskaya	L26	15
Kievskaya	G16	21
Kitay-gorod	K15	20
Kolomenskaya	M23	15
Komsomolskaya	L12	7
Krasnopresnenskaya	G14	17
Krasnoselskaya	M12	7
Krasnye vorota	L13	20

Metro	Coord.	Pg.
Kropotkinskaya	I16	23
Kurskaya	L14	20
Kutuzovskaya	D16	9
Kuznetsky most	I14	19
Leninskiye gory	F20	14
Leninsky pr.	H20	14
Lubyanka	L14	20
Marksistskaya	L16	24
Mayakovskaya	I13	19
Mendeleevskaya	I12	6
Nagatinskaya	I23	14
Nagornaya	I24	14
Nakhimovsky pr.	I25	14
Noviye Cheremushki	F24	14
Novo-Alekseevskaya	K9	7
Novokuznetskaya	J16	23
Novoslobodskaya	I12	6
Okhotny ryad	J14	19
Oktyabrskaya	I17	23
Oktyabrskoye pole	B10	5
Otradnoye	I2	3
Park Kultury	H17	22
Paveletskaya	K18	24
Pechatniki	P21	16
Petrovsko-Razumovskaya	G5	3
Ploshchad Ilyicha	N16	11
Ploshchad Revolyutsii	J14	19
Polezhayevskaya	C12	5
Polyanka	J17	23
Preobrazhenskaya ploshchad	P10	8
Profsoyuznaya	F23	14
Proletarskaya	M17	11
Prospekt Mira	K12	7
Prospekt Vernadskovo	C23	13
Pushkinskaya	I13	19
Rechnoy vokzal	A3	4
Rizhskaya	K10	7
Savelovskaya	H10	6
Semyonovskaya	P12	8
Serpukhovskaya	J18	23
Sevastopolskaya	H26	14
Shabalovskaya	I19	10
Smolenskaya	G15	17
Sokol	C9	5
Sokolniki	N17	11
Sportivnaya	F18	21
Studencheskaya	E16	9
Sukharevskaya	K13	20
Sviblovo	L4	2
Taganskaya	L16	24
Teatralnaya	J14	19
Tekstilshchiki	Q20	16

NOBODY COVERS RUSSIA BETTER

BUSINESS & TRAVEL GUIDES

Russia Survival Guide
The essential guide to doing business in the new Russia, now in its 4th edition. (March 1994, $18.50)

Where in Moscow
Essential directories and color city street map, now in its third edition. (March 1994, $13.50)

Where in St. Petersburg
Essential directories and color city street map, updated and now in its 2nd edition. (March 1994, $13.50)

LANGUAGE

Business Russian
The practical Russian you need to know for doing business in Russia. (May 1993, $16)

MAPS

New Moscow City Map & Guide
A meticulously-accurate color map of the capital city. (March 1994, $6.95)

New St. Petersburg City Map & Guide
The first new Western city map of St. Petersburg in decades. (April 1993, $6.95)

TRAVEL INFORMATION

Russian Travel Monthly
What to read to keep up-to-date on the latest business and independent travel news. (Monthly, $36/yr.)

REFERENCE INFORMATION

Russian News Abstracts
Indexed abstracts of over 1900 key articles from the Russian press during 1993 (1992 volume also avail.). (April 1994, $48)

LEGAL INFORMATION

Business Legal Materials: Russia
A monthly listing of current Russian legal acts related to trade and investment. (Monthly, $225/yr)

Russian Business Legal Materials: 1993
A comprehensive, indexed listing of over 1000 Russian laws related to foreign trade with, and investment in, Russia. (February 1994, $68)

ACCESS RUSSIA CATALOGUE

Be sure to also ask for a copy of *Access Russia,* our catalogue of over 130 publications on Russia by over 40 US and European publishers.

FOR MORE INFORMATION,

OR TO PLACE AN ORDER, CONTACT:

RUSSIAN INFORMATION SERVICES, INC.

89 Main St., Box 2
Montpelier, VT 05602
ph. (802) 223-4955
fax (802) 223-6105

B. Kondratyevskiy per. 4
Moscow, Russia
ph./fax (095) 254-9275

Our way of saying Thank You!

We appreciate that you have chosen to purchase an RIS travel or business guide. As a way of expressing our thanks, and to help you keep up-to-date on the most recent changes in Russia and the CIS, we would like to offer you a free two-month subscription to our acclaimed newsletter, **Russian Travel Monthly.** Designed as a monthly update to our annual guides on Russia, Moscow and St. Petersburg, **RTM** is full of important news, feature articles, inside information and directories. Find out why thousands of readers have come to depend on **RTM** to keep them current on events in Russia. Tear out the card below and send it in to us today to begin receiving your complimentary issues. If, after two months, you decide you would like to continue your subscription, we'll bill you at our low annual subscription rate of just $36. Again, thank you, and we look forward to hearing from you!

Two FREE months of Russian Travel Monthly!

☐ **YES!** Please send me **Russian Travel Monthly**, absolutely free, for two months. I understand that I may continue my subscription for the low annual rate of just $36 (12 issues).

☐ **YES!** Please send me information about other Russian Information Services publications.

☐ **YES!** Please send me a copy of **Access Russia**, your catalogue of over 120 books, maps and other items produced by over 50 companies and all related to traveling in and doing business in Russia.

Please send my issues/information to:

Name: _____

Company: _____

Address: _____

_____

City: _____

State/Zip: _____

Country: _____

Where you purchased this guide: _____

_____

R   M

See the reverse side of this card for a coupon good for two FREE issues of *Russian Travel Monthly*

RUSSIAN INFORMATION SERVICES, INC.
89 MAIN STREET, SUITE 2
MONTPELIER, VT 05602
U.S.A.